The Lost Tomb
of
Alexander the Great

by

Andrew Michael Chugg

2007

First Edition December 2007

Revised May 2012

© 2007 by Andrew Michael Chugg. All rights reserved.
ISBN 978-0-9556790-6-3

Dedicated to the Agathos Daimon

Keeper of the Catacombs

The Quest for the Tomb of Alexander the Great
Contents

	Dramatis Personae and Prologue	1
1.	Introduction: Entombment and Apotheosis	9
2.	Death in Babylon	12
3.	Funeral Games	39
4.	The Capital of Memory	70
5.	The Shrine of the Caesars	92
6.	Vanished from History	112
7.	The Mysteries of the Mosques	132
8.	The Astronomer's Chart	154
9.	Alexander's City	172
10.	Famous Alexandrian Mummies	192
11.	The Sword in the Stone	210
12.	Exequies	227
	Appendix A: The Journal of Alexander the Great	233
	Appendix B: The Sarcophagus of Alexander the Great?	254
	Appendix C: A Candidate for the First Tomb of Alexander	266
	Appendix D: The Tomb of Alexander in Alexandria	279
	Bibliography	297
	Acknowledgements	310
	Index	311

Dramatis Personae & Prologue

Part of the special fascination of this story is that it extends across 25 centuries and weaves through ancient Egyptian, Greek, Roman, Arab and modern European cultures. A consequence of this diversity and longevity is that the reader will meet a kaleidoscopic cast of characters on their journey through these pages. It has therefore seemed appropriate to devote this Prologue to a concise but informative introduction of the principal persons on whose testimony this fresh account relies. These have loosely been sub-divided into ancient and modern sources and they are listed in alphabetical order, so that these pages also serve as a type of glossary, for occasional reference.

This book mainly concerns itself with Alexander's death and his afterlife with its focus resting on his famous tomb. Since, however, Alexander himself is undoubtedly the most important figure of all, this section will conclude with a short summary of his astonishing and scintillating career.

ANCIENT SOURCES

Achilles Tatius: Alexandrian Greek erotic novelist most probably of the 2nd - 3rd century AD, though his date is still disputed. His surviving work *Clitophon and Leucippe* includes a brief but remarkable description of ancient Alexandria. A partial papyrus manuscript has been found in Egypt.

Aelian (Claudius Aelianus): Greek writer who taught rhetoric in Rome c. AD220.

Alexander Romance: a semi-legendary account of Alexander's career, compiled by a native Egyptian editor from older stories and fables in the early 3rd century AD. Although hopelessly disjointed and inaccurate as a work of history, it is nevertheless valuable in that it preserves some traditions lost from the more authoritative ancient accounts. It is also good on Alexandria, since its creator was probably a resident of the ancient city. It is also known as Pseudo-Callisthenes, because some of its manuscripts falsely attributed it to Alexander's court historian Callisthenes. It survives today in a wide number of variant versions, of which the oldest and most faithful to the original are a Greek manuscript of the 3rd century AD, the Armenian translation and the Latin edition of Julius Valerius.

Ammianus Marcellinus: Born in Antioch and active in the second half of the 4th century AD, he was virtually the last of the secular Latin historians of Rome. His accounts of Alexandria are particularly valuable, since he seems to have visited the city in the aftermath of the great earthquake of AD365.

Dramatis Personae & Prologue

Aristobulus: Accompanied Alexander in his campaigns, perhaps in the capacity of an engineer or architect. Subsequently penned an influential but lost history of Alexander's reign, which was a major source for Arrian, Plutarch and Strabo.

Arius Didymus: Prolific and respected Alexandrian scholar of the 1st century BC. He was a close friend of Octavian/Augustus and probably accompanied him during his visit to Alexander's tomb in 30BC. Likely to be the source for the construction of a new mausoleum for Alexander by Philopator.

Arrian (Flavius Arrianus Xenophon): Rose to become Governor of Cappadocia under the Emperor Hadrian in the early 2nd century AD. An experienced military commander, he wrote his Campaigns of Alexander to rescue the King's reputation as a general and a conqueror from a morass of misconceptions and inaccuracies then current in Roman literature. In doing so, he tended to suppress biographical details and anecdotes in favour of troop dispositions, military logistics and strategic intent. His lost *History of Events after Alexander*, which survives only in fragments and a partial epitome, probably contained the most authoritative account of the movements of Alexander's remains after his death.

Caesar (Gaius Julius Caesar): Author of two books – The Civil War and The Alexandrine War - describing a military campaign in Alexandria in 48BC, although the second of these was ghostwritten by Hirtius. A recorded visitor to Alexander's tomb in the same year. Also Dictator of Rome.

Curtius (Quintus Curtius Rufus): The most important Latin historian of Alexander's reign. His date is uncertain but the era of the Emperor Claudius in the 1st century AD seems likely, when a man of the same name was Proconsul of Africa. The work is highly rhetorical and struggles to project a progressive deterioration onto Alexander's character, reminiscent of that exhibited by Gaius Caligula. Curtius' facts are usually reliable, but his interpretations of the facts are hopelessly distorted by his preconceptions.

Dio Cassius (Cassius Dio Cocceianus): Born in Nicaea c. AD155, he was an eminent Greek politician and governor under the Severan emperors. He was twice raised to the consulship and died c. AD235. Author of an important *History of Rome*, some of which only survives in an epitome.

Diodorus Siculus: A Sicilian Greek of the 1st century BC, he wrote a universal history incorporating a volume dedicated to Alexander. He visited Alexandria and the precinct of Alexander's tomb, probably during the reign of Cleopatra VII.

Ephemerides (Alexander's Royal Journal): Our main source for the course of Alexander's fatal illness. Some have tried to show that it is a forgery, but Ephippus of Olynthus seems to have written a five-book commentary upon the *Ephemerides* within decades of Alexander's death. Similar official diaries seem to have been kept by earlier Macedonian kings and by the Ptolemies. Aelian attributes the *Ephemerides* to Eumenes of Cardia, Alexander's Chief Secretary

Quest for the Tomb of Alexander by Andrew Chugg

(and co-written by a certain Diodotus of Erythrae, perhaps a mistake for Diognetus of Erythrae).

Ibn Abdel Hakim: Arab writer of the mid-9th century AD. He knew Alexandria just before the so-called medieval walls were finalised by the Sultan Ahmed Ibn Tulun and he provides tantalizing hints of its topography and a medieval mosque of Alexander.

Herodian: A Greek historian of the 3rd century AD he wrote some time around the year AD240.

John Chrysostom: Pupil of Libanius and subsequently archbishop of Constantinople around AD398-404 (died AD407). Among his sermons is a passage believed to be the earliest assertion that Alexander's tomb had disappeared.

Josephus (Flavius Josephus): Jewish historian of the 1st century AD. He makes frequent mention of Alexandria due to the large Jewish community in the city in his time.

Justin: The 4th century AD epitomiser of a history of the world by a 1st century BC Latin writer called Pompeius Trogus. Trogus was a dedicated Republican and therefore highly antagonistic to absolute monarchy, a prejudice which he makes little attempt to conceal in his account of Alexander's career.

Libanius: Greek sophist and rhetorician of Antioch (born AD314 – died c. AD394). Though of pagan sympathies and a friend of Julian the Apostate, he also taught St John Chrysostom q.v. and received an honorary Praetorian Prefecture from the Christian emperor Theodosius.

Lucan (Marcus Annaeus Lucanus): The nephew of Seneca (who was Nero's tutor and the author of a book about Egypt). Recalled from Athens to join the court of the Emperor, Lucan's instinctively Republican sentiments were nurtured by the spectacle of Nero's descent into cruelty and debauchery. In AD65 at the age of 25, he was implicated in Calpurnius Piso's plot to assassinate the Emperor. When the conspiracy failed, Nero required him to commit suicide. His legacy was the *Pharsalia*, an unfinished poem recounting the civil war between Caesar and Pompey and recognised as a jewel of Latin literature. It contains two passages, which provide the most detailed description of Alexander's tomb.

Lucian: Syrian Greek writer and satirist of the second half of the 2nd century AD.

Nearchus of Crete: Admiral of Alexander's fleet for the voyage through the Indian Ocean and the Persian Gulf. Author of a lost history concentrating on India and his famous voyage, which was the principal source for Arrian's *Indica*.

Onesicritus (of Astypalaea): A pupil of Diogenes the Cynic, he was Alexander's helmsman on the voyage down the Indus. He wrote a lost biography of Alexander, which teemed with anecdotes and local colour. His work was an

Dramatis Personae & Prologue

influential source for Plutarch, Strabo and perhaps parts of the Alexander Romance.

Parian Marble (*Marmor Parium*): A Greek inscription carved in about 263/2BC found on the Aegean Island of Paros and giving a chronology of events. The last surviving entry is for 299/8BC, but there are major lacunae. However, the last fragment is complete until 309BC. It was found in 1897 and is now in the Paros museum. Paros was part of the Ptolemaic Empire, ruled by Philadelphus, when the Marble was set up.

Pausanias: Greek travel writer of the mid-2nd century AD, perhaps from Lydia. His principal work is the *Description of Greece*.

Plutarch: Greek essayist and scholar of the 1st to early 2nd century AD. His Life of Alexander is the most biographical of the surviving ancient sources and drew upon a wider range of primary sources than any other work. His earlier essays on the Virtue or Fortune of Alexander are also important biographical sources on the King.

Pseudo-Callisthenes: see Alexander Romance.

Ptolemy (Ptolemaios I Soter): Author of the most detailed and accurate contemporaneous history of Alexander's campaigns. Though now lost, this work was the most important source for Arrian's *Campaigns of Alexander*. It is believed by some that his accuracy and detail rely upon his acquisition of Alexander's *Ephemerides* (Royal Journal), when he took possession of Alexander's body. At least three ancient sources independently assert that he was Alexander's illegitimate half-brother. Also one of Alexander's most senior officers (a *somatophylax*) and later Pharaoh of Egypt.

Strabo: Greek geographer of the late 1st century BC and early 1st century AD. He lived in Alexandria for around 5 years and gave the most important description of the city as it was when he saw it in about 20BC in his 17th book.

Suetonius (Gaius Suetonius Tranquillus): Author of *The Twelve Caesars*, which is a scandalous, but accurate, set of biographies of the first twelve Roman Princes from Julius Caesar to Domitian. He wrote when they were safely dead in the early 2nd century AD.

Zenobius: Greek sophist who taught rhetoric in Rome under Hadrian and compiled a book of 'proverbs' by Lucillus of Tarrha in Crete and Arius Didymus of Alexandria (according to the Suda).

MODERN SOURCES

Achille Adriani: Director of the Graeco-Roman Museum in Alexandria from 1932-1940 and again from 1948-1952. Author of the theory that the Alabaster Tomb is the antechamber of a tomb of Alexander the Great.

Quest for the Tomb of Alexander by Andrew Chugg

Giuseppe Botti: Founder of the Graeco-Roman Museum in Alexandria and its Director from 1892-1904. Author of numerous archaeological works on Alexandria including a reconstructed map of the ancient city.

Georg Braun and Frans Hogenberg: Cartographers from Cologne, who sought to emulate the success of Ortelius' *Theatre of the World* by publishing an atlas of plans of *Cities of the World*. They included a beautiful chart of Alexandria, which, despite some distortions, contains much valid information on the early 16th century city.

Evaristo Breccia: Director of the Graeco-Roman Museum in Alexandria from 1904-1932. Author of *Alexandrea ad Aegyptum*, an important guide book to the ancient city and the remains in the Museum and an article on the tomb (1930).

Louis-François Cassas: French artist and traveller. Visited Alexandria and drew many important vistas and a map in 1785.

Edward Daniel Clarke: English scholar and traveller. Commissioned by Lord Hutchinson to retrieve the antiquities garnered by the French in 1801, he discovered an ancient sarcophagus in the hold of the French hospital ship, *La Cause*, and established that there was a local tradition that it had once contained Alexander's corpse. Author of *The Tomb of Alexander* published in 1805.

Vivant Denon: Associate of Napoleon and foremost among the scholars who accompanied the French expedition to Egypt in 1798. Author of *Travels in Egypt*. Later Director of the Louvre.

Jean-Yves Empereur: Founder in 1990 and Director of the Centre d'Etudes Alexandrines (CEA). Author of numerous books and scholarly articles on Alexandria including *Alexandria Rediscovered* and *Hoi Taphoi Tou Megalou Alexandrou*.

P. M. Fraser: Author of Ptolemaic Alexandria, a mine of information on the ancient city.

David George Hogarth: English archaeologist of the late 19th and early 20th century. Author of an influential report in 1895, which concluded that archaeological resources were better directed elsewhere than Alexandria.

Jean-Philippe Lauer: Leading French Egyptologist of the 20th century and a specialist in the Memphite necropolis of Saqqara.

Leo Africanus: Moorish traveller in Africa, who was captured by pirates in 1520 and ended up in the service of Pope Leo X, who converted him to Christianity. His *Description of Africa* remained the best general account of the continent for centuries, and it included a description of Alexandria, which he probably visited several times between c.1515 – 1520.

Mahmoud Bey El Falaki: Sent by Mohammed Ali to train as an engineer in France, he spent seven years studying at the Ecole des Arts et Métiers. In 1865 he was commissioned by the Khedive Ismaïl, as a favour to Napoleon III of

Dramatis Personae & Prologue

France, to excavate to determine the layout of ancient Alexandria. He succeeded brilliantly in defining the basic street grid and outline of the Roman metropolis, but argued ineffectually for the Nabi Daniel Mosque as the site of Alexander's tomb. He published his book *L'Antique Alexandrie* describing his investigations whilst resident in Copenhagen in 1872.

Auguste Mariette: Discoverer and excavator of the Serapeum at Saqqara. First Head of the Egyptian Antiquities Commission and the greatest Egyptologist of the 19th century.

Luigi Mayer: Artist employed in 1792 by Sir Robert Ainslie, British Ambassador in Constantinople, for a project to draw a large collection of scenes from around the Ottoman Empire. The fruits of the expedition were published between about 1801-1804 as a magnificent series of aquatinted engravings, including many views of Alexandria.

Napoleon Bonaparte: Instigator of the *Description de l'Egypte*, simply the greatest work on ancient and medieval Egypt ever published. Also Emperor of France.

Richard Pococke: Early 18th century English antiquarian and traveller. Author of the *Description of the East* published in 1743, he had paced around the walls of Alexandria in 1737.

Alan John Bayard Wace: English professor of archaeology, who published an obscure article on *The Sarcophagus of Alexander the Great* in the Bulletin of the Faculty of Arts of Farouk I University in Alexandria in 1948.

Alexandre-Max de Zogheb: Member of a prominent Alexandrian family, who published his *Etudes sur l'Ancienne Alexandrie* containing a chapter on Alexander's tomb in 1909. The main source for Ambrose Schilizzi's implausible tale of the discovery of Alexander's tomb beneath the modern Nabi Daniel Mosque.

ALEXANDER'S EXPLOITS IN LIFE

Alexander was born the son of King Philip II of Macedon and his Molossian Queen Olympias in July of 356BC. During Alexander's childhood and youth Philip gradually established Macedon as the dominant power in Greece. In 338BC Philip destroyed opposition to his authority from Athens and Thebes at the battle of Chaeronea, where Prince Alexander led a dashing charge and annihilated the Theban Sacred Band, who had been considered the finest soldiers in Greece. When his father was assassinated by Pausanias in 336BC, Alexander succeeded to the throne. He crushed insurrections among the tribes to the north, marching as far as the Danube. Thebes and Athens took advantage of his absence to foment rebellion among the city-states, but he retaliated with lightning speed, bringing his army south by forced marches through the mountains. Thebes was besieged, captured and razed to the ground in accordance with a vote of Alexander's allies.

Quest for the Tomb of Alexander by Andrew Chugg

In 334BC Alexander led a Greek coalition in an attack upon the Persian Empire with the initial aim of freeing the Greek cities of the Ionian coast. In May he decisively defeated the Persian armies of the region of modern Turkey at the River Granicus. By the Summer of the following year all the Greek states had duly been liberated, but Alexander continued to prosecute the war by marching towards the heart of the Persian Empire. Darius, the Great King, had gathered an enormous Persian host and the armies clashed on the shores of the Gulf of Issus, which was the highway into Syria. Alexander routed his opponent's forces by a combined assault with his cavalry and the ferocious Macedonian phalanx. Darius fled back to Persia to raise a further army. Alexander marched down the Levantine coast, besieging and capturing Tyre and Gaza and closing all the Mediterranean ports to the Persian fleet, which was eventually compelled to surrender. In Egypt, where Persian rule had been particularly oppressive since its conquest ten years earlier, Alexander was welcomed as a deliverer. Having founded Alexandria near the westernmost mouth of the Nile, Alexander took his army north again for the final showdown with Darius. The climactic battle of the war was fought on the wide, flat plain of Gaugamela in October 331BC. For a third time Alexander triumphed through a perfectly executed stratagem to weaken the Persian centre. Once again Darius fled the field, whilst Alexander proceeded to capture Babylon and the palaces of Susa and Persepolis, declaring himself to be "King of Asia".

Alexander resumed the pursuit of Darius in the summer of 330BC, heading north towards the Caspian Sea. Darius' entourage panicked and executed the deposed Great King. Alexander pressed the pursuit of the dregs of Persian resistance into the region of modern Afghanistan, successively defeating Bessus and Spitamenes. After a series of hard-fought campaigns stretching over two years the ancient nations of Bactria and Sogdiana were finally pacified. In the summer of 327BC Alexander crossed the Hindu Kush and commenced the invasion of India. At the Battle of the Hydaspes Alexander defeated the army of the Rajah Porus, despite his deployment of a large number of war elephants against the Macedonians. Alexander marched ever eastwards, heading now towards the Ganges, but continual drenching by the Indian monsoon and rumours of vast armies with thousands of elephants on the road ahead combined to sap the morale of his troops. Beside the river Beas, the army refused to advance further, forcing Alexander to agree to turn back. Nevertheless, he declined to retrace his steps, but instead led his forces down the Indus to the Indian Ocean, attacking and conquering several large native kingdoms on the way. Nearchus was appointed to command a fleet, which was to sail back to the heart of the Empire via the Straits of Hormuz and the Persian Gulf, whilst Craterus was appointed to lead a large fraction of the army and baggage train back via a circuitous but safe northern route. Alexander himself attempted to lead a third contingent directly back to Persia by crossing the near waterless Gedrosian desert. Due partly to a noble but misguided effort to stay in touch with his fleet, Alexander's force suffered grievous losses to the harshness

Dramatis Personae & Prologue

of the terrain. However, discipline never faltered, so the King was able to lead the survivors in a triumphant, Dionysiac procession through Carmania in the Autumn of 325BC and spirits were lifted even further when contact was finally re-established with Nearchus' fleet.

In 324BC Alexander held court in Susa, where he arranged his own marriage to a daughter of Darius. Around a hundred of the most senior Macedonians and Greeks were also given Persian noblewomen as brides in the same ceremony. But clouds were gathering. In the autumn at Ecbatana Alexander's friend and deputy Hephaistion died suddenly of a feverish illness. Alexander was devastated, but found solace in a campaign against bandit tribes in the mountains. In the spring of 323BC he retuned to Babylon to organise a campaign to circumnavigate and conquer the Arabian Peninsula. But he fell ill with a raging fever at the end of May and expired less than two weeks later.

Embracing the full range of the ancient sources Alexander emerges as an almost Hamlet-like figure, more sinned against than sinning. In a sense Alexander, too, was haunted and motivated by his father's ghost. Arrian comments particularly that his most unique attribute was the expression of genuine conscience and remorse for misdeeds that appear rather slight relative to those of other Graeco-Roman kings. He may well have saved more lives than he destroyed and was rarely gratuitous in the use of violence. Dying young, he left his surviving family dreadfully exposed to the machinations of his enemies, such that virtually all his immediate relations, including both his sons, had been murdered by 15 years after his death. Nevertheless, his legacy is enormous. He was the founder of the Hellenistic Age, which in turn has bequeathed us the foundations of our modern art, science and culture.

This second edition has been revised in May 2012 with the addition of several new figures together with updates and extensions of the accounts of various strands of the story, most notably developments in the investigation of the nature and origins of the starshield block in Venice.

1. Introduction: Entombment and Apotheosis

The conquests of Alexander the Great loom among the towering events of world history. The story has launched a thousand books in a hundred languages. Yet this account will instead focus on Alexander's no less eventful afterlife and the enduring mysteries of his lost corpse and vanished mausoleum. The aim is significantly to elaborate and extend my previous book, *The Lost Tomb of Alexander the Great*, published in 2004, which was the first book length account of the subject in English, since the appearance of the dissertation on *The Tomb of Alexander* by Edward Daniel Clarke in 1805. Not only has Clarke's tome become an expensive rarity, but it is also hopelessly out of date and even *The Lost Tomb* has edged towards obsolescence through the pace of developments. Therefore it is the purpose of this new version to update the quest and enthrall its readership with fresh revelations and novel propositions. More clearly than ever, it will be demonstrated that a detailed knowledge of Alexander's afterlife is integral to a proper appreciation of his impact on history.

This book takes up the tale where conventional histories of Alexander close with the events surrounding his death in Babylon late in the evening of the tenth of June 323 BC. It describes the preparation of the catafalque meant to return his body to his homeland of Macedon, but diverted to Egypt by Ptolemy, who was acting, it is argued, to fulfil Alexander's own wishes. It is shown that Ptolemy's hijacking of the corpse was probably the decisive reason for the subsequent attack on Egypt by Perdiccas, the Regent, who was assassinated there by his own men, having twice failed to force the crossing of the Nile.

Ptolemy's initial entombment of Alexander at the old Egyptian capital of Memphis is investigated with regard to the iconography and possible location of this sepulcher and it is demonstrated that, contrary to previous scholarly opinion, the Memphite tomb very probably existed for three or four decades. Ptolemy's son, Philadelphus, eventually relocated the tomb to Alexandria. There Alexander achieved the apotheosis he had consciously pursued in life. An enormous temple precinct was established at the heart of the city and a high priest was appointed annually to orchestrate his worship.

The tomb returned to the centre-stage of world history in the time of Cleopatra as the Romans embellished their nascent empire through the acquisition of Egypt. For Caesar's faction Alexander was an icon of successful kingship and his tomb a place of pilgrimage. It was correspondingly reviled by the Republican opposition, who resorted to assassinating the populist Caesar in an ultimately vain attempt to ensure that government of the Senatorial class, by the Senatorial class, for the Senatorial class did not perish from the earth. Cleopatra still dreamt of re-establishing Alexander's empire, through the pliable medium of Mark Antony and his military prowess, but Rome would not brook a rival near her throne, so the lovers perished by suicide in the ignominy of their defeat.

Entombment and Apotheosis

The Roman emperors saw in Alexander an exemplar for their autocratic rule, so the tomb basked in their patronage for several centuries more. However, in the late third and fourth centuries AD Alexandria suffered a series of violent upheavals, in one of which the mausoleum overlying the tomb was destroyed. A case is made that almost the last of these shocks, a devastating earthquake closely followed by a roiling tsunami in AD365, is the most likely culprit. Any restoration of the tomb was precluded by the growing political power of the Christian church, which could only see in the deified Alexander a potent pagan rival. The erstwhile famous tomb and sacred corpse vanished mysteriously from history; seemingly at the same time that Christianity finally outlawed paganism.

The forces of Islam secured Alexandria in AD642 and inaugurated a lingering decline of the greatest of Greek cities. For nearly a millennium almost nothing was said of the tomb in the written sources. By the late medieval period the urban area of the city had shrunk to less than a third of its extent in the time of Cleopatra and almost all that remained lay in ruins. However, from the early sixteenth century visitors began once again regularly to report the existence of a tomb of Alexander amidst the wasted vestiges of antiquity (Figures 1.1 & 1.2). Evidence is presented here, which firmly links this medieval tomb with a sarcophagus now displayed in the British Museum. Furthermore, there are intriguing connections between this relic and the Memphite tomb and also with the late Roman period when the Alexandrian tomb was destroyed.

Figure 1.1. Panorama across the Great Harbour of Alexandria in 1681: engraving after a sketch by Cornelius de Bruyn (author's collection)

In the modern era the search for the tomb is inextricably connected with the struggle of the archaeologists to reconstruct ancient Alexandria from fragments in the dust. Progress is seriously hampered by the fact that the modern city has spread to encompass the entire ancient ruin field. Some of the best evidence was gathered in the mid-nineteenth century just barely before the developers sealed over the deeply buried foundations of the Roman and Ptolemaic cities. Through integrating the archaeological material with information from written and cartographic sources, a new hypothesis for the nature and location of the

The Quest for the Tomb of Alexander by Andrew Chugg

Alexandrian tomb has been formulated. If this fresh theory is correct, not only may it provide the key to comprehending the detailed layout of the ancient city, but it also implies that a substantial fragment of the wall that surrounded the precinct of Alexander's tomb has survived unrecognised to the present day.

Figure 1.2. View of Alexandria looking west past Cleopatra's Needle from the Tower of the Romans in 1681: engraving after a sketch by Cornelius de Bruyn (author's collection)

The history of Alexander's tombs is a complex and intricate tapestry, for the threads of evidence are fragmentary, diverse and interwoven through twenty-four centuries. But to unravel the mystery is a thrilling experience, offering as it does glimpses of the vanished glories of the ancient world together with telling insights into the minds of Alexander, the people who followed him and those who succeeded to the kingdoms of his empire. Some admired and worshipped him, whilst others detested and denounced everything that he stood for. The polarity and strength of opinion many centuries after his death is the most impressive testament to the enduring potency of his influence. What though, we might wonder, would Alexander himself have made of the reactions he has stirred?

I should like, Onesicritus, to come back to life for a little while after my death to see how men read these present events then. If now they praise and welcome them, do not be surprised, for they think, every one of them, that this is a fine bait to catch my goodwill.

Alexander quoted by Lucian, How to Write History, 40

2. Death in Babylon

Then the sky was dimmed with mist; and a lightning bolt fell from the heavens into the sea and with it a great eagle. The bronze effigy of Ahura-Mazda in Babylon trembled and resonated; and the lightning rose back into the heavens and the eagle also, bearing a radiant star; and as the star faded into the sky, so Alexander closed his eyes forever.

Alexander's death in the *Alexander Romance*

In the Spring of the year 323 BC, Alexander the Great, in the company of Ptolemy and a task-force of several crack regiments, descended from the cool of the Zagros mountains of western Persia into the already sweltering Mesopotamian plains (see the map in Figure 2.1). He had recently successfully fought a winter campaign against the Cossaeans, a tribe of mountain bandits, who had been in the habit of preying on travellers, whenever unrestrained by royal bribes.[1] His route probably passed through Susa, where he had established his Persian Queen, Stateira, and the rest of the family of Darius, the former Great King, in the palace. Then he headed for his capital, the metropolis of Babylon straddling the river Euphrates, where the original Tower of Babel, its seven-storey ziggurat, dominated the skyline (Figure 2.2) and the Hanging Gardens still bloomed on terraces above an artificial lake fed from the river (Figure 2.3).

Before he reached the river Tigris he was met by embassies from cities and nations beyond his empire in the west including Ethiopia, North Africa, Spain, Italy, perhaps even the Romans,[2] and territories north of the Danube. They congratulated him upon his victories, presented him with golden crowns, and invited his arbitration in various disputes.[3] Following his spectacular and triumphal return from India a little over a year before, there was a burgeoning anticipation that Alexander would soon be moving west, therefore gathering intelligence on his precise intentions would have been the covert mission of these envoys.

After crossing the river Tigris, but still forty miles short of Babylon, Alexander was met by a deputation of Chaldaean astrologers from the temple of the god Marduk in the city. Their leader, Belephantes, reported an unfavorable oracle from their deity to Nearchus, Alexander's admiral, who relayed the warning to

---

[1] Arrian, *Anabasis* 7.15; Plutarch, *Alexander* 72; Diodorus Siculus 17.111.4; Polyaenus 4.3.31; Alexander actively led this mountain campaign during the winter months, dedicating those Cossaeans he killed as offerings to the shade of Hephaistion, which is difficult to reconcile with any significant personal debilitation.
[2] Arrian, *Anabasis* 7.15.5 is corroborated by a fragment of Cleitarchus preserved by Pliny, *NH* 3.57.
[3] This and the rest of the account up to Alexander's death mainly follows Arrian from *Anabasis* 7.15 onwards, except where otherwise indicated.

the King.[4] The Chaldaeans had divined from the inauspicious configuration of the heavens that Alexander's entry into Babylon would certainly be fatal to him, particularly if he entered the city from the west. However, Alexander was suspicious of the motives of these priests: he quoted them a cynical line from a lost play by Euripides, "Prophets are best, who make the truest guess".

The cause of Alexander's scepticism was the failure of the Chaldaeans to make significant progress on the restoration of the shrine of Marduk, the Esagila, which Alexander had ordered on his first visit to Babylon over seven years earlier. Greek sources claimed this shrine had been razed by the Persian king, Xerxes, in the early fifth century BC, but perhaps it was just suffering from the ravages of time.[5] Alexander's revised plan was to employ his army rapidly to clear the foundations in preparation for the reconstruction. He suspected the Chaldaeans might be attempting to delay this project further by keeping him from the city, because they benefited from the revenues of the temple estates, so long as these monies were not required for the upkeep of the shrine. Nevertheless, the King was initially willing to comply with the second part of the priests' advice: to enter the city from the east. However, he quickly discovered that his route was made impassable by swamps, so he failed to assuage the god in this respect either.

There was, in fact, some sense in avoiding the metropolis, since Babylon was on the verge of its stifling summer, when the combination of dank heat and the diseases of a crowded populace posed a considerable danger to visitors in particular, due to their lesser natural immunity. However, Alexander was especially anxious to enter the city at this time. This was partly in order to oversee the final preparations for his Arabian campaign. He planned to sail around the Arabian Peninsula with his fleet, accompanied by an army marching along the coastline. A harbour was under construction to dock a thousand vessels and a fleet of triremes was being fabricated from the cypresses of Babylonia. It was now mid-April and the departure was scheduled for early June.[6] Of still greater significance was the fact that the massive funeral pyre for Hephaistion, Alexander's erstwhile deputy, closest friend and probable lover, was nearing completion across a levelled section of the city's walls. Alexander's lieutenant, Perdiccas, had brought the preserved corpse and the main army down from Ecbatana in the mountains, where Hephaistion had died of a fever in November of the previous year.

---

[4] From Diodorus Siculus 17.112.3; "Belephantes" seems to mean "Mouthpiece of Baal".
[5] Strabo, *Geography* 16.1.5; cf. Michael Wood, *In The Footsteps of Alexander The Great*, p.95.
[6] Strabo 16.1.5 implies that the task of clearing the temple site was expected to take 2 months, but states that this project was unfinished at Alexander's death. This suggests Alexander arrived at Babylon less than two months prior to his death. Diodorus (17.112) states that the fighting with the Cossaeans lasted no more than forty days, so it was probably concluded around the end of February. He then says that Alexander marched in easy stages to Babylon. Allowing for a stopover at Susa, this could easily have taken six or seven weeks.

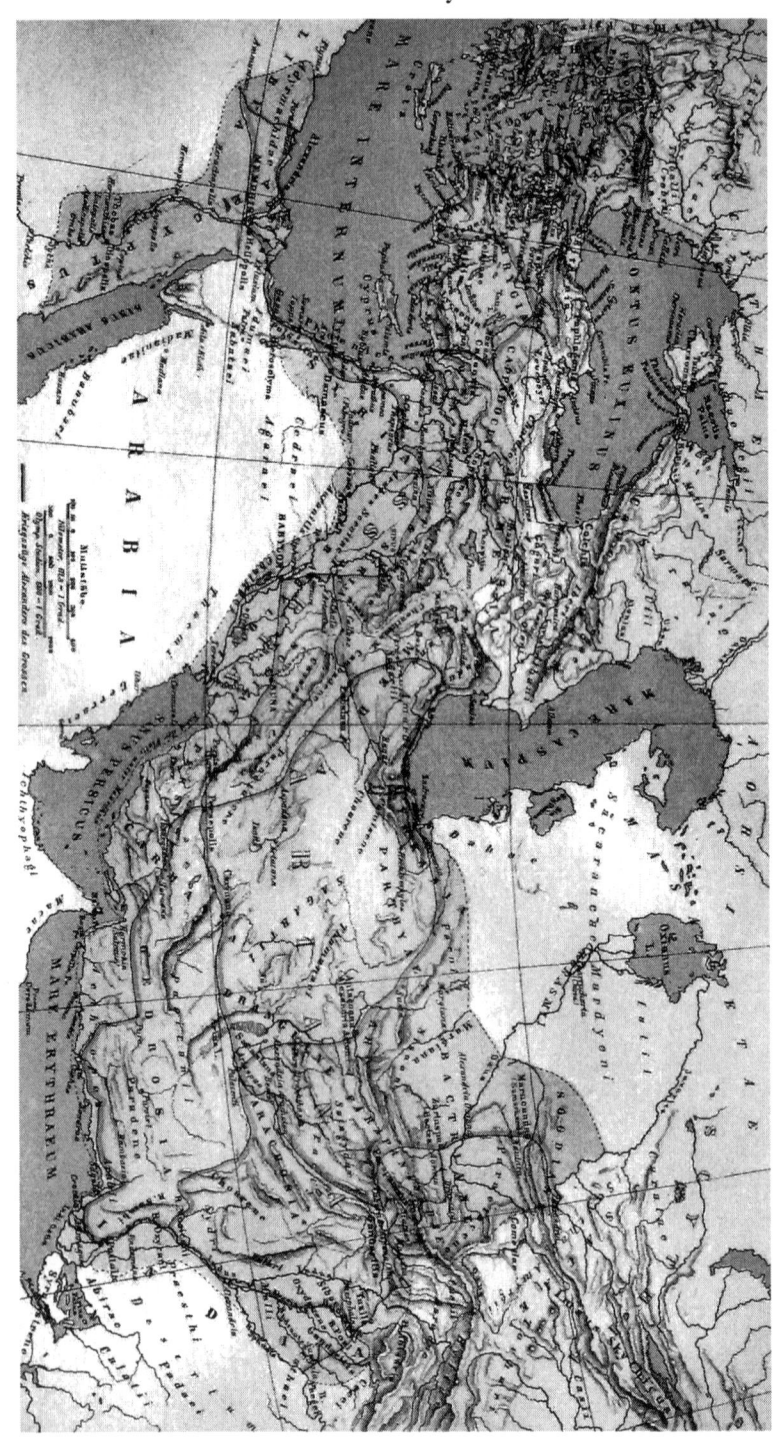

Figure 2.1. Conquests of Alexander (author's collection)

The Quest for the Tomb of Alexander by Andrew Chugg

At Babylon Alexander held court in the Palace of Nebuchadnezzar (Figure 2.4) in the northern sector of the city not far from the Ishtar Gate on the eastern bank of the Euphrates (see map in Figure 2.5). In the second half of April his time was divided between planning for the Arabian expedition, holding audiences with embassies from Greece and preparations for the funeral (an outline chronology for the first half of 323 BC is given in Table 2.1). In what were to be his final months Alexander seems to have planned everything on a breathtaking scale and Hephaistion's obsequies were the most extraordinary manifestation of his extravagance. The pyre was designed by Alexander's court architect, Deinocrates, who seems to have been inspired by the step-pyramid form of the nearby Tower of Babel. Although constructed in wood rather than brick, it was of comparable size (about 70 metres high and 180 metres wide) to the ziggurat and similarly comprised seven stages, each decorated with marvellous gilded sculptures. The first stage had the prows of 240 galleys each with five banks of oars, two kneeling archers and a pair of hoplites.[7] Red felt banners billowed between each vessel. The second level was decorated with flaming torches surmounted by soaring eagles peering at serpents wound about the shafts. The next stage consisted of wild beasts and men composed into royal hunting scenes and the fourth depicted a war of the centaurs. Lions and bulls alternated around the fifth level and at the sixth there were arrayed panoplies of Greek and Persian arms. Most splendid of all at the apex stood the mythical Sirens of Homer's Odyssey, each hollowed out to accommodate a living singer keening out rhapsodic laments. A mile-long section of the city wall had been torn down to form a baked tile foundation for this gleaming edifice, the centrepiece of the most spectacular funeral ever recorded (see Figure 2.6). It all cost a reputed total of 12,000 talents, which was equivalent to about 25 tonnes of gold. It remains the most lavish funeral in history and a physical testament to the depth of Alexander's sorrow and affection. A poignant detail is related by Diodorus: during the period of mourning Alexander ordered that the sacred fires should be extinguished in the temples. This rite was normally only performed upon the death of the king, so the Persians considered it a grim omen. However, it recalls the Greek definition of a friend as a second self and also the King's most famous quote concerning Hephaistion, "He too is Alexander".[8]

In the wake of the funeral around the beginning of May Alexander was probably finding the atmosphere both physically and mentally oppressive at Babylon. He had become aware of a problem with the canal system built by the

---

[7] Diodorus Siculus 17.115; the archaeologist Robert Koldewey has located a possible site for the pyre at a scorched and reddened platform beneath a mound of brick rubble close to the inner wall of Babylon due east of the "Southern Palace" of Nebuchadnezzar; Robert Koldewey, *Das Wieder Erstehende Babylon*, Leipzig, 1913, pp.301-302; Joan Oates, *Babylon*, London, 1979, p.159.

[8] E.g. Diogenes Laertius, *Zeno* 124; Plutarch, *Moralia* 93E; cf. Achilles of Patroclus, "The companion whom I valued above all others and as much as my life." Homer, *Iliad* 18.81: Alexander paraphrases this in Arrian, *Anabasis* 7.14.6.

Assyrian kings to divert the annual spate of the Euphrates away from the metropolis.[9] This occurred as spring turned to summer and the snows melted in the Armenian mountains, thus threatening to burst the river's banks. A little way upstream from Babylon a canal called the Pollacopas (or Pallacotta) had been dug to redirect the flood southwards from the river towards an area of lakes and marshes bordering on the Arabian Desert a hundred miles from the city (see Figure 2.1). The flaw in this system lay in the sogginess of the soil at the junction of the canal with the river. This made it easy to open up the channel in the spring, but it required two months' effort from ten thousand labourers to close it up again in the autumn. Alexander therefore embarked upon an engineering expedition with a small section of the fleet to seek a solution to this conundrum. He sailed upriver on the Euphrates, then down the Pollacopas to the lake district. En route 5km from the soggy mouth he spotted an area of stonier ground, where a new channel might be dug, through which the flow could more easily be controlled. Among the lakes the King located a well-appointed site, where he instigated the establishment of a new city, the last of a couple of dozen such foundations undertaken by Alexander. However, on returning to Babylon via the marshes, several members of his flotilla went astray among the maze of channels, until a pilot he sent to rescue them eventually tracked them down. His own vessel must have dawdled among the reeds as menacing clouds of mosquitoes whined about in the sultry air.

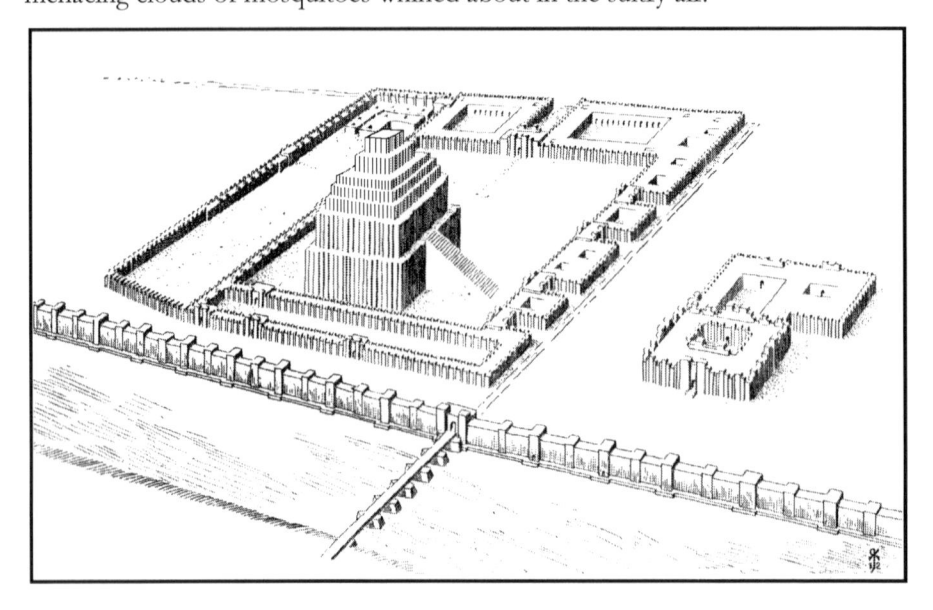

Figure 2.2. The Babylonian Ziggurat & Temple of Marduk (after Koldewey)

---

[9] Cf. Strabo 16.1.9-11 who adds that Alexander wished to make it easier to move his warships closer to Arabia via the lakes and marshes.

The Quest for the Tomb of Alexander by Andrew Chugg

In another part of the wetlands the flotilla happened across some of the tombs of the Assyrian kings. Alexander had taken the tiller of his ship, when a rare gust of wind flipped his cap from his head and onto a patch of reeds growing beside one of these silent sepulchers. The royal diadem was bound about this cap, so its entanglement with a royal grave was considered a dreadful portent. However, a Phoenician oarsman dived into the water and swam to recover the errant headgear. Thinking to keep it dry for the King, he placed the cap on his own head before returning. Unfortunately, the law dictated death for subjects who wore the royal insignia, whatever the reason. Nevertheless, according to Aristobulus,[10] who as one of Alexander's engineers and the main source of our information was probably in attendance, the sailor was merely flogged to avert the omen, then rewarded with the gift of a Talent, equal to a generous 26 kilograms of silver.

By the time of Alexander's return to Babylon well into the second half of May several army groups had arrived to reinforce the Arabian expedition including 20,000 Persians under Peucestas. At the palace, sacred envoys from the Greeks were waiting to present Alexander with golden crowns. Athens and Sparta had voted to award "divine honours" to Alexander the previous year, probably as a placatory gesture, since these states were considered to be the most antagonistic to Alexander's rule among the Greeks. Precedents for this exalted form of recognition had included the worship of Lysander as a god in many Greek cities after his victory over the Athenians at Aegospotami in 404 BC and heroic honours for Dion, Plato's protégé, upon his triumphant return to Syracuse in 357 BC.[11] In letting the Greek city-states know that he would be amenable to accepting such honours, Alexander had probably sought to emulate his putative maternal ancestor, Achilles, who had received divine honours from the Epirotes.[12] Paradoxically, his own Macedonians seem to have refused Alexander these honours, although they had been accorded his father, Philip, during his lifetime.[13] The mission of the envoys in Babylon may have been formally to confer his honours upon Alexander.

Emissaries from the god Ammon in Egypt had also arrived to deliver an oracular verdict on the King's enquiry as to how the spirit of the deceased Hephaistion might be honoured. The god had determined that Hephaistion might be offered sacrifice as a hero, so Alexander began to plan the establishment of his cult throughout the empire.

---

[10] Other historians seem to have accentuated the dramatic irony of the story by claiming the sailor was rewarded with a talent then executed.

[11] See discussion in A.B. Bosworth, *Conquest and Empire: The Reign of Alexander The Great*, p. 280; A. B. Bosworth, "Heroic Honours in Syracuse" in *Crossroads of History: The Age of Alexander*, California, 2004, pp. 11-28.

[12] Plutarch, *Pyrrhus* 1.

[13] Curtius 10.5.11; Diodorus 16.92.5 notes that Philip included a statue of himself among those of the twelve Olympian gods in the procession at the celebration of his daughter's marriage just before his assassination.

Figure 2.3. Reconstruction of the Hanging Gardens of Babylon (author's collection)

Sometime in the next week or so yet another ominous incident transpired. Alexander and his companions had left the throne room to play ball according to Plutarch, to be rubbed down with oil in Diodorus' account or simply because they were thirsty in Arrian's version. During his absence a deranged prisoner from Messenia called Dionysius approached the throne, settled himself upon it and attired himself in the royal diadem and robes, which had been left close at hand.[14] When questioned, the man was unable to offer any excuse for his behaviour, which only blackened the omen. In accordance with the law Alexander had him executed. All this was recorded by the Greek writers. However, it is interesting to note that this scenario bears a striking resemblance to the ancient ritual of having a criminal play-act the role of the king in times of misfortune. This custom traditionally climaxed with the execution of the substitute, thus supposedly diverting the bad luck.[15]

Figure 2.4. Reconstruction of the Palace in Babylon (R. Koldewey)

Most of the known details of Alexander's fatal illness are summarised in Table 2.2. In particular, from the 30th May onwards we have edited extracts from the *Ephemerides*, Alexander's Royal Journal, which Aelian[16] attributes to Eumenes of Cardia, the King's Chief Secretary, but also co-written by a certain Diodotus of Erythrae, who is otherwise unknown. I have shown in an article first published in the Ancient History Bulletin and reproduced here as Appendix A, that "Diodotus" is probably a manuscript error for Diognetus of Erythrae, who, as one of Alexander's surveyors, is likely to have contributed records of the daily marches to this journal, whilst the army was on the move. Both Arrian and Plutarch cite the *Ephemerides* for their versions of the King's final days. Nonetheless, some scholars have disputed the authenticity of this document.[17]

---

[14] From Plutarch, *Alexander* 73.
[15] Michael Wood, *In The Footsteps of Alexander The Great*, p. 225.
[16] Aelian, *Varia Historia* 3.23; Athenaeus, *Deipnosophistae* 434B.
[17] N. G. L. Hammond and C. A. Robinson have championed the authenticity of the Journal in modern scholarship, whilst A. B. Bosworth has conceded that it may have been written and published by Eumenes, but he continues to hold out for the possibility that it was edited to the

Death in Babylon

For example, it makes reference to the Egyptian bull-god Serapis, supposed to have been invented by Ptolemy after Alexander's death.[18] Yet the Greeks were an ecumenical people in that they commonly renamed foreign deities with the nearest familiar equivalent. It is entirely likely that a scholar in Alexandria in the context of one of the inevitable transcriptions of the scrolls changed the name of some Babylonian deity, perhaps the bull-god Marduk, to be more recognisable to his readership. There is a second instance of this apparent anachronism in Plutarch's account, where Serapis appears to the prisoner who sat on the throne. It is also known that Alexander's successors in Egypt as well as other kings of Macedon kept similar diaries of their affairs. In general, the very banality of many of the details from the Journal, the self-consistency of the medical case history it provides and the fact that its references to Babylonian topography seem to be consistent with modern excavations of the city all lend it considerable credence.[19]

In particular the Suda names Strattis of Olynthus as the author of a five book commentary on the *Ephemerides* and states that he was also responsible for an account of Alexander's death. I have shown that this is almost certainly a mistake for Ephippus of Olynthus, whose lost work on the death of the King is extensively quoted in the surviving writings of Athenaeus. Ephippus compiled his commentary within a generation of Alexander's death, which strongly vindicates the authenticity of the *Ephemerides* themselves (see Appendix A).

The 30th May was a day of festivities culminating in a formal banquet in honour of Nearchus. After the meal the King bathed and then attended a private drinking party organised by his friend, Medius of Larissa. On leaving this symposium he again bathed, then seems to have slept until the following evening, when he dined with Medius, who afterwards hosted a second drinking party deep into the night in the company of twenty or so leading Macedonians.[20] More probably on this occasion than the previous evening,

---

point of distortion. L. Pearson, A. E. Samuel and E. Badian have claimed that the Journal is an outright forgery, though their theories on its origins vary markedly.

[18] See Tacitus, *Histories* 4.83-4; it is most probable that Serapis was derived by Ptolemy from Egyptian traditions: the sacred Apis bulls at Memphis were identified with Osiris after their death and worshipped as "Osor-Hapi", hence perhaps "Serapis" in Greek; it has been suggested that there was an Egyptian shrine of this nature in Babylon, but this is a rather intricate hypothesis; R. Koldewey suggested that the Greeks later associated Ea, the father of Marduk, with Serapis and he identified his sanctuary on the northern side of the temple of Marduk.

[19] N. G. L. Hammond, *Alexander the Great*, 1981, Introduction for the Macedonian practice: P. A. Brunt in Section 14 of his Introduction to the Loeb edition of Arrian's *Anabasis* for the Ptolemies, referring to Ulrich Wilcken's seminal article on this issue: "Hypomnematismoi", *Philologus* 53, 1894, pp. 84-126 and especially p.117.

[20] A figure of twenty was given by the mysterious Nicobule, who is quoted by Athenaeus (see Lionel Pearson, *The Lost Histories of Alexander the Great*, p. 67). Nicobule also says that Alexander recited a scene from Euripides' *Andromeda* at the final banquet and it is known from Plutarch, Arrian and others that the King really was fond of quoting this playwright. The Armenian version of the Alexander Romance gives the most extensive list of the names of the guests: Perdikkas, Pithon, Leonatos, Pokestes [Peucestas], Ptlomeos [Ptolemy], Lysimachos, Ariston[ous?],

The Quest for the Tomb of Alexander by Andrew Chugg

Alexander drank undiluted wine from a large cup in commemoration of the death of Heracles, whereupon Arrian, Diodorus, Justin and Plutarch all mention that the King felt a sharp pain as though pierced by a dagger or spear. Plutarch mentions an account, which located the pain in Alexander's back,[21] though he dismissed the story as a fiction. Justin writes rather melodramatically that the King "was carried half-dead from the table; he was wracked with such agony that he asked for a sword to put an end to it and felt pain at the touch of his attendants as if he were all over wounds."[22] The Journal merely records that Alexander bathed and ate lightly (or scantily) following this party, afterwards sleeping in the bathroom as he was starting to feel feverish.

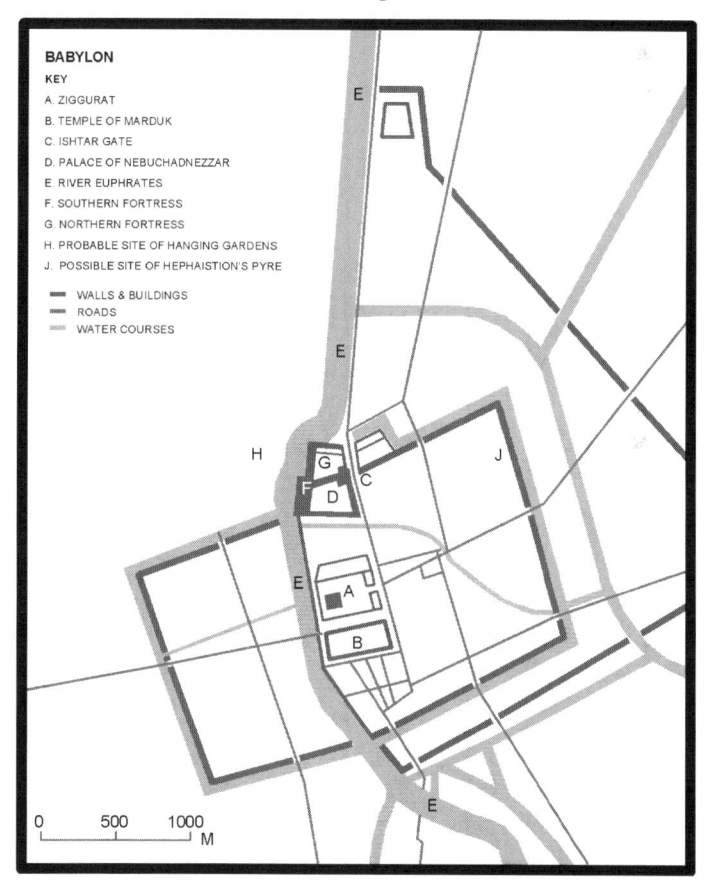

BABYLON
KEY
A. ZIGGURAT
B. TEMPLE OF MARDUK
C. ISHTAR GATE
D. PALACE OF NEBUCHADNEZZAR
E. RIVER EUPHRATES
F. SOUTHERN FORTRESS
G. NORTHERN FORTRESS
H. PROBABLE SITE OF HANGING GARDENS
J. POSSIBLE SITE OF HEPHAISTION'S PYRE

― WALLS & BUILDINGS
― ROADS
― WATER COURSES

Figure 2.5. Plan of Babylon (after Koldewey)

Eumenes, Nearchos, Kassandros [Cassander], Olkias, Meleandros, Philip, Philip the doctor, Philip the engineer, Heraclides, Europpeos, Pharsalios, Philotas, Dardana. It adds Asander to a list of those who were innocent of the poisoning plot (as well as Perdikkas, Ptlomeos, Lysimachos, Olkias and Eumenes). Other versions of the Romance give more garbled and less complete lists.

[21] Plutarch, *Alexander* 75.
[22] Justin, *Epitome of the Philippic History of Pompeius Trogus* 12.13.9.

Death in Babylon

On the 1st June the King was borne on a couch to perform the daily sacrifices. Afterwards he lay in the men's apartments of Nebuchadnezzar's palace until dusk, whilst playing dice with Medius and issuing instructions to his officers: the land army was scheduled to depart for Arabia in three days and the fleet would sail in four. In the evening he had himself ferried across the river to the gardens, where he bathed and reclined. These gardens most probably lay just north of the inner walls on the west bank of the Euphrates opposite the palace and may well have been the famous terraced Hanging Gardens, which Strabo placed on the banks of the Euphrates and which are believed to have been constructed by Nebuchadnezzar II for his queen – Figures 2.3 & 2.5.[23] Plutarch and Arrian both mention that Alexander had his bed set beside a "great diving pool" whilst he was in the gardens, which may refer to the reservoir at the base of the terraces from which water was drawn up to irrigate the foliage. The next day the King bathed and sacrificed as usual, then lay down in his canopied bed, conversed with Medius and was entertained by listening to Nearchus telling tales of his Indian Ocean voyage. After instructing his officers to meet with him at dawn, he dined, once again "lightly", and was carried back to the canopied bed. He was in a high fever the whole night.

Figure 2.6. Reconstruction of Hephaistion's funeral pyre by F. Jaffé (author's collection)

---

[23] Strabo 16.1.5; Diodorus Siculus 2.7.3 & 2.10.1; Josephus, *Contra Apion* 1.141-142; Philo of Byzantium, *Concerning the Seven Wonders* 1.

The Quest for the Tomb of Alexander by Andrew Chugg

On the 3rd June after bathing and sacrificing he explained his plans for the Arabian voyage, still scheduled to start on the 5th, to Nearchus and the other senior officers, but his fever grew more intense towards evening and he had a bad night. The following day after bathing and sacrificing it was stated by the *Ephemerides* that he no longer had any rest from the fever (οὐκέτι ἐλινύειν πυρέσσοντα). Nevertheless, he summoned his officers to discuss appointments to vacant army commands and ordered them to finalise the preparations for the voyage. After bathing in the evening he was very ill. However, the next morning he was again carried to the house near the diving pool, where he dutifully offered the appointed sacrifices and issued further instructions concerning the voyage to his most senior officers. On the 6th June he just managed to perform the sacrifices, yet persisted in instructing the officers further concerning the Arabian voyage, but his fever grew worse. That evening or possibly early the next day he ordered his generals to wait in the courtyard of the palace and the battalion and company commanders to gather outside the gates. On the 7th June he was carried back from the gardens to the palace. Being now extremely ill, though he still recognised his officers, he said nothing: he was voiceless (ἄναυδον). His fever burned high that night and all the next day, and ever more intensely during the following night and throughout the day of the 9th June.

By this time the rumour had spread among his troops that the King might already have died. To allay their fear and suspicion they yearned to see him one last time and thronged about the gates of the palace shouting threats at the King's Companions, who eventually relented and admitted them to file past his bedside (Figure 2.7). His voice was failing, but he acknowledged them by raising his head or signing with his eyes. Perhaps he was still capable of a hoarse whisper, for Curtius quotes the King asking, "After my death will you find a king who deserves such men?" and says that Alexander collapsed in exhaustion after everyone had passed. Shortly after he took his ring from his finger and handed it to Perdiccas. Curtius and Justin claim he commanded that his body be taken to Ammon, the Egyptian god.[24] When his Companions asked him to whom he bequeathed his kingdom, he replied, "To the strongest" (ὅτι τῷ κρατίστῳ), and some of the sources add that he foresaw great funeral games (see Table 2.2). When, finally, Perdiccas asked him at what times he wished his divine honours to be paid to him, he answered, "When you are happy".

Five of the King's Companions: Pithon, Seleucus, Attalus, Peucestas and Menidas, together with the seers, Demophon and Cleomenes, held an overnight vigil in the temple of Serapis (Marduk?), enquiring whether it would be desirable for Alexander to be brought there to be cared for by the god, but the shrine's

---

[24] Curtius 10.4.4; Justin 12.15.7 & 13.4.6; Diodorus 18.3.5; *Liber de Morte* 119; Lucian, *Dialogues of the Dead* 13.

Death in Babylon

oracle indicated that he should remain where he was. Aristobulus[25] has written that Alexander, made thirsty by his fever, became delirious after drinking wine and this detail might be fitted to around the 9th June. The next day, the 10th June,[26] towards evening, Alexander was pronounced dead. He was not quite 33 years old.

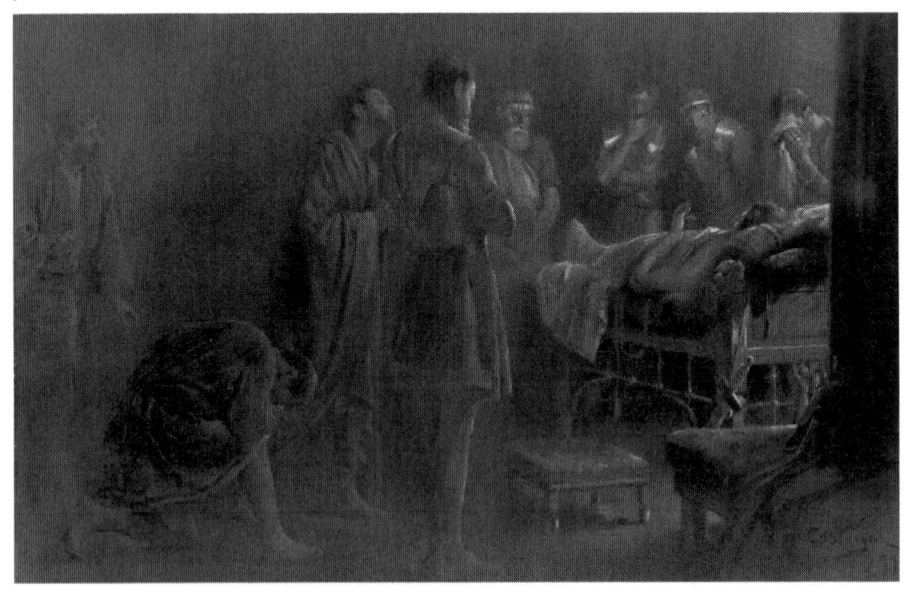

Figure 2.7. The Death of Alexander by A. Castaigne (author's collection)

At first the sounds of lamentation, weeping and the beating of breasts echoed throughout the royal quarters. Then a sad hush fell, enveloping all in a still silence like that of desert wastes, as from grief they turned to considering what would happen now. The young noblemen who formed his customary Bodyguard could neither suppress their bitter anguish nor confine themselves to the vestibule of the royal canopy. They wandered around like madmen, filling the whole city with the sound of their mournful grieving, foregoing no kind of lament that sorrow suggests in such circumstances. Accordingly, those who had been standing outside the royal quarters rushed to the spot, barbarians and Macedonians alike, and in the general grief

---

[25] Quoted by Plutarch, *Alexander* 75.4.

[26] Plutarch gives the 28th of Daisios, which is the 10th June in the Julian calendar, and Arrian's version is consistent with this date. A Babylonian tablet confirms 10th/11th June beyond reasonable doubt (29th day of 2nd month of Babylonian year – see A. E. Samuel, *Ptolemaic Chronology*, Munich, 1962). However, Plutarch also mentions that Aristobulus recorded the date as 30th Daisios, which is the 11th June, because Daisios was a "hollow" month of the Macedonian calendar and had no 29th (see *Ptolemaic Chronology*, p. 46). The disparities are best explained by assuming Plutarch was citing the *Ephemerides* for the accurate date and time, whereas Aristobulus and the Babylonian priests only heard the news announced the following morning. Pseudo-Callisthenes (Alexander Romance) gives 4th Pharmouthi, which is 13th June according to the Egyptian calendar: this cannot be the day that Alexander was pronounced dead, but may be closer to the actual date, if he had entered a profound coma.

The Quest for the Tomb of Alexander by Andrew Chugg

conqueror and conquered were indistinguishable. The Persians recalled a master of great justice and clemency, the Macedonians a peerless king of outstanding valour; together they indulged in a kind of contest in mourning.

Quintus Curtius Rufus[27]

The sincerity of much of the shocked grief in reaction to Alexander's death is epitomised by the behaviour of Sisygambis, Darius' mother and latterly Alexander's grandmother-in-law, who, upon hearing the news, turned to face the wall and refused sustenance until she died five days later.[28]

On the 16th June, when Egyptian and Chaldaean embalmers arrived to treat and preserve Alexander's corpse, despite the summer heat they found it uncorrupted and retaining a lifelike complexion. At first they did not dare touch the body, but after praying to gain the gods' consent they cleaned out the cadaver and laid it in a golden sarcophagus crammed with exotic spices and perfumes.[29] The Armenian Alexander Romance 283 mentions that Alexander's body was preserved in "island-honey and *hipatic* aloe" and "a mixture of honey and spices was added to the coffin" according to the *Liber de Morte* in Section 113 of the *Metz Epitome*. This might well have been an effective preservative. Plutarch records in his *Life of Agesilaus* 40 that the Spartan king died on the coast of Libya[30] in 360BC, but his companions, due to their custom of returning their kings' bodies to Spartan soil for burial, wished to preserve his corpse in honey. However, they had to make do with melted wax, since there was insufficient honey to hand.

* * * * * * * *

What then was the cause of Alexander's death? It remains one of the most tantalizing mysteries of the ancient world, for we lack sufficient details to make a certain diagnosis. Nevertheless, on the basis of the assumption that the Journal account is authentic, it is possible to argue that one scenario fits the case history significantly better than any other.

At the time of the King's death there was no suspicion of poisoning.[31] After all the account given by the Journal is a classic case history for death through disease. However, within about a year at most and probably sooner the story emerged that Alexander had been treacherously poisoned by order of Antipater, his regent in Macedon. A certain Hagnothemis, who is otherwise unknown, is supposed to have claimed to have heard the tale from Antigonus, Alexander's governor of Phrygia. Alexander had ordained in 324 BC that Craterus should

---

[27] Curtius 10.5.7.
[28] Curtius 10.5.19-25; Diodorus 17.118.3.
[29] Curtius 10.10.9 and Plutarch, *Alexander* 77; cf. Diodorus 18.26.3.
[30] Libya anciently meant Africa west of the Nile.
[31] This version of the poisoning story is principally derived from Plutarch, *Alexander* 77, who was skeptical: so too Arrian, *Anabasis* 7.27, whilst Curtius 10.10.14 and Diodorus 17.118 were more neutral; Justin 12.14 accepted the story as fact and the *Liber de Morte* reported the poisoning as true history.

Death in Babylon

take over the regency of Macedon, thus providing Antipater with a basic motive. The poison is variously described as having been provided by Aristotle, Alexander's former tutor, or having been mere water collected from the River Styx. This was considered deadly by virtue of its extreme chill and was said to have been transported to Babylon in a mule's hoof, the only vessel capable of withstanding its legendary caustic properties. Cassander, Antipater's son, was the supposed emissary and he had indeed joined Alexander late in 324 BC or early in 323 BC. A story is told that, being new to the court, he was foolish enough to laugh at a Persian performing proskynesis (a form of obeisance) before the King. Alexander was furious and dashed his head against the wall. Plutarch says that when Cassander caught sight of a statue of Alexander at Delphi many years later he shook uncontrollably.

In the classic version, as related by the *Liber de Morte*, the poison was administered at Medius' party by Iollas, Alexander's cup-bearer, Cassander's younger brother and reputedly Medius' lover. On the strength of this same rumour, Hypereides, an Athenian orator and a bitter enemy of Macedon, proposed a vote of thanks to Iollas not very long after Alexander's death[32] and Olympias, Alexander's vengeful mother, destroyed the cup-bearer's grave in 317BC.[33]

An initial problem with this story is that it contains some obviously fictitious elements, such as the river water and the mule's hoof. If some parts of it are invention, then the rest must also be suspect. Arrian was aware of several fantastical versions of the tale, and an account with close similarities to the *Liber de Morte* has come down to us among the fables of the Alexander Romance.[34] Both Arrian and Plutarch were deeply sceptical, and even Curtius and Diodorus hedge their bets, although Justin accepted the story and extended the scope of the plot by implicating Alexander's officers. A second reason to be dubious is that this story emerged at a time of continual warfare between the Diadochi, Alexander's successors, among whom Antipater and subsequently Cassander were prominent leaders. Anything that might have helped to estrange the Macedonian troops from these commanders would have been potent propaganda for their opponents. In other words, even if Alexander had not really been poisoned, circumstances would have dictated that such a story be fabricated. Thirdly, it is very difficult to make any sensible poisoning scenario fit the case history from the Journal account. For this reason those who favour the poisoning theory have traditionally been leading critics of the Journal's authenticity. However, even Justin, in treating the poisoning story as fact, gives

---

[32] Plutarch, *Moralia* 848.
[33] Diodorus 19.11.8 & 19.35.1.
[34] E.g. R. Stoneman (translator), *The Greek Alexander Romance* 3.31; A M Wolohojian (translator), *The Romance of Alexander the Great by Pseudo-Callisthenes* 264-268.

a duration of more than a week for Alexander's illness,[35] whereas any poison potent enough to produce the reportedly sharp and incapacitating pains should really have been promptly fatal. Nonetheless, slow strychnine poisoning has been proposed,[36] but the risks associated with such a complex and protracted plan requiring multiple dosings would seem prohibitive given that Alexander himself had some knowledge of herbal medicine.[37] Engels has also pointed out that the lethal variety of strychnine has an extremely bitter taste and that Alexander's reported symptoms do not fit the physiological effects of either slow or fast administration of strychnine.[38] Finally, Antipater on his deathbed showed considerable loyalty to Alexander's wife and son by placing them in the care of Polyperchon, rather than leaving his own son, Cassander, in power.[39] In summary, whereas poisoning cannot be excluded as a possibility, it may reasonably be considered an unlikely scenario.

For completeness mention should be made of a couple of recent books, which have embraced the theory that Alexander was murdered, whilst discarding all the ancient evidence on the likely perpetrators.[40] Each author appears to have been motivated by the whodunit principle of pinning the crime on the least likely suspect. In one case Queen Roxane is fingered, despite the fact that she was reliant on Alexander as guarantor of her status and for the safety of both herself and her unborn child. In the other, Ptolemy is accused, though several ancient sources suggest he was Alexander's illegitimate half-brother (and none denies it). Furthermore, Alexander had personally saved his life in India and had raised him to a rank, such that he was second only to Perdiccas in Babylon when the King died. Such was Ptolemy's loyalty, that he later wrote an important history of Alexander, which sought to rescue the King's reputation from the gossip of his detractors. In neither of these modern books is there any tangible evidence to support their convoluted hypotheses. Though these works might have some entertainment value as amusing fictions, and indeed one author is also a novelist, they lack any historical rigour.

Did Alexander drink himself into an early grave? There is no dispute that the King sometimes drank heavily, but this was by no means unusual among high-ranking Greeks in those times (nor, it might be added, among most social groups in most epochs). Ephippus, a hostile and sensationalist chronicler,

---

[35] Justin 12.15.12: "On the sixth day Alexander's voice failed." Justin mentions another period of three days at 12.15.1: "After three days Alexander felt that his death was certain…" It appears doubtful whether these periods are meant to be consecutive, but allowing that Alexander survived perhaps several days after his voice failed, then Justin is more or less in agreement with the Journal account regarding the duration of his illness.
[36] R. D. Milns, *Alexander the Great*, London, 1968, p. 257.
[37] Plutarch, *Alexander* 8
[38] D. W. Engels, "A note on Alexander's death," *Classical Philology* 73, pp. 224-8.
[39] Diodorus 18.48.4.
[40] Graham Phillips, *Alexander the Great: Murder in Babylon*, 2004; Paul C. Doherty, *Alexander the Great: Death of a God*, 2004.

attributed Alexander's death to the anger of Dionysus, the god of wine, who was particularly associated with the city of Thebes, which had been destroyed by Alexander's allies.[41] This may therefore be a wishful case of poetic justice. Aelian gives another edited extract from the Royal Journal, which details various drinking parties attended by Alexander in a three-week period around October 324 BC.[42] The passage appears to have been selected with the purpose of demonstrating that Alexander drank excessively, yet it reports drinking bouts confined to just four evenings in the period. This hardly sounds notably intemperate during a time of relative relaxation. Aristobulus, who will have been an eyewitness, wrote that Alexander only sat long over his wine for the sake of conversation with his Companions.[43] Alcoholic hepatitis might sometimes be associated with fever and could terminate in coma. However, it would almost invariably be accompanied by jaundice and evidence of profound malnutrition, neither of which was observed. The possibility of incidental contamination of Alexander's wine with lead or methanol has also been raised, but neither would be expected to produce a raging and escalating fever.[44] It is therefore most unlikely that Alexander's drinking was the direct cause of his demise, though alcohol may possibly have exacerbated another disease.

Other popular candidate diagnoses include Schachermeyr's suggestion that it might have been leukaemia,[45] though the King's illness seems to have been too short and sudden for this to be at all likely. In all probability, Alexander's death was genuinely the consequence of infection by some biological organism. Typhus is an old favourite. It is transmitted by fleas, lice, mites and ticks and can become epidemic in the context of crowded and unsanitary living conditions. It presents with fever, back and muscle pain, severe headache, a cough and a prominent rash. Some districts of Babylon were probably densely populated, but Alexander's personal living conditions were obviously spacious and he was in the habit of bathing at least once a day. Furthermore, there is no evidence of any rash. On the contrary, his corpse is described as pure and fresh by Plutarch.

Oldach and Richards have recently proposed a diagnosis of typhoid fever with the rare complication of ascending paralysis and coma.[46] Unfortunately, however, their case rests heavily upon a supposition that abdominal pain "in the right upper quadrant" was a key symptom. The only evidence for this comes

---

[41] Athenaeus 434A-B; see Lionel Pearson, *The Lost Histories of Alexander the Great*, p.62.
[42] Aelian, *Varia Historia* 3.23.
[43] Arrian, *Anabasis* 7.29.4.
[44] David W. Oldach, MD and Robert E. Richard, MD, PhD, "A Mysterious Death", *The New England Journal of Medicine*, Volume 338, Number 24, June 11, 1998; John Maxwell O'Brien, *Alexander the Great: the Invisible Enemy*, makes the case for the rôle of drink in Alexander's downfall, but even he does not see alcohol as much more than an exacerbating factor in the King's death.
[45] Fritz Schachermeyr, *Alexander der Grosse*, p. 563: he also suggests falciparum malaria.
[46] David W Oldach, MD and Robert E Richard, MD, PhD, "A Mysterious Death", *The New England Journal of Medicine*, Volume 338, Number 24, June 11, 1998.

The Quest for the Tomb of Alexander by Andrew Chugg

from the unreliable and frequently downright fictional Alexander Romance of Pseudo-Callisthenes,[47] which states that Alexander "suddenly shouted with pain as if struck through the liver with an arrow" at Medius' party. Setting aside the fact that the liver pain is expressed as a mere simile, the Greeks considered the liver to be the seat of the passions, so being struck through the liver has the same poetical overtones in the original Greek of the Romance as being pierced through the heart does in English, thus it ought not to be taken literally. In general, the credibility of the Romance is fatally undermined by episodes such as Alexander's conversations with prophetic trees, which foretell his death in Babylon and the subsequent murder of his mother and wife. Another problem for the typhoid theory is that the Persian kings had their drinking water boiled and there is no reason to suppose that this practice was discontinued at the royal palaces following Alexander's accession.[48] Furthermore, the marshes he navigated in May seem to have been fed by the Pollacopas Canal, which is believed to have branched from the Euphrates upstream of Babylon, so there is no *prima facie* reason to suppose that the King was exposed to the unspeakable horrors of Babylonian sewage effluent. Whilst the Typhoid hypothesis cannot be ruled out, a water-borne disease does not appear to fit the evidence particularly snugly.

In the aftermath of an epidemic of West Nile Virus in the United States in 2002, John Marr and Charles Calisher proposed in 2003 that Alexander's cause of death was encephalitis resulting from infection by this disease.[49] In the course of the US outbreak dead birds had been discovered lying beneath trees, so Marr & Calisher's article in *Emerging Infectious Diseases* drew special attention to an incident reported by Plutarch, when dead birds had fallen at Alexander's feet as he entered Babylon in 323BC.[50] However, Plutarch was explicit that these ravens had been fighting one another, so it is superfluous to infer the intervention of any disease. Furthermore, in modern outbreaks the disease has a mortality of only a few percent among reported cases and many additional mild cases go unreported. Its fatal victims are normally elderly or already debilitated by some other illness. Finally, in a letter responding to Marr & Calisher's article, Massimo Galli, Flavia Bernini and Gianguglielmo Zehender of the University of Milan presented genetic analyses of the virus, which show that it could not have infected humans before the 8th century AD and probably not before ~AD1000. They concluded that the molecular dating of the origin of West Nile Virus acquits it of any responsibility for Alexander's death.[51]

---

[47] Stoneman, *The Greek Alexander Romance* 3.31; cf. Robin Lane Fox, *Alexander the Great*, Ch. 32.
[48] Mary Renault, *The Nature of Alexander*, p.228.
[49] John S. Marr & Charles H. Calisher, "Alexander the Great and West Nile Virus Encephalitis", *Emerging Infectious Diseases*, Vol. 9, No. 12, December 2003, pp. 1599-1603.
[50] Plutarch, *Alexander* 73.1.
[51] Massimo Galli, Flavia Bernini and Gianguglielmo Zehender, "Alexander the Great and West Nile Virus Encephalitis [letter]", *Emerging Infectious Diseases*, Vol. 10, No. 7, July 2004.

Death in Babylon

Early in 325 BC Alexander had suffered a grievous arrow wound to his chest, whilst personally leading the storming of a Mallian town, possibly Multan, in India. Ptolemy stated that air was seen to escape from the wound as well as blood when the arrow was withdrawn, implying perforation of the lung.[52] On the strength of this and Alexander's voicelessness in the late stages of his final illness, pleurisy has been considered a likely complication. However, Ptolemy himself recorded that he was not present at this siege, having been engaged in a mission elsewhere.[53] The rest of the ancient accounts suggest the arrow actually lodged in Alexander's breast-bone, which would also be more medically consistent with the reported speed and completeness of the King's recovery from the wound.[54] The two-year span between the arrow wound and Alexander's demise also renders pleurisy less likely than is sometimes portrayed.

A TV documentary entitled "Alexander the Great's Mysterious Death" and first aired in 2004 proposed that the King might have overdosed on herbal medicine, specifically hellebore. I have found it difficult to trace any authenticated cases where individuals have managed fatally to poison themselves using this plant. It is especially preposterous to suggest that Alexander did so, since Aristotle's teachings on herbal medicine would undoubtedly have extended to the potential dangers of hellebore in large doses.

A recent paper by Hutan Ashrafian in the Journal of the History of the Neurosciences has discussed the possibility that Alexander died due to aggravation of a cervical neck deformity.[55] It cites reports that that he habitually cocked his head to the left and sometimes directed his gaze slightly upwards, although the ancient sources maintain that these were mere mannerisms. Ashrafian argues that reports that Alexander was epileptic, that one of his pupils was nearly black and the other blue-grey and that he had horns might all be worked into his hypothesis via various rare medical conditions. However, the source evidence on all three points is defective. Epilepsy is never specifically attested for Alexander by ancient writers. Its association with the King seems to have been inspired by a passage in the *Physiognomonika* of Adamantios: "Small and tremulous eyes… display the height of boldness and elevation but also susceptibility to anger and drink, boasting, mental instability, and near-epilepsy, and they yearn for superhuman glory, as in the case of Alexander the Macedonian."[56] Since this author only mentions "near-epilepsy", he implicitly clears Alexander of having suffered from actual epilepsy. The eye-colour asymmetry is sourced from the semi-legendary Alexander Romance, where the same passage confides that Alexander had pointed teeth "like a snake". Though

---

[52] Arrian, *Anabasis* 6.10.1.
[53] Arrian, *Anabasis* 6.11.8; Curtius 9.5.21.
[54] Plutarch, *Moralia* 327B, 341C, 344C-D, 345A; Plutarch, *Alexander* 63.6; Arrian, *Anabasis* 6.9.10; Diodorus 17.99.3; Curtius 9.5.9-32; Strabo 15.1.33; A. B. Bosworth, *Alexander and the East*, p. 62.
[55] Hutan Ashrafian, "The Death of Alexander the Great – A Spinal Twist of Fate," *Journal of the History of the Neurosciences*, Vol. 13, Issue 2, June 2004, pp. 138-142.
[56] Adamantios, *Physiognomonika* 1.14 (4th century AD).

coins and statues depict Alexander wearing horns, they were not real, but symbolized deification as Ammon. Ephippus wrote that Alexander wore them as fancy dress at a party, which would hardly have been necessary had he sprouted a pair of his own![57] Death from neck deformities is improbable and especially so in a physically active individual, who had survived into his thirties without ill effect.

Almost all real deaths can be attributed to one among a small range of common causes. Few people die of rare causes and virtually nobody ever dies of a unique cause. On statistical grounds alone, rare or unique causes for Alexander's death are not worth considering unless all common explanations have been securely ruled out.

Among all the disparate diagnoses we are left with just one common cause of death, which provides a perfect fit to virtually every known feature of Alexander's final illness. It was first suggested as long ago as the 19th century[58] and is endorsed by many modern writers (notably Engels[59]), but it never seems to have been put forward with quite as much force and detail as it merits. We can be fairly confident that Alexander will have been exposed to malaria-infected mosquitoes in the swamps south of Babylon some time around the middle of May, since malaria has been endemic to Mesopotamia since very ancient times. There are four species of malaria parasite, but only one of these, plasmodium falciparum, is commonly promptly fatal. The nature of the illness produced by falciparum malaria is succinctly described in the following extracts from an article and a book dealing with this subject:-

Malaria is a parasitic disease endemic in many tropical and sub-tropical parts of the world. It is usually transmitted by the bites of infected anopheline mosquitoes. Falciparum malaria… is associated with the highest levels of parasites in the blood and is the most severe form of malaria, sometimes fatal. The incubation period of Falciparum malaria is usually nine to fourteen days during which the parasites develop silently in the liver before they mature, multiply and invade the red blood cells…. According to an expert consulted by the Medical Protection Society in a recent case, one of the chief characteristics of infection is the extreme variability of signs and symptoms of the attack. Classical symptoms of malaria such as cold and rigors followed by high fever and sweating repeated at regular intervals are rare. The early symptoms of malaria include tiredness, depression headache, pains in the back and limbs, loss of appetite and nausea. In about thirty per cent of patients the illness starts with a rigor; mild diarrhoea, perhaps accompanied by slight jaundice or cough. Although the spleen is often enlarged it is often not palpable. The development of severe malaria is variable. Most often the patient is not very ill during the first three or four days of the illness but deteriorates rapidly towards the end of the first week and this deterioration can occur over the course of a few hours…. The symptoms of severe malaria vary depending on which of the patient's organs are

---

[57] Athenaeus, *Deipnosophistae* 537E.
[58] The French physician, Emile Littré, diagnosed Alexander's fatal illness as falciparum malaria in *Médecine et Médecins*, Paris, 1872, pp. 406-415.
[59] D. W. Engels, "A note on Alexander's death," *Classical Philology* 73, pp. 224-8.

Death in Babylon

damaged by the dividing form of the parasite, which situates itself in small blood vessels within the organs. The brain, kidneys and lung are often involved. Cerebral malaria may develop slowly or rapidly. Headache, agitation or drowsiness, abnormal behaviour or coma can ensue. Temperature is usually high but may be subnormal. In such cases death is likely to be the outcome unless there is skilled intervention in hospital at an early stage.[60]

...in practice the characteristic periodicity is not in fact observed in many cases, owing to infections with multiple generations of parasites whose development cycles are not synchronized. Experiments... were carried out for many years at Horton Hospital in Epsom in England. These experiments proved that in malaria caused by P. falciparum, the most dangerous species of malaria, most attacks take the form of subcontinuous or quotidian (peaking every twenty-four hours) fevers.[61]

It is worthwhile enumerating the parallels between the circumstances and symptoms of Alexander's illness and a typical case history for falciparum malaria, for there are many:-

i) Alexander was very probably sailing and sleeping in malaria infested swamps south of Babylon between one and two weeks prior to his falling ill, which is precisely consistent with the incubation period of falciparum malaria.

ii) The Journal account implies that Alexander slept right through the day following Medius' first party. Fatigue and lethargy are typical of the onset of many serious infections, but this is especially true of falciparum malaria.

iii) Plutarch describes Alexander experiencing a stabbing back pain, whilst quaffing wine from a Cup of Heracles at Medius' party, whilst Justin has him carried from the party experiencing pains all over. It is ironic that both these writers believed they were citing evidence in favour of poisoning, whilst their accounts are in fact more cogently consistent with the pains in the back and the limb joints that are a common precursor symptom of falciparum malaria.

iv) There are two references in the ancient accounts to Alexander eating lightly in the early days of his illness, which may hint at a suppressed appetite as expected in the early stages of falciparum malaria.

v) Arrian's version of the Journal states that Alexander "no longer had any rest from fever" after 4th June. The implication is that the fever had been intermittent for most of the first week of illness. Such an

---

[60] Dr P. D. Clarke (Medical Director of the UK Medical Advisory Service for Travellers Abroad) & Dr A. Bryceson (Hospital for Tropical Diseases, London), *The Medical Protection Society, Casebook (GP) No. 4*, London, 1994, pp. 4-5.
[61] Robert Sallares, *Malaria and Rome*, 2002, p. 11.

intermittent fever fits in well with the details of the King instructing his officers, playing dice and discussing the filling of vacant army posts, which are interspersed with references to serious bouts of fever setting in during the evenings and continuing overnight. A pattern of fever peaks and remissions on a daily cycle (a so-called quotidian fever) is highly characteristic of falciparum malaria. This also helps to explain why Alexander failed to postpone the imminent Arabian expedition during the first week of his illness. If he had a malarial fever, he probably felt he was starting to recover every morning in the initial phases and his optimism may have lasted until nightfall. Furthermore, it is expected that the fever should eventually become pseudo-continuous, because different broods of the parasite start to overlap like runners on a racetrack over many laps.

vi) Alexander was not very ill during the first three or four days of his illness, but he deteriorated rapidly towards the end of the first week, which is the classic pattern for falciparum malaria.

vii) Falciparum malaria provides two possible causes for the reported voicelessness. It could either be a consequence of a pulmonary complication or the beginning of neurological effects. In severe cases of falciparum malaria the brain and the lungs are the most commonly affected organs.

viii) Aristobulus says the King became delirious, probably towards the end. This would fit with the agitation, confusion and fitting which typify the onset of cerebral malaria.

ix) The reports that Alexander's body remained pure and uncorrupted for days after his supposed death, despite the heat of the Babylonian summer, have led many to infer that the King may actually have been in a state of profound coma. It is potentially difficult to distinguish coma from death without sophisticated medical tests, because breathing can become so shallow as to be nearly undetectable. Diseases such as typhoid might have terminated in coma, but in this context it is a rare complication. Conversely, cerebral malaria is a common complication of falciparum malaria in the case of patients with low innate immunity, which group would especially include most visitors to a malaria-infested region. Cerebral malaria almost invariably terminates in coma and is rapidly fatal, unless there is skilled medical intervention.

x) A diagnosis of falciparum malaria has the additional advantage of not requiring any exacerbating circumstance for it to prove fatal. Heavy drinking and a debilitating chest wound would certainly not have helped, but falciparum malaria could easily have killed Alexander, even if he was as fit and healthy as his exploits during the preceding Cossaean campaign suggest.

Death in Babylon

It might be added that the malarial explanation has the special charm of reconciling the details in the so-called vulgate sources with the information from the *Ephemerides* in Arrian and Plutarch. Nevertheless, medical experts have often been curiously dismissive of malaria. For example, Marr & Calisher have written, "Some of Alexander's symptoms are comparable with malaria... however... intermittent fevers were not reported... absence of P. falciparum's dramatic signature fever curve diminishes the possibility of malaria as a probable cause."[62] We have seen that in fact there is clear evidence of an intermittent fever from the best source: Arrian's citations from the *Ephemerides*. Why then should Marr & Calisher think otherwise? Unfortunately, the relevant phrase in Arrian is rather badly translated in some of the bestselling modern editions of his Anabasis. Instead of the literal translation that Alexander "no longer had any rest from the fever" the Penguin version states that he "was afterwards in constant fever", which skillfully camouflages the information in the original Greek that the fever had previously been intermittent. Much of the controversy regarding Alexander's death relies on such misunderstandings.

It would not be surprising if so mundane an explanation as malaria should prove unpopular with those sensationalists who prefer to portray Alexander's career as some kind of theatrical tragedy and with those moralists who like to see the great undone by their personal weaknesses, but we are dealing with real life here rather than romantic fiction.

* * * * * * * *

In the course of his reign Alexander made mistakes. On balance he should have intervened to save Thebes from the retribution of his allies,[63] even though the city had twice broken peace treaties with him and had murdered members of the Macedonian party at the start of the revolt. In retrospect it was an over-reaction to attack the camp of the Indian mercenaries at Massaga,[64] even though they may have been attempting to desert and could have posed a threat to him in the future. In addition, Alexander ought probably to have modified his policies in the face of the fanaticism of the Brahmins on the Indus to avoid much futile bloodshed. Furthermore, crossing the Gedrosian desert with so large a force was an excessive risk, which led to the unnecessary deaths of many of his followers, though probably fewer than has usually been believed. Above all, the killing of Cleitus the Black following a drunken argument at a party in Samarkand was reprehensible, despite the fact that Cleitus had insulted him.[65] This is not just because Cleitus was a senior officer and the King's friend, but also because he was the brother of Alexander's nurse and had saved the King's life during the battle at the Granicus.

---

[62] John S. Marr & Charles H. Calisher, "Alexander the Great and West Nile Virus Encephalitis", *Emerging Infectious Diseases*, Vol. 9, No. 12, December 2003, pp. 1599-1600.
[63] Arrian, *Anabasis* 1.9.9.
[64] Arrian, *Anabasis* 4.27.
[65] Plutarch, *Alexander* 50-52; Curtius 8.1.22.

However, these failings should be weighed against Alexander's immense achievements and enduring legacy.

In contrast to the insular prejudice of most Greeks at the time, which labelled all foreigners and their cultures as barbarous, Alexander operated a relatively enlightened multiracial policy. This included the regular reinstatement of local rulers, adoption of some Persian, Egyptian and Indian customs, marriage to Bactrian and Persian princesses, patronage of Indian philosophers and recruitment of tens of thousands of Persian and mixed-race youths, the so-called *epigoni* (afterborn), into his army. Alexander was largely responsible for the spread of Greek culture across the Middle East as far as India, where its influence is still discernible today. He saw money and treasure as commodities to be utilised rather than hoarded and sought to open up trade routes between the Mediterranean and the Far East, especially by means of the foundation of strings of new cities and the exploration of the sea-lanes of the Gulfs of Persia and Oman. These policies collectively engendered a huge economic boom in the Eastern Mediterranean in the decades following his death. They resulted in a significant rise in the standard of living of millions and financed the construction of spacious and gleaming Hellenistic cities all around the Mediterranean seaboard. During the next few centuries these cities fostered a great flowering of art, literature and science, much of which survived to stimulate the renaissance in medieval Europe. The greatest of these cities was Alexandria, which had been founded by Alexander at the western end of the Nile Delta in 331 BC. Its lighthouse, the Pharos, became recognized as one of the Seven Wonders of the World, whilst its Great Library sheltered the knowledge of mankind. But there was a third building of equal fame, which dominated the heart of the city for at least five centuries. It was known as the Soma, which is the Greek word for a body, since it housed Alexander's embalmed corpse.

Ultimately, Alexander deserves to be judged in terms of the ideals of his own culture and times. It is by definition anachronistic to analyse his career in terms of modern moral and ethical codes that would have been ridiculed in his own society. His personal ideals are epitomised by Xenophon's *Cyropaedia* and Homer's *Iliad*, a copy of which he kept beneath his pillow.[66] These books present parables lauding the heroism of combat, the immortality of fame and the chivalry of befriending worthy enemies after their defeat. Alexander was not always a perfect exemplar of these virtues, but on the whole he came close enough to deserve his epithet of greatness.

---

[66] Plutarch, *Alexander* 8.

Table 2.1. Outline of Alexander's final months

323BC DATE	EVENTS	KEY SOURCES
February-March	Conclusion of campaign against Cossaeans in the Zagros Mountains	Arrian, Plutarch, Diodorus, Polyaenus – forty day campaign
Mid April	Arrival at Babylon – orders clearance of temple site over two months; work unfinished at Alexander's death	Strabo 16.1.5
Mid to Late April	Receives embassies from the Greeks	Arrian
Late April – Early May	Funeral of Hephaestion	Diodorus, Aelian
Several Weeks in May	Expedition to Pollacopas marshes, foundation of new city	Arrian, Strabo, Diodorus
3rd or 4th Week of May	Return to Babylon past tombs of Assyrian Kings	Arrian, Diodorus
Late May	Receives word that Hephaestion may be worshipped as a Hero - deranged prisoner sits in Alexander's throne	Arrian, Plutarch, Diodorus
30th May	Festivities in honour of Nearchus	Plutarch
Evening of 31st May	Alexander begins to feel feverish after 2nd symposium of Medius	Arrian & Plutarch, quoting Ephemerides by Eumenes
Evening of 10th June	Death of Alexander	Aristobulus, Ephemerides, Babylonian tablet
16th June	Embalming of corpse begun	Curtius, Plutarch

The Quest for the Tomb of Alexander by Andrew Chugg

Table 2.2. Alexander's illness (A=Arrian, P=Plutarch, D=Diodorus, C=Curtius, J=Justin)

323 BC DATE	EVENTS	SYMPTOMS
30th May (Julian)	Banquet in honour of Nearchus followed by a bath (J, P)	
Night	Medius' drinking party (*comus*) (A, D, P) Rose, bathed and slept (A)	
31st May, 18th Daisios	Dined with Medius after rising (A)	Implies slept until evening (A)
Night	Drank till late (A, J, P), bathed, ate a little (A), slept in bathroom (A, P)	Sharp pain in back drinking cup of Heracles (Athenaeus, A, D, J, doubted by P) Began to feel feverish (A, P)
1st June, 19th Daisios	Carried to sacrifices on couch, lay in men's apartments, instructed officers on Arabian voyage (A) Bath, moved to bedchamber, dice with Medius (P)	
Night	Carried on couch across river to garden, bathed and rested (A) Bathed, sacrificed, dined (P)	Feverish throughout night (P)
2nd June, 20th Daisios	Bathed, offered sacrifices (A, P), went into canopied bed, conversed with Medius (A), entertained by listening to Nearchus' account of his voyage lying down in bathroom (P)	
Night	Instructed officers to meet him at dawn, dined lightly, carried to canopied bed (A)	High fever (A)
3rd June, 21st Daisios	Bathed, sacrificed, explained plans for Arabian voyage to Nearchus and other officers (A): Entertained by listening to Nearchus' account of his voyage lying down in bathroom (P)	Fever grew more intense (P)
Night		Bad night (P)
4th June, 22nd Daisios	Arabian expedition: planned departure of foot (A) Bathed, sacrificed, summoned officers and ordered them to see that all was ready for the voyage (A) Bed moved to be beside great diving pool, discussed filling vacant posts in the army with his officers (P)	No longer any rest from fever (A) Fever high throughout day (P)
Night	Bathed	Very ill after bathing (A)
5th June, 23rd Daisios	Arabian expedition: planned departure of fleet (A) Carried to house near great diving pool, sacrificed, summoned most senior officers and gave instructions for the voyage (A)	
6th June, 24th Daisios	Carried to offer sacrifices (A, P), continued to instruct officers (A)	Fever still worse (P)
Night	Ordered generals to wait in courtyard & officers outside (P)	

Death in Babylon

Table 2.2 (Continued). Alexander's illness

323 BC DATE	EVENTS	SYMPTOMS
7th June, 25th Daisios	Still offered sacrifices, ordered generals to wait in the courtyard and commanders of brigades and battalions to wait before the gates, carried (through them) from garden to palace (A) Moved back to palace across river, slept a little (P)	Very ill, then extremely ill (A) Knew officers, but said no more, now speechless (A, P) Fever did not abate (P)
Night		High fever (A)
8th June, 26th Daisios		High fever (A), speechless (P)
9th June, 27th Daisios	Troops file past (A, C, D, J, P, *Liber de Morte*) having suspected that news of Alexander's death was being withheld (A) "After my death will you find a king who deserves such men?" (C, J) Handed ring to Perdiccas (C, D, J, Nepos, Lucian, *Liber de Morte*) Instructed that his body be transported to Ammon (C, J, Lucian, *Liber de Morte*) "To whom do you leave your kingdom?"-"To the best" (A, C, D, J) Foresaw great funeral games (A, C, D, J, P[Moralia]) Perdiccas asked him when he wished divine honours paid him – "When you are happy" (C)	Speechless (A) Voice failing (C, J) Collapsed from exhaustion when troops left (C) Delirious after drinking wine to quench thirst (P from Aristobulus, day uncertain)
Night	Pithon, Attalus, Demophon, Peucestus, Cleomenes, Menidas, Seleucus spent night in temple of Serapis, enquiring whether Alexander should be moved, god replied no (A, P)	
10th June, 28th Daisios	Died (A), died towards evening (P), died on 11th June according to a Babylonian tablet	Pronouncement of death to the Friends & Bodyguards (including Secretary Eumenes)
11th June, 30th Daisios	Died according to Aristobulus (P) – note that Daisios had no 29th day, so there is little real disagreement here: late on the 10th June might be the 11th June or the announcement was made the next morning (the Greeks used Lunar months running between successive New Moons – since the Lunar month is 29.53 days long, nearly half of all months only have twenty-nine days, so Greek practice was usually to give the 29th day the name of the 30th in such "hollow" months)	Announcement of death to the troops (?)
16th June	Embalmers arrived, no decay of corpse despite heat, did not dare touch him at first, due to lifelike appearance (C) Body uncorrupted for days (P)	Coma (?)

3. Funeral Games

Bedford:	*Hung be the heavens with black, yield day to night!*
	Comets, importing change of times and states,
	Brandish your crystal tresses in the sky,
	And with them scourge the bad revolting stars
	That have consented unto Henry's death!
	King Henry the Fifth, too famous to live long!
	England ne'er lost a king of so much worth.
Gloucester:	*England ne'er had a king until his time.*
	Virtue he had, deserving to command:
	His brandish'd sword did blind men with his beams;
	His arms spread wider than a dragon's wings;
	His sparkling eyes, replete with wrathful fire,
	More dazzled and drove back his enemies
	Than mid-day sun fierce bent against their faces.
	What should I say? his deeds exceed all speech:
	He ne'er lift up his hand but conquered.
Exeter:	*We mourn in black: why mourn we not in blood?*

Henry VI, Part 1, Act 1, Scene 1

Thus Shakespeare foreshadowed the Wars of the Roses with three royal dukes lamenting the demise of Henry V. So, too, the Wars of the Successors broke out in Babylon with Alexander's passing. His Macedonian marshals mourned their King in torrents of blood.

On the 11th June 323 BC Perdiccas called an emergency council of the senior officers to address the issue of the succession. However, word leaked out and many of the rank and file crowded into the hall, so that the event escalated into an *ad hoc* session of the Assembly of the Macedonians. The atmosphere was tense and fractious. Curtius gives a near verbatim account of increasingly ill-tempered arguments, which culminated in a schism between the infantry, led by an officer called Meleager, and the cavalry, commanded by Perdiccas and loyal to Alexander's Bodyguards.[1]

The pleas of Perdiccas and the Bodyguards that the Macedonians should await the birth of Alexander's child by his queen Roxane, who was six months pregnant, were met with antagonism and hostility. The ordinary troops were loath to risk acclaiming an infant monarch of half barbarian blood. The infantry preferred to proclaim Arrhidaeus, Alexander's mentally impaired half-brother, as their new king under the regnal name of Philip III. But setting aside the claim

---

[1] They were Alexander's eight most senior army officers at Babylon: Perdiccas himself, Ptolemy, Leonnatus, Pithon, Aristonous, Peucestas, Lysimachus and (probably) Seleucus.

Funeral Games

of Alexander's unborn heir offended against the instinctive loyalty to the deceased still felt by his Bodyguards and Friends among the cavalry.

The impasse sparked fierce fighting in the palace and even around Alexander's deathbed.[2] Outnumbered, the cavalry withdrew from Babylon to camp out in the surrounding plains, where they instigated a siege by cutting all supplies to the city. Meleager was forced within days to negotiate and he quickly settled for an offer of the position of Perdiccas' deputy. However, Perdiccas tricked him by coaxing the imbecilic Philip-Arrhidaeus to denounce Meleager's supporters, who were summarily put to death before a parade of the army by being trampled by the elephants. Meleager himself was eliminated shortly afterwards, as he sought sanctuary in a temple precinct.

Alexander's body seems to have been left virtually unattended in the Royal Apartments until Perdiccas reasserted his authority. Aelian says,[3] "While his followers argued about the succession… he was left unburied for thirty days", but Curtius' more detailed account,[4] which has the embalmers treat the corpse about a week after the pronouncement of death, is probably more accurate. By that time the cadaver should have been putrid and foetid in Babylon's summer heat, but the embalmers found the corpse to be remarkably pure, fresh and lifelike. The ancient stories remembered this as a sign of Alexander's divinity, but medically speaking it is a strong indication that death occurred much later than was believed at the time. As already discussed, Alexander had probably entered a profound, terminal coma due to the onset of cerebral malaria. He may not actually have expired until shortly before the embalmers began their ministrations.

Perdiccas now called upon an official Assembly of the Macedonians to endorse a string of key decisions. Justin writes that Alexander's body was placed in their midst whilst they deliberated.[5] The Assembly voted for the abandonment of Alexander's ambitious Last Plans and approved the division of the kingdoms of the empire among his Bodyguards and Companions. Notably, Ptolemy was awarded the Governorship of Egypt, probably at his own instigation. Both Diodorus and Justin state at this juncture that Alexander's corpse was to be transported to a temple of the Egyptian god Ammon, which reflected Alexander's expressed wishes. These writers and also Arrian[6] name the officer appointed to take charge of the preparation and escort of the catafalque as Arrhidaeus, although Justin mistakenly confuses him with Philip-Arrhidaeus, the new king.

---

[2] Curtius 10.7.16-19.
[3] Aelian, *Varia Historia* 12.64.
[4] Curtius 10.10.9.
[5] Justin 13.4.
[6] Diodorus Siculus 18.3.3; Justin 13.4; Arrian, *Events after Alexander*, summarised by Photius 92.

The Quest for the Tomb of Alexander by Andrew Chugg

The principal primary source for events after Alexander's death was the history of Hieronymus of Cardia,[7] who was a friend, countryman and perhaps the nephew of Eumenes, Alexander's Secretary.[8] His work has not survived except in fragments, but it seems to have been relatively reliable and authoritative. It is likely that Diodorus and possibly also Trogus (Justin's source) derived their comments about the decision to transport Alexander's body to Ammon from Hieronymus. This is particularly interesting, because Curtius and Justin, in reporting Alexander's last request that his body should be taken to Ammon, were probably using a different primary source: namely Cleitarchus' History of Alexander.[9] Lucian and the *Liber de Morte* speak of a plan to send the corpse to Egypt, but without mentioning Ammon. If the references to a planned entombment at a temple of Ammon can be traced back to several different and largely independent primary sources, then they gain considerable credence.

Furthermore, Alexander's request is thoroughly consistent with our knowledge of his personality and beliefs. He deferred to Ammon's authority in matters such as the worship of the dead Hephaistion as a Hero and he seems genuinely to have considered himself to be the "Son of Ammon" in a religious (but probably not a literal) sense.[10] Plutarch has the following regarding Alexander's visit to the Oracle of Ammon at Siwa:

In the shrine of Ammon he was hailed by the prophetic priest as the son of Zeus. "That is nothing surprising," said he; "for Zeus is by nature the father of all, and he makes the noblest his own."[11]

Above all, Alexander knew that in Egypt he stood to achieve the apotheosis, which was perhaps always the ultimate motive for his pursuit of superhuman achievements. He will have been well aware that his exemplar, Achilles, had been awarded divine honours in his mother's land of Epirus.[12] In this vein Lucian puts the following words into Alexander's mouth in one of his Dialogues of the Dead:-

I have lain in Babylon for three[13] whole days now, but Ptolemy of the Guards is pledged, as soon as he can get a moment's respite from present disturbances, to take and bury me in Egypt, there to be reckoned among the Gods.[14]

---

[7] See, for example, M.M. Austin, *The Hellenistic World from Alexander to the Roman Conquest*, CUP, 1981, note 3 to excerpt 22; Hieronymus is cited by Diodorus as a source for his books 18 - 20.
[8] Diodorus 18.50.4; Eumenes' father was another Hieronymus according to Arrian, *Indica* 18.7.
[9] See in general N.G.L. Hammond, *Three Historians of Alexander the Great*, CUP, 1983; Introduction to Loeb edition of Diodorus Siculus, Vol. IX, trans. Russel M. Geer; L. Pearson, *The Lost Histories of Alexander the Great*, American Philological Association, 1960.
[10] See, for example, Plutarch, *Alexander* 27; A.B. Bosworth, "Alexander and Ammon", *Greece and the Eastern Mediterranean in Ancient History and Prehistory*, ed. K.H. Kinzl, Berlin 1977.
[11] Plutarch, *Moralia* 180D; this recalls the first line of the Lord's Prayer, "Our Father which art in Heaven…"
[12] Plutarch, *Pyrrhus* 1.
[13] The manuscript read "three", but Du Soul emended it to "thirty" on the (very weak) basis of the Aelian story.

Funeral Games

It is therefore highly credible that Alexander really did ask to be buried under the auspices of Ammon in Egypt and that the Assembly of the Macedonians initially acquiesced to this request in the emotive atmosphere that prevailed shortly after his death.

* * * * * * * *

In the late summer of 323BC Roxane gave birth to a son, who was named Alexander after his father. We know him as Alexander IV, since he had three eponymous predecessors as king of Macedon. Sometimes he is called Alexander Aegus, but this stems from the misreading of an antique manuscript by a modern editor.[15] He shared in a joint-kingship with Philip-Arrhidaeus, whilst Perdiccas administered the empire as their Regent. Athens fomented a serious rebellion against Macedonian hegemony in Greece and simultaneously the Greeks whom Alexander had settled in the eastern satrapies rose up in revolt. Various of Alexander's Bodyguards set out to counter these threats. Ptolemy left to take up his governorship of Egypt, whilst Perdiccas himself, accompanied by the kings, marched the Grand Army against the king of Cappadocia, who had refused to acknowledge Macedonian supremacy.

Remaining at Babylon Arrhidaeus now spent over a year preparing a splendid catafalque for Alexander. In fact Diodorus writes that Arrhidaeus "spent nearly two years in making ready this work",[16] but this seems a little too long.[17] It probably reached Syria in the winter of 322-321 BC and cannot have travelled much further than a few miles per day, despite being "accompanied by a crowd of road-menders and mechanics". It may, therefore, have left Babylon as early as the summer of 322 BC. Diodorus gives an exceptionally detailed description of the carriage and its contents,[18] which manifestly derives from an eyewitness account, and indeed a surviving fragment of Hieronymus implies that he is Diodorus' source for these passages.[19]

---

[14] Lucian, *Dialogues of the Dead* 13 (about 165 AD).
[15] A misreading of *aigou* for *allou* in the manuscript of the Astronomical Canon of Claudius Ptolemy; hence "another Alexander" became "Alexander Aegus".
[16] Diodorus Siculus 18.28.2.
[17] I follow "high chronology", but there are serious difficulties with the chronology of the years 321-319BC. Some historians have even ventured so far as to defer Perdiccas' attack on Egypt until 320BC (so-called "low chronology"). The arguments are complex. However, the later dating appears to leave Perdiccas and the Grand Army marking time for a year and implies that Craterus and Antipater failed to challenge Perdiccas' supremacy for three years after Alexander's death. It would also suggest that Diodorus' duration of "nearly two years" for the preparation of Alexander's catafalque is actually an underestimate: unusual for an author afflicted elsewhere with a tendency to exaggerate for effect. See Hans Hauben, "The First War of the Successors - Chronological and Historical Problems," *Ancient Society*, 8, 1977, pp.85-120; Edward Anson, *Classical Journal*, 80, 1985, pp.303-316; see also the four recent articles by Pat Wheatley, Edward Anson, Tom Boiy and Boris Dreyer in W. Heckel, L. Trittle & P. Wheatley (Editors), *Alexander's Empire: Formulation to Decay*, Regina Books, California, 2007.
[18] Diodorus Siculus 18.26-27.
[19] Jacoby, *FGrH*, No. 154, fragment 2 = Athenaeus 206E.

The Quest for the Tomb of Alexander by Andrew Chugg

Diodorus begins by describing the coffin, which was of "hammered gold" and "fitted to the body", which is suggestive of a form like an Egyptian mummy-case. The space around the body was packed with preservative spices to keep it sweet and uncorrupted. This coffin was destined to survive for over 240 years after Alexander's death and is mentioned by several other ancient authors including Strabo[20] and Curtius.[21] The latter confirms that it was crammed with perfumes and notes that Alexander's corpse was crowned with the royal diadem, details which also appear in *Metz Epitome* 113. We have already seen that the Armenian Alexander Romance is specific that Alexander's corpse was preserved in honey and hipatic aloe. Additionally, most early versions of the Alexander Romance have a reference to the coffin in the section which purportedly quotes from "Alexander's Will":-

I command the administrators of the kingdom to build a golden sarcophagus, weighing 200 talents, to hold the body of Alexander, the King of Macedonia.[22]

Much of this will is a blatant forgery, probably by a Rhodian pen, and it is badly corrupted in surviving versions. Nevertheless, it contains some striking references, which suggest that it was originally composed within a generation or two of Alexander's death.

Diodorus continues by describing the coffin draped with a pall of gold-embroidered purple (*Metz Epitome* 113 also mention a purple pall over the coffin) and stacked about with the panoplies and arms of the deceased in the traditional fashion. The carriage itself took the form of an Ionic temple about twenty feet long and fourteen wide having a colonnade with scrolled capitals supporting a pediment and a vault fashioned from fish-scale tiles of gem-encrusted gold. Golden acanthus plants spiralling up the length of each column and water-spouts to drain rain from the roof were spaced around the pediment, taking the form of goat-stag masks biting on rings, from which were suspended swags of a brightly coloured garland. At each corner of the pediment were perched statues of the winged goddess of victory, Nike, each proffering a trophy. Slung from tassels beneath their feet, sonerous golden bells tolled mournfully to proclaim from afar the approach of the cortège. Within the colonnade thick golden cords had been woven into nets to curtain and seclude the plinth where the coffin lay. Suspended from these meshes were series of sculpted and painted tablets running the length of each side. In the front panels the King was shown parading in a chariot and wafting his sceptre surrounded by Macedonian and Persian bodyguards and preceded by a vanguard of his troops. Around the corner, formations of Alexander's cavalry galloped down the side panels, whilst a herd of war elephants charged down the opposite side

---

[20] Strabo 17.1.8.
[21] Curtius 10.10.13.
[22] Wolohojian (translator), *The Romance of Alexander the Great by Pseudo-Callisthenes (Armenian manuscripts)*, Section 274; Stoneman (translator), *The Greek Alexander Romance*, Section 3.32 (Manuscript A).

of the vehicle and a flotilla of warships patrolled the sea-lanes at its rear. Guarding the entrance a pair of golden lions glared forth imperiously over the backs of sixty-four mules hitched to four poles in the Persian fashion. Even these beasts were each richly caparisoned with gilded crowns, bejewelled collars and a pair of golden bells. The temple rumbled along on four gilded wheels borne by a pair of axles, from the centres of which an ingenious suspension system supported the carriage and protected its precious cargo from the joltings of the unmetalled highway. As a finial touch a mast jutted skywards from the centre of the roof bearing a banner of royal purple with a vast olive wreath done in gold leaf that glinted vibrantly in the sunlight, each flash seeming from a distance like a thunderbolt cast by Zeus.

…[The catafalque] appeared more magnificent when seen that when described. Because of its widespread fame it drew together many spectators; for from every city into which it came the whole population went out to meet it and again escorted it on its departure, never becoming sated with the pleasure of beholding it.

Diodorus Siculus, Book 18, Section 28

Some modern reconstructions of the carriage depict it with a barrel roof (Figure 3.1). This is firstly because Diodorus uses the word καμάρα, which usually refers to something with a vaulted or arched roof, but can also simply mean a covered carriage. Secondly, it has been proposed that its architects were imitating the barrel-vaulting used in the funeral chambers of Macedonian tumulus tombs,[23] although any structural engineer will readily explain that the motive for adopting this form is principally to provide the strength required to support the weight of the overlying earth. The rest of Diodorus' description is reminiscent of a classical Greek temple of the Ionic order, so a roof with a squat Λ cross-section would perhaps have been more appropriate. The so-called Alexander Sarcophagus, found in the royal necropolis of Sidon in 1887 and very probably created for Abdalonymus, whom Alexander appointed to rule Sidon in 333BC, has a lid that imitates the roof of a classical temple (See Figure 3.2). There has been speculation that its design was partly inspired by Alexander's catafalque, which had passed close to Sidon a decade or so before it was sculpted.[24]

---

[23] Katerina Rhomiopoulou, "An Outline of Macedonian History and Art," *The Search for Alexander: an Exhibition*, New York Graphic Society, 1980.
[24] E.g. Andrew Stewart, *Faces of Power: Alexander's Image & Hellenistic Politics*, California 1993, p.296.

The Quest for the Tomb of Alexander by Andrew Chugg

Figure 3.1. Barrel-vaulted reconstruction of Alexander's catafalque (author's collection)

Figure 3.2. End view of the Alexander Sarcophagus from Sidon (albumen photo taken ~1890 from the author's collection)

Funeral Games

The sequence of events whereby Alexander's body was conveyed upon its spectacular carriage from Babylon ultimately to arrive in Egypt is shrouded in a fog of apparent discrepancies and contradictions among the surviving accounts from the ancient writers. The story of these events is like a smashed vase with some shards altogether lost. Had we only a few fragments, then they would be unlikely to share common edges, so they could be arranged to fit many different reconstructions. But in fact we have many pieces, so it is only possible to fit them *all* back together harmoniously in a single way.

An initial area of superficial disagreement among the sources is whether Perdiccas intended to bury Alexander in Egypt or in Macedonia. As we have seen, there is persuasive evidence that the plan was to take the body to Ammon in Egypt at the time Arrhidaeus was appointed. However, Pausanias writes of Ptolemy:-

The Macedonians who had been entrusted with the task of carrying the corpse of Alexander to Aegae, he persuaded to hand it over to him.[25]

Aegae was the site of the Royal Cemetery in Macedon, where in 1977 Professor Andronikos discovered the intact tomb of an important king beneath the Great Tumulus. It is widely accepted that this was the grave of Philip II, Alexander's father, so Aegae was indeed the obvious alternative to Egypt.[26] In addition, a summary of a lost history by Arrian bolsters the idea that Perdiccas had some other destination that Egypt in mind:-

And Arrhidaeus, who guarded the body of Alexander, led it, against the orders of Perdiccas, from Babylon via Damascus to bring it before Ptolemy, son of Lagus, in Egypt. Despite the opposition of Polemon, an associate of Perdiccas, Arrhidaeus managed to achieve his design.[27]

Finally, the Alexander Romance[28] also states that the Macedonians wanted to take Alexander's body to Macedonia.

Clearly, in order to reconcile the two traditions it seems to be necessary to infer that Perdiccas changed his mind at some point. In fact it is easy to understand how Perdiccas and the Assembly may initially have been swayed by grief, sympathy and respect for the Alexander's wishes to confirm his orders that he be buried in Egypt. But is equally apparent that a mix of practical and superstitious considerations may subsequently have caused the Regent to regret such a decision. For example, under the Macedonian constitution it seems to

---

[25] Pausanias 1.6.3.
[26] There is an alternative view that Tomb II at Aegae is that of Philip III (Arrhidaeus), but I find it impossible to doubt that the youthful prince at the center of the fresco on its façade is Alexander the Great at the time of his accession, in which case the bearded lion-hunter on the right is Philip II, who must be the occupant.
[27] Arrian, *History of Events after Alexander*, summarised by Photius 92.
[28] Wolohojian (translator), *The Romance of Alexander the Great by Pseudo-Callisthenes (Armenian manuscripts)*, Section 282; Stoneman (translator), *The Greek Alexander Romance*, Section 3.34.

have been the prerogative of the new monarch to bury his predecessor.[29] Consequently, Perdiccas would have been most reluctant effectively to cede this honour to Ptolemy. Ironically, there was a prophecy, attributed to an early Macedonian king also named Perdiccas, that the royal line would end when the kings ceased to be buried at Aegae.[30] Perhaps most worryingly of all Perdiccas stood to bring the full wrath of the baleful Olympias down upon himself should he fail to return her son's remains to her in Greece. How, though, might the volte-face have been presented to the army without losing face?

Perhaps the most colourful account of the journey of Alexander's body to survive from antiquity is the story given by Aelian in his *Varia Historia*. This is so pertinent as to be worth quoting in full:-

Alexander, son of Philip and Olympias, lay dead in Babylon – the man who said he was the son of Zeus. While his followers argued about the succession he lay awaiting burial, which even the very poor achieve, since the nature common to all mankind requires a funeral for those no longer living. But he was left unburied for thirty days, until Aristander of Telmissus, whether by divine inspiration or for some other reason, entered the Assembly of the Macedonians and said that of all kings in recorded history Alexander was the most fortunate, both in his life and in his death; the gods had told him that the land which received his body, the former habitation of his soul, would enjoy the greatest good fortune and be unconquered through the ages.

On hearing this they began to quarrel seriously, each man wishing to carry off the prize to his own kingdom, so as to have a relic guaranteeing safety and permanence for his realm. But Ptolemy, if we are to believe the story, stole the body and hurriedly made off with it to Egypt, to the city of Alexander. The other Macedonians did nothing, whereas Perdiccas tried to give chase. He was not so much interested in consideration for Alexander and due respect for his body as fired and incited by Aristander's prediction. When he caught up with Ptolemy, there was quite a violent struggle over the corpse, in some way akin to the one over the phantom at Troy, which Homer [Iliad 5.449] celebrates in his tale, where Apollo puts it down among the heroes to protect Aeneas. Ptolemy checked Perdiccas' attack. He made a likeness of Alexander, clad in royal robes and a shroud of enviable quality. Then he laid it on one of the Persian carriages, and arranged the bier sumptuously with silver, gold and ivory. Alexander's real body was sent ahead without fuss and formality by a secret and little used route. Perdiccas found the imitation corpse with the elaborate carriage, and halted his advance, thinking he had laid hands on the prize. Too late he realised he had been deceived; it was not possible to go in pursuit.[31]

Aristander had been Alexander's principal soothsayer. He features prominently in the extant histories, where his prognostications are normally found to be supportive of the King's objectives. In the context of Babylon a month after Alexander's death the prophecy described by Aelian provides a perfect

---

[29] W.W. Tarn, *Cambridge Ancient History*, Vol. 6, p. 482.
[30] Justin 7.2.
[31] Aelian, *Varia Historia* 12.64.

Funeral Games

explanation of how the army might have been swayed to demand that the corpse be returned to Macedonia for burial. If this is true, then the period of thirty days may indicate the timing of Perdiccas' change of heart, rather than the delay before the commencement of the embalming process.

As regards the rest of Aelian's tale, many of the essential facts are corroborated elsewhere, but some of the interpretations he places on these facts are more dubious. The story probably reflects an underlying truth, which has become garbled through contraction and errors introduced in transmission.

It is virtually certain that a difference of opinion arose between Perdiccas and Ptolemy concerning the destination and ultimate fate of the cadaver. Ptolemy consequently made covert arrangements for the catafalque to be diverted to Egypt as soon as it reached Syria in defiance of Perdiccas' orders. Strabo concurs with Aelian, Pausanias and Arrian in stating this:-

For Ptolemy, the son of Lagus, forestalled Perdiccas by taking the body away from him when he was bringing it down from Babylon and was turning aside towards Egypt, moved by greed and a desire to make that country his own.[32]

However, he wrongly conflates the hijacking of the corpse with Perdiccas' ensuing attack on Egypt and therefore incorrectly implies that Perdiccas personally escorted the catafalque.

Diodorus, though silent concerning the controversy, nevertheless hints at the potential for conflict in mentioning Ptolemy's army:-

…Arrhidaeus… brought the body of the King from Babylon to Egypt. Ptolemy, moreover, doing honour to Alexander, went to meet it with an army as far as Syria, and, receiving the body, deemed it worthy of the greatest consideration.[33]

The means by which Ptolemy arranged for the diversion of the cortège was evidently the collaboration of its commander, Arrhidaeus: Arrian states this explicitly, whilst Pausanias agrees that Ptolemy suborned the escort. Diodorus and Arrian provide a further indication that Ptolemy and Arrhidaeus were in league through their reports that the former shortly afterwards nominated the latter to be one of two Guardians for the joint-kings.[34] This appears to have been intended as a reward for services rendered.

But specifically how did Perdiccas react to the provocation? Fortunately, a second less well known but more detailed summary of Arrian's lost account of the hijack has survived in a palimpsest; it describes the Regent's irate response:-

The partisans of Perdiccas, Attalus and Polemon, sent out by him to prevent the departure, returned without succeeding and told him that Arrhidaeus had deliberately given the body of Alexander to Ptolemy and was carrying it to Egypt. Then, even more, he wanted to march to

---

[32] Strabo 17.1.8.
[33] Diodorus 18.28.2-3.
[34] Diodorus 18.36.6-7; Arrian in Photius' abridgement, Section 92.

The Quest for the Tomb of Alexander by Andrew Chugg

Egypt in order to take away the rule from Ptolemy and put a new man in his place (one of his friends) and retrieve the body of Alexander. With this intention he arrived in Cilicia with the army.[35]

From this it would seem clear that Polemon and Attalus were both sent off in pursuit of the catafalque by Perdiccas, as soon as he received word of Arrhidaeus' treacherous southwards diversion. They failed in their attempt to thwart the heist, perhaps because Ptolemy's army arrived on the scene, but there may well have been actual skirmishes as suggested by Aelian.

This was the winter of 322-321 BC and Perdiccas and the Grand Army were in Pisidia (southwestern Turkey).[36] The cortège must have been in Northern Syria, since that was where the routes from Babylon to Macedon and to Egypt diverged and Arrian mentions that it was driven southwards past Damascus. Such momentous news probably reached Perdiccas at a gallop, in which case he knew it within a week or two. Conversely, Arrhidaeus and Ptolemy will have been greatly hampered by the ungainly carriage and its gangling train of mules. Perdiccas may have calculated that a cavalry force might just overtake them before they reached Egypt. In this context Aelian's story of the chase can be seen to make reasonable sense. Hard-pressed by the pursuit, Ptolemy might well have decided either to create a decoy or to sacrifice the real carriage in favour of retaining its precious cargo. Aelian's description of the decoy carriage and its contents closely resembles Diodorus' more elaborate account of the real catafalque: for example, a "Persian" carriage meant one with a roof or cover and the "shroud of enviable quality" is consistent with the "pall of gold-embroidered purple" that Diodorus recorded based on Hieronymus' eyewitness details. It is such hints as these that suggest that, despite its legendary flavour, Aelian's story may embody the essential truth.

*   *   *   *   *   *   *   *

It is certain that Perdiccas attacked Egypt with the Grand Army in the immediate aftermath of the hijacking of Alexander's corpse. His invasion is one of the key events of classical history. Diodorus gives the most detailed surviving account, but there are also outlines by Arrian, Justin, Nepos, Pausanias, Plutarch and Strabo.[37] A near contemporaneous inscription[38] from the island of Paros dates the offensive to the year commencing in July 321 BC, but it very probably began with the opening of the campaign season in the spring. To what extent was this momentous assault triggered by the theft of Alexander's corpse?

---

[35] See Walter J Goralski, "Arrian's Events After Alexander," *Ancient World*, 19, (1989); this palimpsest Fragment of Arrian's *Events after Alexander* is labelled 10A by F. Jacoby.
[36] Diodorus 18.25.6.
[37] Diodorus 18.33-37; Arrian in Photius' abridgement, Section 92; Justin 13.8; Cornelius Nepos, *Eumenes* 3 & 5; Pausanias 1.6.3; Plutarch, *Life of Eumenes* 5 & 8; Strabo 17.1.8.
[38] Parian Marble, FGrH 239, dating to 263-262 BC.

Funeral Games

The reason there is any ambiguity on this point is that Diodorus, whose account of this period is the most detailed and widely read, seems to have used a source that eulogised Ptolemy for much of this section of his history.[39] Consequently, he ignores the illegality and drama of the hijack and instead treats the event as a stately procession. This in turn deprives him of the option of using Ptolemy's provocation as the motive for Perdiccas' aggression, however circumstantially likely this might appear. Diodorus resorts instead to the lame explanation that Perdiccas' supporters advised him to "defeat Ptolemy first in order that there might be no obstacle in the way of their Macedonian campaign".[40] The same strategically dubious excuse is cited by Justin: "…it seemed more to the purpose to begin with Egypt, lest, while they were gone into Macedonia, Asia should be seized by Ptolemy".[41] But the reverse of this reasoning would make equal sense. At the time Perdiccas marched away to Egypt, Antipater, Regent of Macedon, was on the verge of invading Asia across the Hellespont, ably supported by Craterus.

There is, of course, a strong implication in Aelian's tale of hot pursuit that the attack upon Egypt was the consequence of the theft of Alexander's body. More particularly, the palimpsest summary of Arrian's version makes this motivation quite explicit, whilst hinting that relations between Perdiccas and Ptolemy had already taken a downturn. Notice especially that Perdiccas and the Grand Army are said to have moved into Cilicia directly he knew that Ptolemy had succeeded in hijacking the corpse. This constituted a decisive eastwards march from Pisidia, clearly directed against Egypt. The threat from Antipater and Craterus was focused on the Hellespont in the opposite direction. Furthermore, the account by Pausanias also implicitly supports this version of events. He writes that, after persuading the escort of the catafalque to hand the corpse over to him, Ptolemy "proceeded to bury it with Macedonian rites in Memphis, but knowing that Perdiccas would make war, he kept Egypt garrisoned; and Perdiccas took Arrhidaeus, son of Philip, and the boy Alexander, whom Roxane, daughter of Oxyartes, had borne for Alexander, to lend colour to the campaign, but really he was plotting to deprive Ptolemy of his kingdom in Egypt."[42]

If Perdiccas had been indifferent to the fate of the corpse, his best strategy would have been to seek to appease Ptolemy in order to concentrate upon tackling the imminent threat from Europe. That he chose instead to assault Egypt suggests that the hijack must have been the decisive influence on his plans, even though it was not the only source of antagonism between him and Ptolemy.

---

[39] See Introduction to Loeb edition of Diodorus Siculus, Vol. IX, trans. Russel M Geer.
[40] Diodorus 18.25.6.
[41] Justin 13.6.
[42] Pausanias 1.6.3.

The Quest for the Tomb of Alexander by Andrew Chugg

The invasion of Egypt was an abject failure. Perdiccas failed twice to force the crossing of the Nile with disastrous loss of life among his troops. In particular, his bungling of an attempt to ford the river led to many of his men being swept away by the current and becoming fodder for crocodiles. Ultimately, his officers led by Seleucus and Antigenes mutinied and Perdiccas was stabbed to death with sarissas, the exceptionally long Macedonian pike-spears.[43] The triumphant Ptolemy graciously declined the Army's offer of the Regency. Instead, he nominated Pithon and Arrhidaeus as co-regents for the joint-kings. These commanders led the Grand Army back north, whilst Ptolemy turned his attention to completing Alexander's memorial.

*   *   *   *   *   *   *   *   *

In describing Alexander's entombment in Egypt, Diodorus weighs in by attributing a sudden change of policy to Ptolemy:-

He decided for the present not to send [the body] to Ammon, but to entomb it in the city that had been founded by Alexander himself, which lacked little of being the most renowned of the cities of the inhabited earth. There he prepared a sacred enclosure worthy of the glory of Alexander in size and construction.[44]

The reference to Alexandria as the greatest city on Earth is a glaring anachronism. In 321 BC it was only ten years old and still for the most part a building site.[45] Memphis remained the Egyptian capital[46] and Alexandria's days of glory lay decades into the future. However, Alexander was undoubtedly entombed in Alexandria within a large sacred enclosure in the time of the famous Cleopatra, when Diodorus himself visited the city.[47] It appears that Diodorus may here be making a rather inept attempt to reconcile the statements he found in his sources (Cleitarchus and Hieronymus?) concerning the intention to deliver Alexander to Ammon with the evidence of his own eyes.

However, Aelian also claims that Ptolemy took the body to Alexandria and Strabo asserts, "the body of Alexander was carried off by Ptolemy and entombed in Alexandria, where it still now lies."[48] But he too is probably drawing on his eyewitness experience, obtained during his residence in the city for several years in the time of Augustus.

In fact there is overwhelming evidence from elsewhere that these three writers are bypassing the complexities of the actual events, for it is virtually certain that Memphis was Alexander's initial resting place and that the body was only transferred to Alexandria some years later. In the first place, Pausanias

---

[43] Strabo 17.1.8; Diodorus 18.35.6-36.5; Arrian, *Events after Alexander* (Photius 92); Cornelius Nepos, *Eumenes* 5.
[44] Diodorus 18.28.3.
[45] E.g. the construction of Alexandria's walls is ascribed to Ptolemy by Tacitus, *Histories* 4.83.
[46] See P.M. Fraser, *Ptolemaic Alexandria*, note 28 to chapter 1.
[47] Diodorus mentions his own visit at 17.52.6.
[48] Strabo 17.1.8.

Funeral Games

maintains that Ptolemy buried Alexander "with Macedonian rites in Memphis" and Curtius buttresses this version in the closing sentence of his history:-

Alexander's body was taken to Memphis by Ptolemy, in whose power Egypt had fallen, and transferred thence a few years later (paucis post annis) to Alexandria, where every mark of respect continues to be paid to his memory and his name.[49]

The Alexander Romance also makes great play of the role of Memphis, blending as usual a tantalizing seasoning of historicity into a thick soup of fable:-

...Then Ptolemy addressed them: 'There is in Babylon an oracle of the Babylonian Zeus. Let us consult the oracle about the body of Alexander; the god will tell us where to lay it to rest.' The god's oracle was as follows: 'I tell you what will be of benefit to us all. There is a city in Egypt named Memphis; let him be enthroned there.' No one spoke against the oracle's pronouncement. They gave Ptolemy the task of transporting the embalmed body to Memphis in a lead coffin. So Ptolemy placed the body on a wagon and began the journey from Babylon to Egypt. When the people of Memphis heard he was coming, they came out to meet the body of Alexander and escorted it to Memphis. But the chief priest of the temple in Memphis said, 'Do not bury him here but in the city he founded in Rhakotis [i.e. Alexandria]. Wherever his body rests, that city will be constantly troubled and shaken with wars and battles.'[50]

But none of these, nor all of them combined, could be considered decisive. The indisputable evidence comes from the chronology inscribed in Greek upon a slab of marble on the Aegean island of Paros in the year 263-262BC, when it was part of the empire of the Ptolemies. The Parian Marble states unambiguously that "Alexander was laid to rest in Memphis"[51] in its entry for the year 321-320 BC. It is virtually inconceivable that such a public document made within living memory of the events could be mistaken, the more so since most of the rest of the information it contains is verifiably accurate and it is corroborated by the accounts of Pausanias, Curtius and Pseudo-Callisthenes.

* * * * * * * * *

In the light of the persuasive evidence that Ptolemy stole Alexander's body in defiance of Perdiccas, entombed it at Memphis and readied his defences against an anticipated onslaught, it is fascinating to enquire why he should knowingly have taken such a tremendous risk in this matter? That it was a truly perilous risk is underlined by the fact that Perdiccas came within a hairsbreadth of forcing the crossing of the Nile. Had he succeeded, Ptolemy should certainly have lost his kingdom and most probably his life as well.

There is a suggestion in Diodorus that Ptolemy had already been contacted by Antipater with a view to forging an alliance against Perdiccas. The *casus belli* was that Antigonus, the Governor of Phrygia, had fled to Macedon and disclosed a

---

[49] Curtius 10.10.20.
[50] Richard Stoneman (trans.), *The Greek Alexander Romance* 3.34.
[51] F. Jacoby, FGrH 239.

plot by Perdiccas to marry Alexander's sister and seize the throne in his own name.[52]

Nevertheless, had Ptolemy behaved less provocatively, it is likely that Perdiccas would have preferred to march against Antipater, especially since this had been a feature of Perdiccas' original plan as alleged by Antigonus. Ptolemy might easily have spared himself the wrath of Perdiccas at a time when the Regent had just won a minor war in Cappadocia and was supremely powerful in the empire. Significantly, the rashness of the hijacking contrasts starkly with the carefully conceived strategies and alliances, which characterised the rest of Ptolemy's career. How then have historians sought to explain this curious aberration?

A naïve view is that Ptolemy was motivated by the monetary value of the elaborate hearse: that he needed to realise its cash value to hire troops to secure his position in Egypt. Yet Diodorus records that Ptolemy had found 8000 talents in the treasury when he arrived to take control of the country[53] and St Jerome attributed an annual income of over 14800 talents to Ptolemy's son, Philadelphus.[54] Furthermore, the most valuable item in the funeral cortège was the golden sarcophagus and Strabo notes that this survived intact for another 240 years.[55] In short, the representation of Ptolemy as a glorified highwayman is thoroughly incongruous.

A more reasonable opinion, commonly expressed by scholars, is that Ptolemy was seeking to bolster his position through the prestige he might hope to derive from custody of the corpse. For example, Robin Lane Fox refers to the catafalque as "the spoils that would justify Ptolemy's independence"[56] and Richard Stoneman calls the body a "symbol of power".[57] But the sort of prestige which would normally accrue from burying the previous monarch in the eyes of both the Egyptians and the Macedonians would be uniquely suited to underpinning a claim to the throne.[58] However, in 321 BC Ptolemy nurtured no such ambitions, for he refused even the role of Regent, when offered it after the murder of Perdiccas, and he scrupulously maintained the fiction that he governed Egypt on behalf of Philip-Arrhidaeus and Alexander IV for a further 16 years. Philip-Arrhidaeus was murdered by Olympias in 317 BC and Cassander secretly poisoned Alexander IV and his mother Roxane in about 310 BC. Even Alexander's other illegitimate son, Heracles, was murdered by Polyperchon at Cassander's behest whilst attempting to acquire the vacant throne in 309BC. Yet it was not until 305 BC that Ptolemy had himself proclaimed as pharaoh and issued the first coins bearing his own distinctive

---

[52] Diodorus 18.25.3-4.
[53] Diodorus 18.14.1.
[54] Alan K. Bowman, *Egypt after the Pharaohs*, British Museum Press, 1986, Chapter 2.
[55] Strabo 17.1.8.
[56] Robin Lane Fox, *Alexander the Great*, 1973, Chapter 33.
[57] Richard Stoneman, *Alexander the Great*, 1997, p. 91.
[58] *Cambridge Ancient History*, Vol. 6, p. 467.

Funeral Games

portrait. Even then it was only done as a counterblast to the assumption of royal titles by Ptolemy's arch-enemies, Antigonus and Demetrius. Evidently, the political aspirations that might have made sense of the hijacking were demonstrably absent from Ptolemy's plans in 321 BC.

To discover a compelling and convincing motive for Ptolemy's actions, however, it is only necessary to pay heed to the statements of the ancient sources on the issue. Curtius and Justin state that Alexander commanded that his body be taken to Ammon shortly before he expired, whilst Lucian makes Alexander's ghost claim that Ptolemy had vowed to fulfil this dying wish in his thirteenth Dialogue of the Dead. The Armenian Alexander Romance has Alexander say quietly to Ptolemy seated beside him as he was dying, "And you, go to Egypt and you shall take care of our body."[59] Quite simply, we are being told that Ptolemy diverted the catafalque to Egypt in order to keep faith with his dead King. No ancient source disputes this motive.

Historians familiar with the treacherous and cynical behaviour of most of Alexander's commanders after his death are bound to be sceptical of this touching tale of loyalty beyond the grave. However, there are some special factors in Ptolemy's case, which lend credence to this version of events. For example, some believe that Ptolemy composed his history of Alexander's campaigns late in life to rescue the King's reputation from the malicious exaggerations and fanciful fabrications of earlier accounts.[60] In this behaviour we begin to discern a pattern of fidelity to Alexander's interests, which begs further explanation.

In an assault upon a town in southern India, Ptolemy received a slight wound to his shoulder, but the swords of the natives had been smeared with poison and he soon grew gravely ill. Curtius, Diodorus and Strabo have recorded Alexander's personal intervention to save his companion:-

Indeed, [the Macedonians'] concern for Ptolemy was no less than the King's. Exhausted though he was from battle and anxiety, Alexander kept watch at Ptolemy's side and ordered a bed brought in on which he himself might sleep. As soon as he lay upon it, a deep sleep immediately overcame him. On waking, he declared that he had had a dream about a serpent carrying a plant in its mouth, which it had indicated was an antidote to the poison. Alexander also described the colour of the plant claiming that he would recognise it if anyone found it. It was subsequently located – for it was the object of a large-scale search – and Alexander applied it to the wound. Ptolemy's pain immediately ceased and within a short time a scab formed.[61]

---

[59] Wolohojian (translator), *The Romance of Alexander the Great by Pseudo-Callisthenes (Armenian manuscripts)*, Section 277.
[60] See Hammond, *Three Historians of Alexander the Great*, pp. 83-5, with whom I am inclined to agree. But the issue has been hotly disputed, e.g. by Badian.
[61] Curtius 9.8.25-27 (whence the quotation); cf. Diodorus, 17.103; cf. Strabo, 15.2.7.

The Quest for the Tomb of Alexander by Andrew Chugg

Curious as it may seem to find Alexander acting as his friend's doctor, this is in fact a perfectly sensible story, because we know from elsewhere that the King had studied herbal medicine under Aristotle and regularly prescribed cures for sick members of his entourage.[62] The technique of seeking cures in dreams is also a familiar Greek medical practice.

From this it might reasonably be inferred that Ptolemy felt he owed Alexander his life, which is in itself a sufficient reason for special loyalty. However, there was yet another singular bond between them, of which several ancient reports survive: Ptolemy may well have been an illegitimate son of Philip II and therefore Alexander's half-brother:-

The Macedonians consider Ptolemy to be the son of Philip, the son of Amyntas, though putatively the son of Lagus, asserting that his mother was with child when she was married to Lagus by Philip.

Pausanias 1.6.2

He [Ptolemy] was a blood-relative of Alexander and some believe he was Philip's son (it was known for certain that he was the child of a concubine of Philip's).

Curtius 9.8.22

And Perdikkas thought that Alexander would leave all his goods to Ptlomeos because he had often spoken to him of Ptlomeos' lucky birth. And Olympias, too, had made it clear that Ptlomeos had been fathered by Philip.

The Romance of Alexander, Armenian version, Section 269[63]

Modern historians have expressed doubts. Fraser, for example, speaks of Ptolemy's "fictitious relationship with Alexander",[64] but Pausanias and Curtius are well-informed writers. They ought not lightly to be dismissed and there does not seem to be any tangible evidence to contradict them. In fact several other ancient sources confirm that Ptolemy was of illegitimate birth and only adoptively the son of Lagus.[65] However, the sceptics' argument runs that

---

[62] Plutarch, *Alexander* 8.
[63] The *Syriac Alexander Romance* 3.20 has a corrupted version of the same story, which shows it was in the archetypal "alpha" recension of the Romance, because that is the only common ancestor of the Armenian and Syriac versions.
[64] P.M. Fraser, *Ptolemaic Alexandria*, p. 215.
[65] Plutarch, *Moralia* 458A-B; *Suidae Lexicon* s.v. Lagos (citing Aelian); Plutarch, *Demetrius* 2, points out that Demetrius was only adoptively the son of Antigonus, though he is commonly referred to as Antigonus' son without further explanation by most ancient sources – for this reason references to Πτολεμαῖος ὁ Λάγου in Arrian and elsewhere do not constitute evidence of Ptolemy's legitimacy; see also N.L. Collins, "The Various Fathers of Ptolemy I", *Mnemosyne* 50.4, 1997, pp.436-476 who thinks that the connection was invented by Ptolemy Ceraunus when he claimed to be the heir to the throne of Macedon in 281BC – however the mention of the rumour in the *Liber de Morte* section of the Alexander Romance mitigates against Collins, since it is generally agreed that the *Liber de Morte* was composed in the 4th century BC; Collins also errs in believing that the acclamation of Arrhidaeus after Alexander's death makes it impossible for Ptolemy to have been Philip's illegitimate son, because Arrhidaeus must have been recognized

55

Funeral Games

Ptolemy encouraged a false rumour of his paternity by Philip to enhance his standing among his followers, but since such a rumour also impugned the honour of his beloved mother, Arsinoë, this is innately dubious. Most of Ptolemy's supporters would have been close enough to the Macedonian court to have known the truth anyway. Ptolemy's public stance seems merely to have been to claim a common descent from Heracles with the Macedonian royal family. For instance, Theocritus describes Ptolemy as Lagus' son, but also says that Alexander and Ptolemy both "traced back their line to Heracles". That this was the official version need not be questioned, because it was part of an Encomium to Ptolemy performed at the court of his son Philadelphus.[66]

The clear message from the ancient writers is therefore that Ptolemy found himself obligated by a multi-faceted debt of honour to his dead King, of such potency as to compel him to place his kingdom and his life in jeopardy for the sake of the fulfilment of Alexander's dying wish. An immediate test of their veracity will be to explore whether this motivation can help us to understand what happened to Alexander's body after it reached Egypt.

*   *   *   *   *   *   *   *

Many modern authors[67] suggest that the ancient writers have stated that there was an intention to bury Alexander at the Oasis of Siwa in the desert far to the west of the Nile, but in doing so they are, whether knowingly or innocently, glossing over a major ambiguity, which may even have originated with Alexander himself. What the ancient sources[68] actually wrote was that the body was to be conveyed to Ammon or the Temple of Ammon. It is often assumed that this means Siwa, because the ancient geographers called this oasis *Ammonium* after the god, whose oracle lay there. It is also a natural assumption, because of Alexander's famous visit to this oracle in 331 BC and because he was in communication with the oasis to gain endorsement of Hephaistion's status as a Hero in the months preceding his death.

There is wide agreement that Alexander's "voice was failing" or that he was "voiceless" in his final few days. If any of his last words are genuine, they cannot have been uttered in anything more than a hoarse whisper. The brevity of the reported phrases ("to the strongest"; "when you are happy") might be symptomatic of struggle in expressing even a few syllables.[69] Perhaps, in a rare

---

and therefore legitimized by Philip II to make him viable as a marriage pawn in the Pixodarus affair.
[66] Theocritus, *The Idylls* 17; see also Satyrus, FGrH 631, F1, which gives a suspiciously circumlocuitous explanation of the ancestry of the Ptolemies; see also OGIS 54, lines 1-5.
[67] E.g. Richard Stoneman, Michael Wood, Robin Lane Fox…
[68] Diodorus 18.3.5, 18.28.3; Curtius 10.5.4; Justin 12.15, 13.4 – it appears that Justin did assume it was Siwa that was meant, but Justin was easily confused on such matters.
[69] Mary Renault, *The Nature of Alexander* p.231 has plausibly suggested that *kratisto* (strongest) might actually have been Kratero (Alexander's leading general, Craterus) by reason of Alexander's failing voice.

interval of lucidity, he said something like, "Take me to Ammon". The interpretations that might have been placed on such a wish in this a context are various. One possibility would have been an immediate transfer to a temple in Babylon of a god considered to be the local equivalent of Zeus-Ammon, for the Greeks habitually associated foreign gods with their nearest Olympian counterparts.[70] This could explain, for example, what prompted the delegation of the King's Companions, said to have spent the night of 9th June in the temple of "Serapis", to ask whether Alexander should be moved there. Alternatively, Alexander might have intended either that his body be taken to Siwa or to another temple explicitly dedicated to Ammon in Egypt. The name could refer either to the oasis or more vaguely to the god at any of his temples. There was in fact a temple of Ammon in most Egyptian cities and the centre of the cult lay at Thebes. It was its oracular prowess that made Siwa special, but oracles are too late at funerals.

Ptolemy might well have considered that an Egyptian temple on the Nile met the spirit of Alexander's dying wish, but even had he wished to transport Alexander's body to so remote a location as Siwa, he would probably have been thwarted by the circumstances. The oasis was strategically isolated and would have been exposed to an attempt by Ptolemy's enemies to send an expedition by sea to snatch back the corpse. The oasis lacked the resources to sustain the army that would have been required to defend it for any length of time.

*   *   *   *   *   *   *   *

There are but few hints as to the form and precise location of the tomb at Memphis. Apart from Pausanias' mention of burial "with Macedonian rites" and the purported involvement of the chief priest of a Memphite temple according to the Alexander Romance, another clue is the possibility of a link with the worship of Ammon, given Alexander's reported last wish and Ptolemy's determination to implement it.

However, there is also another independent piece of evidence for a connection between the Memphite tomb and the god Ammon. In around 319BC Ptolemy became the first of the successors to deviate from Alexander's standard coinage by minting a series of silver tetradrachms with a completely new obverse design.[71] In place of the famous head of Heracles wearing a lion-scalp headdress, Ptolemy substituted an explicit portrait of Alexander wearing an elephant scalp and the ram's horns of Ammon (Figure 3.3 – the ram's horn is

---

[70] This is known as syncretism and "Zeus-Ammon" is of course a case in point.
[71] A "Gold Porus Medallion" has recently come to light with the same obverse design. It has been claimed that it was minted by Alexander himself – see Osmund Bopearachchi & Philippe Flandrin, *Le Portrait d'Alexander le Grand*, 2005; however, I have shown in "Is the Gold Porus Medallion a Lifetime Portrait of Alexander the Great?" *The Celator*, vol. 21, no. 9, September 2007 that it appears to be a modern forgery; cf. Silvia Hurter, "Review of Le Portrait d'Alexandre le Grand", *Swiss Numismatic Review*, Vol. 85, 2006, pp. 185-195.

Funeral Games

the crescent-shaped feature curving up from the end of the eyebrow and continuing beneath the elephant skin).[72]

This is particularly significant because it is the earliest known depiction of Alexander wearing ram's horns, although Ephippus, who may once have served Alexander as an overseer of mercenaries,[73] has described how the King used to dress up in this guise at banquets:-

...Alexander also used to wear sacred clothing at his dinners, sometimes the purple robe of Ammon and slippers and horns like the god ... most of it indeed he wore all the time, the purple chlamys and chiton with a white stripe...[74]

Figure 3.3. Alexander wearing the elephant's scalp and ram's horns (crescent ascending from the left end of the eyebrow) on a tetradrachm of Ptolemy I (author's collection)

The ram's horns motif received its most memorable expression in the sensational series of tetradrachms issued by Lysimachus between about 298-281 BC in the cities of Ionia (see front cover). The elephant-scalp theme enjoyed enduring popularity, as shown by the surviving fragments of various statuettes from Egypt and a portrait head of Alexander, made in North Africa in the 2nd century AD, now in the Copenhagen National Museum. The most complete statuette was found in the Nile Delta at Athribis, about 40 miles downstream from Memphis (see Figure 3.4). It represents Alexander on horseback, though

---

[72] For details of the transition see Orestes H. Zervos, "Early Tetradrachms of Ptolemy I," *ANS Museum Notes* 13, 1967, pp. 1-16.
[73] Arrian, *Anabasis* 3.5.3.
[74] Ephippus of Olynthus, quoted by Athenaeus 537E-538B; cf. Curtius 3.3.17, Darius' "tunic was purple, interwoven with white at the centre"; *Metz Epitome* 2 (4th century AD) translated by Stewart in *Faces of Power: Alexander's Image & Hellenistic Politics*, "Alexander... adopted the diadem, the tunic with the central white stripe, the sceptre, the Persian girdle, and all the royal regalia that Darius had used"; cf. Diodorus 17.77.5, who uses ζώνη for the girdle, which is strictly a word for a female supporting belt, but just such a sash appears in some of the Alexandrian coins of Hadrian; identical clothing, including the sash-belt, is worn by the "Demetrio" Alexander statuette from Egypt, 1st century BC, Fig. 144 in Stewart; see also the Alexander Sarcophagus from Sidon; Darius wears the royal white stripe in the Alexander Mosaic from Pompeii.

his steed is missing, and is believed on stylistic grounds to date from the early Ptolemaic period.[75]

The emergence of the new tetradrachms in the immediate aftermath of the entombment of Alexander at Memphis and the evidence of the sculptures, has led Otto Mørkholm to infer the creation of an archetypal funerary statue of Alexander to embellish the Memphite tomb at this time.[76] This attractive theory both bolsters and in turn is itself reinforced by the indications from the literary evidence that we should expect a relationship between Alexander and Ammon at the first tomb. This in turn prompts the question of whether there might have existed a temple dedicated to Ammon at Memphis in 321 BC?

Figure 3.4. Early Ptolemaic statuette depicting Alexander wearing an elephant skin found in the Nile Delta (sketch by the author)

The answer is affirmative, for there is an early Ptolemaic papyrus, No. 50 in the first volume of the British Museum catalogue, which mentions the presence of an "Imensthotieion" (i.e. a temple of Ammon and Thoth) in the Hellenion

---

[75] See *The Search for Alexander: an Exhibition*, New York Graphic Society, 1980, exhibit 46.
[76] Otto Mørkholm, *Early Hellenistic Coinage*, CUP, 1991, Chapter 6.

district of Memphis. The Hellenion was the Greek quarter of the city, which is believed to have been founded by mercenary troops in the service of a Late Period pharaoh prior to Alexander's conquest. Claire Préaux argues that the papyrus cannot be later than the 3rd century BC on the internal evidence of the valuations of two properties.[77] Consequently, it is probable that this temple was available to Ptolemy, when he was seeking a site in Memphis at which to lay Alexander to rest.

Where were the Imensthotieion and the Hellenion? The evidence is scant. Memphis was abandoned well over a thousand years ago and stone robbing has left few visible remains. The main New Kingdom cult sites of Ammon-Re at Memphis are connected with Perunefer, the city's port, which may have been at or near the eastern side of the mound, at the heart of the ruin field (see the archaeological map in Figure 3.5). Greek and Phoenician dedicatory inscriptions were found here in the late 1890s and early 1900s. However, Dorothy Thompson, on the basis of the "Memphis dyke repair papyrus",[78] suggests that the Hellenion lay in the northwestern quadrant of the site.[79] This may also be consistent with the location of Petrie's "camp" (a possible barracks) around the Apries palace foundation. Petrie considered this to have been built to house the king's foreign (Greek?) bodyguard.[80] The most likely vicinity for the Imensthotieion is therefore the area within a few hundred metres to the north and west of the Palace of Apries.

Nevertheless, an entombment in the heart of the city with any degree of permanence would have conflicted with the Egyptian demarcation between the land of the living on the irrigated flood plain of the river and the land of the dead in the nearer parts of the desert above the western escarpment of the Nile Valley. In particular, the ancient city of Memphis had gradually developed a gargantuan necropolis just beyond the limit of the vegetation. We know this archaeological paradise as North Saqqara.

* * * * * * * *

What form might the Memphite tomb have taken? It is possible that Ptolemy literally created a full-scale Macedonian Royal Tomb at Memphis, in which case the Royal Tombs at Aegae may provide the best prototypes. The tomb of Alexander's father, Philip II, comprised stone chambers with a painted temple façade and a barrel-vaulted roof to support the great weight of earth, which was piled up over it, forming a huge tumulus. This would be the best model if Pausanias' mention of burial according to "Macedonian rites" were taken to refer to the type of tomb. However, a Macedonian interment would normally

---

[77] Claire Préaux, *L'Économie Royale des Lagides*, 1939, pp. 298-9.
[78] PSI 488.
[79] Dorothy Thompson (formerly Crawford), *Memphis under the Ptolemies*, Princeton 1988, pp. 13-16.
[80] David Jeffreys, *The Survey of Memphis*, Egypt Exploration Society, London, 1985.

have involved the prior incineration of the corpse on a pyre, which certainly did not happen.

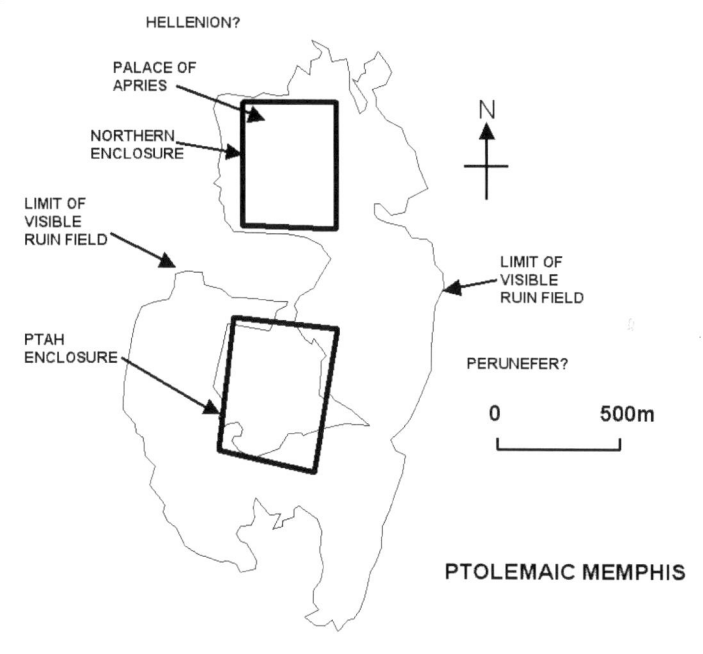

Figure 3.5. Archaeological plan of Ptolemaic Memphis

In Egypt it was a tenet of faith that the dead would have need of their corpses once again, when they were reborn into the afterlife. Such was the logic that justified the complexity and expense of the mummification process. Consequently, incineration of the corpse of the previous pharaoh would have been a terrible act of sacrilege in Egyptian eyes. If he were to preserve any chance of winning much-needed support for his rule from the Egyptian populace, Ptolemy could not allow Alexander to be cremated. However, this decision will have stirred up a degree of antipathy towards the satrap from some of his fellow Macedonians, who will have agreed with Homer that they should "bring wood and make ready all that is right for a dead man to have when he goes beneath the murky darkness, so that unwearied fire may burn him quickly from our eyes."[81] The Iliad goes on to explain the procedure: "Many noble sheep and many sleek cattle of shambling gait they flayed and dressed before the pyre; and from them all great-hearted Achilles gathered the fat, and enfolded the dead in it from head to foot," thus ensuring a hot and even flame.[82] When the blaze died down "they quenched the pyre with ruddy wine, so far as the flame had spread,"[83] thereby producing, through the thermal shock of the splashes of

---

[81] Homer, *Iliad* 23.50-53.
[82] Homer, *Iliad* 23.166-169.
[83] Homer, *Iliad* 23.250-251.

Funeral Games

cold liquid, the unusual transverse fractures seen among the cremated bones of Philip II from Tomb II at Aegae.

Most likely, it is the failure to cremate Alexander in Egypt of which Olympias complained in Aelian's anecdote:

When Alexander's mother Olympias learned that her son lay unburied for a long time, she groaned deeply and cried in a high-pitched voice: "My child," she said, "you wanted to reach heaven and you made it your aim, but now you do not enjoy even what are surely common rights shared by all men, the right to earth and to burial." Thus she lamented her own fate and criticized her son's arrogance.[84]

In fact we know from later reports that Alexander's body remained intact within the same golden coffin as was fashioned for it at Babylon for centuries. Furthermore, there are many hints that Alexander's remains almost immediately became the object of religious veneration in a temple context. Therefore, Pausanias must only have been referring to superficial religious ceremonies, such as the sacrifices and funeral games, which were organised by Ptolemy according to Diodorus.[85] Even this soon after his death, Alexander's corpse was probably treated more as a sacred relic than as an ordinary human cadaver. His deification had, after all, begun in his lifetime and was perfectly consistent with pharaonic precedent and tradition in Egypt.

* * * * * * * *

The most intriguing possibility regarding the character of the Memphite tomb relates to a surviving antiquity found in Alexandria and now on display in the British Museum. In about 341BC the last native pharaoh of Egypt, Nectanebo II, fled to Ethiopia to escape a Persian invasion. He was thereby forced to forsake his magnificent stone sarcophagus, which had been readied in the traditional fashion in anticipation of his eventual burial. Ten years later Alexander ousted the Persians from Egypt and a decade later still Ptolemy brought his body back to Memphis. In all probability the sarcophagus still stood empty and abandoned at that time. There are strong circumstantial reasons to suppose that Ptolemy decided to adopt it for Alexander's entombment.

Firstly, it is most likely that the sarcophagus lay at Memphis in 321BC, since the city had been the capital of Nectanebo II and of the preceding pharaohs of the 30th Dynasty.[86] He had undertaken an extensive building program in the Memphite necropolis at North Saqqara, which may have been motivated by an intention to make it the site of his tomb. Late Period pharaohs were generally

---

[84] Aelian, *Varia Historia* 13.30.
[85] Diodorus 18.28.4.
[86] The locations of the tombs of the 30th Dynasty are not known – see Aidan Dodson, *After the Pyramids*, London, 2000, p.162-3; speculation has centred on Sebennytos, but simply because the founder of the dynasty, Nectanebo I, was a native of that town; fragments of the sarcophagus of Nectanebo I have been found embedded in walls in medieval Cairo; there is a complete shabti of Nectanebo II in Turin and some ten fragments also, but all unprovenanced.

The Quest for the Tomb of Alexander by Andrew Chugg

buried in the precincts of major temple complexes, typically in a deep vault beneath a cult chapel.[87] Nectanebo had added temples to the Serapeum (excavated by Auguste Mariette in 1850-1) and to the Sacred Animal Necropolis, adjoining the Sanctuary of the Mother Cows of the Apis Bulls at Saqqara (Figure 3.6). His predecessor, Nectanebo I, is believed to have embellished the processional route to the Serapeum with an Avenue of Sphinxes and there is a major cemetery of the 30th Dynasty in its vicinity. It is clear that the 30th dynasty pharaohs identified themselves closely with the cult of the Apis Bull, which was mummified and preserved in a giant sarcophagus in the subterranean vaults of the Serapeum. This highlights the importance for the Egyptians of Alexander's act of sacrificing to the Apis Bull when he reached Memphis in 332BC.[88]

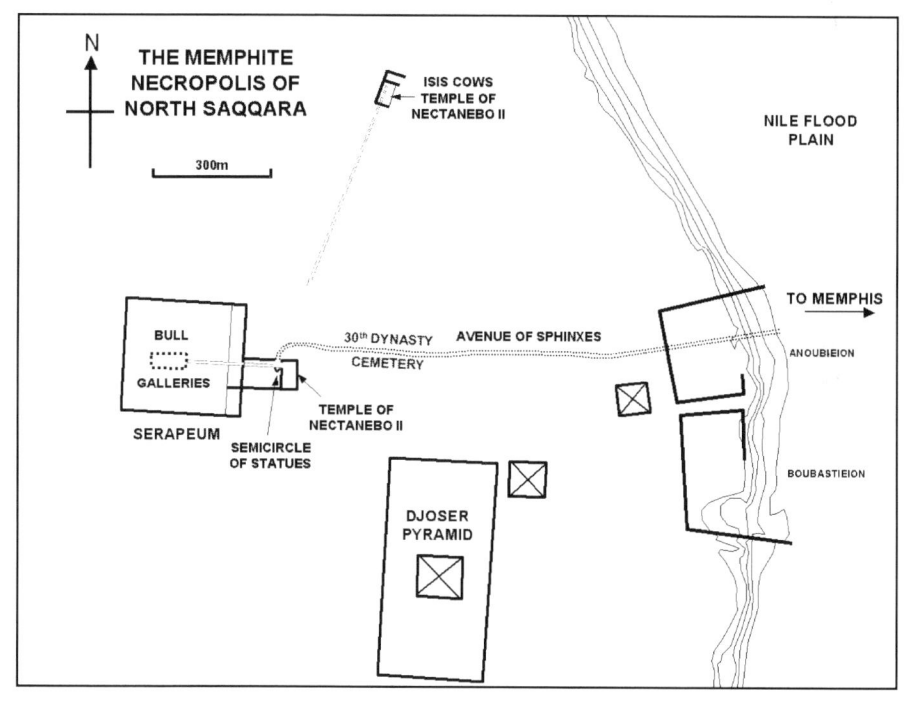

Figure 3.6. The Serapeum and the temples of Nectanebo II at North Saqqara

Most strikingly, there is a semicircle of eleven limestone statues of Greek sages and poets, which guards the entrance to the Nectanebo II temple at the Serapeum (Figures 3.7 & 3.8). The central figure seems to be Homer, for whom

---

[87] Examples are the 26th dynasty tombs at Sais and those of the 29th dynasty at Mendes. This type of tomb was one element of a Late Period revival of Old Kingdom styles and traditions; see B.G. Trigger, B.J. Kemp, D. O'Connor and A.B. Lloyd, *Ancient Egypt: A Social History*, Cambridge, 1983, p.321.

[88] Arrian, *Anabasis* 3.1.4; Nectanebo II began his reign by officiating at the funeral of the Apis Bull at the Serapeum, see Nicolas Grimal, *A History of Ancient Egypt*, Blackwell, 1994, p. 379.

Funeral Games

Alexander expressed a passionate appreciation.[89] Another is Pindar, whose house and descendants Alexander intervened to preserve from destruction at Thebes. Yet another is Plato, the preceptor of Alexander's own tutor Aristotle. Lauer & Picard have even speculated that a twelfth statue representing Aristotle himself is missing from the end of the semicircle closest to the temple.[90] Opinions differ over the date of these sculptures: various scholars have favoured dates from the late 3rd through to the 2nd century BC mainly on stylistic grounds,[91] but Lauer & Picard have proposed a date early in the third century under Ptolemy I.[92] They argue that the statue at the western end of the semicircle represents Demetrius of Phalerum, the leading philosopher at Ptolemy's court. Under Philadelphus, Demetrius was exiled to the countryside and eventually died through the bite of an asp, because he had supported a rival faction in the struggle over the succession.[93]

Figure 3.7. Photo of the semicircle of statues at the Serapeum (~1850)

---

[89] E.g. Plutarch. *Alexander* 8.2 & 26.1.
[90] J-P. Lauer & C. Picard, *Les statues Ptolémaiques du Sarapieion de Memphis*, Paris, 1955, p. 153.
[91] E.g. F. Matz, "Review of Lauer & Picard; Les statues Ptolémaiques du Sarapieion de Memphis," *Gnomon* 29, pp. 84-93; Fraser, *Ptolemaic Alexandria*, Note 512 to Chapter 5, says an early date is not impossible, but prefers a later one, as does Dorothy Thompson, *Memphis after the Ptolemies*, p. 212.
[92] J-P. Lauer & C. Picard, *Les statues Ptolémaiques du Sarapieion de Memphis*, Paris, 1955, p. 149.
[93] Diogenes Laertius, *Demetrios* 5.76; Cicero, *Pro Rabirio Postumo* 23.

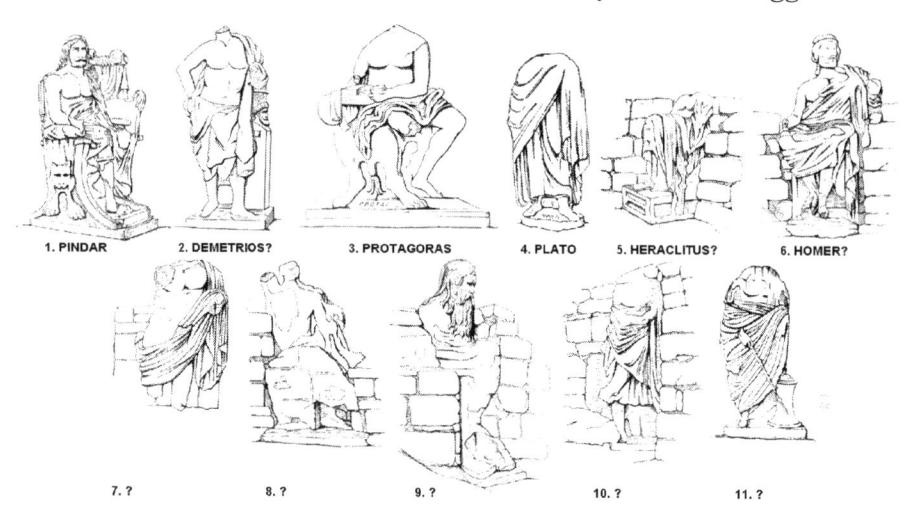

1. PINDAR 2. DEMETRIOS? 3. PROTAGORAS 4. PLATO 5. HERACLITUS? 6. HOMER?

7. ? 8. ? 9. ? 10. ? 11. ?

Figure 3.8. Drawings by Auguste Mariette of the statues of the semicircle at the Serapeum

In 1951 Lauer discovered a fragment of an inscription in the neighbourhood of some other Greek statues standing further down the dromos of the Serapeum. It appears to be an artist's signature in Greek characters of form dating to the early third century BC.[94] It therefore seems likely that all the Greek statuary at the Serapeum was sculpted under Ptolemy I, hence these statues were contemporaneous with Alexander's Memphite tomb. Dorothy Thompson has speculated that they "guarded a shrine of some importance – the site once perhaps of Alexander's tomb."[95] If so, then the shrine in question almost certainly lay within the Nectanebo II temple, as may be inferred from Auguste Mariette's detailed plan (Figure 3.9).[96] The association of Alexander's tomb at Memphis with the temple of Nectanebo II at the Serapeum derives from evidence that is entirely independent of an association of the sarcophagus of Nectanebo II with Alexander's tomb in Alexandria (Chapter 7). The duplication of a connection with Nectanebo II is therefore likely to prove significant.

A cryptic oracle given to Alexander by the god Serapis in the Alexander Romance may also be relevant:-

You, a callow young man, shall subdue all the races of barbarian nations; and then, by dying and yet not dying, you shall come to me. Then the city of Alexandria… is to be your grave.[97]

---

[94] J-P. Lauer & C. Picard, *Les statues Ptolémaiques du Sarapieion de Memphis*, Paris, 1955, p. 182.
[95] Dorothy Thompson, *Memphis after the Ptolemies*, 1988, p.212, though she believed the statues to be too late in date to have been created for Alexander's tomb.
[96] J-P Lauer & Ch. Picard, *Les Statues Ptolémaiques du Sarapieion de Memphis*, Paris, 1955, Plate 26; see also Ulrich Wilcken, "Die griechischen Denkmäler vom Dromos des Serapeums von Memphis," *JDAI* 32, pp.149-203.
[97] *Armenian Romance* 93; Sesonchousis repeats part of the same oracle at *Armenian Romance* 249.

Funeral Games

Coming to Serapis reads like a euphemism for dying and indeed Serapis is believed to have derived from Osiris-Apis, a manifestation of Osiris, who was lord of the afterlife. However, such prophecies characteristically had double meanings, so here we might discern a further hint that Alexander's first tomb was located at the Memphite temple of Serapis.

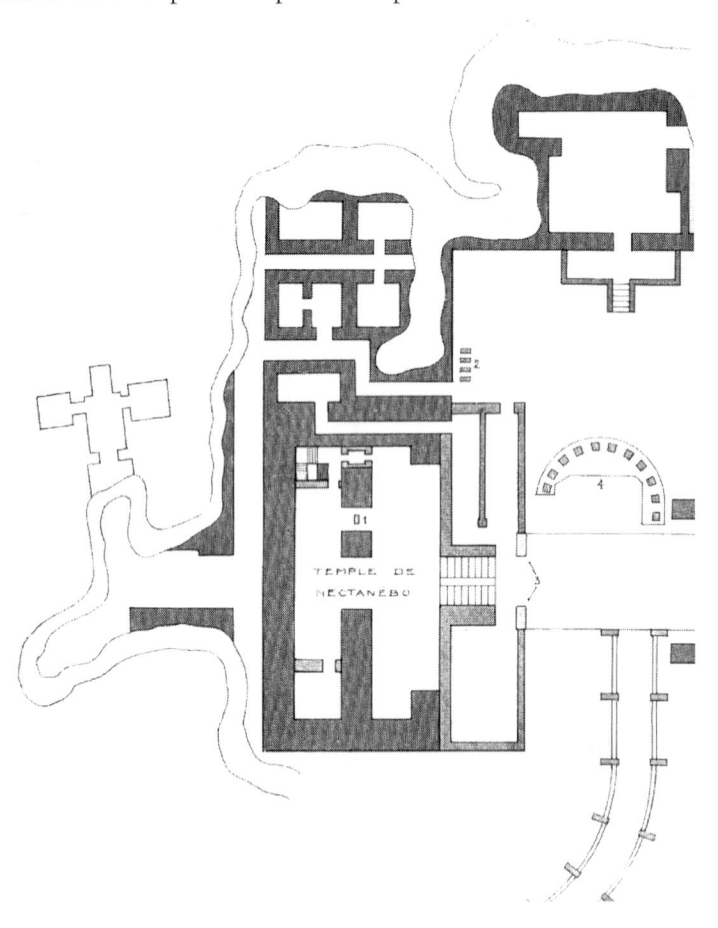

Figure 3.9. Buildings at the eastern end of the Serapeum showing the semicircle guarding the entrance to the Nectanebo II temple from a plan by Auguste Mariette

Most versions of the Alexander Romance mention that an Egyptian priest at Memphis advised that Alexander's body should be moved to Alexandria. Unfortunately, the affiliation of this priest is lost from the better-known manuscripts. However, the Syriac Alexander Romance seems to preserve the information that this advice was given by the "priests of Serapis".[98] This

---

[98] E.A.W. Budge, *The History of Alexander the Great: Being the Syriac Version of the Pseudo Callisthenes*, Cambridge, 1889, 3.23, p. 142.

constitutes direct ancient evidence that Alexander's first tomb was located at the Memphite Serapeum.

However, the Nectanebo sarcophagus re-enters the story at a much later date, at which point it will be possible to provide a more complete evaluation of its claim and the implications for the location and form of the Memphite tomb of Alexander.

* * * * * * * *

In 1996 Andreas Schmidt-Colinet published a laconic German article entitled "The Tomb of Alexander the Great in Memphis?" with the objective of building on the ideas of Thompson concerning a tomb of Alexander at the Memphite Serapeum.[99] He mentions the possible associations between Alexander's tomb and the semicircle ("Exedra") of statues and also (more tenuously) the Dionysiac statuary located further west on the *dromos* of the Serapeum. He additionally connects the Nectanebo II temple with the story in the Alexander Romance of Nectanebo having fathered Alexander. However, he does not seem to notice the fact that the intended sarcophagus of Nectanebo II was found in Alexandria, where it was traditionally recognized as the tomb of Alexander. Schmidt-Colinet's article nevertheless serves perfectly to indicate that the associations between Alexander's tomb and the Serapeum have been considered strong enough to excite interest by scholars and their editors, even without the smoking gun of the sarcophagus now in the British Museum.

* * * * * * * *

The duration of the Memphite entombment remains in dispute among scholars. It is relatively certain that the body was moved to Alexandria within half a century of its arrival, but Fraser has argued that Ptolemy made the transfer as soon as two or three years after his defeat of Perdiccas in support of his contention that Ptolemy moved his capital to Alexandria at an early date during his rule of Egypt. However, we shall shortly find, after careful analysis of the evidence, that this view is virtually untenable. Rather the statement by Pausanias that the relocation was effected by Ptolemy's son, Philadelphus, should be believed. We have already found Pausanias to be precisely accurate in everything else he writes concerning this history, so it would be surprising if he were mistaken on this solitary point and there is nothing to contradict him in the ancient evidence. If he is correct, then the transfer can hardly have occurred much before the second decade of the third century BC Since Philadelphus was not even born until 309-308 BC.

* * * * * * * *

---

[99] Andreas Schmidt-Colinet, "Das Grab Alexanders d. Gr. In Memphis?", *The Problematics of Power: Eastern & Western Representation of Alexander the Great*, M. Bridges & J. Ch. Bürgel (eds.), Peter Lang, 1996, 87-90; I was unaware of this article until 2008 and did not obtain a copy until March 2009 – hence it was not mentioned in the first edition of this book published in 2007.

Funeral Games

On the basis of the preceding autopsy of the surviving fragments of evidence concerning Alexander's corpse, the shards of the history of its journey from Babylon and the nature and origins of his first tomb at Memphis may now be reconstructed as a vessel that will hold water.

Alexander was pronounced dead on the evening of the tenth of June 323 BC. Perdiccas called a meeting of army officers the next day, which escalated into an ad hoc session of the Assembly of the Macedonians. The Assembly was emotive and fractious. It gave rise to a schism between the cavalry, led by Perdiccas and the rest of the Bodyguards, and the infantry, led by Meleager. The dispute culminated in fighting in the palace and bloodshed beside Alexander's deathbed.

After nearly a week Perdiccas regained control and had Meleager and his chief supporters executed. During the interim Alexander's body had lain virtually unattended. By that stage it should have grown putrid in Babylon's summer heat, but the embalmers found the corpse to be pure, fresh and lifelike. In the ancient sources this was remembered as a sign of Alexander's divinity, but medically speaking it is a strong indication that death occurred much later than was thought at the time. Alexander had probably entered a profound, terminal coma due to the onset of cerebral malaria.

Alexander's last wish had been that his body should be taken to the god Ammon in Egypt. The Assembly of the Macedonians probably initially agreed to this request, but Perdiccas subsequently overturned this decision in favour of a traditional funeral and burial at Aegae in Macedon, possibly with the aid of an opportune prophecy from the Royal Seer. Perdiccas appointed an officer called Arrhidaeus to be responsible for the preparation of a catafalque and the transport of the body back to Aegae.

The catafalque was a richly ornamented masterpiece of jaw-dropping splendour in the form of an elegant Ionic temple. The body was placed in a coffin fashioned from 200 talents of gold, fitted to the corpse like an Egyptian mummy case and filled with preservative honey mixed with rich incense and perfumes. It took over a year to design and construct the hearse and its trappings. It eventually set out on its long journey in the late summer or autumn of 322 BC.

Ptolemy had received the governorship of Egypt in the initial settlement of the administration of the empire in the aftermath of Alexander's death. He was probably an illegitimate half-brother of Alexander. The King had personally saved his life in India, and he is said to have sworn an oath to the dying Alexander to fulfil his wish that his body be taken to Ammon. In an uncharacteristically reckless act of rebellion inspired by fierce loyalty to his dead monarch, Ptolemy suborned Arrhidaeus and intercepted and hijacked the cortège in Syria in the Winter of 322-321 BC, whilst Perdiccas was 700 miles away in Pisidia. Perdiccas sent his henchmen Polemon and Attalus in hot pursuit, but Ptolemy fought them off or eluded them, possibly by exploiting the carriage as a decoy. He brought the body to Memphis on the west bank of the Nile and readied his defences. In the spring of 321 BC a vengeful Perdiccas marched against him at the head of the Grand Army. However, having twice failed to force the crossing of the Nile with disastrous loss of life among his troops, Perdiccas was murdered by his own officers. Ptolemy made peace with the Grand Army and sent it back north to meet Antipater, who took over the Regency of the empire on behalf of the joint-kings: the infant Alexander IV and the imbecilic Philip-Arrhidaeus.

Ptolemy now completed the entombment of Alexander at Memphis in the Nectanebo II temple of the Serapeum precinct in the necropolis of North Saqqara. He may have commissioned a large statue of Alexander riding a charger, heroically nude except for an elephant skin aegis and deified with the ram's horns of Ammon. Soon afterwards the head of this statue was adopted as the design for the obverse of a new series of tetradrachm coins. Over two decades later, in the early 3rd century BC, Ptolemy commissioned the surviving semicircle of statues of Alexander's favourite poets and sages to decorate the entrance to the tomb.

In the next chapter it will be argued that the Memphite tomb existed for three or four decades, but Ptolemy's son, Philadelphus, eventually transferred the body to Alexandria, probably in the 280's BC. In his eponymous city Alexander was worshipped as a god and his high priest was the chief official of the metropolis. In Egypt under the Ptolemies the years were named after this Priest of Alexander, just as they were named for the archon at Athens.

4. The Capital of Memory

Your name from hence immortal life shall have,
Though I, once gone, to all the world must die.
The earth can yield me but a common grave,
When you entombed in men's eyes shall lie.

William Shakespeare, Sonnet LXXXI

In the three centuries before Christ Alexandria was the largest, loveliest and most learned and luxurious city in the world. The writer Lawrence Durrell has nostalgically alluded to this Alexandria as "the capital of memory".[1] Alexander had wished to found a port that would provide an interface between the ancient civilisation of the Nile Valley and the Mediterranean world of the Greeks. A site in the delta was impractical because of the marshy nature of the ground and the annual Nile flood. He therefore chose a location just to the west on a strip of rocky ground about a mile and a half wide sandwiched between the Mediterranean and Lake Mareotis, a freshwater lagoon connected by canals with the Canopic branch of the Nile.

Souvenir coin issues minted in Roman Alexandria appear to commemorate Alexander's foundation of the city. On the reverse of various bronze drachms minted under Trajan, Hadrian and some of their successors an elephant headdress is worn by a naked male figure driving a chariot drawn by two winged serpents (Figure 4.1). The charioteer casts seeds about him from a bag draped over his left arm. He probably has to be a pharaoh, because the serpents wear the skhent crown of Upper and Lower Egypt in some examples. Arrian writes of Alexander's expedition to the Siwa oasis:

Now Ptolemy son of Lagus says that two serpents preceded the army giving voice, and that Alexander told his leaders to follow them and trust the divinity; and the serpents led the way to the oracle and back again.[2]

Most probably on the way back from Siwa, Alexander founded Alexandria, famously marking the outline of its walls with barley seeds. The iconography of these coins is also reminiscent of representations of Triptolemus, the Greek god of agriculture. However, it is known that the type was revived specifically in the year of the 500th anniversary of Alexandria. This tends to confirm that they are an allegorical celebration of Alexander's foundation of the city and that the charioteer is both Alexander as Triptolemus and Alexander as pharaoh and founder.[3]

---

[1] First paragraph of *Clea*.
[2] Arrian, *Anabasis Alexandri*, 3.3.5.
[3] For more details see A.M. Chugg, "A Double Entendre in the Alexandrian Bigas of Triptolemos," *The Celator Journal*, Vol. 17, No. 8, August 2003, pp. 6-16.

The Quest for the Tomb of Alexander by Andrew Chugg

Figure 4.1. Alexander wearing his elephant scalp cap dispenses seeds from a serpent *biga* on a bronze Alexandrian drachm minted under Hadrian (author's collection)

Strabo has provided a detailed description of the layout of Ptolemaic Alexandria, based on his personal observations during a long stay in Egypt beginning in 25 BC.[4] The street plan was a rectangular grid oriented so that the cooling Etesian winds[5] that blow onshore from the northwest in the summer flowed down through the streets that ran between the sea and the lake (see the reconstructed street plan, Figure 4.2). Two principal streets, twice as wide as the rest and lined by colonnades of marble and polished granite, intersected at the centre of the city. The longer of these, often called Canopic Way, ran for some three miles between the Gate of the Sun in the northeastern wall, which faced towards Canopus at the nearest mouth of the Nile, and the Gate of the Moon, which looked out over the city's necropolis to the southwest. The intersecting highstreet ran from the Lochias peninsula on the Mediterranean seaboard to the harbour on the lake,[6] although its identification is still disputed. A causeway called the Heptastadion, because it was seven stades (nearly a mile) long, connected the city with the offshore island of Pharos. It also divided the eastern Great Harbour from the Eunostos, the Harbour of Happy Returns. The famous Pharos lighthouse, the seventh wonder of the ancient world, towered about four hundred feet over the entrance to the Great Harbour on the eastern tip of the island (Figures 4.3 & 4.10).

---

[4] Strabo 17.1.6-10 gives by far the most detailed contemporaneous description of the ancient city, which is the basis of the account given here, except where otherwise indicated.
[5] Diodorus 17.52.
[6] Mahmoud Bey El-Falaki, *L'Antique Alexandrie...*, Copenhagen, 1872; this identification has been disputed, e.g. by F. Noack, "Neue Untersuchungen in Alex.," *Athen-Mitteil.*, 1900, from p. 215.

71

The Capital of Memory

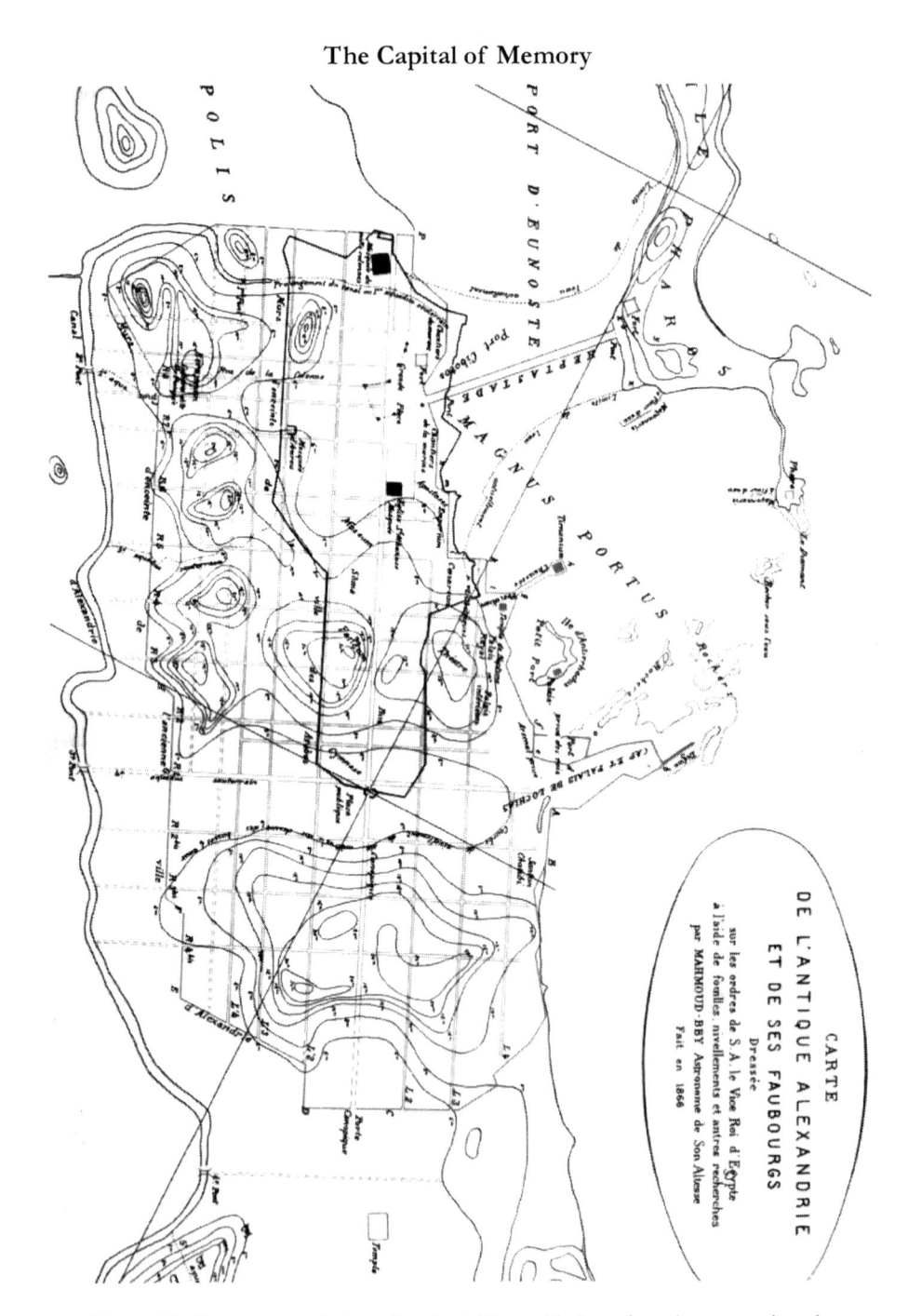

Figure 4.2. Reconstructed plan of ancient Alexandria based on the excavations by Mahmoud Bey in 1865

The Quest for the Tomb of Alexander by Andrew Chugg

Diodorus quotes a census recording the number of free citizens as exceeding 300,000 at the end of the Ptolemaic period.[7] This suggests a total population of around half a million, when slaves are taken into account. Philo has written that the city comprised five quarters.[8] They were designated Alpha (for Ἀλεξάνδρος = "Alexander"), Beta (for βασιλεύς = "king"), Gamma (for γένος = "descendant"), Delta (for Δίος = "Zeus") and Epsilon (for ἔκτισε πόλιν ἀείμνηστον = "founded an ever-memorable city") according to Pseudo-Callisthenes,[9] who also asserts that these names were supplied by the Founder himself. Alpha, the district named after Alexander, probably lay around the central crossroads.[10] Beta was the Royal District containing the palaces of the kings, roughly co-extensive with the district that the Romans later called the Bruchium. It stretched from the Lochias peninsula along the shore as far as the middle of the Great Harbour and southwards to the border of Alpha. Strabo refers to a Royal District, which incorporated between a quarter and a third of the whole city, though he probably included some areas that did not strictly lie within the traditional bounds of Beta. The Royal District contained a theatre built above a private Royal Harbour in the lee of the Lochias promontory. Yet another palace had been squeezed onto Antirrhodos, an islet in the Great Harbour just beyond the entrance to the private harbour. The Museum and its Library, the famous centre of learning for the whole Greek world, also lay somewhere in or near the Royal District, presumably close to the shore, since, when Julius Caesar set fire to a fleet of ships in the harbour, the Library accidentally caught alight. The Egyptian quarter lay either in Gamma or Epsilon, but it has also been called Rhakotis, which some believe to have been the name of the pre-existing Egyptian port at the site. However, it may alternatively come from the words for "building site" in Egyptian (Demotic), so it could just be the name given to the new city by the native inhabitants of fishing villages on this shore.[11] It apparently remained a name used by the Egyptian populace throughout the Ptolemaic and Roman periods.[12] The Egyptian quarter lay behind the shipyards at the western end of the Great Harbour, perhaps extending from the southwestern corner to the Eunostos Harbour. There was also a Jewish quarter, almost certainly lying behind the seafront east of Lochias, which may have been Delta.[13] The final quarter, of unknown character, but by

---

[7] Diodorus 17.52.
[8] Philo of Alexandria, *In Flaccum* 55; see also P.M. Fraser, "A Syriac Notitia Urbis Alexandrinae," *JEA* 37.
[9] Pseudo-Callisthenes, *The Romance of Alexander*, e.g. Stoneman (trans.), *The Greek Alexander Romance* 1.32.
[10] Achilles Tatius, *Clitophon and Leucippe* 5.1.
[11] M. Chauveau, *L'Egypte au temps de Cléopâtre*, Daily Life Series, Hachette, 1997, p.77.
[12] Stoneman (translator), *The Greek Alexander Romance* 1.31 and 3.34.
[13] Josephus, *Contra Apion* 2.33, places the Jewish quarter near the Royal Palaces on a harbourless stretch of the coast; he also speaks of the Jews being concentrated in Delta in *The Jewish War*, 2.495; however, Philo, *In Flaccum* 55, states that two of the five quarters were predominantly Jewish; there is also a papyrus (BGU 1151, lines 40-41) which seems to assert that Delta was near

elimination bordering the shores of the lake south of Canopic Way, was perhaps occupied by citizens of predominantly Greek extraction in view of the ethnic demarcation associated with the other districts.

Figure 4.3. The goddess Isis Pharia holds a billowing sail on a bronze drachm minted in Alexandria under Hadrian with the Pharos lighthouse to the right (author's collection)

Among the great buildings of the Ptolemaic city Strabo records a Temple of Poseidon at the centre of the Great Harbour with the Emporium, where duties on goods were collected, sited a little further to the west. The principal temple of the city, the Serapeum, was situated on rising ground in its southwestern corner. Somewhere near the middle of the city there was an artificial hill known as the Paneum in the shape of a fir cone with a spiral track ascending to a viewpoint at its summit. This used to be identified with the hillock of Kom el-Dikka, just south of Canopic Way about half way between the gates, but this mound has been substantially excavated away and has proved to be made of waste from the medieval pottery industry and underlain by Roman remains. Two hundred metre porticoes facing onto Canopic Way, probably towards the centre of the city, fronted a splendid Gymnasium. The tribunal (*dicasterion*) and the groves were also situated nearby. Here too within the walls of a vast sacred precinct and adjoining the palace complex lay Alexander's tomb.

*   *   *   *   *   *   *   *

The date for the transferral of Alexander's embalmed corpse from Memphis to Alexandria remains uncertain, but various lines of argument tend to converge on a range between about 290 - 280 BC. Pausanias attributes this act to Ptolemy Philadelphus, the son and heir of the first Ptolemy, whose epithet is Soter, meaning the Saviour.[14] He places it near the beginning of his brief summary of Philadelphus' reign: "... and [Philadelphus] it was who brought down from

---

the Kibotos harbour (ἐν τῶι Δ... πρὸς τῆι Κειβωτῶι), which Strabo places firmly in the west of Alexandria.

[14] Ptolemy I was rarely called the son of Lagus by Alexandrian sources, but was usually distinguished from his eponymous descendants solely by his epithet.

The Quest for the Tomb of Alexander by Andrew Chugg

Memphis the corpse of Alexander".[15] The Parian Marble places Philadelphus' birth in the year 309-8 BC. He reigned jointly with his father from 28th December 285 BC until Soter's death in the first half of 282 BC,[16] and later with his sister, Arsinoë, whom he married in the incestuous Pharaonic tradition, although the union proved childless. His epithet means "brother/sister-loving" and it was intended to refer to this marriage, but it is also darkly ironic, since he killed at least two of his brothers and made war against another in order to secure his throne. However, his reign was long and magnificent, lasting until 246 BC and spanning the apex of Ptolemaic power in the eastern Mediterranean.

In the previous chapter Pausanias emerged as a reliable authority on matters concerning Alexander's corpse. Although he also cites the spurious story that Ptolemy had helped to save Alexander's life in the land of the Oxydracae, even this shows he was well-read, because it derives from the lost work of Cleitarchus, who was one of the earliest and most influential historians of Alexander. If Pausanias is correct in making Philadelphus responsible for the transfer to Alexandria, then it would be difficult to date it much before about 290 BC, when Philadelphus was eighteen. Nevertheless, the authority of a single source is always open to doubt in the absence of corroboration. Of the other sources which mention the move from Memphis to Alexandria, Curtius is too vague and the Alexander Romance too fantastical to be helpful. In the Parian Marble there is no mention of any transfer of Alexander's corpse up to the last surviving entries around 300 BC. There are a few lacunae in the entries for the last few years of the 4th century BC, but the record is complete up to 309 BC. This prompts the question of whether it is at all likely that, having taken the trouble to note the initial entombment at Memphis, the author of the Parian Marble, writing in 263-262 BC when the body almost certainly lay in Alexandria, would not subsequently have noted the transfer to Alexandria. In fact it is clear that he would at least have bewildered his contemporaries by such an omission, so it must be considered highly improbable. Conversely, if the body was moved by Philadelphus in the early 3rd century, then it is transparent that the Marble is citing the initial burial as a means of setting the scene for a subsequent entry on the transfer to Alexandria in order to flatter the monarch who still reigned over Paros, when it was sculpted. This is an argument from silence, but the silence is significant, because the mention of the Memphite entombment under the entry for 321/320BC must have been followed up with a note of the transfer to Alexandria in some later entry. Since there is no sign of such a note up to the last surviving entries, the relocation must have taken place in the third century BC. Hence the Parian Marble provides the requisite independent near-contemporaneous corroboration of Pausanias' version. The argument for an

---

[15] Pausanias 1.7.1.
[16] Alan K. Bowman, *Egypt After The Pharaohs*, Appendix I.

The Capital of Memory

early transfer to Alexandria (i.e. within a decade of Alexander's death) is therefore virtually untenable in the evidence.

This merits emphasis, because the mainstream of modern scholarship has often expressed the opposite opinion on this point, though more by accident than through careful analysis. In particular, Fraser became embroiled in an argument with Welles in which he sought to prove that Ptolemy transferred the Egyptian capital from Memphis to Alexandria as early as circa 320 BC.[17] In support of this hypothesis, he found it convenient also to advocate an early date for the transfer of Alexander's corpse. He later conceded that the case for an early transfer of the capital cannot be proven, but his incidental opinion on the duration of the Memphite entombment has nevertheless been influential. His feeling was that Ptolemy should logically have been eager to embellish his new capital with the tomb of its founder.[18] However, if in fact Ptolemy's principal motivation in the matter was to fulfil a personal promise made to Alexander to deliver his body to Ammon, then it is easy to understand why the new pharaoh might actually have been reluctant to disturb a burial at the most sacred precinct in the Memphite necropolis.

It is nonetheless feasible that Philadelphus acted whilst Ptolemy still lived, since he seems to have progressively taken over the government of the country as his father edged into extreme old age. There is also papyrus evidence suggesting that Menelaus, Ptolemy's brother, became the first high priest of Alexander in Alexandria, probably between 290-85 BC.[19] It would be fitting if this priesthood was established in association with the origins of the plan to move Alexander's body. However, Pausanias' words are more literally in keeping with the move having occurred shortly after Ptolemy's death. Relieved of his father's inhibitions, Philadelphus will have been keen to adorn the new capital with the powerful symbolism of its founder's tomb, so an early transfer date within his reign is to be preferred.

The antechamber of a tomb of the early Ptolemaic period constructed of monumental blocks of alabaster was unearthed at Alexandria in the early 20th century by Breccia in the catholic cemetery of Terra Santa. It was more extensively excavated by Adriani, his successor as director of the Graeco-Roman Museum, who confirmed that the main burial chamber and all other traces are missing. The tomb was built in a style vaguely reminiscent of a Macedonian tumulus tomb of the late 4th century BC. On the basis of the royal quality of this tomb and its style, location and early date, Adriani proposed that it might be part of a tomb of Alexander in the city.[20] However, a number of the

---

[17] P.M. Fraser, *Ptolemaic Alexandria*, Ch. 1, note 28.
[18] P.M. Fraser, *Ptolemaic Alexandria*, Ch. 1, note 79.
[19] P.M. Fraser, *Ptolemaic Alexandria*, Ch. 5 & note 215 to Ch. 5.
[20] Nicola Bonacasa, "Un Inedito di Achille Adriani Sulla Tomba di Alessandro," *Studi Miscellanei – Seminario di Archaeologia e Storia dell Arte... dell Universita di Roma*, Vol. 28, 1991; Achille Adriani (posthumously), *La Tomba di Alessandro*, L'Erma di Bretschneider, Rome, 2000.

The Quest for the Tomb of Alexander by Andrew Chugg

Ptolemies themselves died or were killed in the relevant timeframe, so it might equally have belonged to one of them or some other prestigious individual. There is as yet nothing to link it specifically with Alexander.

It is known with certainty that the Ptolemies set up a cult at the royal tombs in Alexandria for the worship of Alexander and their own ancestors. For example, Athenaeus has preserved an account by Callixinus of Rhodes of a procession through Alexandria in 271-0BC under Philadelphus, in which statues of Alexander and Ptolemy Soter were paraded through the streets in the company of images of the gods Dionysus and Priapus and the goddess Virtue.[21] Even the names of most of the high-priests of Alexander have come down to us thanks to the practice of invoking them in the preambles of inscriptions and papyri bearing Ptolemaic decrees and contracts, partly as a means of recording their date.[22] In August 256 BC the priest's name is given as Alexander son of Leonidas.[23] For 251 BC Neoptolemus son of Phrixius had been appointed according to one of the Hibeh papyri,[24] whilst an inscription of Ptolemy III Euergetes dated 4th March 238 BC names the priest of Alexander and his forebears as Apollonides son of Moschion.[25] It is instructive that these documents consistently invoke the predicate *theos*, meaning "divine", to sanctify the dead Ptolemies, whereas Alexander seems to have been considered a fully-fledged deity who did not need such a careful introduction.

The Alexander Romance mentions a "Grand Altar of Alexander" built by the King "opposite" the shrine and tomb of Proteus on Pharos Island.[26] This could indicate a wide range of locations on the mainland in Alexandria proper. The Romance is generally considered relatively reliable concerning Alexandrian topography (e.g. by P. M. Fraser, *Ptolemaic Alexandria* p. 4), since Pseudo-Callisthenes (whatever his real identity) was probably a resident. Such an altar, which is reminiscent of the contemporaneous Great Altar at Pergamum, may have been closely associated with Alexander's tomb. The Romance subsequently essays a job description for the priesthood of Alexander:-

There is to be an administrator of the city [Alexandria], who will be known as the Priest of Alexander and will attend all the city's great festivals, adorned with a golden crown and a purple cloak; he is to be paid a talent per annum. His person is to be inviolate and he is to be free of all civic obligations; the post shall be the preserve of the man who excels all in nobility of family, and the honour shall remain in his family thereafter.[27]

* * * * * * * *

---

[21] Athenaeus, *Deipnosophistae* 5.201B-F, 202F-203.
[22] Most are known from 272-1 BC onwards; see W. Clarysse & G. van der Veken, *The Eponymous Priests of Ptolemaic Egypt*, E.J. Brill, Leiden, 1983.
[23] P. Col. 54.
[24] P. Hib. 98. (Elsewhere "son of Kraisis")
[25] OGIS 56.
[26] Stoneman (translator), *The Greek Alexander Romance* 1.33.
[27] Stoneman (translator), *The Greek Alexander Romance* 3.32.

The Capital of Memory

The fourth Ptolemy, known as Philopator (Father-Loving), came to the throne at about the age of 23 late in 222 BC upon the death of his father, Ptolemy Euergetes (Ptolemy the Benefactor). However, he was an habitual hedonist with little interest in the day-to-day business of government. Consequently, much power devolved upon his principal minister, Sosibius. The Queen-Mother, Berenice II, sought to undermine this man, but was herself poisoned on the minister's orders early in the reign. One of the most important of ancient references to Alexander's tomb relates to the period after the assassination of Berenice. It comes from the third book of the *Proverbia*,[28] which was an epitome of the proverbs of Didymus and Tarrhaeus by Zenobius the Sophist, who taught in Rome under the emperor Hadrian. Arius Didymus was a famous Alexandrian scholar and a friend of the emperor Augustus, so this reference has an authoritative pedigree. Zenobius writes:-

Ptolemy Philopator... built in the middle of the city [of Alexandria] a memorial building (μνῆμα οἰκοδομήσας), *which is now called the Sema* (Σῆμα), *and he laid there all his forefathers together with his mother, and also Alexander the Macedonian.*

Bevan in his History of the Ptolemaic Dynasty also mentions that the priesthood of the Saviour-Gods, Ptolemy Soter and his wife Berenice I, became incorporated under the priesthood of Alexander in the year 215-214BC, according to a change in the dating formula in papyrus documents.[29] Bevan seems to have been unaware of the Zenobius reference, so he missed the significance of this observation. However, this not only provides excellent corroboration of Zenobius' information, but it also dates either the commencement or the completion of the construction of the new Soma Mausoleum to this year. The original Alexandrian tomb was therefore vacated at this time and it was Philopator's new edifice that became the famous tomb that is mentioned by numerous subsequent ancient writers. Strabo states that this structure was part of the Royal District (literally βασιλείων = "king-town") of the city and describes it as a walled enclosure (περίβολος) that contained the graves (ταφαὶ) of Alexander and the kings (i.e. the Ptolemies):-

μέρος δὲ τῶν βασιλείων ἐστὶ καὶ τὸ καλούμενον Σῶμα, ὃ περίβολος ἦν ἐν ᾧ αἱ τῶν βασιλέων ταφαὶ καὶ ἡ Ἀλεξάνδρου

A standard translation (slightly adapted from the Loeb, but with the manuscript reading of *Soma* replacing the modern emendation *Sema*) would be:

The Soma also, as it is called, is a part of the royal district. This was the walled enclosure, which contained the burial-places of the kings and that of Alexander.[30]

---

[28] Zenobius, *Proverbia* 3.94; according to the Suda s.v. *Zenobios* these were the proverbs of Arius Didymus (see Plutarch, *Antony* 80) and Tarrhaeus (Lucillus of Tarrha in Crete).
[29] Edwyn Bevan, *A History of Egypt under the Ptolemaic Dynasty*, Methuen & Co, 1927, p. 231.
[30] Strabo 17.1.8.

The Quest for the Tomb of Alexander by Andrew Chugg

However, an alternative and perhaps more literally correct translation could be:

Also a part of the Royal quarter is the so-called Soma that used to be the Enclosure Wall [of the city], which contains the Royal tombs and that of Alexander.

This infers a standard Greek grammatical construction called a zeugma (one verb governing several clauses to either side) and rescues us from the problem that Strabo is otherwise using the past tense to refer to structures that almost certainly still existed in his era (~25BC). As we shall see in the chapter on *Alexander's City* (below), there is a strong possibility that the Soma was indeed simply the part of Alexandria enclosed by Alexander's original walls, which had become a district of temples and tombs as Alexandria grew enormously beyond its original bounds in the 3rd century BC.

Diodorus also mentions this enclosure, calling it a sacred precinct (τέμενος), which was "worthy of the glory of Alexander in size and construction",[31] whilst Herodian[32] (Ἀλεξάνδρου μνῆμα) and Dio Cassius[33] (μνημεῖον) simply refer to the "memorial" of Alexander. The location of the precinct at the middle of the city is further supported by Achilles Tatius, an Alexandrian writing before AD300, who describes a place or district named after Alexander (ἐπώνυμον Ἀλεξάνδρου τόπον) at the main crossroads:-

After a voyage lasting three days we arrived at Alexandria. I entered by the Sun Gate, as it is called, and was instantly struck by the splendid beauty of the city, which filled my eyes with delight. From the Sun Gate to the Moon Gate – these are the guardian divinities of the entrances – led a straight double row of columns, about the middle of which lies the open part of the town, and in it so many streets that walking in them you would fancy yourself abroad while still at home. Going a few stades further [stade = 165m], I came to the place called after Alexander, where I saw a second town; the splendour of this was cut into squares, for there was a row of columns intersected by another as long at right angles.[34]

The Sun Gate and the Moon Gate are also mentioned by John, Bishop of Nikiu in the Nile Delta in his chronicle of c. AD690.

Aelius Antoninus Pius… built two gates in Alexandria on the west and on the east (of the city), and he named the eastern gate Ἡλιακή *[Sun] and the western gate* Σεληνιακή *[Moon].*[35]

Achilles Tatius therefore appears to be describing his characters entering Alexandria by its eastern gate and walking westwards along Canopic Way to its

---

[31] Diodorus 18.28.
[32] Herodian 4.8.9.
[33] Dio Cassius, *Roman History*, Epitome of Book LXXVI, 13.2.
[34] Achilles Tatius, *Clitophon and Leucippe* 5.1; the manuscripts of Achilles Tatius state that the author was an Alexandrian as does the entry on Achilles Tatius in the Suda Lexicon.
[35] John of Nikiu, *Chronicle*, Robert Henry Charles (trans.), Text and Translation Society 3, Amsterdam, reprint of London edition of 1916, Chapter LXXIV, p.56.

centre, where they saw the place of Alexander, which is likely to mean the sacred precinct of the Soma.

Taken together these testimonies make it clear that the tombs of Alexander and the Ptolemies were probably contained within one or more mausoleums, which in turn lay within a sacred walled precinct of significant size and grandeur. This precinct may also have contained one or more temples dedicated to their worship, together with the Grand Altar of Alexander. Furthermore, if the accounts of Strabo, Zenobius and Achilles Tatius are to be reconciled, then this enclosure was probably situated athwart the central crossroads or at least adjacent to this vicinity beside Canopic Way.

Another intriguing issue raised by these sources is the question of the name of Alexander's tomb. Zenobius says it was called the Sema (Σῆμα), which is simply a Greek word meaning "Tomb" in this context.[36] However, all the manuscripts of Strabo's *Geography* called it the Soma (Σῶμα), which means "Body" or "Corpse", but this has been "corrected" to Sema in many modern editions by their editors. Additionally, the Armenian text of Pseudo-Callisthenes declares: "And Ptolemy made a tomb in the holy place called 'Body of Alexander', and there he laid the body, or remains, of Alexander" and this is corroborated by the β recension of the Alexander Romance.[37] Only the later (and usually less accurate) Syriac version reads: "and they call that place 'The tomb of Alexander' unto this day".[38] It should also be mentioned that John Chrysostom, Bishop of Constantinople from AD398 until his exile in June AD404, referred to the sema of Alexander, but he seems to have used the word as an ordinary noun, rather than as a name.[39] Similarly, Dio Cassius refers to the soma of Alexander, but appears literally to mean his corpse.[40] Among Strabo, Zenobius and Pseudo-Callisthenes, where Soma/Sema is stated to be the name, it may be concluded that either Soma is being corrected to Sema or vice versa by the ancient scribes and copyists, who transmitted these accounts down the ages. In fact we have the behaviour of the modern editors of Strabo and of Kroll, who similarly emended Pseudo-Callisthenes, to demonstrate what is anyway fairly obvious: that an emendation from Soma to Sema is inherently

---

[36] More broadly it means a marker, its use for "tomb" seemingly deriving from the archaic Greek practice of using tumuli to mark significant graves; e.g. see Homer, *Iliad* 2.814 "but the immortals call it the grave-mound (sema) of Myrine, light of step" and 6.419 "heaped over him a mound (sema)" - Loeb translations.

[37] Wolohojian (translator), *The Romance of Alexander the Great by Pseudo-Callisthenes (Armenian manuscripts)*, Section 284; Leif Bergson, *Der Griechische Alexanderroman Rezension β*, 3.34, p. 190; this passage is absent from manuscript A.

[38] E.A.W. Budge, *The History of Alexander the Great: Being the Syriac Version of the Pseudo Callisthenes*, Cambridge, 1889, 3.23, p. 142.

[39] Homily XXVI of St John Chrysostom on the second epistle of St Paul the Apostle to the Corinthians.

[40] Dio Cassius, *Roman History* 51.16.5.

more likely than the reverse. Conversely, it would be perverse if several ancient authors were really taking the trouble explicitly to state that a tomb was called *The Tomb*. The fact that they bother to give the name suggests it was distinctive, rather than bland. For these reasons it is probable that the name of the sacred precinct was indeed the Soma and that those who have emended the manuscripts have erred.

However, notwithstanding the enclosure being called the Soma, it is feasible that the mausoleum that stood within it was separately known as the Sema.

Two Latin authors have provided some details of the architecture of the Soma. Suetonius, in describing a visit to the tomb by Augustus in 30 BC, refers to the sarcophagus and corpse of Alexander being brought out from a *penetrali*, which translates as something like an inner sanctum, but which could also suggest a chamber accessed via a passage or shaft.[41] Much more important, however, are certain verses by Marcus Annaeus Lucanus, who is usually abbreviated to Lucan.

He was born into a prominent Roman family in AD39. Seneca the Elder was his grandfather and Seneca the Younger, the mentor and advisor of Nero, was his uncle. He seems himself to have been a boyhood friend of the Emperor, first achieving fame as a poet at Nero's court. However, he evidently harboured nostalgic Republican sympathies, which were amply nourished by the spectacle of the Emperor's descent into despotism and debauchery. In AD65 he joined Calpurnius Piso's plot against Nero, which was subsequently betrayed. In the aftermath Nero required him to commit suicide and his *magnum opus*, the Pharsalia, was left unfinished. Nonetheless, ten books of this epic of the Roman civil war between Caesar and Pompey have come down to us. Having been composed in the last four years or so of his life, it is imbued with a keen contempt for kings and emperors, doubtless inspired by his personal experience of absolute power inexorably evolving into absolute corruption.

It is indeterminate whether Lucan personally visited Alexandria, but the city figures prominently in his poetry and Suetonius has mentioned that he was recalled to Rome from as far away as Athens by Nero.[42] Alexandria was a voyage of a mere week from Athens[43] and must have exerted an almost irresistible allure for a youthful Roman scholar. Even if Lucan never visited the city himself, his uncle, Seneca, had certainly been there and could have provided detailed information.[44] Two passages in Lucan's Pharsalia[45] constitute the only detailed description of the Soma that survives from the ancient world:-

---

[41] Suetonius, *Lives of the Caesars* 2.18.
[42] Suetonius, *Lives of Illustrious Men, On Poets, Life of Lucan*.
[43] L. Casson, "Speed under Sail of Ancient Ships," *TAPhA* 82, 1951, pp. 136-148.
[44] H. Thiersch, "Die alexandrinische Königsnekropole," *Jahrbuch d. K. D. Archaeol. Instituts* 25, 1910, pp. 68-69.
[45] Lucan, *Pharsalia*; adapted for literalness from the Loeb translation of J. D. Duff.

The Capital of Memory

Cum tibi sacrato Macedon servitur in antro
Et regem cineres extructo monte quiescant,
Cum Ptolemaeorum manes seriemque pudendam
Pyramides claudant indignaque Mausolea,...

Though you preserve the Macedonian in consecrated grotto
and the ashes of the Pharaohs rest beneath a loftily constructed edifice,
though the dead Ptolemies and their shameful dynasty
are covered by unseemly pyramids and Mausoleums,...
Lucan, Pharsalia, Book VIII, Lines 694-697

...Tum voltu semper celante pavorem
Intrepidus superum sedes et templa vetusti
Numinis antiquas Macetum testantia vires
Circumit, et nulla captus dulcedine rerum,
Non auro cultuque deum, non moenibus urbis,
Effossum tumulis cupide descendit in antrum.
Illic Pellaei proles vaesana Philippi,...

Then, with looks that ever masked his fears,
Undaunted, he [Caesar] visited the temples of the gods and the ancient shrines
of divinity, which attest the former might of Macedon.
No thing of beauty attracted him,
neither the gold and ornaments of the gods, nor the city walls;
but in eager haste he went down into the grotto hewn out for a tomb.
There lies the mad son of Philip of Pella [i.e. Alexander]...
Book X, Lines 14-20

The first passage exerts a seductive temptation to formulate the equation: pyramids plus tombs plus Egypt equals Giza. It looks at first sight as though the Ptolemies had been indulging in some kind of emulation of the pharaohs of the Old Kingdom and the use of the Latin word for a mountain in describing the buildings tends to reinforce this prejudice in modern readers. Furthermore, according to his Last Plans,[46] Alexander himself intended to bury Philip, his father, in "a tomb comparable with a pyramid" and the mausoleum of Cestius built at Rome under Augustus, where Egyptian influence was felt, has the form of a modest pyramid. Nevertheless, first impressions are often deceptive and there is an alternative model for the architecture of the Soma, which fits Lucan's words more precisely, but is quite unrelated to the monuments of earlier pharaohs. The Great Pyramid at Giza was counted among the Seven Wonders of the World by Philo of Byzantium, but he also included a Greek funerary monument in his list. This was the tomb of King Mausolus of Caria at Halicarnassus on the Ionian coast of the Aegean.

---

[46] Diodorus, 18.4.5.

The Quest for the Tomb of Alexander by Andrew Chugg

Mausolus' sepulcher was an architectural and sculptural tour-de-force largely constructed after his death by Artemisia, his disconsolate Queen, between about 352-350 BC. It became known as the Mausoleum and it is, of course, the ancestor, in name at least, of all subsequent mausoleums. Coincidentally, Alexander besieged and captured Halicarnassus in 334 BC and, intriguingly, Halicarnassus was among the Aegean possessions of the Ptolemies at the time the Soma mausoleum was built. The Mausoleum survived largely intact until an earthquake damaged its roof and part of its colonnade some time between the 12th and 15th centuries. Unfortunately, the ruins of the building were largely eradicated in 1522 by the Knights Hospitaller of St John, who robbed its masonry in reinforcing their nearby castle. However, detailed ancient descriptions of its architecture exist[47] and Sir Charles Newton identified the foundations in 1857 in recovering some of its sculptures on behalf of the British Museum, where they can still be seen today. Consequently, the general appearance of the Mausoleum can be reasonably accurately reconstructed (see Figure 4.4).

The rectangular podium measured about 100 by 120 feet and was decorated with bands of sculpture by the leading artists of the age. It was surmounted by a colonnade of 36 ionic columns, which supported a stepped, pyramidal roof. At its apex 140 feet above the ground stood a statue group of Mausolus and Artemisia in a four-horse chariot. Beneath this structure lay the only trace of the Mausoleum that remains in place today, a subterranean vault or crypt, measuring about 7 metres square, which formed the actual burial chamber. This edifice stood near the north-east corner of a walled enclosure or *temenos*, which measured about 240 x 100 metres.[48]

The Mausoleum is an intrinsically strong candidate for having been the inspiration for the design of the Ptolemies' funerary monuments in the 3rd century BC by virtue of its size, beauty and renown and also because it lay in the middle of another port city within their empire.[49] Apart from such generalities, however, there are evidently some striking parallels between the Mausoleum and Lucan's lines on the Soma:-

i) Both the Soma and the Mausoleum had a pyramidal superstructure.

ii) Lucan literally says Caesar "eagerly descended into the grotto of a hewn-out tomb". This clearly indicates a subterranean vault like that found at the site of the Mausoleum. Suetonius' use of the word *penetrali* is also consistent with an underground burial chamber. It might also be added that an underground chamber would maintain a cool and constant temperature all year long, whilst Alexandria's

---

[47] E.g. Pliny, *Natural History* 36.30-31; Vitruvius, *On Architecture*, Praef. 12-13.
[48] Kristian Jeppesen, "Tot Operum Opus, Ergebnisse der Dänischen Forschungen zum Maussolleion von Halikarnass seit 1966," *Jahrbuch des Deutschen Archäologischen Instituts*, Bd. 107, 1992, pp. 59-102.
[49] Alan K. Bowman, *Egypt After The Pharaohs*, pp. 28-9.

iii)	The Latin *extructo monte* translates literally as a "loftily constructed mountain". This is the line taken by some translators and it would seem to pose a problem for the Mausoleum prototype. However, Cicero (with whose works Lucan was probably familiar) in Section XXI of his speech *Against Piso* uses *montem* to mean a tall and splendid villa: *...ad hunc Tusculani montem exstruendum*, which translates, "in order to raise that edifice at Tusculum". It is therefore most apposite to translate Lucan's meaning as a "tall edifice", which fits the Mausoleum model well.
iv)	Lucan explicitly uses the word *Mausolea* to describe the buildings, which provides a direct allusion to Mausolus' tomb.[50]
v)	In the line, "covered by unseemly pyramids and Mausoleums", the Latin does not seem to favour the interpretation that the pyramids are the mausoleums. Possibly some kings were in pyramids and others in mausoleums, but what Lucan really seems to be saying is that the tombs have both a pyramidal superstructure and a supporting mausoleum. This makes perfect sense if the Mausoleum of Halicarnassus is their model, but it is an odd way to describe tombs that were straightforward Egyptian-style pyramids.

So the Pharsalia references seem to agree in five distinct ways with a Mausoleum prototype and to agree less explicitly or even to contradict an Egyptian pyramid model. It might also be added that both the Mausoleum and the Soma stood within a large, walled enclosure at the heart of a port city within the Ptolemaic Empire. Furthermore, an Egyptian-style solid pyramid sufficiently tall as to impress Lucan would have been extremely rugged, so its rapid and complete disappearance would be relatively more difficult to explain. Conversely, had it been hollow, then the support of its faces would have posed significant structural engineering problems. Instead, on the best interpretation of the scanty available evidence, it should be concluded that the Soma was most probably a close architectural relative of the Mausoleum at Halicarnassus.

---

[50] Suetonius, *Lives of the Caesars* 2.100-101, similarly refers to the "Mausoleum" of Augustus.

Figure 4.4. Reconstruction of the Mausoleum at Halicarnassus (1872 - author's collection)

There exists one other tantalizing line of evidence in the form of several two and three metre tall funerary monuments from the Chatby necropolis in an eastern district of ancient Alexandria (Figure 4.5). Similar, larger scale Hellenistic and early Roman funerary monuments are found throughout the eastern Mediterranean: examples from Cyrene and Kalat Fakra in Lebanon are sketched in Figure 4.6.[51] The design of these memorials would certainly appear to have been influenced by the Mausoleum at Halicarnassus. It might be argued that such influence is more readily explained, if it echoes the lost royal tombs in Alexandria. At the very least, the Chatby monuments provide a precedent for the introduction of the form of the Mausoleum into the architecture of Alexandrian funerary monuments of the Ptolemaic era.

---

[51] For the Chatby monuments see Achille Adriani, *Repertorio d'Arte del'Egitto Greco-Romano*, Series C, Vol. I-II, pp.117-118, Tav. 39; Anna Maria Bisi Ingrassia, "Influenze Alessandrine Sull'Arte Punica: Una Messa A Punto," *Alessandria e il mondo ellenistico-romano - Studi in onore di Achille Adriani*, III, Roma, 1984, p. 837; for the Cyrene tomb (N_{180}) & Kalat Fakra see Janos Fedak, *Monumental Tombs of the Hellenistic Age*, Toronto, 1990, figs. 168 & 223.

The Capital of Memory

Figure 4.5. Funerary monument of Ptolemaic Alexandria from the Chatby necropolis – sketch showing the condition when excavated and photo taken in 2001 by the author

Figure 4.6. Greek mausoleums from Cyrene (left) and Kalat Fakra in Lebanon (right); sketches by the author with human figures for scale

*   *   *   *   *   *   *   *   *

The Quest for the Tomb of Alexander by Andrew Chugg

A single authentic, quality image of ancient Alexandria might prove invaluable in helping to interpret the few thousand words of descriptive evidence on the cityscape that have survived in the ancient sources. However, the handful of highly stylised ancient representations that have been identified as possible depictions of the city all have dubious pedigrees.

Firstly, there are several dozens of Roman lamps of the first century AD with seemingly related harbour scenes. An example in the Hermitage has been thought to depict Alexandria: among a throng of tall buildings that loom up behind the harbour front in its background, the leftmost has a pyramidal roof and has been proposed as a possible representation of the Soma.[52] However, both the date and the location of the scene have been questioned by Bailey, who argues confidently that these lamps show early 3rd century AD views of other North African (e.g. Carthage) or Italian (e.g. Ostia) ports or else are outright forgeries by a 20th century workshop in Naples (e.g. the Hermitage lamp).[53]

The sculpted cover of the sarcophagus of Julius Philosyrius of Ostia, the ancient port of Rome, appears to depict a Pharos-style lighthouse tower and a column very like "Pompey's Pillar", a monument erected in Alexandria by the Emperor Diocletian in AD298 and still standing today. There is also a tower with a pointed roof, which might just possibly represent the Soma (Figure 4.7). Doubt arises from the fact that there was a lighthouse designed to resemble the Pharos at Ostia itself, which might seem to suggest that this scene actually depicts Ostia, given its provenance. However, there are a number of hints that the sculptor, who may never have seen Alexandria, intended to evoke the Egyptian port.[54] Firstly, the date-palm tree on the extreme left is used as part of the symbolism for Alexandria in an ancient mosaic at Jerash (see Figure 4.8). A palm forest outside the eastern gateway remained a captioned feature of the 16th century maps of Alexandria by Belon and Braun & Hogenberg (Figure 7.2). Secondly, two Tritons, fishtailed sons of Poseidon, the sea god, are shown blowing conch shells on top of the triple-arch monument. The most famous ancient reference to these mythical deities shown trumpeting on shells is as sculptural adornments at the corners of the parapet of the first stage of the Pharos lighthouse (discernible in Figure 4.3 opposite the top of the sail). But Strabo also records a temple of Poseidon at the centre of the Alexandrian harbour front. Thirdly, the name of the deceased may allude to a connection with the Eastern Mediterranean. Finally, the monuments appear in approximately the correct order as at Alexandria, if left to right corresponds to the east-west direction. If it is supposed that the tower with the pointed roof is a highly schematic representation of the Soma, then this sarcophagus provides evidence for the survival of the mausoleum into the early fourth century AD.

---

[52] E.g. Michael Grant, *Cleopatra*, London, 1972, Figure 8.
[53] D.M. Bailey, "Alexandria, Carthage and Ostia," *Alessandria e il mondo ellenistico-romano - Studi in onore di Achille Adriani*, 2, Roma, 1984, pp. 265-272.
[54] Ch. Picard, "Quelques représentations nouvelles du Phare d'Alexandrie," *BCH* 76, 1952.

The Capital of Memory

However, this supposition is tenuous. It is anyway clear that the sculptor has imbued his work with a strong flavour of Ostia, though perhaps because his knowledge of Alexandria was gleaned verbally rather than pictorially.

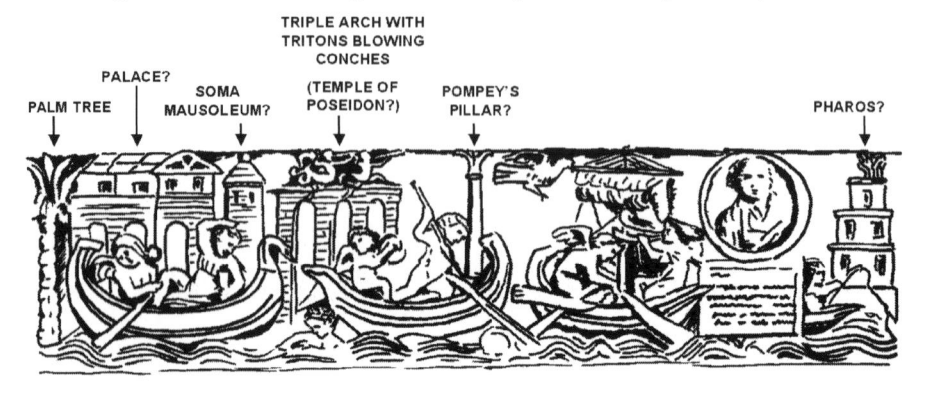

Figure 4.7. Harbour scene on the cover of the sarcophagus of Julius Philosyrius (sketch by the author)

Figure 4.8. Stylised representation of Alexandria in a sixth century AD mosaic at Jerash

There are several mosaics of Byzantine date that show named representations of Alexandria. In particular, the aforementioned sixth century AD pavement from the Church of St John at Jerash ("paved and roofed" in December AD531) depicts a walled city with the inscription "ΑΛΕΞΑΝΔΡΙΑ" (ALEXANDRIA) accompanied by a separate tower, which must be the Pharos. A building with a cupola might be the old church of St Mark, whilst another with a tholos (domed) roof allegedly represents the Soma. But this is at odds with Lucan's description. In addition, there is other evidence, which will be discussed in a later chapter, which suggests that the aboveground parts of the Soma at least had been destroyed some two centuries before this mosaic was laid.

Finally, and perhaps most enigmatically, two images of the Soma have been proposed by the Spanish scholar, Alberto Balil. A fragment of a glass cup of the 3rd or 4th century AD (Figure 4.9) found in the nineteenth century at Carthage bears an image of a prominent peristyle monument in the background of a harbour scene with a cane fisherman and his basket of fish.[55] The term peristyle refers to the row of columns around a temple, court or cloister, and can also describe the colonnade of the Mausoleum at Halicarnassus. In 1962 Balil proposed that this image might be a representation of the Soma, but his arguments were mainly stylistic.[56]

Later, in 1984, Balil presented an analysis of a Roman mosaic from Toledo in Spain, which probably dates from the 3rd century AD.[57] He argued that many of its elements, such as cane fishermen and various harbours are reminiscent of other possible depictions of the port of Alexandria. Most concretely, it contains a multi-stage lighthouse linked with the mainland by an arched causeway, recalling the Pharos accessed via the Heptastadion. There are also several tall, temple-like buildings with domed or pointed roofs, one of which, Balil suggested, might be a representation of the Tomb of Alexander.

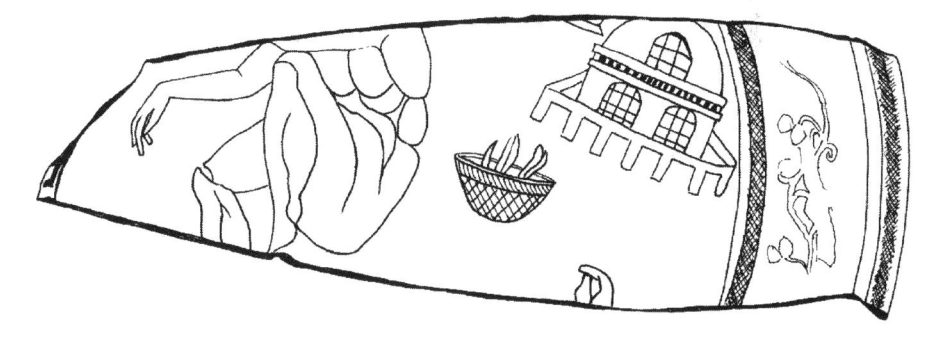

Figure 4.9. Fragment of a Roman glass cup of the 3rd-4th century AD depicting a harbour scene with a peristyle monument in which Balil saw the Soma (sketch by the author)

*   *   *   *   *   *   *   *

In the thousand-year history of ancient Alexandria almost everything about the city changed, yet one theme was recurrent throughout the period: the rampages

---

[55] J. Ferron and M. Pinard, *Cahiers de Byrsa* 8, 1958-9, pp.103-9.
[56] A Balil, "Una nueva representación de la tumba de Alejandro," *Archivo. Españ. Arqueol.* 35, 1962, pp.102-3.
[57] Alberto Balil, "Monumentos Alejandrinos y Paisajes Egipcios en un Mosaico Romano de Toledo (España)," *Alessandria e il Mondo Ellenistico-Romano - Studi in Onore di Achille Adriani*, Vol. III, Roma, 1984.

The Capital of Memory

of the Alexandrian mob regularly exerted a decisive influence in religious and political disputes. It was characteristically indiscriminate in its choice of victim, sometimes overthrowing a bloodstained monarch or a poisonous minister, but on other occasions cruelly dismembering a venerable scholar or an architectural masterpiece on some wild religious whim. This menacing rabble first intersected the story of the Soma in 89 BC, when the populace finally lost patience with the hideous and bloated drunkard, who had ruled over them as Ptolemy X Alexander I on and off for over twenty years. The rioters won over the army to their cause and Ptolemy X was forcibly expelled. He fled to Syria, where he recruited a force of mercenaries with promises of plunder and riches and marched them straight back to Egypt.

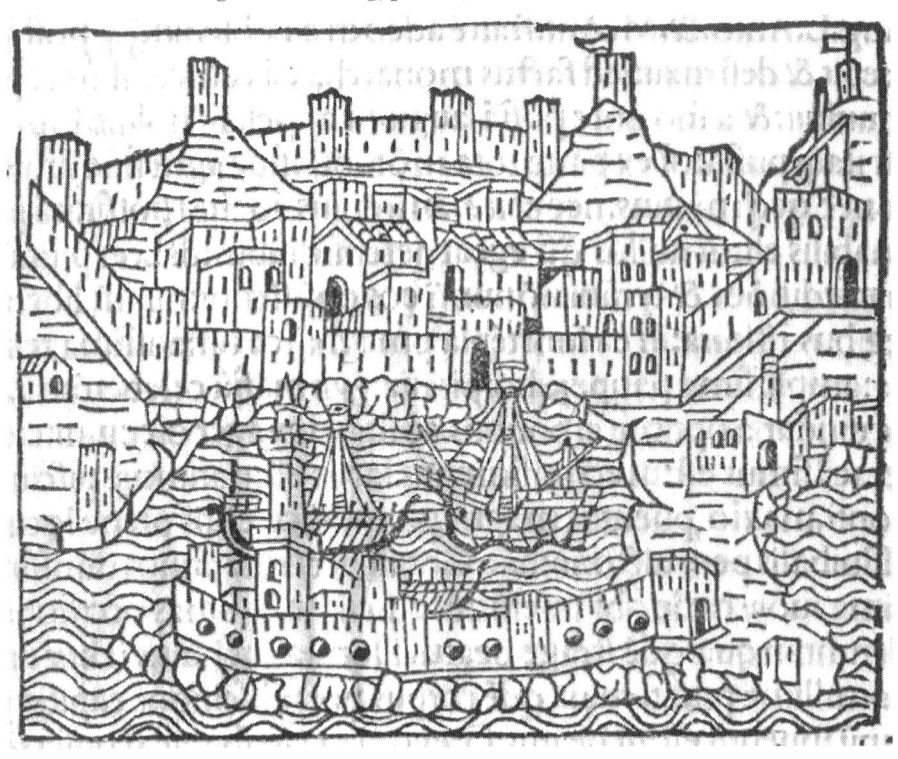

Figure 4.10. Authentic woodcut plan of Alexandria published in Italy in 1513 by Foresti di Bergamo: depending on the date of the information used to produce this illustration, the tower on the peninsula might be the Pharos lighthouse or merely an exaggerated version of the minaret of the later Qait Bey fortress (author's collection)

Having retaken Alexandria with little trouble, Ptolemy X was confronted with the trickier problem of making good the compact with his troops. His solution, as recorded by Strabo 17.1.8, was to pillage the Soma and steal Alexander's golden sarcophagus, probably the same one hammered out to fit the corpse in Babylon twenty-three decades earlier. The body was afterwards housed in a substitute of glass or else some similar translucent crystalline substance, possibly alabaster, since the Greek word ὑαλίνη is potentially ambiguous in this context. Nevertheless, in the eyes of the Alexandrians the desecration of the Founder's tomb was an extreme act of sacrilege and nobody was surprised when the mob rose again to expel the defiler of Alexander's grave within the year. Ptolemy X fled once more, heading towards Myra in Lycia, but Alexandrian naval squadrons pursued him and he was drowned in a sea fight, as he was attempting to land at Cyprus.

Writing eighty years after these events, Strabo continued to reflect the unrelenting contempt of the Alexandrians for the pilferer of the Soma by omitting both Ptolemy X Alexander I and his son Ptolemy XI Alexander II from his genealogy of the dynasty.

5. The Shrine of the Caesars

Like Alexander I will reign,
And I will reign alone;
My thoughts did evermore disdain
A rival on my throne.
He either fears his fate too much,
Or his deserts are small,
That dares not put it to the touch
To gain or lose it all.

James Graham, Marquis of Montrose

In the middle of the first century before Christ the tide of world history began to surge dramatically. In the eastern Mediterranean the Hellenistic kingdoms of Alexander's successors had dominated the region almost unchallenged for nearly three centuries. Grown indolent and soft on the prosperity of the peace, they made attractive prey for the hawks of the Roman Republic, which had recently emerged triumphant and battle-hardened from the ferocious struggles of the Punic Wars. By 50 BC Rome stood on the threshold of empire and only Ptolemaic Egypt retained a nominal independence under the juvenile Pharaoh Ptolemy XIII and his charismatic elder sister Cleopatra VII.

It was at this juncture that Julius Caesar chose to cross the Rubicon, sparking a civil war with his rival Pompey. In 48 BC at the battle of Pharsalus in Thessaly Pompey was vanquished and fled to his erstwhile friends in Egypt with Caesar in hot pursuit. But Ptolemy's ministers, disdaining to espouse a lost cause, treacherously murdered the supplicant general. When Caesar arrived in Alexandria a few days later he was greeted in the Great Harbour by Ptolemy's tutor, Theodotus, who graciously presented the signet ring and severed head of Pompey to the Roman dictator. More revolted than appeased by this intended act of friendship, Caesar decided to enact the role of guardianship over the youthful Egyptian monarchs appointed to Rome by the will of their father, the late Pharaoh Ptolemy XII Auletes. This was the occasion of Caesar's visit to the Soma, which was later celebrated in Lucan's epic poem.[1] Once again Alexander's tomb found itself at the centre of events, and not just geographically, but also in a symbolic and political sense, for the scene was now set for two epic ideological conflicts, that were destined to settle the control of the Mediterranean world for the next half millennium: Republicanism versus Dictatorship and domineering Roman nationalism versus Graeco-Roman collaboration and confederation.

---

[1] Lucan, *Pharsalia*, Book 10, lines 14-20.

The Quest for the Tomb of Alexander by Andrew Chugg

In Rome a great schism was opening between the supporters of the traditional republican constitution and those who advocated normalizing the powers of dictatorship. Most Romans were aware that their political system was showing distinct signs of strain under the pressures of ruling almost the entire Mediterranean world, but they differed over the best cure. A populist faction, of whom Caesar was the champion, believed that the new circumstances demanded a decisive central authority, which could only be achieved by resting much of the power of the state in a single person. However, a significant senatorial constituency considered that the problems were attributable to the constitutional compromises that had already been allowed and therefore sought a return to a purer form of republicanism. In this struggle Alexander's career became potently symbolic. As an exemplar of successful absolutist rule he was a propaganda dream from the point of view of Caesar's party. Conversely, the Republicans found it correspondingly expedient to revile his memory by emphasising his excesses and supposed megalomania. One of the earliest surviving histories of Alexander was originally penned at the close of this period by a Roman called Pompeius Trogus. His name itself alludes to the fact that his family was originally allied with Pompey and the senatorial faction, though they seem ultimately to have switched sides. Trogus, whose history only survives in a 4th century epitome by Justin, took a relatively hostile line on Alexander, which was probably influenced by its author's Republican sympathies.

Caesar's contrasting attitude was amply demonstrated by his eagerness to grasp the opportunity for a pilgrimage to the tomb of his hero provided by his arrival at Alexandria. In his own account he describes how he landed and processed through the city with the full pomp and regalia of a Roman Consul.[2] Partly, his intention was to overawe the fiercely anti-Roman populace, but this elaborate degree of ceremony may also have been inspired by his desire to honour and celebrate Alexander through his visit to the Soma.

* * * * * * * * *

At the time of Caesar's arrival in Egypt, Cleopatra had been evicted from Alexandria in the course of a power struggle with her brother. On learning of the Roman Dictator's declared intention to mediate in the dispute, she returned secretly to the Royal Palaces to lobby for a favourable judgement. Caesar seems to have been enraptured by the young Queen and they soon became lovers. Ptolemy's faction retaliated by besieging the Romans in the Palace district, but a few months later Caesar's main army arrived via the long land route. Ptolemy's forces were routed in a pitched battle and he drowned in the Nile, whilst attempting to flee. When Caesar finally departed from Egypt in the summer of 47 BC, he left the Queen as its undisputed monarch. Shortly afterwards she gave birth to his son, whom the facetious Alexandrians nicknamed *Caesarion* or "Little Caesar". Her master plan to save her dynasty and to resuscitate the

---

[2] Julius Caesar, *The Civil War* 3.106.

The Shrine of the Caesars

political fortunes of the Greek world relied upon persuading Caesar to declare Caesarion to be his heir, thereby cementing a grand alliance of the Greeks and the Romans. The stakes were enormous. Success would have meant a realistic chance of realising the elusive dream of re-creating Alexander's long vanished empire. Failure might engender the extirpation of her dynasty.

The most famous cinematic appearance of the Soma was set during Caesar's sojourn in Alexandria by Joseph Mankiewicz in his epic 1963 version of "Cleopatra". In this scene, Caesar, played by Rex Harrison, is taunted by the Queen, played by Elizabeth Taylor, both of them standing before an enormous glass sarcophagus. Alexander's embalmed corpse is dimly glimpsed through the misty crystal, as Cleopatra urges the Roman dictator to take up his sword and re-conquer Alexander's lost domains. But it was never to be. A few years later Caesar was struck down in Rome, the victim of a Republican conspiracy among the senators (Figure 5.1). His great-nephew Octavian was discovered to be the principal beneficiary of his will. For the time being Cleopatra's ambitions were thwarted.

Figure 5.1. Assassination of Julius Caesar, 15th March 44BC (1872 – author's collection)

*   *   *   *   *   *   *   *

Octavian formed an alliance with Caesar's erstwhile lieutenant, Mark Antony, in order to oppose and confront his uncle's assassins. Thanks largely to Antony's military prowess, Cassius and Brutus, the leaders of the conspiracy, were finally defeated and killed at Philippi in northern Greece in 42 BC. In retrospect the Republican cause died with them. The victors divided the Roman world between them, Octavian taking Rome and the west and Antony choosing the

The Quest for the Tomb of Alexander by Andrew Chugg

alluring east, which had the effect of bringing Egypt within his immediate sphere of influence. Naturally enough he sought a meeting with Cleopatra, who sailed to visit him in a galley of famous splendour. Antony was speedily infatuated, whereas Cleopatra discerned a fresh opportunity to fuse an enduring alliance with the foremost surviving Roman general. For a year they were inseparable, until Antony was reluctantly dragged from the Queen's embrace by the pressure of events elsewhere. In the autumn of 40 BC Cleopatra gave birth to twins by Antony. They were named Alexander Helios for the Sun and Cleopatra Selene for the Moon in anticipation of a glorious revival of the Greek empire in the east. It was, however, to be another three years before their father first set eyes on them, thanks to Antony's political impotence in the face of an offer of the hand of Octavian's sister in marriage. He was obliged to accept, lest his patriotism be deemed suspect by the Roman populace.

The flame of his romance with the Egyptian goddess-incarnate guttered but could not be extinguished. He was eventually drawn back by her divine magnetism and this time he was committed to the pursuit of her political ambitions. They fought a series of wars in Persia and Armenia with mixed success, but the Greek speaking nations rallied enthusiastically to their cause, so they grew immensely powerful. Rome was seriously antagonised when Antony allowed Cleopatra to divide the eastern provinces among their offspring in 34 BC, declaring, "Let it be known that the greatness of Rome lies not in what she takes, but in what she gives." However, an irrevocable break with Octavian was delayed until 32 BC, when Antony formally divorced his sister. At that point Antony commanded a seasoned army of 30 legions and a fleet of 500 warships. All Rome believed he was poised to invade Italy and most considered that such an enterprise would readily succeed. Fatally, he dithered and demurred. In the following year Octavian's admiral, Marcus Agrippa, was able to use his superior naval skills to turn the tables on the East. By the cumulative effects of a series of small defeats Antony and his Egyptian Queen found themselves virtually besieged in the Ambracian Gulf at Actium. They themselves were successful in an attempt to break out, but three quarters of their fleet was annihilated in their wake. Antony's marooned legions found it expedient to accept a generous offer of terms from Octavian, by virtue of which Cleopatra's romantic vision of Graeco-Roman partnership became a tragically lost cause.

* * * * * * * *

Antony and Cleopatra fled straight back to Egypt as the magnitude of their defeat at Actium unfolded behind them. In a black mood of despondency Antony shut himself away in a tower at the end of a pier in the Great Harbour at Alexandria. He called it the Timonium, likening himself to the famous misanthrope, Timon of Athens. Cleopatra, however, continued feverishly to pursue desperate plans for the preservation of her kingdom and her dynasty. In particular according to Dio Cassius the Queen "proceeded to gather vast wealth from her estates and from various other sources, both profane and sacred, sparing not even the most holy shrines...".[3] The particular shrines in question are identified by Josephus, a Jewish writer who was hostile to the Queen. He accuses Cleopatra of having "plundered her country's gods and her ancestors' sepulchers" without offering any explanation of the circumstances.[4] Presumably, she appropriated part of the gold and valuables stored up in the temples and the tombs of the precinct of the Soma in a desperate attempt to fund the hire of a fresh army or the construction of a new fleet.

Yet all the while Octavian was meticulously closing in with armies grown irresistibly vast. He still feared Antony enough to deny him an opportunity to fight back until overwhelming force could be brought to bear. As Octavian approached Alexandria, Antony finally despaired and fell upon his sword. He died in Cleopatra's arms, whilst she was ensconced in her mausoleum in Alexandria. Plutarch refers to the construction program which included this building:

She had caused to be built, joining to the temple of Isis, several tombs and monuments of wonderful height and remarkable workmanship.[5]

This passage provides further evidence for the hypothesis that tallness was a notable feature of Alexandrian mausoleums and temples. Plutarch adds that these structures, were close by the sea, but unfortunately the site of the particular temple of Isis is unknown. It seems very likely that this complex was separate from the precinct of the Soma and there is a good explanation for this.[6]

When Caesar was besieged in the palaces at Alexandria, his men set fire to many of the enemy's vessels in the Great Harbour. It is easy to imagine clouds of cinders blown onshore by Alexandria's famous Etesian winds. A stretch of dockside warehouses caught alight and the fire reportedly engulfed the bookstores of the Great Library.[7] Livy mentions the destruction of 400,000 books or scrolls, although this may be an exaggeration.[8] The most likely location was the central stretch of the Great Harbour, since the ships must have been docked beyond the coastal stretch occupied by the palaces, but not so far from Caesar's positions as to lie out of range of a sortie. This general vicinity is also consistent with Strabo's remark that the library and museum adjoined the palaces. Furthermore, it is known that Cleopatra subsequently began the construction of one of the most opulent of the city's temples, known as the Caesareum or Sebasteum, in just this location. It is reasonable to infer that an area razed by the fire near the central stretch of the harbour was the main focus of Cleopatra's subsequent architectural redevelopments.

---

[3] Dio Cassius, *Roman History* 51.5.3.
[4] Josephus, *Contra Apion* 2.58.
[5] Plutarch, *Life of Antony* 74.
[6] Dio Cassius 51.8.6 says that Cleopatra was constructing her tomb in the royal grounds; cf. Zenobius, *Proverbia* 5.24.
[7] Plutarch, *Life of Caesar* 49.
[8] P.M. Fraser, *Ptolemaic Alexandria*, Chapter 6 and Notes.

The Quest for the Tomb of Alexander by Andrew Chugg

* * * * * * * *

Octavian's agents tricked the Queen into surrendering with vague promises that she might negotiate for her throne to pass to her children, so she was taken into captivity.

Octavian himself entered the city in the company of Arius Didymus, an Alexandrian scholar. In the Gymnasium he announced to the crowd that he proposed to spare them all, firstly for the sake of Alexander, their founder, secondly, for the beauty of their city and finally, in response to the pleas for clemency made on their behalf by his friend Arius.[9] This man was the probable author of the statement in Zenobius' *Proverbia* that Ptolemy Philopator had built the Soma. He is very likely now to have accompanied Octavian in his visit to the Soma (Figures 5.2 & 5.3), which has been recorded by Suetonius:-

Per idem tempus conditorium et corpus Magni Alexandri, cum prolatum e penetrali subiecisset oculis, corona aurea imposita ac floribus aspersis veneratus est consultusque, num et Ptolemaeum inspicere vellet, regem se voluisse ait videre, non mortuos.[10]

About this time [Octavian] had the sarcophagus and body of Alexander the Great brought forth from its inner sanctum, and, after gazing on it, showed his respect by placing upon it a golden crown and strewing it with flowers; and being then asked whether he wished to see the tomb of the Ptolemies as well, he replied, "My wish was to see a king, not corpses."

And the same event is also described by Dio Cassius:-

He next viewed the body of Alexander, and even touched it in such a fashion that, so it is said, a piece of the nose was broken off. Yet he went not to see the corpses of the Ptolemies, despite the keen desire of the Alexandrians to show them to him, retorting, "I wished to see a king not dead people."[11]

Cleopatra was now given to understand that Octavian intended to parade her as the highlight of his triumph in Rome. This was an intolerable indignity and it is possible that Octavian knew it and was therefore complicit in her suicide. The story that she accomplished her death by means of an asp is quite likely to be true. Before she expired she sent a message to Octavian begging that she should be buried next to Antony. Perhaps fearing to be ensnared by her dying wish, the future emperor sent his men to find her. One of them, seeing the Queen already dead, angrily turned on her dying handmaiden: "Charmion, was this well done?" and she replied, "Extremely well! And as became the descendant of so many kings." Her words have become the epitaph of the Ptolemies.

---

[9] This is Plutarch's version: Dio Cassius gives the god Serapis, instead of the beauty of the city.
[10] Suetonius, *Lives of the Caesars, Augustus* 2.18.
[11] Dio Cassius, *Roman History* 51.16.5.

The Shrine of the Caesars

Figure 5.2. Octavian viewing the corpse of Alexander in 30BC (drawn by Fragonard and engraved by Masquelier in 1803 after Bourdon's painting of ~1643 – author's collection)

* * * * * * * *

Octavian was left the undisputed master of the Mediterranean world. He completed Cleopatra's mausoleum and entombed her there beside Antony as she had desired. In 27 BC the Senate declared him its Leader or Prince (*Princeps Senatus*) and he was awarded the honorary title of *Augustus*.[12] Subtly but surely the Roman Republic became the Roman Empire. Even before this in 28 BC he had begun the construction of a monumental mausoleum for his family in the *Campus Martius* at Rome. The timing strongly suggests that the Alexandrian tombs had been a major source of inspiration, although the essential form of this mausoleum is usually supposed to have been derived from Etruscan tumulus tombs.[13] A significant part of the supporting structure survives today and descriptions of it in its heyday are also extant. Consequently, its reconstructed form (Figure 5.4) can be compared with that of the Mausoleum at Halicarnassus and several plausible parallels may be drawn between them. In particular, credible reconstructions suggest an elevated peristyle rotunda with a

---

[12] David Shotter, *Augustus Caesar*, 1991, Chapter 4.
[13] Amanda Claridge, *Oxford Archaeological Sites: Rome*, 1998.

large bronze statue of the emperor at the apex of its roof.[14] However, the earthen in-fill between the concentric, cylindrical walls of the structure and the planting of cypress trees over the top probably reflect the Etruscan influence. It is also clear that Augustus' mausoleum had a far more squat profile than its tall, rectangular Greek antecedents. The actual burial chamber was a cylindrical hall with niches in its walls, which formed the innermost ring of masonry. It was above ground level, but thermally insulated by the surrounding mass of earth to the same effect as the subterranean funerary vaults of the Greeks.

Figure 5.3. Octavian crowning Alexander's mummy (by Showmer/Schommer - author's collection)

*   *   *   *   *   *   *   *

The Civil War between Antony and Octavian engendered the birth of the imperial system of government and the complete subjugation of the Greek

---

[14] The colonnaded rotunda has been inferred on the basis of the extraordinary thickness (5.7m) of the concentric wall, which remains at this radius: structurally, it looks as though it supported something heavy. However, no such superstructure is mentioned by Strabo, who gives the best early description; see L. Richardson, *A New Topographical Dictionary of Ancient Rome*, John Hopkins University Press, 1992.

The Shrine of the Caesars

kingdoms to the will of Rome. Fortuitously, these outcomes combined to enhance the fame and significance of the Soma in the succeeding centuries. In Alexander the Roman emperors recognised an exemplar of absolutist rule, in whom their crushing power and extravagant wealth were amply vindicated. His tomb became a frequent site of pilgrimage and veneration by the new masters of the East. Prior to the seizure of power by the Christians in the 4th century his body was probably the most important religious relic in the Empire.

Figure 5.4. Reconstruction of the Mausoleum of Augustus (sketch by the author)

*   *   *   *   *   *   *   *

In AD19 the Roman Prince Germanicus, a grandson of Antony, had lately vanquished the king of Armenia and reduced Cappadocia to the form of a Roman province. He now decided to undertake a pleasure cruise up the Nile by way of relaxation, taking in the sights of Alexandria on the way.[15] It is likely that his wife, Agrippina, the daughter of Agrippa, and also their seven year old son, Gaius, accompanied him on this expedition, since they are known to have been with him in the East.[16] His parents were fond of dressing the child up in a miniature army uniform, which had inspired his father's troops to nickname the boy "Little Boots", or in Latin "Caligula", after his military style footgear.[17] It is an innocent enough origin for a name, which later came to live in infamy.

Germanicus was rapturously received by the Alexandrians, who still harboured fond memories of his grandfather. He addressed them in the Hippodrome: the crowd yelled, "Bravo! May you live all the longer." The Prince replied, "I am mindful of what is common knowledge and also of the way in which I have

---

[15] Tacitus, *Annals* 2.59-61; Arthur Ferrill, *Caligula, Emperor of Rome*, 1991, p.51.
[16] Suetonius, *Lives of the Caesars, Gaius Caligula* 4.10.
[17] Suetonius, *Caligula* 4.9.

The Quest for the Tomb of Alexander by Andrew Chugg

found your greetings multiplied through being stored in your prayers."[18] He is referring (probably with a hint of sarcasm) to the fact that the Alexandrians had exposed him to the wrath of his jealous uncle, the emperor Tiberius, by offering him worship as a god. Suetonius says of Germanicus that, "Wherever he came upon the tombs of distinguished men, he always offered sacrifice to their shades."[19] It is therefore a near certainty that he visited the Soma in the course of his stay and Caligula may well have accompanied him, since it would have been regarded as an edifying experience for any Roman princeling.

Germanicus died mysteriously later the same year, probably by poison and possibly with the emperor's collusion.[20] Although Tiberius subsequently murdered two of his other sons, Caligula became one of the emperor's favourites. This vicious old man liked to say that he was nurturing a viper in his bosom that would eventually strike at the Romans after his death.[21]

When Tiberius had grown so decrepit that the act seemed less risky than further patience, Caligula, with a little help from his ally Macro, the commander of the Praetorian Guard, hastened Tiberius on his way to Hades by means of smothering.[22] In this inauspicious fashion Caligula took the purple in 37 BC. At first the Romans were optimistic at this change of ruler, for Tiberius had been hated almost as avidly as Caligula's father had been loved. However, the symptoms of a murderous strain of insanity were not long in bursting forth.

Many of his conceits were relatively harmless. His childhood habit of dressing-up and play-acting remained a fundamental of his character, but now he occupied so exalted a position that the boundaries between fact and fiction might easily become blurred. Of particular relevance is Suetonius' statement:-

He frequently wore the dress of a triumphing general, even before his campaign, and sometimes the breast-plate of Alexander the Great, which he had taken from his sarcophagus.[23]

This breast-plate or cuirass may have been the same as that which Alexander is shown wearing in the mosaic of the battle of Issus from Pompeii or else one very like it.[24] A very similar cuirass was found in the tomb of Alexander's father, Philip.[25] Caligula wore it on the occasion that he had a three and a half mile bridge of boats built across the bay of Naples, which he then rode across in military garb imitating a Roman triumph as described by Dio Cassius:-

---

[18] Oxyrhynchus papyrus, P.Oxy. 25.2435 recto.
[19] Suetonius, *Caligula* 4.3.
[20] Suetonius, *Caligula* 4.2.
[21] Suetonius, *Caligula* 4.11.
[22] Suetonius, *Caligula* 4.12.
[23] Suetonius, *Caligula* 4.52.
[24] The original painting from which the "Alexander Mosaic" derives was created within living memory of the Battle of Issus, which it probably depicts, so Alexander's cuirass is authentic.
[25] E.g. *Greece: Temples, Tombs & Treasures*, Time Life Books, Lost Civilizations Series, 1994, p.155.

The Shrine of the Caesars

Gaius [Caligula]... was eager to drive his chariot through the sea, as it were, by bridging the waters between Puteoli and Bauli... When all was ready, he put on the breastplate of Alexander (or so he claimed), and over it a purple silk chlamys, adorned with much gold and many precious stones from India; moreover he girt on a sword, took a shield, and donned a garland of oak leaves. Then he offered sacrifice to Neptune... and entered the bridge from the end at Bauli... and he dashed fiercely into Puteoli as if in pursuit of an enemy.[26]

The purple chlamys echoes Ephippus' description of Alexander's attire, which is probably not coincidental in this context. The garland of oak leaves also has an indirect association with Alexander, because an exquisite gold oak wreath was among the most spectacular artefacts from the tomb of Philip II at Aegae.

The darker side of Caligula's character was reflected in his opening of a brothel in the palace at which Roman matrons and freeborn youths were prostituted to raise cash for an exchequer bankrupted by his extravagances. He also perpetrated a wide range of casual murders, including the decapitation of his adoptive son, Gemellus, who had annoyed him through taking medicine to cure a persistent cough. Smelling the substance on his breath, Caligula accused him of taking an antidote to poison. The youth famously retorted, "How can there be an antidote to Caesar?" but his fate had been sealed. Ptolemy of Mauretania, the last known descendant of Cleopatra VII, being her grandson via Cleopatra Selene, was another of the emperor's victims. To nobody's great surprise Gaius Caligula was assassinated in the fourth year of his reign by two tribunes of the Praetorian Guard, whom he had persistently aggravated by setting lewd watchwords that they had been forced to repeat to one another all night long.

*　　*　　*　　*　　*　　*　　*　　*

Two decades later the emperor Nero planned to visit Alexandria in AD64 and again in AD66, although in the event it seems he approached no nearer than Greece.[27] Nevertheless, he perpetrated a royal piece of chicanery upon the Egyptian populace by calling in all the Ptolemaic tetradrachm coins still in circulation and re-issuing them in new types at the same denomination, but containing a lower weight of silver.[28] One of the new issues from the Alexandrian mint bore a personification of the city wearing the elephant scalp headdress (Figure 5.5). It could be a crude imitation of Ptolemy Soter's tetradrachms. Certainly, it is likely that a direct reference to Alexander was intended.

Following Nero's deposition and suicide in AD68 several generalissimos seized the purple in quick succession. AD69 became the Year of Four Emperors as they vied for the throne. In the eastern provinces the hierarchy favoured Vespasian, the Governor of Syria. In July the Egyptian legions became the first

---

[26] Dio Cassius, *Roman History* 59.17; Suetonius, *Caligula* 4.19; Arthur Ferrill, *Caligula, Emperor of Rome*, 1991, p.115.
[27] Suetonius, *Nero* 6.35; Dio Cassius 58.18.1.
[28] Erik Christiansen, *The Roman Coins of Alexandria*, 1988, Aarhus University Press, Chapter 1.

The Quest for the Tomb of Alexander by Andrew Chugg

to declare for him at the urging of their prefect, Tiberius Alexander. Vespasian transferred his headquarters to Alexandria,[29] since Egypt was strategically vital due to its corn supplies, which substantially fed Rome. The new emperor is known to have visited the Serapeum and a visit to the Soma is also very likely given that he was based in the city for a number of months. His armies triumphed over his rival Vitellius at the battle of Cremona and he reigned securely for a decade. His son Titus, who had accompanied his father in AD69, also revisited Alexandria in AD71 and he inherited the Empire upon his father's death in AD79.[30]

Figure 5.5. Tetradrachm minted in Alexandria in the 12th year of Nero

*   *   *   *   *   *   *   *

In AD115 under Trajan the Alexandrian Jews staged a major revolt against both the Romans and the Alexandrian Greeks, but they were brutally subdued and a large proportion of them were massacred.[31] From this time on the Jewish community in the city was never more than a shadow of its former self. It is believed that the centre of gravity of Alexandria began to drift westwards at about this time, which may be a critical factor in understanding the topography of the ancient metropolis. The city was anyway suffering a long, lingering decline from its pre-eminence as the Ptolemies' capital and the devastation of the Jewish suburbs in the eastern districts in the course of the suppression of the rebellion may well have exacerbated this process.

Just two years later Hadrian, the philhellene emperor, succeeded Trajan. In AD122 there were further disturbances in Alexandria, but the new monarch managed to quell them from afar through diplomacy and exhortation, whilst based in the province of Narbonensis in Southern Gaul. It was not until early August AD130, escorted by his empress, Sabina, and his handsome young

---

[29] Suetonius, *Vespasian* 8.6-7.
[30] Dio Cassius, *Roman History* 65.8; Oxyrhynchus papyrus, P.Oxy. 34.2725.
[31] E.g. Eusebius, *Ecclesiastical History* 4.2.1-5; Dio Cassius 68.32.1-3.

The Shrine of the Caesars

favourite, Antinous, that he began perhaps the most renowned and dramatic of all the Roman imperial visits to Egypt.[32]

Following the emperor's formal entry into Alexandria riding in a four-horse chariot (known as a quadriga), he engaged in a round of sight-seeing, which undoubtedly took in the Soma, probably in the company of Antinous. The imperial party was enthusiastically fêted by the Greek population, which saw in this "Greekling" emperor a potential benefactor and an ally against their Jewish antagonists. The emperor in turn lavished his patronage upon the city and its monuments. A life-size statue of a bull in black basalt, dedicated by Hadrian, has been found in the ruins of the Serapeum.[33] However, the emperor promptly managed to alienate much of the initial goodwill by appointing outsiders of his own acquaintance to lucrative sinecures at the Museum and by refusing entreaties to allow the city to reconstitute its ancient council, which had been dissolved by Augustus. The atmosphere soured to the extent that Hadrian wrote to a friend at this juncture describing the Alexandrians as "seditious, vain and spiteful".

A tangible link survives between Hadrian's visit and the Soma story in the form of several coin types, which the emperor issued in Alexandria to commemorate the event. A description of one of these is given in the Dictionary of Roman Coins:-

The genius of Alexandria, or of Egypt in general, is figured in a brass medal of Hadrian (struck in Egypt) as a man, wearing on his own head the skin of an elephant's, and holding in his right hand a bundle of corn ears. He takes with his left hand that of the emperor, and lifts it to his lips, as if to kiss it, in acknowledgement of Hadrian's benefits to the city and country. Round the coin is engraved ALEXANDREA and in the field LIE (Year XV [of the emperor]).[34]

The three types from this series are depicted in Figure 5.6: firstly, the bronze drachm type described by the Dictionary; secondly, the emperor greeted by the same figure on a billon tetradrachm; finally, the emperor in a quadriga, also greeted by the "genius of Alexandria". The character in the elephant headdress has sometimes been identified as a young woman.[35] This seems to be by analogy with a separate group of coins from Hadrian's reign, on which there is a personification of Africa as a reclining or kneeling woman wearing an elephant scalp. However, the Africa coins were minted in Rome and conform to general types used to commemorate visits to a range of provinces, whereas the Alexandrian coins were a special local issue. Also the figure in the Alexandrian

---

[32] For details of the story of Hadrian and Antinous in Egypt see Royston Lambert, *Beloved and God*, 1984.
[33] Jean-Yves Empereur, *Alexandria Rediscovered*, p.88.
[34] S.W. Stevenson, C. Roach Smith & F.W. Madden, *Dictionary of Roman Coins*, George Bell & Sons, 1889, p.35: the left and right hands are interchanged in the examples of which I am aware and the inscription *ALEXANDREA* exists only on other elephant-scalp types (e.g. Galba).
[35] E.g. Alan K. Bowman, *Egypt after the Pharaohs*, Chapter 7.

The Quest for the Tomb of Alexander by Andrew Chugg

coins is dressed in a chiton (tunic) and sometimes a chlamys (cloak). This is precisely the apparel that Ephippus describes as constituting the habitual garb of Alexander. Furthermore, as we have seen, there was an enduring association of the elephant scalp motif with Alexander dating from the earliest period of the Ptolemaic kingdom. Perhaps the clinching detail is the inclusion of a belt just beneath Alexander's breast in some examples. This is clearly the "Persian Girdle" (Περσικὴν ζώνην[36] or *zonam Persicam*[37]), which Alexander also wears in the "Alexander Sarcophagus" reliefs from Sidon and in the "Demetrio Alexander" statuette from 1st century BC Egypt (now at Athens). What could be more natural than for Hadrian to portray himself being greeted as an equal by the personification of Alexandria in the guise of the city's deified founder?[38]

Figure 5.6. The series of coins minted to celebrate Hadrian's visit to Alexandria in AD130: Alexander/Alexandria greets the emperor (author's collection)

---

[36] Diodorus 17.77.5.
[37] *Metz Epitome* 2, an anonymous 4th century AD text, quoted by Andrew Stewart, *Faces of Power: Alexander's Image & Hellenistic Politics* (1993, University of California Press) p. 356, item T46.
[38] For more details see A.M. Chugg, "An Unrecognised Representation of Alexander the Great on Hadrian's Egyptian Coinage," *The Celator Journal*, Vol. 15, No. 2, February, 2001, pp. 6-16.

The Shrine of the Caesars

If Otto Mørkholm is correct in his hypothesis that the representation of Alexander wearing the elephant headdress derives from a funerary statue at the Memphite tomb, then in these evocative series of coins we glimpse the transfer of the iconography of the Memphite tomb to Alexandria and the persistence of this symbolism deep into the Roman period.[39] Quite possibly the funerary statue of Alexander wearing elephant spoils had accompanied his body in its move to the new capital and still stood in the Soma Mausoleum in Hadrian's day.

In early October the imperial party embarked upon a flotilla of barges for a pleasure cruise up the Nile. Even today with most of the monuments in ruins and glimpses of modernity around every bend this remains an atmospheric voyage. But in the second century AD most of the ancient architecture remained relatively intact and the priests of the old gods still practised their mystical rituals as they had since the dawn of civilisation. For the Romans, Egypt was a land steeped in potent magic and the emperor and his entourage will have been engulfed by an almost tangible sense of sorcery and the occult. Hadrian had been suffering intermittently from a serious haemorrhagic illness, so he had planned the trip as a kind of pilgrimage to seek a cure by the magicians and diviners in this most supernatural of his realms.

The warlocks and diabolists assured the emperor that all the evils that beset him might be averted, if a willing human victim could be persuaded to sacrifice himself in Hadrian's stead, thus deflecting the bad luck. But no suitable volunteer could be found among the emperor's retinue.

Another shadow oppressing the voyage was the spectre of famine hanging over the land in the wake of two successive failures of the Nile flood: a third drought would bring catastrophe. According to immemorial tradition the sacrifice of a youth or a virgin to the river gods was the only sure means of appeasing their wrath and the proper occasion would be the festival to celebrate the Nile's flood on 22nd October.

Antinous may also have been depressed by signs of a cooling in his relationship with the emperor. It seems likely, although the exact circumstances are shrouded in mystery, that the combination of these pressures led this impressionable youth to commit suicide by drowning himself in the river during the week following the Nile festival. Hadrian recognised in this act a gesture of supreme sacrifice and was profoundly moved. He plunged into an orgy of mourning, founding the city of Antinoopolis at the spot where the body was washed ashore (Figure 5.7) and establishing a cult for the worship of the deified Antinous throughout his empire. The emperor seems to have modelled his new city in conscious imitation of Alexander's foundation of Alexandria.[40] The

---

[39] O. Mørkholm, *Early Hellenistic Coinage*, Cambridge, 1991, pp. 63-4.
[40] Orsolina Montevecchi, "Adriano e la fondazione di Antinoopolis, Neronia IV, Alejandro Magno, modelo de los emperadores romanos," *Collection Latomus*, Vol. 209, 1990.

The Quest for the Tomb of Alexander by Andrew Chugg

worship of Antinous came to parallel that of Alexander himself in the succeeding centuries: some time around AD400 St John Chrysostom denounced the Roman Senate for recognising Alexander and "the favourite of Hadrian" as gods.[41]

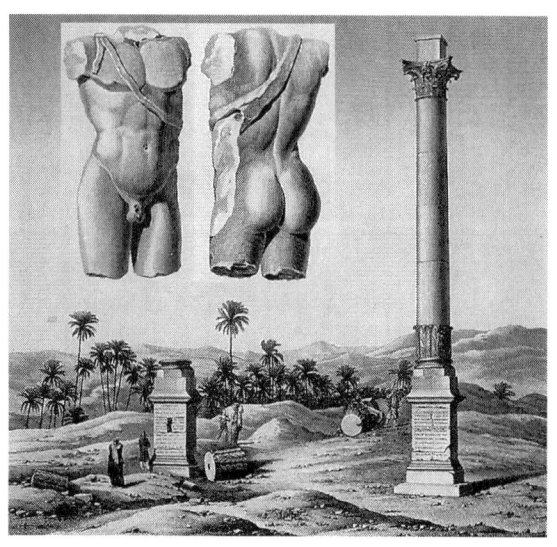

Figure 5.7. Ruin field of Antinoopolis as seen by Napoleon's expedition in 1799 with views of the torso of a statue of Antinous inset (author's collection)

Hadrian himself died seven years later and was buried at Rome in a mausoleum of similar design to that of his predecessor Augustus. This monument still looms over the river Tiber, having been transmogrified in the medieval period into the papal fortress of Castel Sant'Angelo. The location of the tomb of Antinous, however, is another of antiquity's enthralling sepulchral mysteries. Some would place it in his eponymous city beside the Nile, but the obelisk now standing on the Pincio in Rome bears Hadrian's own epitaph for his favourite and claims to mark his burial. Unfortunately, its original location is unknown, but in a crucial sentence its hieroglyphs translate:-

O, Antinous! This deceased one, who rests in this tomb in the country estate of the Emperor of Rome.

This appears to be a reference to Hadrian's villa at Tibur (Tivoli) just outside Rome. If Antinous was entombed there, then the Canopus section, which the emperor modelled on the city of Canopus at the western mouth of the Nile, is a likely site.

* * * * * * * *

---

[41] St John Chrysostom, Bishop of Constantinople, *Homily 26 on the second epistle of St Paul the Apostle to the Corinthians.*

The Shrine of the Caesars

The next emperor who is known to have visited the Soma was Septimius Severus in the course of his visit to Egypt in AD199-200.[42] He courted popularity in Alexandria by finally granting the city permission to reconstitute its town council and thereby administer itself. According to Dio Cassius, Augustus had dissolved this body 230 years earlier as a means of punishing the Alexandrians. Severus may also have removed a bar on Alexandrians serving in the Roman Senate, for Egyptians appear in the lists of its membership from early in the 3rd century AD.[43]

This emperor was a disciplinarian by style and temperament, keen to root out potentially subversive influences. He seems to have been particularly intolerant of the Egyptian predilection for sorcery and the occult. We have a papyrus record of his edict against the magical divination of future events:-

Therefore let no man through oracles, that is, by means of written documents supposedly granted under divine influence, nor by means of the parade of images or suchlike charlatanry, pretend to know things beyond human ken and profess (to know) the obscurity of things to come, neither let any man put himself at the disposal of those who enquire about this or answer in any way whatsoever.[44]

Part of the enforcement adopted by the emperor seems to have been to command the seizure of all the "written documents", the secret books of magic lore, that his soldiers and officials could lay their hands on.

Severus came from North Africa, but his empress, Julia Domna, hailed from Syria. Doubtless partly on account of these roots in the Greek East, the Severan family identified themselves especially closely with Alexander and his legacy. Septimius Severus seems to have been shocked by the accessibility of the mortal remains of his hero and he ordered that the burial chamber should be sealed up to inhibit further tourism. Dio Cassius 76.13.2 implies that the emperor decided to take this opportunity also to seal up the confiscated secret books in the tomb of Alexander:-

[Severus] *inquired into everything, including things that were very carefully hidden; for he was the kind of person to leave nothing, either human or divine, uninvestigated. Accordingly, he took away from practically all the sanctuaries all the books that he could find containing any secret lore, and he sealed up the tomb of Alexander* (Ἀλεξάνδρου μνημεῖον συνέκλεισεν); *this was in order that no one in future should either view his body or read what was mentioned in the aforesaid books.*

These facts are important, because of their implications for the preservation of the underground funerary chamber and its contents. Sealing in this context can hardly have meant a simple lock on the door. Rather we should look to the example of the sealing of the burial chamber of Mausolus at Halicarnassus,

---

[42] This visit is recounted by Dio Cassius, *Roman History (Epitome)* 76.13.
[43] Dio Cassius 51.17.1-4.
[44] J.R. Rea, "A New Version of P.Yale inv. 299," *ZPE* 27, pp.151-6.

which was accomplished by inserting a huge block of masonry in the entrance passage. In this case there would be more hope that the burial chamber and the sarcophagus might have survived the destruction of the building above it.

* * * * * * * *

Septimius Severus had two sons by Julia Domna. The elder, named Antoninus, was a year older that his brother Geta. It is likely that they accompanied their father on his visit to Alexandria, at which time Antoninus would have been about 12 years old. It is easy to imagine how awe-inspiring the Soma would have been for a boy at such an impressionable age. As he grew up Antoninus came to identify himself closely with Alexander, but in ways that came to be seen as additional symptoms of a terrifying megalomania.[45] He also acquired a faintly deprecatory nickname: Caracalla, because of his habit of wearing a short military style of cloak. Although it was never used officially in his lifetime, it is by this agnomen that he is known to history.

In AD211 Severus died at York leaving the empire under the joint rule of his sons. However, the young men had by then become irreconcilably estranged. After a period of escalating tension Caracalla arranged to have Geta murdered in AD212. His brother expired in their mother's arms, having been mortally wounded by Caracalla's henchmen.[46] Yet this was just the most prominent of a long litany of murders and executions. It was a source of pride for Caracalla that an oracle had once referred to him as "the Ausonian beast".[47]

Caracalla's emulation of Alexander plumbed new depths after he became emperor. He wrote to the Senate advising them of his conviction that his hero had been reincarnated in his own person, and he raised a phalanx of sixteen thousand Macedonians, kitting them out as authentically as he could in old-fashioned armour and with long pikes like a set of life-size toy soldiers. He is also said to have acquired certain cups and weapons, which he believed to have been owned by Alexander.[48] The Soma Mausoleum was a possible source for these artefacts, just as it had been for the cuirass sported by Caligula.

In AD215 Caracalla announced his intention to bless Alexandria with his presence, since he longed to see the city founded by his idol.[49] He arrived in the summer amidst clouds of perfume, sweet music and showers of flowers thrown by the enthusiastic crowd, who anticipated generous benefactions from an emperor so much obsessed with anything connected with Alexander. An

---

[45] Dio Cassius 78.7-8 7.
[46] Herodian, *History of the Empire* 4.4; Dio Cassius 78.
[47] Dio Cassius 78.23.4.
[48] Dio Cassius 78.17.1-2.
[49] The visit is recounted by Herodian 4.8.6-9.8 and by Dio Cassius 78.22-23, though only the former mentions the Soma visit. The visit is also mentioned by John of Antioch (7th century) in C. Müller, *Fragmenta Historicorum Graecorum*, Paris, 1868, Vol. 4, p. 590, but this appears to be derived from Herodian.

The Shrine of the Caesars

account of his visit to the Soma was penned by Herodian within a few decades of the event:-

As soon as Antoninus entered the city with his whole army he went up to the temple, where he made a large number of sacrifices and laid quantities of incense on the altars. Then he went to the tomb (μνῆμα) of Alexander where he took off and laid upon the grave the purple cloak he was wearing and the rings of precious stones and his belts and anything else of value he was carrying.

Another ancient reference to the same visit has survived in an anonymous 4th century manuscript ascribed to Sextus Aurelius Victor:-

After he had inspected the body of Alexander of Macedon, he [Caracalla] ordered that he himself should be called 'Great' and 'Alexander', for he was led on by the lies of his flatterers to the point where, adopting the ferocious brow and neck tilted towards the left shoulder that he had noted in Alexander's countenance, he persuaded himself that his features were truly very similar.[50]

These accounts have the particular significance of being the last definite mentions of the existence of the tomb and the body in recorded history. Caracalla must have ordered the burial chamber to be unsealed for his visit, but it is likely that he had it re-sealed afterwards, for he will have been even more jealously protective of its contents than his father.

The emperor set up his headquarters in the temple of Serapis, overlooking the city, where he plotted the most despicable of his crimes against the unsuspecting citizens of Alexandria. He had in fact been receiving reports from his spies for several years regarding the behaviour of the Alexandrians, who had been indulging in their customary lampooning of the reigning monarch. This emperor had presented a broad target on account of his fratricide, rumours of incest with his mother and his emulation of Alexander, but the humour had been lost on Caracalla, who nurtured a foetid anger against the perpetrators of these casual witticisms.

Accordingly, he assembled all the young men of the city in an open space, under the pretext of recruiting a regiment for his army. Whilst he strolled among them smiling and chatting inconsequentially, his soldiers completed an encirclement of the parade ground. As the emperor withdrew with his guards he gave a pre-arranged signal and the trap was sprung. A ring of gnashing steel closed in upon the panic-stricken youths and methodically hacked them to pieces. This, however, was but the prelude to a more generalised massacre as the troops were loosed upon the streets to rape, pillage and slaughter the unfortunate inhabitants without restraint.

The emperor lingered several months in the city, probably until early in AD216 (according to two papyri: P.Flor. 382 and BGU 1.266). He was overseeing a

---

[50] Epitome de Caesaribus Sexti Aureli Victoris 21.4.

plan to concentrate the main garrisons of Egypt in a fortress in the old palace quarter of the city known as the Bruchium.[51] A great wall was constructed through the heart of the city to cordon off this district (Dio Cassius 78.23.3). Its imposing towers completed the intimidation of the terrorised populace.

Caracalla was now so steeped in the blood of friend and foe alike that he became increasingly fearful of assassination. He wrote to a friend in Rome asking him to consult the seers to discover any plots against him. The friend wrote back that he should beware of Macrinus, one of his military prefects. However, Caracalla asked Macrinus to deal with the very batch of dispatches that included this reply. Naturally enough, the imaginary plot consequently became an urgent reality. Macrinus recruited to his cause a centurion whose brother had recently been put to death by the emperor. When Caracalla was suffering from a bout of diarrhoea during a desert journey, he halted to relieve himself and his guards drew aside to allow him some privacy. The vengeful centurion saw his chance. When the emperor's breeches were around his ankles, the assassin ran up to him as though responding to a summons and delivered a fatal stab wound with military precision.[52] It was a fittingly ironic end for an emperor who revelled in opportunities to catch his victims off their guard.

* * * * * * * *

The last of the Severan dynasty was named Alexander in keeping with his family's traditional affiliation with the conqueror's memory. After his murder in AD235 the Roman Empire entered an era of serious political instability, which was sorely aggravated by the opportunistic incursions of various neighbouring nations. The Empire was only saved from complete disintegration by a succession of powerful, authoritarian emperors, who imposed radical changes in the way it was governed and defended. At first Alexandria was relatively unaffected by these troubles, but in the second half of the century it became embroiled in a grievous series of wars and rebellions, from which it emerged terribly scarred and demoralised.

---

[51] John Marlowe, *The Golden Age of Alexandria*, Gollancz, 1971, p. 219, who mentions that the Roman garrison was moved from Nicopolis into the Bruchium at this time.
[52] Herodian 4.12-13.

6. Vanished from History

"Yet you will know my lover, though you live far away:
And you will whisper where he's gone, that lily boy to look upon,
And whiter than the spray."
"How should I know your lover, Lady of the Sea?"
"Alexander, Alexander, King of the World was he!"
"Weep not for him, dear lady, but come aboard my ship.
So many years ago he died, he's dead as dead can be."
"O base and brutal sailor to lie this lie to me.
His mother was the foam-foot star-sparkling Aphrodite;
His father was Adonis, who lives away in Lebanon,
In stony Lebanon, where blooms his red anemone.
But where is Alexander, the soldier Alexander,
My golden love of olden days, the King of the World and me?"
She sank into the moonlight and the sea was only sea.

               Santorin (A Legend of the Aegean), James Elroy Flecker

The legend of Alexander and the mermaid tells of a beautiful yet perilous marine enchantress, who waylays ships to beg their crews for news of the conqueror. So long as they reply, "He lives and reigns" she departs satisfied. If, however, they should venture to mention his death, then she springs into a terrible rage and summons up a storm to drown them.

This fable seemingly owes its genesis to the fantastical version of Alexander's career known as the Alexander Romance, which its redactor attributed quite implausibly to Callisthenes, a great-nephew of Aristotle who travelled with Alexander as court historian. In particular, the Romance has a story of how Alexander dived to the bottom of the sea in a glass jar held within a cage, where he saw all kinds of fish and an especially large specimen took the cage in its mouth and ferried the King to the shore.[1] In later versions an angel acted as Alexander's guide on his undersea adventure and the large fish grew into a gargantuan sea-monster.[2] The Romance seems to have been compiled in Greek through an uncritical conflation of earlier documents and legends some time in the 3rd century AD by a native of Egypt, most probably a citizen of Alexandria.[3] It became an international best seller, proliferating rapidly in Europe and the Middle East. It is is known to have appeared in Latin, Armenian, Syriac, Coptic,

---

[1] Stoneman (translator), *The Greek Alexander Romance* 2.38.
[2] Gwen Benwell and Arthur Waugh, *Sea Enchantress: The Tale of The Mermaid and Her Kin*, Hutchison, 1961, Chapter 4.
[3] It is difficult, by virtue of some relatively late additions, to date the redactor (i.e. "Pseudo-Callisthenes") of the archetypal α recension of the Romance before the 3rd century AD, but it is fairly certain that it existed by AD300, because the A manuscript almost certainly derives from the 3rd century AD. However, many of the components of the tale are clearly much older, and the section on Alexander's death probably originated in the late 4th century BC.

The Quest for the Tomb of Alexander by Andrew Chugg

Hebrew, Persian, Turkish, Arabic and Ethiopic versions by the medieval period.[4]

Herodian probably wrote his account of Caracalla's visit to Alexandria in the late AD240's. He may himself have been a native of Alexandria, because an Alexandrian grammarian, Aelius Herodian, who was a friend of the Roman emperor, Marcus Aurelius, may have been his father.[5] His *History* came to a close in AD238 without any hint of the destruction of the Soma. We would expect him to have mentioned so dramatic an event in view of his colourful account of Caracalla's visit to the building just a few decades before he wrote, so his silence indicates that the Soma still stood at least until about the middle of the 3rd century AD. However, the Syriac version of the Romance explicitly mentions the contemporaneous existence of Alexander's tomb: "and they call that place the 'Tomb of Alexander' unto this day."[6] This version of Pseudo-Callisthenes is likely to be later than Herodian in its origins, in which case it is the last piece of documentary evidence that attests to the continuing existence of the Soma Mausoleum.

*   *   *   *   *   *   *   *

Although the Soma Mausoleum probably survived until at least the second half of the 3rd century AD, it is equally likely that it had been destroyed by the end of the 4th century of the Christian era. The most explicit evidence for this comes from a section of a sermon by John Chrysostom, a cleric from Antioch who eventually rose to become the Bishop of Constantinople between AD398-404. This man lived from the 340's until AD407, so his homily may be dated to the last quarter of the 4th century or very early in the 5th. His words are fascinating for the light they cast on the battle for hearts and minds, which raged at that time between the Church and the disparate pagan forces, spearheaded by the Senate in Rome:-

For thus it was that idolatries gained ground at first; men being held in admiration beyond their desert. Thus the Roman senate decreed Alexander to be the thirteenth God,[7] for it possessed the privilege of electing and enrolling Gods. For instance, when all about Christ had

---

[4] Of most historical significance is the single manuscript A, which is a relatively close copy of the α recension, the common ancestor of all later versions. There are, however, significant lacunae in A, which have to be filled from the Armenian manuscripts, the Latin version of the 4th century by Julius Valerius and various manuscripts of the β recension. The Syriac and medieval western European versions derive from the δ* recension, but are later, more fabulous and of less historical interest.

[5] C.R. Whittaker, *Introduction to Loeb edition of Herodian, History of The Empire*.

[6] E.A.W. Budge (trans.), *Syriac Alexander Romance* 3.23; Budge thought the Syriac relatively late (7th-9th century), but he notes that Zacher dated it to the 5th century – its prototype δ* (of which no Greek manuscript survives) may well be 4th century in origin.

[7] So too Clement of Alexandria, *Exhortation to the Greeks* 10: "For these are they who have dared to deify men, describing Alexander of Macedon as the thirteenth god, though 'Babylon proved him mortal.'" The Babylon quote may be from *Sibylline Oracles* 5.5-9; cf. Lucian, *Dialogues of the Dead* 13.

been reported, the ruler of the nation sent to inquire, whether they would be pleased to elect Him also a God. They however refused their consent, being angry and indignant that previous to their vote and decree, the Power of the Crucified flashing abroad had won over the whole world to its own worship. But thus it was ordered even against their will that the Divinity of Christ was not proclaimed by man's decree, nor was He counted one of the many that were by them elected. For they counted even boxers to be Gods, and the favourite of Hadrian; after whom the city Antinous is named. For since death testifies against their immortal nature, the devil invented another way, that of the soul's immortality; and mingling therewith that excessive flattery, he seduced many into impiety. And observe what wicked artifice. When we advance that doctrine for a good purpose, he overthrows our words; but when he himself is desirous of framing an argument for mischief, he is very zealous in setting it up. And if any one ask, 'How is Alexander a God? Is he not dead? and miserably too?', 'Yes, but the soul is immortal,' he replies. Now thou arguest and philosophizest for immortality, to detach men from the God Who is over all: but when we declare that this is God's greatest gift, thou persuadest thy dupes that men are low and grovelling, and in no better case than the brutes. And if we say, 'the Crucified lives,' laughter follows immediately: although the whole world proclaims it, both in old time and now; in old time by miracles, now by converts; for truly these successes are not those of a dead man: but if one say, 'Alexander lives,' thou believest, although thou hast no miracle to allege. 'Yes,' one replies; 'I have; for when he lived he wrought many and great achievements; for he subdued both nations and cities, and in many wars and battles he conquered, and erected trophies.' If then I shall show [somewhat] which he when alive never dreamed of, neither he, nor any other man that ever lived, what other proof of the resurrection wilt thou require? For that whilst alive one should win battles and victories, being a king and having armies at his disposal, is nothing marvelous, no, nor startling or novel; but that after a Cross and Tomb one should perform such great things throughout every land and sea, this it is which is most especially replete with such amazement, and proclaims His divine and unutterable Power. And Alexander indeed after his decease never restored again his kingdom, which had been rent in pieces and quite abolished: indeed how was it likely he, dead, should do so? but Christ then most of all set up His after He was dead. And why speak I of Christ? seeing that He granted to His disciples also, after their deaths, to shine? For, tell me, where is the tomb of Alexander? show it me and tell me the day on which he died. But of the servants of Christ the very tombs are glorious, seeing they have taken possession of the most loyal city; and their days are well known, making festivals for the world. And his tomb even his own people know not, but this man's the very barbarians know. And the tombs of the servants of the Crucified are more splendid than the palaces of kings; not for the size and beauty of the buildings, (yet even in this they surpass them,) but, what is far more, in the zeal of those who frequent them. For he that wears the purple himself goes to embrace those tombs, and, laying aside his pride, stands begging the saints to be his advocates with God, and he that hath the diadem implores the tent-maker and the fisherman, though dead, to be his patrons.[8]

---

[8] St John Chrysostom, Bishop of Constantinople, "Homily 26 on the second epistle of St Paul the Apostle to the Corinthians," in *Patrologia Graeca*, vol. 61. p. 581 (English translation by J.H. Parker, 1848); elsewhere in St John Chrysostom, *Instructions to Catechumens (Ad Illum. Catech.)* 2.5 he rails against the pagan habit, then prevalent among the people of Antioch, of making talismans to hang about the neck and the ankle out of coins bearing Alexander's portrait: "And what is one to say

The Quest for the Tomb of Alexander by Andrew Chugg

It is appears that the bishop was suggesting that Alexander's tomb did not exist in his time, particularly when he asserted, "his tomb even his own people know not". By contrast he noted the adoration of the faithful for the tombs of major Christian figures: that of St Paul, the subject of his sermon, had recently been established in Rome; furthermore, Saint Helena, the mother of Constantine the Great, had undertaken a pilgrimage to Jerusalem in around AD326, where she had "rediscovered" various biblical sites including the (empty) tomb of Jesus.[9]

Chrysostom's mention of the emperor worshipping the relics of prominent Chistians in this sermon recall the behaviour of Theodosius in his ultra-religious phase between about AD390 and his death in AD395. It will subsequently prove to be of interest to our story that this emperor had built a grand Basilica of St Paul the Apostle in about AD390 near the Appian Way just outside the walls of Rome, where it was believed that the saint had been buried.[10] It appears that Theodosius also identified a specific set of remains. Vatican archaeologists have recently (2002-2006) excavated this tomb, although the sarcophagus has not yet been opened.

It is possible to interpret Chrysostom's words as an expression of complete ignorance about the Soma, which would mitigate in favour of the building having been destroyed long before he spoke. However, it is also possible to take the view that this educated and cosmopolitan man chose the example of the Soma just because he had some knowledge of its destruction and therefore knew it would be impossible for his audience to respond to his rhetorical request that they show it to him. In this case he would have been more likely to be mindful of the event, if the destruction had been relatively recent. On balance, therefore, his words are ambiguous regarding how recently the Soma had ceased to exist.

Theodoret, writing around the middle of the fifth century, also listed Alexander among famous men, whose last resting places were then unknown.[11]

It may therefore be inferred that the monument's destruction probably occurred some time in the interval between the mid-third century and the close of the fourth. It is consequently apposite to sieve though the history of Alexandria in that period to identify candidates for the cause of its obliteration. There is certainly no shortage of such events, for in this era the city suffered several of the most tumultuous upheavals in its lengthy and continuing history.

*　　*　　*　　*　　*　　*　　*　　*

---

about them who use charms and amulets, and encircle their heads and feet with golden coins of Alexander of Macedon. Are these our hopes, tell me, that after the cross and death of our Master, we should place our hopes of salvation on an image of a Greek king?"
[9] Socrates Scholasticus, *Ecclesiastical History* 1.17.
[10] Prudentius, *Peristephanon* 12.
[11] Theodoret, *Graecarum Affectionum Curatio* 8.61 in *Patrologia Graeca*, vol. 83, J-P Migne (trans.), Paris, 1864, cols. 1029-1030.

Vanished from History

Alexandria's troubles in the second half of the 3rd century are said to have been sparked in AD260 by an incendiary argument between a servant and a legionary over a pair of shoes. This trivial dispute escalated into a classic Alexandrian mob riot. Marcus Julius Aemilianus, the Roman Prefect of Egypt, resorted to deploying his garrison troops to quell the disorder. However, the Empire had just suffered the ignominious defeat and capture of Valerian, the Augustus (senior emperor), by the Persians in Syria. His son, Gallienus, who had been left to rule in the West as Caesar (junior emperor), had therefore recently assumed supreme power. He seems to have been notably unpopular with the army contingents in Egypt, so they seized the opportunity presented by Aemilianus' reliance on their services to prevail upon him to become their rival candidate for the purple.[12] The rebellion of Aemilianus lasted for two years, until Gallienus sent his leading general, Theodotus, into Egypt to destroy the usurper. Aemilianus seems to have been besieged for a couple more years in the Bruchium fortress behind Caracalla's lofty walls, but he was eventually defeated, captured and strangled. Consequently, much of Alexandria was a virtual battlefield in the years AD262-4. Eusebius has preserved a (rather hyperbolical) description of the consequences of the sedition of Aemilianus for the city of Alexandria:-

It would be easier for one to go, not only beyond the limits of the province, but even from the East to the West, than from Alexandria to Alexandria itself. For the very heart of the city is more intricate and impassable than that great and trackless desert which Israel traversed for two generations. And our smooth and waveless harbors have become like the sea, divided and walled up, through which Israel drove and in whose highway the Egyptians were overwhelmed. For often from the slaughters there committed they appear like the Red Sea.[13]

He goes on to describe an outbreak of pestilence, possibly plague, which killed a third of the population of Alexandria in the grim aftermath of the insurrection.

Meanwhile in Syria the Roman frontier was being preserved from disintegration by the wealthy merchant city of Palmyra. Its king, Odenath, was nominally an ally of the Empire and shared the Romans' enmity for the expansionist Persians: they were definitely not good for business. He organised and led a highly successful counter-offensive against Shapur, the Persian monarch, which succeeded in driving him back across the Euphrates. Impressed by this achievement Gallienus diplomatically moved to ensconce Odenath within the Roman fold by appointing him "Roman" commander in the Orient.[14] This ploy seems to have been successful whilst Odenath lived, but in the late 260's he perished and was succeeded by Zenobia, his ambitious and formidable queen. She is said to have claimed descent from Cleopatra, which may help to explain her actions. She broke the alliance with Rome in dramatic fashion by invading

---

[12] John Marlowe, *The Golden Age of Alexandria, 1971*, Chapter 10, p. 220.
[13] Eusebius, *Ecclesiastical History* 7.21.
[14] Stephen Williams, *Diocletian and The Roman Recovery*, Routledge, 1985, Chapter 2: *Virtus Illyrici*.

and capturing Egypt in AD269-270. The Roman garrison just barely managed to hold out in the Bruchium fortress, behind Caracalla's sturdy ramparts.[15]

Rome, however, had just acquired its most heroic emperor of the century. His name was Aurelian and it was through his dauntless campaigning that the Empire, then assailed on all fronts, was retrieved from the brink of collapse. He had been a member of an elite corps of senior officers, the *Protectores*, who had begun to develop a novel military strategy based on mobility and the ability to strike fast and hard across great distances. They were in effect practitioners of a kind of archetypal blitzkrieg. In AD272 Aurelian deployed these tactics in a war against the troublesome Palmyrenes. He led his armies on forced marches across vast tracts of desert and routed Zenobia's forces in two climactic battles. Palmyra itself was besieged, but capitulated on equitable terms proffered by the emperor. As part of the deal Zenobia was compelled to parade through the streets of Rome as the centrepiece of Aurelian's triumph.[16]

One of Zenobia's supporters in Alexandria, an immensely wealthy merchant called Firmus, is said to have instigated a fresh rebellion after the queen's defeat by having himself declared emperor.[17] Unsurprisingly, he was speedily routed, taken captive, tortured and put to death.[18] Aurelian may have led the attack upon this upstart in person, for a papyrus from the town of Oxyrhynchus in Upper Egypt records the decision of its council to present a golden statue of the goddess Victory to the emperor to commemorate his successes.[19] Writing over a century later, probably during the late AD380's, the historian Ammianus Marcellinus deplored the devastation of Alexandria and particularly the Bruchium district in Aurelian's eastern wars:-

But Alexandria herself, not gradually (like other cities), but at her very origin, attained her wide extent; and for a long time she was grievously troubled by internal dissension, until at last, many years later under the rule of Aurelian, the quarrels of the citizens turned into deadly strife; then her walls were destroyed and she lost the greater part of the district called Bruchium, which had long been the abode of distinguished men.[20]

For a quarter of a century after Aurelian's wars Alexandria seems to have basked in relative tranquillity, but in AD297 during the reign of the great reforming emperor, Diocletian, the empire came under a renewed threat from the East in the person of Narses, then king of Persia. Egypt had been provoked by an unpopular tax reform and a simmering mood of nationalism suddenly saw an opportunity to express itself, whilst the imperial armies were preoccupied by the Persian emergency.[21] The entire nation rose up in revolt in the name of a

---

[15] John Marlowe, *The Golden Age of Alexandria*, 1971, Chapter 10, pp. 220-1.
[16] Stephen Williams, *Diocletian and The Roman Recovery*, Chapter 2.
[17] Alan K. Bowman, *Egypt After The Pharaohs*, Chapter 2.
[18] Gibbon, *The Decline and Fall of the Roman Empire*, Chapter 11.
[19] Oxyrhynchus Papyrus, P.Oxy. 1413 (AD271/2?).
[20] Ammianus Marcellinus, *Res Gestae* 22.16.15.
[21] Stephen Williams, *Diocletian and The Roman Recovery*, Chapter 6, Victory and Consolidation II.

new Egyptian emperor, Lucius Domitius Domitianus. He remained, however, little more than a figurehead, since the real power was wielded by a certain Achilleus, the self-styled "Corrector of Egypt".

In Syria, despite an initial victory over the Romans, the Persians had been fought to a standstill and an uneasy stalemate prevailed. Whilst hostilities were interrupted by the summer heat, Diocletian led a large detachment by forced marches to counter the rebellion in Egypt. They joined up with the remnants of the former Roman garrisons and commenced a systematic campaign to reduce the rebel-held towns. By early winter Diocletian's army was arrayed before the walls of Alexandria itself. Nevertheless, Achilleus maintained a stubborn and desperate resistance, perhaps hoping against hope that the siege might be relieved by the Persians, although in fact Galerius, Diocletian's deputy, was successfully maintaining the Roman position in Syria. Diocletian simply cut the subterranean aqueducts supplying fresh water to Alexandria and bided his time. After eight months of dreadful hardship the city capitulated in the spring of AD298. The vengeful emperor commanded that a terrible example should be made of the city and that all those who had supported the sedition should be put to the sword. Only when the blood flowed above his horse's knees, he vowed, should the killing stop. But when his mount suddenly stumbled so that its knees actually touched the earth, the superstitious Diocletian saw it as an omen and prematurely relented. With their characteristic black humour, the Alexandrians subsequently erected a bronze statue of the emperor's steed to commemorate their deliverance.

Within the precinct of the Serapeum, Diocletian erected a great granite column, which was surmounted by a twice life-size porphyry statue of the victorious emperor (Figure 6.1). This is virtually the only major monument from ancient Alexandria to survive to the present day, although the statue has long since disappeared and the pillar is erroneously named after Julius Caesar's rival, Pompey.[22]

*   *   *   *   *   *   *   *   *

Scholarly opinion has been inclined to endorse the idea that the Soma was demolished or razed to the ground during one of the three calamitous periods of warfare during the second half of the 3rd century. The favourite culprit has been Aurelian in the context of his offensives against Zenobia and Firmus. The reasoning behind this is that Strabo located the Soma in what he called the "Royal Quarter",[23] which is known to have corresponded somewhat with the district known to the Romans as the Bruchium, although the latter was probably rather smaller than the former. Ammianus observed that "under the rule of Aurelian, the quarrels of the citizens turned into deadly strife; then Alexandria's

---

[22] Jean-Yves Empereur, *Alexandria Rediscovered*, Chapter 5 gives a detailed account of Pompey's Pillar; a mosaic from Sepphoris in Israel shows the Pillar with its statue still in place.
[23] Strabo, *Geography* 17.1.8.

walls were destroyed and she lost the greater part of the district called Bruchium."[24] Epiphanius confirmed that the Bruchium was a wilderness at about the same date.[25] However, there are problems with this ostensibly straightforward theory.

Figure 6.1. Pompey's Pillar at the site of the Serapeum in an aquatint sketched by Luigi Mayer in ~1792 (author's collection)

The boundary of the Bruchium district in late Roman times was probably defined by the wall built by Caracalla. Although the exact location of this wall is unknown, the line of the Tulunid walls, built by the Sultan Ahmed Ibn Tulun in the ninth century (c. AD868-84), is marked as "Murs d'enceinte de la ville des Arabes" on the map of Alexandria drawn in 1866 by Mahmoud Bey (Figure 4.2).[26] A northeastern stretch of these walls ran from the Tower of the Romans near the coast towards the eastern gate of the city. A long stretch ran more or less along the course of one of the major east-west streets of ancient Alexandria, which Mahmoud designated L2.[27] The Tower of the Romans, which stood until the beginning of the twentieth century (Figures 6.2 and 6.3), seems to have been built in the Hellenistic style, which means it probably dated from no later than the beginning of the Roman period (Augustan era). Therefore it may well have survived because of successive incorporation in Caracalla's wall and the Tulunid

---

[24] Ammianus Marcellinus 22.16.15.
[25] Epiphanius, *On Weights and Measures* col. 250C.
[26] Mahmoud shows the line of these walls as rebuilt by Galice Bey in the 1820's, which differs in some details from the true course of the medieval circuit.
[27] According to Mahmoud Bey's labelling convention for the longitudinal streets.

walls. Furthermore, this section of the Tulunid walls is indented from the coastline so as to exclude a section of the Bruchium district from the Byzantine and medieval bounds of Alexandria. On the basis of these clues, it would seem a reasonable conjecture that the Tulunid walls in their northeastern sector followed the line of Caracalla's wall. If so, then the central crossroads of Ptolemaic Alexandria lay at least several hundred metres further south than the Bruchium.[28] Since the evidence of Achilles Tatius and Zenobius suggests that this crossroads is the most likely location of the Soma, Ammianus' report of the destruction of the Bruchium is consequently not necessarily directly relevant to the fate of Alexander's tomb. There are in fact strong reasons to believe that Strabo's "Royal District" *did* extend southwards to beyond the central crossroads, but we will return to this complex issue in a later chapter.

The sarcophagus of Julius Philosyrius (Figure 4.7) provides a further hint that the Soma may still have existed after Diocletian erected Pompey's Pillar and therefore survived all three episodes of warfare. Additionally, the shard of a glass goblet from Carthage (Figure 4.9) dates to the 4th century AD (though the claim that it depicts the Soma Mausoleum is weak). Furthermore, Ammianus tells two other intriguing stories about Alexandria, which can be interpreted as suggesting that the Soma was a victim of an entirely natural disaster some sixty-five years into the 4th century AD. The first of these accounts concerns the downfall of a certain Bishop Georgius, who was appointed Patriarch of Alexandria late in the reign of Constantius, one of Constantine the Great's sons. Ammianus describes how Georgius had made himself disastrously unpopular with the Alexandrians by acting as an informer against them to the emperor:-

And, among other matters, it was said that he maliciously informed Constantius also of this, namely, that all the edifices standing on the soil of the said city [Alexandria] had been built by its founder, Alexander, at great public cost, and ought justly to be a source of profit to the treasury. To these evil deeds he added still another, which soon after drove him headlong to destruction. As he was returning from the emperor's court and passed by the splendid temple of the Genius [speciosum Genii templum], attended as usual by a large crowd, he turned his eyes straight at the temple, and said: 'How long shall this tomb [sepulcrum] stand?' On hearing this, many were struck as if by a thunderbolt, and fearing that he might try to overthrow that building also, they devised secret plots to destroy him in whatever way they could. [29]

Soon after, following the death of Constantius and the accession of the pagan emperor Julian, probably in December AD361, the Alexandrian mob seized Georgius and gleefully tore him limb from limb.[30]

---

[28] Probably at the intersection of L1 with R1, but anyway somewhere on L1.
[29] Ammianus Marcellinus, *Res Gestae* 22.11.7.
[30] Socrates Scholasticus, *Ecclesiastical History* 3.2..

The Quest for the Tomb of Alexander by Andrew Chugg

Figure 6.2. The obelisks known as Cleopatra's Needles (one fallen in the foreground) with the Tower of the Romans standing on the shore behind them in an engraving from a drawing of 1785 by L-F Cassas (author's collection)

Vanished from History

Figure 6.3. The standing member of Cleopatra's Needles with the remains of the Tower of the Romans on the shore in an albumen photo of ~1870 and the Tower in a postcard of ~1900 after the Needle and the 19th c. buildings had been removed (author's collection)

Ammianus' description of a "splendid temple of the Genius", which Georgius calls a tomb, is obviously very tantalizing in that it sounds exactly like a description of the Soma Mausoleum according to the Halicarnassus prototype.

The Quest for the Tomb of Alexander by Andrew Chugg

In Latin the word Genius normally refers to a tutelary deity or the sacred and spiritual essence of a place, person or thing. It is very rare for Latin authors to use it to refer to *intellectual* genius, its most common form in English. It would appear reasonable that Ammianus should refer to the deified Alexander as the Genius or guardian spirit of a city which he had founded, especially since he had mentioned the conqueror by name a couple of sentences beforehand. After all, Alexander seemingly appears in precisely this guise in some of the Alexandrian issues of Hadrian (Figure 5.6). However, this suggestion, first made by Hogarth in 1895,[31] has met with dubiety in some quarters, because there was a serpent-spirit called the Agathos Daimon, which also fulfilled this type of role in some contexts.[32] Nevertheless, it is doubtful whether Ammianus was sufficiently familiar with the cultural niceties of Alexandrian tradition as to be aware of the ambiguity. He came from Antioch, and, although he probably visited Alexandria in the late AD360's,[33] he makes various blunders concerning the city's history: for example, he asserts that Cleopatra built the Pharos lighthouse, although we know it was constructed over two centuries earlier. Furthermore, Ammianus probably wrote his history in Rome, where the Genius of the emperor Augustus is known to have been worshipped.[34] The suggestion that the tutelary deity of Alexandria is always the Agathos Daimon is anyway exploded by the fact that the Christian writer Sozomenus, also writing in the late Roman period, attributes this particular status to Serapis.[35] Then again, Christopher Haas identifies Ammianus' Genius as the Tyche of Alexandria, a female personification of the city's Fortune derived from Isis.[36] It would therefore seem that there are at least four deities that have variously been recognised as the Genius of Alexandria, yet only one of these satisfies the further criterion of having been entombed in a splendid temple in the city. On balance, the most credible interpretation of Georgius' remarks is that he was referring to the Soma Mausoleum. If so, the building survived until at least AD361.

The other significant story told by Ammianus is a gripping account of a gargantuan earthquake followed by a devastating tidal wave (i.e. tsunami), which struck the eastern Mediterranean in AD365. The quake probably occurred on one of the major geological fault lines that lie beneath the sea to the south of Crete and Alexandria seems to have been particularly badly hit:-

On the 21st of July in the first consulship of Valentinian with his brother, horrible phenomena suddenly spread through the entire extent of the world, such as are related to us neither in fable

---

[31] D.G. Hogarth, "Report on Prospects for Research in Alexandria," *Egypt Exploration Fund* 1894-5, note 3 on p. 23; Lily Ross Taylor, "The Cult of Alexander at Alexandria," *Classical Philology*, 22, 1927, p. 168.
[32] P. Fraser, *Ptolemaic Alexandria*, Chapter 5.
[33] See the Introduction to Loeb edition of Ammianus Marcellinus by John C. Rolfe.
[34] W.W. Tarn, "The Hellenistic Ruler Cult and the Daemon," *Journal of Hellenic Studies* 48, 1928, p. 216.
[35] Sozomenus, *Ecclesiastical History* 5.7.
[36] Christopher Haas, *Alexandria in Late Antiquity*, p. 287.

nor in truthful history. For a little after daybreak, preceded by heavy and repeated thunder and lightning, the whole of the firm and solid earth was shaken and trembled, the sea with its rolling waves was driven back and withdrew from the land, so that in the abyss of the deep thus revealed men saw many kinds of sea-creatures stuck fast in the slime; and vast mountains and deep valleys, which Nature, the creator, had hidden in the unplumbed depths, then, as one might well believe, first saw the beams of the sun. Hence, many ships were stranded as if on dry land, and since many men roamed about without fear in the little that remained of the waters, to gather fish and similar things with their hands, the roaring sea, resenting, as it were, this forced retreat, rose in its turn; and over the boiling shoals it dashed mightily upon islands and broad stretches of the mainland, and levelled innumerable buildings [aedificia] in the cities and wherever else they are to be found; so that amid the mad discord of the elements the altered face of the earth revealed marvellous sights. For the great mass of waters, returning when it was least expected, killed many thousands of men by drowning; and by the swift recoil of the eddying tides a number of ships, after the swelling of the wet element subsided, were found to have been destroyed, and the lifeless bodies of shipwrecked persons lay floating on their backs or on their faces. Other great ships, driven by the mad blasts, landed on the tops of buildings – as happened at Alexandria – and some were driven almost two miles inland, like a Laconian ship which I myself in passing that way saw near the town of Motho, yawning apart through long decay.[37]

A parallel description of this disaster, which also underlines its dire consequences at Alexandria, has been provided by Sozomenus, although he incorrectly attributes it, being a Christian writer, to the wrath of God during the reign of Julian the Apostate, who had in actuality been assassinated two years beforehand in AD363:-

It is, however, very obvious that, throughout the reign of this emperor [Julian], God gave manifest tokens of His displeasure, and permitted many calamities to befall several of the provinces of the Roman Empire. He visited the earth with such fearful earthquakes, that the buildings were shaken, and no more safety could be found within the houses than in the open air. From what I have heard, I conjecture that it was during the reign of this emperor, or, at least, when he occupied the second place in the government, that a great calamity occurred near Alexandria in Egypt, when the sea receded and again passed beyond its boundaries from the re-flux waves, and deluged a great deal of the land, so that on the retreat of the waters, the sea-skiffs were found lodged on the roofs of the houses. The anniversary of this inundation, which they call the birthday of an earthquake, is still commemorated at Alexandria by a yearly festival; a general illumination is made throughout the city; they offer thankful prayers to God, and celebrate the day very brilliantly and piously.[38]

To these compelling contemporaneous and near-contemporaneous accounts may be added some knowledge of the geography of ancient Alexandria gleaned from Mahmoud Bey's map. The central crossroads seems to have lain in a shallow declivity in the landscape, which stretched from the Mediterranean

---

[37] Ammianus Marcellinus, *Res Gestae* 26.10.15-19.
[38] Sozomenus, *Ecclesiastical History* 6.2.

The Quest for the Tomb of Alexander by Andrew Chugg

coast near the Lochias peninsula right the way across the city to lake Mareotis on its southern side. Buildings in this slight valley would have been particularly exposed to the destructive effects of a major tsunami approaching from the north. If, as Ammianus suggests, innumerable buildings were levelled by the surging waters, then the devastation in this area of the city might even have been so extensive that it was subsequently difficult to recognise the precise location of Alexander's tomb. Ammianus' account of Georgius' rhetorical question, "How long shall this tomb stand?" also acquires extra resonance, if indeed the building was destined to be destroyed, as it was believed by divine wrath, just a few years later. In the devastation wrought by this calamity we may recognise perhaps the most convincing explanation of why the Soma Mausoleum subsequently vanished so completely from the historical record.

* * * * * * * *

Until recently the reference by Ammianus was believed to be the latest text to allude to the continued existence of Alexander's remains in ancient Alexandria. But now, thanks to the diligent research of Judith McKenzie, a previously unrecognised comment by a late fourth century writer pertaining to the fate of Alexander's corpse has come to light. This occurs in an oration addressed to the emperor Theodosius I (AD 378-95) by the pagan scholar Libanius, a prominent resident of the great metropolis of Antioch in Syria. Intriguingly, he had been both a friend of Julian the Apostate and the tutor of John Chrysostom. His 49th Oration entitled *To the Emperor for the City Councils* seems to have been composed whilst Tatianus was Praetorian Prefect in the East, which dates it to between AD388-392. This dating is secured by a condemnation of the activities of Cynegius as Praetorian Prefect within this Oration at 49.3. Libanius then goes on to mention "our present Prefect", of whose behaviour he broadly approves. This must mean Cynegius' immediate successor, Tatianus, who was Praetorian Prefect in the East between AD388-392. Since Tatianus had evidently been in office long enough to move magistrates into council memberships and for Libanius to evaluate the results, Oration 49 was probably written at least a year or two into Tatianus' term. On the other hand it was probably written before the full ramifications of Theodosius' edicts against the pagans had become clear in the later part of AD391.[39] Libanius was dead by about AD394.

Libanius' address constitutes a fierce attack upon the behaviour and performance of the city councillors in Syria and elsewhere. In the relevant section Libanius speculates whether even tombs are safe from their depredations:

Who could be the friend of such as these? When they behave like this for money's sake, would they keep their hands off temple offerings or tombs? If they were travelling with some companion who had a gold piece, would they not kill him and rob him of it, if they had the

---

[39] S. Williams & G. Friell, *Theodosius: The Empire at Bay*, London, 1994, Ch. 9: "Contra Paganos", pp. 119-133.

Vanished from History

chance. And this evil, King, is universal, whether you mention Paltus or Alexandria where the corpse of Alexander is displayed, whether Balaneae or our own city [Antioch]. They may differ in size, but the same ailment afflicts them all.

Libanius, Oration 49.11-12

In this context, the mention that the corpse of Alexander was displayed in Alexandria appears to be a deliberate illustration of the threat posed by city councillors to the sanctity and integrity of tombs. It implies that the body had been extracted from its tomb to be publicly exhibited by the orders of such councillors.

It is necessary to express some caution regarding the identity of this "corpse of Alexander", since Libanius was mainly discussing the situation in his home provinces of Syria. The other three towns he mentions are all in Syria and there was an Alexandria in Syria located near the site of Alexander's battle at Issus. Furthermore, there were a number of important individuals named Alexander who lived in the East in that epoch. In particular, there was an Alexander who had been Governor of Syria in the early 360's under Julian the Apostate. Letters by Libanius survive, which were addressed to that Alexander. Nevertheless, Libanius is seeking to demonstrate the universality of the problem in this passage and he seems to be referring to Alexandria in Egypt as a parallel case to his own city of Antioch. The Emperor Theodosius, who was the intended recipient of the address, could not readily have understood Libanius to mean any other than the most renowned corpse of an Alexander in the principal Alexandria by such a comment. It may therefore be concluded, on the balance of probabilities, that this is indeed a reference to the corpse of Alexander the Great having been on public display in the Egyptian city of Alexandria in about AD390-391.

It may be added that the idea that the Soma Mausoleum was destroyed by the catastrophe of AD365 is perfectly consistent with this new fragment of evidence. Such a catastrophe would have provided a motive, an opportunity and an excuse to excavate the subterranean burial chamber and rescue the famous remains. The timing of Libanius' oration also provides a ready explanation for the subsequent disappearance of the corpse. Shortly after he composed this speech in AD391 the roof fell in on the pagans and literally so in the case of many of their temples and shrines, for that year marked the end of official tolerance of paganism in the Roman Empire. Drastic measures would have been required to save so sacred a pagan relic as Alexander's corpse from oblivion at the hands of Christian zealots.

There are some who believe that the Soma Mausoleum itself may have survived even the disaster of AD365. They point to the rioting and religious violence at the end of the 4th century to explain its disappearance. At this time the remaining vestiges of the pagan past were systematically suppressed and destroyed as the new Christian orthodoxy became ever more intolerant of rival religions. In AD385 Theophilus became Patriarch in Alexandria and began to

The Quest for the Tomb of Alexander by Andrew Chugg

pursue a rabidly anti-pagan policy, backed up by a militia of zealots known as the *parabolani*.[40] In early AD391 the emperor abandoned his previous policy of religious tolerance and respect for paganism by enacting a series of increasingly radical laws banning sacrifice, closing pagan shrines and temples and outlawing virtually every mode of expression of pagan beliefs.[41] In Alexandria, Theodosius supported Theophilus against the imperial Prefect, who had sought to maintain the peace between the Christian and pagan factions in the city. Theodosius ordered that the Serapeum, which had become the last refuge of the pagans, should be attacked and then demolished, together with all other remaining pagan temples. Theophilus and his henchmen duly tore the magnificent temple apart, exposing the mechanisms of its wonders, such as a life size statue made to float on air by means of magnets, and leaving it as a mere pile of rubble.[42] It can scarcely be doubted that any other surviving pagan shrines either shared its fate at this time or else were converted to churches, as had already happened to the Caesareum. But the fact that no specific mention is made of the fate of the Soma Mausoleum tends to support the perception of John Chrysostom that it had already ceased to exist by this date.

Tantalizingly, Rufinus began his famous account of the destruction of the Serapeum by the ascendant Christian faction by telling of the exposure of pagan relics in caverns found beneath a ruinous basilica by Christian fanatics.[43] Constantius II had given the site to the Church decades earlier, but it had evidently been left undisturbed in the meantime. However, by AD390 the Christian congregation had expanded to the point that more church sites were needed for worship, so the ancient shrines beneath the basilica were being sacked as a prelude to site redevelopment. Rufinus explains that the sacrilegious treatment of their relics incited the pagans to instigate a riot. However, Socrates Scholasticus suggests that the basilica in question was a Mithraeum and that the relics, which the Christians paraded through the agora, were the Phalli of Priapus.[44] Nevertheless, this is indicative of the kind of scenario, which might have been played out in the case of Alexander's mummy. The Christians might similarly have excavated the remains of the funerary chamber of the Soma Mausoleum and exhibited their discoveries before the populace. This explanation fits in well with other strands of the evidence, because it indicates how the body might have become separated from the Nectanebo II sarcophagus at this juncture.

Having sieved through the evidence on the disappearance of Alexander's tomb, it is possible to draw some tentative conclusions concerning its fate. Notwithstanding the lack of any direct evidence for the event, it is possible to

---

[40] John Marlowe, *The Golden Age of Alexandria*, 1971, Chapter 14, pp. 280-1.
[41] Williams and Friell, *Theodosius: The Empire At Bay*, 1994, Chapter 9, Contra Paganos.
[42] Socrates Scholasticus, *Ecclesiastical History* 5.16.
[43] Rufinus, *Ecclesiastical History* 2.22-30.
[44] Socrates Scholasticus, *Ecclesiastical History* 5.16-17.

Vanished from History

be as much as 95% confident that the Soma Mausoleum, that is to say the building overlying the underground burial chamber, was destroyed some time during the century between AD262 and AD365. Whereas the various episodes of warfare in the late 3rd century remain strong possibilities, the earthquake and tsunami at the end of this period is by far the best candidate for its demolition. Nevertheless, this does not necessarily mean that the burial chamber was destroyed at the same time. Indeed, if the Soma was as large a building as the sources imply and if it collapsed due to fire or earthquake over a burial chamber that was already sealed up, then it will have rendered the excavation of Alexander's sarcophagus a major endeavour. The traumatised populace may have had little incentive or inclination to attempt to dig it out, so the destruction of the overlying building might paradoxically have helped to preserve the tomb for posterity or at least for a generation.

* * * * * * * *

In the 5th century AD the Roman Empire, which had for centuries been a force for cohesion, continuity and an unprecedented degree of peace and prosperity, began to crumble. The West was lost to the invasions of barbarian hoards spearheaded by the Goths, whose tragedy was that by grasping too eagerly at the fruits of the Roman peace they inevitably tore the peace itself to shreds. In the East the Greeks finally seized the reins of power that had slipped from Cleopatra's grasp half a millennium earlier, but it was now an introspective, insular, faithfully Christian metamorphosis of Greekness, which frittered away its energies on abstruse and futile arguments about the duality of God and Christ. Literally, the ordinary people in the streets would enthusiastically dispute the finer points of the inter-relationships between the Father, the Son and the Holy Ghost with their friends and neighbours, in much the same way that people nowadays discuss the twists of the plots of their favourite soap operas. Although in places like Alexandria the transition was more or less seamless, the East bereft of Rome and sundered from the West has become known as the Byzantine Empire after the former name of its capital, Constantinople. It is not without justification that "Byzantine" has also become a byword for intricacy.

For two and a half centuries Alexandria, in common with the other great Byzantine cities, was a religious cauldron that regularly boiled over. In the main the disputes were between various factions or sects among the Christians, for paganism was in its death throes. Nevertheless, Procopius (c. AD562), an official under Justinian, the greatest of the Byzantine emperors, has written that up to his time sacrifices were still made "to Ammon and Alexander the Macedonian" in two cities, both called Augila, located in Libya to the west of Alexandria.[45] Procopius is in fact quite specific that they lay four days' journey south of Boreium, which must be "Boreo" as cited in the African section of the Antonine Itinerary, where it is located 125 Roman miles from Benghazi along

---

[45] Procopius of Caesarea, *On Buildings* 6.2.9-20.

the road to Carthage.[46] He describes this place as the most westward city of the Pentapolis, a group of five towns in the vicinity of modern Benghazi. There is a modern town called "El Agheila" on the Gulf of Sirte close to the site of Boreium and an oasis 100 miles SE of it called "Awjilah" in approximately the position described by the Byzantine author. In fact Herodotus also mentions an oasis of Augila ten days' journey west of the oasis of Ammonium (i.e. Siwa).[47] Nonetheless, some have instead confused these cities with the Siwa oasis itself, because of Alexander's visit to receive the oracle of Ammon in 331 BC and by virtue of his deathbed request that his body should be taken to Ammon.[48]

Also in this period there seems to have existed a church in Alexandria dedicated to "Saint Alexander".[49] Naturally enough, this has excited the interest of some tomb-hunters, who deduce that this building may have been erected on the site of the Soma Mausoleum. However, it is singularly improbable that the Alexander in question was the city's founder, since John Chrysostom's attitude to Alexander typifies the hostile opinions of contemporaneous Christian theologians. A much more credible candidate would be the Patriarch Alexander, who was appointed in AD312-313 in the wake of the great persecutions of the Christians by Diocletian and Galerius. He was very popular with the Alexandrians, whom he led in fierce opposition to the so-called Arian heresy.[50]

By the early 7th century Byzantine control of Alexandria was inexorably loosening. In AD618 yet another Persian invasion succeeded in capturing the city. Although it remained in their hands for a decade, the emperor Heraclius eventually managed to drive them out of Egypt and even went so far as to conquer the Persian capital in requital. However, another bitter schism had opened between the Christian factions in Alexandria: the pro-imperial Melkites were implacably opposed to the Jacobites, who were the ancestors of the modern Copts. The Persians had encouraged the latter during their occupation, so they were much in the ascendant when the city was recovered; a factor that significantly weakened Constantinople's commitment to its Egyptian province.[51]

In the 630's with irresistible fervour and honed steel the tribes of Arabia burst upon the Byzantine Empire in full Jihad. The Prophet Mohammed had died in Medina in AD632, having preached a holy war against the Byzantines, and now the followers of the new Islamic religion were determined to convey his revelations to the infidels. After the precipitous fall of Syria and Palestine, in AD639 the Arab general 'Amr ibn al As set out with a small force perhaps just

---

[46] See Otto Cuntz, *Itineraria Romana*, Teubner, 1929.
[47] See Dr John Ball, *Egypt in the Classical Geographers*, Government Press, Cairo, 1942, p. 21.
[48] E.g. Liana Souvaltzis.
[49] John Marlowe, *The Golden Age of Alexandria*, 1971, Chapter 11.
[50] John Marlowe, *The Golden Age of Alexandria*, Chapter 13; there was also a Christian named Alexander, who was martyred at Alexandria in the purges of the mid third century – see Eusebius, *Ecclesiastical History* 6.41.
[51] John Marlowe, *The Golden Age of Alexandria*, Chapter 15.

Vanished from History

4000 strong to march across the Sinai desert under orders from the Caliph Omar to invade Egypt. Coming upon the impressive Roman fortress of Babylon (Figure 6.4) near modern Cairo at the apex of the Nile Delta, he was moved to call for reinforcements. With an enlarged army about 15,000 strong he engaged and vanquished the Byzantine forces near Heliopolis. The remnants of the imperial army retreated to shelter behind Babylon's tall defences. In the light of the difficult military situation the Patriarch Cyrus proposed to Heraclius that Alexandria should be surrendered to the Arabs on terms that permitted the evacuation of the leading citizens and most of the city's treasures. The emperor indignantly refused and recalled the Patriarch to Constantinople. But no imperial reinforcements were dispatched and Heraclius died shortly after Cyrus arrived. Following the storming of Babylon after a prolonged siege on Good Friday AD641 and with Constantinople embroiled in factional disputes over the succession, Cyrus was authorised to negotiate as best he could with the Arabs and so he sailed back to Alexandria in the early autumn. A peace treaty with 'Amr was concluded in November of AD641. It provided for an eleven-month armistice, during which all who wished to do so were permitted to leave the city together with their transportable property. It further guaranteed the status and religious freedom of any who remained. The document was ratified by the new child emperor, Heraclonas, late in November, shortly before his elimination by Valentine, the army chief in Asia Minor.[52]

When 'Amr eventually entered Alexandria in September AD642, he found a city which retained much of the magnificence of its glorious past. His report to the Caliph ran thus: "I have taken a city of which I can but say that it contains 4000 palaces, 4000 baths, 400 theatres, 1200 gardens and 40,000 tributary Jews (actually Christians?)."[53] One of his soldiers was literally bedazzled: "The moonlight reflected from the white marble made the city so bright that a tailor could see to thread his needle without a lamp. No one entered the city without covering over his eyes to veil him from the glare of the plaster and marble."[54] And so it was, after nearly a millennium as the greatest of Greek cities, with the impotent complicity of the Byzantine throne, Alexandria was Greek no more.

As Eliot has written, thus it is that the world ends: not with a bang but a whimper.

---

[52] Alan K. Bowman, *Egypt After the Pharaohs*, Chapter 2; Butler, *The Arab Conquest of Egypt and the Last Thirty Years of the Roman Dominion*, Oxford, 1902, p. 304 *et seq*.
[53] Haas, *Alexandria in Late Antiquity*, p. 113; J. Marlowe, *The Golden Age of Alexandria*, p.13; Butler, *The Arab Invasion of Egypt...*, has "12000 sellers of green vegetables" instead of "1200 gardens".
[54] Butler, *The Arab Invasion of Egypt and the Last 30 Years of the Roman Dominion*, Ch. 24, quoting from the Arab writer Sujuti.

Figure 6.4. The ruins of the Roman fortress of Babylon near Cairo c. 1799 as depicted in the Description de l'Egypte (author's collection)

7. The Mysteries of the Mosques

When suddenly there is heard at midnight
A company passing invisible
With wondrous music, with voices,
Your fortune giving way now, your works
All turned to illusions, do not mourn vainly.
As one long since prepared, courageously,
Say farewell to her, to Alexandria who is leaving.
Above all do not be fooled, never say it was
All a dream, and that your hearing was deceived;
Do not stoop to such vain hopes as these.
As one long since prepared, courageously,
As becomes one worthy as you were of such a city,
Firmly draw near the window,
And listen with feeling, but not
With the complaints and entreaties of cowards,
Listen, your last enjoyment, to the sounds,
The exquisite instruments of the mystic troupe,
And say farewell, farewell to Alexandria you are losing.

Constantine Cavafy, 1911

The character of Alexandria was greatly altered under the auspices of the Islamic Caliphate. The Graeco-Roman city of spacious marble colonnades and monumental classical architecture in a rectilinear street plan was already much decayed in the Byzantine period. But the Christians of the Empire had been energetic builders of illustrious churches with vast, echoing interior spaces capped by domes and vaulted ceilings and embellished with glinting cupolas. With the arrival of the Arabs, however, this architecture too steadily crumbled to rubble to be replaced by the multitudinous mosques and bazaars of a typical Middle-Eastern trading city, all presided over by the continual song of the muezzins perched in the pinnacles of a hundred minarets.

It is thought that the architecture of these minarets – a square base supporting an octagonal middle section surmounted by a cylindrical turret (see Figure 7.1) – was inspired by the design of the Pharos lighthouse, which continued to dominate the skyline of the port. Indeed, the Arabic term *manarah* for the Pharos seems to have been the origin of the word minaret.[1]

Ostensibly surprisingly, the Arabic rulers seem to have been more tolerant of the memory of Alexander than their Christian predecessors. This may be because Alexander appears as a kind of prophet in the Islamic holy book, the

---

[1] Alfred Butler, *The Arab Conquest of Egypt and the Last Thirty Years of the Roman Dominion*, p. 398.

The Quest for the Tomb of Alexander by Andrew Chugg

Koran (or Quran), in the guise of Dulkarnein[2] (or Dhulkarnein or Dzoul Karnein or Dhul-Qarnain… the transliteration of Arabic names into English is notoriously erratic). This title translates to something like "Two-Horned Lord" and evidently derives from Alexander's appurtenances on the widely circulated coins of his generals Ptolemy, Seleucus and Lysimachus, where he variously wears the ram's horns of Ammon, a helmet with bull's horns and a headdress fashioned from the skin of an elephant fully furnished with tusks.[3]

Some time in the 9th century, but prior to his death in 871 AD, the Arab historian Ibn Abdel Hakim compiled an account of the mosques then existing in Alexandria. Among them he recorded, "The Mosque of Dulkarnein, situated near the Gate of the City and its exit."[4] Furthermore, in the next century, AD954 to be exact, the commentator Al-Massoudi wrote: "And his [burial] place made of marble, known as the tomb of Alexander, remains *in situ* in the city of Alexandria in the country of Egypt to this day."[5] Since they wrote within a century of one another, they could be describing the same shrine. Hakim's account is especially interesting, because he probably wrote shortly before the revamping of the walls of Alexandria by Sultan Ibn Tulun.[6] According to Mahmoud Bey's map, the main Graeco-Roman crossroads of Alexandria, which is the most likely vicinity for the Soma, lay just within the main eastern gate in these fortifications. The shrine seems to be too minor to be the Soma Mausoleum itself, which probably no longer existed, but the relatively early date and the tentative association with the location suggested by the Greek accounts makes it feasible that it had indeed been constructed at the remembered site of Alexander's tomb. From the opposite point of view, it also tends to reinforce the theory that the Soma Mausoleum was situated near the main crossroads.

Al-Massoudi's account is even more tantalizing. Was he perhaps referring to the Nectanebo II sarcophagus in mentioning a marble tomb?

---

[2] Surah 18 of the *Koran*, "The Cave"; it should be noted that Al-Maqrizi in his *Khilat* flatly denies the identification of Alexander with Dulkarnein, but Leo Africanus believed Alexander to have appeared in the *Koran*; see in general Vassilios Christides, "The Tomb of Alexander the Great in Arabic Sources" in *Studies in Honour of Clifford Edmund Bosworth, Part I, Hunter of the East*, edited by Ian Richard Netton, 2000, pp. 165-173.
[3] Otto Mørkholm, *Early Hellenistic Coinage from the Accession of Alexander the Great to the Peace of Apamea*, 1991.
[4] P. Fraser, *Ptolemaic Alexandria*, Section 1 of Note 86 to Chapter 1; James Holmes, private communication, November 2005, suggests that Ibn Ayash al-Qitbani noted two mosques of Dulkarnein or "Al-Khadr", one by the city gate and the other by the "Soma" in the old Souq.
[5] Al-Massoudi, *Muruj* I, 253; see Vassilios Christides, "The Tomb of Alexander the Great in Arabic Sources" in *Studies in Honour of Clifford Edmund Bosworth, Part I, Hunter of the East*, edited by Ian Richard Netton, 2000, p. 170.
[6] The dates for Sultan Ibn Tulun are AD868-84 (see, for example, Jean-Yves Empereur, *Alexandria Rediscovered*, p. 86), so the Tulunid walls most probably post-date Hakim. However, there is reason to suppose that the eastern gate of the city was in the same place even before the construction of the Tulunid walls: there remains a fragment of a Ptolemaic/Roman wall abutting the Arab fortifications 200m north of the site of this gate today.

The Mysteries of the Mosques

Following Hakim's and Al-Massoudi's observations there is a gap of fully five centuries before anything more is heard of Alexander's tomb. This was a period of gentle decline for Alexandria, due to the establishment of the new Arab capital of Egypt at Cairo and the diminution of Mediterranean trade in consequence of the political and religious divide between its northern and southern shores. The commercial climate eventually began to improve in the wake of the Veneto-Ottoman Treaty of 1517, when also the Ottoman Sultan took over the government of Egypt from the Mamelukes.

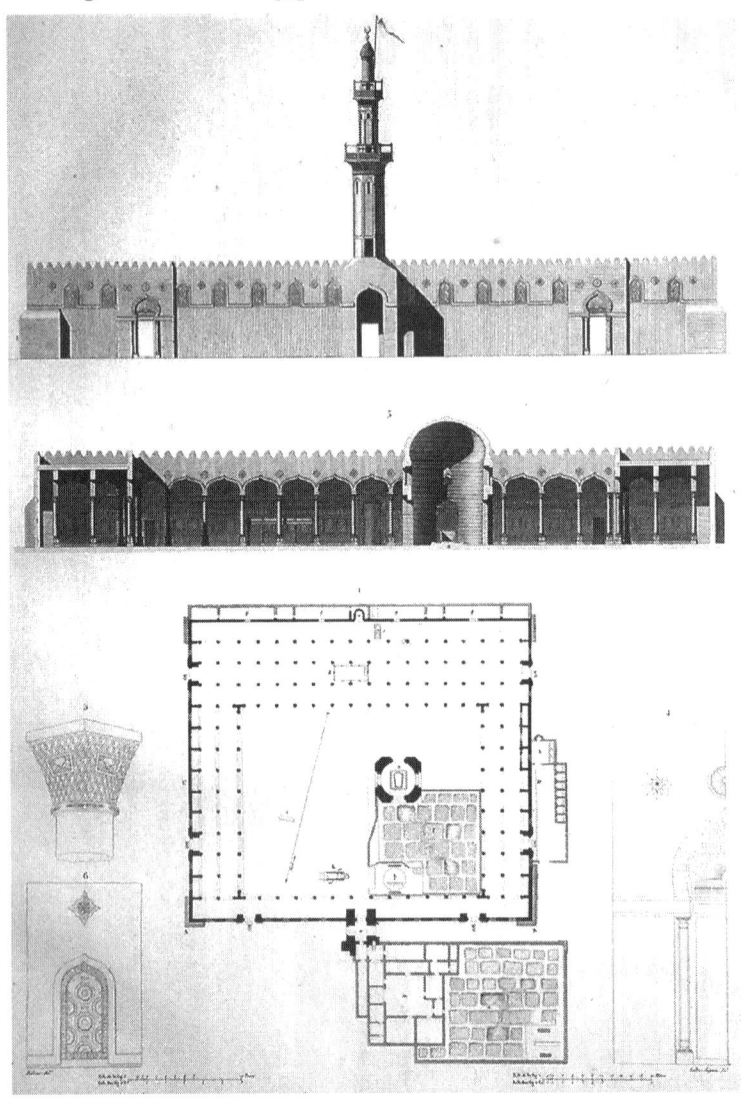

Figure 7.1. Plan, section and side elevation of the Attarine Mosque as seen in Alexandria in 1798 by the scholars of Napoleon's expedition (from the Description de L'Egypte, Planche 38 in Antiquités V – author's collection)

134

The Quest for the Tomb of Alexander by Andrew Chugg

Early in the 16th century another Arab writer, Leo Africanus (1494/5-1552), reported the existence of Alexander's tomb in Alexandria.[7] The following extract derives from an Italian translation made in 1550 of the lost Arabic manuscript of 1526 for his *Description of Africa*:

It should not be omitted, that in the middle of the city amongst the ruins may be seen a little house in the form of a chapel, in which is a tomb much honoured by the Mahometans; since it is asserted that within it is kept the corpse of Alexander the Great, grand prophet and King, as may be read in the Koran. And many strangers come from distant lands to see and venerate this tomb, leaving at this spot great and frequent alms.[8]

The Spanish traveller Marmol visited Alexandria in 1546. His account of the tomb of Alexander, which also locates it in a house in the form of a temple in the centre of the city amongst ruins, almost paraphrases the words of Leo Africanus, adding only that Alexander was called "Escander".[9] However, contrary to several later authors, Marmol did not write that this chapel lay near the Church of St Mark: he merely mentioned the chapel immediately after describing the Church.[10] In addition, George Sandys, who visited the city in AD1611,[11] and Michael Radzivill Sierotka (AD1582-4)[12] have provided much the same account in similar words. The parallels are so striking, in fact, as to suggest a connection between the various descriptions: probably the sixteenth and early seventeenth century visitors were using a version of Leo Africanus as their guidebook.

The most significant feature of Leo's description in comparison with that of Ibn Abdel Hakim is its location of the tomb in the centre of Alexandria. This is difficult to reconcile with a location near an important exit gate, so it seems unlikely that the tomb cited by Leo (and his 16th century plagiarists) is in the same place as Ibn Abdel Hakim's Mosque of Dulkarnein. Leo's mention of the importance of the tomb as a source of alms from tourists indicates that the Alexandrians had a strong financial interest in maintaining a tomb of Alexander. The cynical view might be that a suitable shrine would have been established for the sake of the local tourism industry, whether or not the natives had any genuine knowledge of the tomb's location. Conversely, if a mysterious ancient

---

[7] Leo Africanus made several visits to Egypt between ~1515-20; his account of Alexandria was drafted in 1526; an English translation by J. Pory was republished in London in 1896.
[8] Leo Africanus, *Descrizione dell'Africa*, ed. Ramusio, 1550, f. 89ʳ.
[9] Perrot (translator into French), *L'Afrique de Marmol*, Paris, 1677, Tom. III, liv. xi, c. 14, p. 276; in Arabic translation Alexander is variously rendered: Escander, Iscander, Secander, Iskender, Scander, etc. The reason seems to be that "Al" is the Arabic definite article "the", so it can appear logical to drop it to produce a plain Arabic version of the name.
[10] P. Fraser, *Ptolemaic Alexandria*, Section 1 of Note 86 to Chapter 1.
[11] George Sandys, *Relation of a Journey begun in AD 1610*, London, 1617, p.112: "There is yet to be seene a little Chappell: within, a tombe, much honoured and visited by the Mahometans, where they bestow their alms; supposing his [Alexander's] body to lie in that place: Himselfe reputed a great Prophet, and informed thereof by their *Alcoran*."
[12] *Hierosolymitana peregrinatio illustrissimi domini Nicolai Christopheri Radzivilli,…Ex idiomate Polonica in latinum linguam translate… Thorma trelere interprete*, Brunsbergae, 1601 [and Polish, Krakow, 1925].

The Mysteries of the Mosques

sarcophagus had been preserved with a traditional association with Alexander's sepulcher, then it would surely have remained the focus for religious and commercial exploitation.

* * * * * * * *

In AD1570 Ortelius published his *Theatrum Orbis Terrarum* (Theatre of the World), the first modern atlas. Two years later, apparently as a companion volume to Ortelius' *magnum opus*, Georg Braun and Frans Hogenberg of Cologne published their *Civitates Orbis Terrarum* (Cities of the World), comprising plans of most of the prominent cities then known. Among them was a lovely map of Alexandria (Figure 7.2).

Braun and Hogenberg's plan is not the earliest known. It was preceded by Ugo Comminelli's panorama in the Codex Urbinate of 1472 (Figure 10.2) and several early sixteenth century plans. However, theirs is probably the most seductive of the antique images of the metropolis, providing as it does a vivid, if slightly impressionistic, insight into the layout and atmosphere of the late medieval city. It seems to have been based on reasonably good first-hand information supplied to the cartographers by the Cologne merchant, Constantin van Lyskirchen.[13] Its accuracy is limited by various distortions of scale and perspective, but it faithfully reproduces certain zigzags in the Tulunid walls and numerous other authentic details. Pompey's Pillar is depicted in its top left beyond the walls and the fort of Qait Bey is shown on the right-hand of the two promontories, which enfold the Great Harbour. The Mameluke Sultan whose name it bears erected this fort in AD1477-80 on the foundations of the ruined Pharos lighthouse. The Pharos itself had been progressively damaged and reduced by a succession of earthquakes from AD796 onwards. The most destructive seems to have occurred on 8th August 1303, after which little was left standing.[14]

Close inspection of the exact centre of Braun and Hogenberg's panorama (Figure 7.3) reveals the arcane legend *Domus Alexandri Magni*, which is Latin for

---

[13] A Hanse merchant by the name of Constantin van Lyskirchen, colocated in Cologne with Braun and Hogenberg, supplied views of many towns in Asia and Africa to them including Alexandria. Braun & Hogenberg may have used other sources as well. According to Oscar Norwich in *Norwich's Maps of Africa, an illustrated and annotated carto-bibliography*, edited by Jeffery Stone, Norwich, Vermont, Terra Nova Press, 1997, p. 380: "in the Hanse merchant Constantin van Lyskirchen of Cologne the editors found a willing agent, who supplied views of the towns of India, Asia, Africa, and Persia never portrayed before." According to Norwich, "Lyskirchen obtained these views from the manuscript produced by an unknown Portuguese illustrator." He goes on to say, "apart from these Portuguese views, some of the African illustrations were taken from military plans concerned with the expeditions of the Emperor Charles V in 1535 and 1541 to Tunis and Algeria." Braun's & Hogenberg's plates subsequently passed to Jansson, so the Alexandria map was republished in his famous Atlas of 1619.
[14] Jean-Yves Empereur, *Alexandria Rediscovered*, Chapter 4, The Seventh Wonder of the World; Moustafa Anouar Taher, "Les séismes á Alexandrie et la destruction du Phare" in *Alexandrie Médiévale* 1, ed. Christian Décobert and Jean-Yves Empereur, Institut Français d'Archéologie Orientale, 1998.

The Quest for the Tomb of Alexander by Andrew Chugg

"House of Alexander the Great".[15] This wording especially recalls the accounts of Marmol and Leo Africanus, both of whom describe Alexander's tomb as lying within a house (*casa* in the Italian and Spanish source manuscripts). This caption appears to refer to a modest octagonal building with a domed roof, which sits next to the minaret of a mosque at the righthand corner of the central cluster of buildings a little to the north of the line of Canopic Way (north lying towards the lower margin of the image in this antique plan). Given the fact that this map was engraved just a few decades after Leo's and Marmol's visits, it is very likely that this building is a representation of the same tomb of Alexander to which these travellers had referred.

Figure 7.2. Plan of Alexandria engraved in about 1575 by Braun & Hogenberg (author's collection)

*   *   *   *   *   *   *   *

In the mid-to-late 18th century a number of European travellers reported the existence of a tomb inside a small shrine within the courtyard of the Attarine Mosque in Alexandria (see Figure 7.9 for its location). However, Richard Pococke in 1737 could glean "no account of it", whereas Van Egmont with John Heyman failed to gain entry, since infidels were debarred from admission

---

[15] Some later followers of Braun & Hogenberg appear to have misread this caption as "the big house of Alexandria" and translated it as "maison de ville" (Town Hall): e.g. Dapper 1670; Calmet 1730.

The Mysteries of the Mosques

by the religious authorities at that time. Nevertheless, the intrepid Eyles Irwin managed to enter secretly in 1777 and Sonnini visited the shrine some time a little before 1780 by means of bribery. A little afterwards in 1792 W. G. Browne inspected it. All provided accounts in their travelogues, yet none of them seems to have explicitly linked the shrine with Alexander.[16]

Figure 7.3. Detail of the centre of the plan of Alexandria by Braun & Hogenberg of ~1575 (author's collection)

*   *   *   *   *   *   *   *

Alexandria emerged from its medieval torpor and obscurity, becoming fully accessible to the inquisitive gaze of the modern world in 1798 with the arrival of Napoleon Bonaparte in Egypt. He was escorted by a powerful army and accompanied by a team of scholars and scientists, whom he commissioned to compile a magnificent survey of the country called the "Description de l'Egypte". It incorporates a thousand of the finest engravings ever made, amongst which twenty-nine plates provide a matchless record of Alexandria at the close of the eighteenth century.

Napoleon's expedition came to grief at the "Battle of the Nile", when the English fleet under Nelson virtually annihilated his escorting men o'war whilst they lay at anchor in Aboukir Bay. Nonetheless the French expeditionary force

---

[16] Richard Pococke, *Description of the East*, 1743, vol. i, p. 4; Van Egmont and Heyman's *Travels*, 1759, vol. ii, p. 133; Eyles Irwin, *A Series of Adventures...*, i, 1780, p. 367; Sonnini, *Travels in Upper and Lower Egypt*, vol. i, p. 67, edit. London, 1800; W.G. Browne, *Travels in Africa, Egypt and Syria*, 1799, p. 6.

The Quest for the Tomb of Alexander by Andrew Chugg

remained in Egypt for three years until they were ultimately routed by the English under General Abercrombie in a land battle just to the east of Alexandria in March 1801.[17] In 1799 Napoleon's *savants* discovered the famous Rosetta Stone with simultaneous texts in Hieroglyphs, Demotic and Greek of a proclamation marking the first anniversary of the coronation of Ptolemy V. It was ceded to the British upon the final surrender of Alexandria in September 1801. During their stay, the French scholars, Vivant Denon and Dolomieux, had also discovered the small octagonal building in the courtyard of the Attarine Mosque in Alexandria (Figure 7.4). Circumstances suggest that the Egyptians confided that it was venerated as the tomb of Alexander.[18] It contained a substantial and magnificent, but disappointingly empty green granite-breccia sarcophagus weighing seven tonnes and inscribed across its entire exterior surface with hieroglyphic text (Figure 7.5). Around a dozen holes had been crudely drilled through its sides to the bottom edge of its interior, thus converting it to a cistern for providing streams of water for the ritual ablutions of the worshippers at the mosque. This relic too was subsequently secured by the British and shipped to the British Museum in 1802 by Edward Daniel Clarke, who published his account of it in a book entitled "The Tomb of Alexander" in 1805.[19] Concerning his discovery of the sarcophagus in 1801, he explained how both its whereabouts and its identity were made known to him:-

We had scarcely reached the house in which we were to reside, when a party of the merchants of the place, who had heard the nature of our errand, came to congratulate us on the capture of Alexandria, and to express their anxiety to serve the English. As soon as the room was clear of other visitants, speaking with great circumspection and in a low voice, they asked if our business in Alexandria related to the antiquities collected by the French? Upon being answered in the affirmative, and, in proof of it, the copy of the Rosetta Stone being produced, the principal of them said, 'Does your Commander in Chief know that they have the Tomb of Alexander?' We desired them to describe it; upon which they said it was a beautiful green stone, taken from the mosque of St Athanasius; which, among the inhabitants, had always borne that appellation. Our letter and instructions from Caïro evidently referred to the same monument. 'It is the object,' they continued, 'of our present visit; and we will shew you where they have concealed it.' They then related the measures used by the French; the extraordinary care they had observed to prevent any intelligence of it; the indignation shewn by the Mahometans at its removal; the veneration in which they held it; and the tradition familiar to all of them respecting its origin. I conversed afterwards with several of the Mahometans, both Arabs and Turks, on the same subject; not only those who were natives and inhabitants of the

---

[17] Brian Lavery, *Nelson and The Nile*, Chatham Publishing, 1998, pp. 298-300.
[18] Vivant Denon in the company of Dolomieux arrived with Napoleon's expedition on 4th July 1798: Vivant Denon, *Travels in Upper and Lower Egypt*, 1802; this account omits mention of Alexander's name, but it appears from subsequent events and the great secrecy with which they proceeded that the French were at some point told about the connection between the sarcophagus and Alexander.
[19] E.D. Clarke, *The Tomb of Alexander, a dissertation on the sarcophagus from Alexandria and now in the British Museum*, Cambridge, 1805.

The Mysteries of the Mosques

city, but also dervises and pilgrims; persons from Constantinople, Smyrna, and Aleppo, who had visited, or who resided in Alexandria; and they all agreed in one uniform tradition, namely, ITS BEING THE TOMB OF ISCANDER *(Alexander),* THE FOUNDER OF THE CITY OF ALEXANDRIA. *We were then told it was in the hold of an hospital ship, in the inner harbour; and being provided with a boat, we there found it, half filled with filth, and covered with the rags of the sick people on board.*

In his later travelogue relating his adventures in the eastern Mediterranean Clarke specified that the hospital ship was *La Cause*.[20]

Figure 7.4. The courtyard of the Attarine Mosque in 1798 with the chapel containing the sarcophagus in an engraving from the Description de L'Egypte, Antiquités V, Planche 39 (author's collection)

In the early 19th century many were convinced by Clarke's arguments that the sarcophagus in the British Museum was indeed that of Alexander the Great, although his book does not provide any hard evidence in support of this conclusion beyond the assertions of the local merchants.[21] The edition of *The British Critic* for October 1805 in reviewing Clarke's dissertation summed up, "Thus concludes the evidence adduced by Dr Clarke, which, after all possible deductions, must be allowed to amount to a considerable degree of probability."

---

[20] E.D. Clarke, *Travels in Various Countries of Europe, Asia and Africa, Part 2: Greece, Egypt and the Holy Land*, Section 2 (Vol. 5), 4th Edition, 1817 (original preface dated 24th May, 1814), p.337.
[21] However, criticism from the "Conductors of the Edinburgh Review" prompted Clarke to publish an open 8-page *Letter addressed to the Gentlemen of the British Museum by the Author of the Dissertation on the Alexandrian Sarcophagus*, Cambridge, 28th September, 1807.

The Quest for the Tomb of Alexander by Andrew Chugg

However, a fresh twist in the tale came in 1822, when, through studying the inscriptions on the Rosetta Stone, Champollion deduced how to decipher Egyptian Hieroglyphs, which had remained utterly unintelligible for a dozen centuries. When the hieroglyphs on the sarcophagus were translated, the sacred Egyptian text of the *Amduat* – The Book of What is in the Underworld - was revealed, liberally scattered with the cartouches of Nectanebo II, the last native Egyptian pharaoh. He had been overthrown by the Persians, whilst Alexander was still a boy in 343BC. Since the decipherment, it has usually been assumed that the attribution of the sarcophagus makes its purported use by Ptolemy for Alexander unlikely. However, it may now be shown that there are some striking pieces of circumstantial evidence, which reinforce its association with the King, but of which Clarke was unaware.

Figure 7.5. The sarcophagus inscribed for Nectanebo II found in the chapel in the courtyard of the Attarine Mosque in an engraving from Clarke's *Tomb of Alexander* (author's collection)

Firstly, Clarke's book contains an engraving (Figure 7.6), prepared from a drawing by the French scholar Vivant Denon, of the courtyard of the Attarine Mosque depicting the small octagonal building, which housed the sarcophagus, being venerated by several Islamic worshippers.[22] It bears close comparison with the "House of Alexander the Great" situated beside a mosque at the exact centre of Braun and Hogenberg's map. Furthermore, the location of the mosque in this map matches the actual position of the Attarine Mosque within the Arab city. It would seem that the shrine in the Attarine Mosque and the tomb of Alexander in the "little house in the form of a chapel" described by Leo Africanus are almost certainly one and the same. Previously, this has been

---

[22] There are also a number of views and plans of the Attarine Mosque and the sarcophagus in the *Description de l'Egypte: Antiquités*, Vol. 5, plates 35, 38-41.

The Mysteries of the Mosques

doubted, mainly because the significance of the *Domus Alexandri Magni* legend has not been properly recognized, due to its mistranslation as "Town Hall". However, it should now be clear that the association of the sarcophagus with Alexander dates back at least as far as the medieval period.

Figure 7.6. The octagonal chapel in the courtyard of the Attarine Mosque worshipped by the Arabs in 1798, from *The Tomb of Alexander* by E.D. Clarke (author's collection)

Secondly, in the Byzantine period it is believed that the Church of St Athanasius stood on the site of the Attarine Mosque, the name of which is derivative from Athanasius.[23] Intriguingly, this Athanasius was Patriarch of Alexandria in AD365, when the tsunami struck. The Late Roman church that originally stood on the site of the Attarine Mosque was probably constructed just decades after the most likely date for the destruction of the Soma mausoleum. If Athanasius had arranged for the rescue of Alexander's remains from beneath the rubble of the Soma, then this could explain how the sarcophagus ended up in a church bearing his dedication. However, a skein of doubt arises from the fact that Athanasius had been a protégé of the preceding Patriarch, who had happened to

---

[23] P. Fraser, *Ptolemaic Alexandria*, Section 2 of Note 86 to Chapter 1; the Attarine mosque building seen by Napoleon's scholars was probably an 11th century construction, since its foundation inscriptions give the date AD1084: *Corpus Inscript. Arabic.*, Egypte I, No. 518; *Bull. Inst. Egypt.* XXIV, p.147 et seq.; it remains possible that the courtyard chapel was older; Sonnini, *Travels in Upper and Lower Egypt*, vol. i, p. 67, edit. Lond. 1800, saw a Greek inscription in Roman letters, of which he could read only the single word "CONSTANTINON", on the pavement beside the tomb, which presumably derived from the antecedent church.

be named Alexander.[24] Could the tomb of the Patriarch Alexander have become confused with the tomb of the city's founder? This might seriously be contemplated were it not for the fact that it would have been anathema for a Christian Patriarch to be entombed in the pagan sarcophagus of a pharaoh, whereas there are strong circumstantial links between Nectanebo's sarcophagus and Alexander the Great.

The Attarine tomb languished in the obscurity of disproof and the mosque itself, including the "House of Alexander the Great", was destroyed in 1830, and then entirely rebuilt on an adjacent site in the second half of the 19th century.[25] However, an interesting attempt was made to resuscitate the Attarine tomb theory in 1948 by Wace.[26] He pointed out that the sarcophagus had probably been available in an unused condition at the time of Alexander's death, because Diodorus states that Nectanebo II fled to Ethiopia in about 341BC to escape the Persian invasion and there is no evidence that he ever returned from this exile.[27] Wace suggested that the use of the sarcophagus for Alexander's corpse instead had been the inspiration for a story in the Alexander Romance that Nectanebo was Alexander's father.[28] He proceeded to explain the presence of the sarcophagus at Alexandria by postulating the existence of an otherwise unattested Egyptian Royal Cemetery on the site prior to the foundation of the Greek city by Alexander.

This Royal Cemetery hypothesis is rather dubious. On the authority of Strabo and the Alexander Romance we know that the town of Rhakotis plus a few other fishing villages occupied the future site of Alexandria in the Late Pharaonic Period.[29] Yet there is no tangible indication of anything of royal status in the vicinity prior to the Ptolemaic era. The main sources on the foundation of Alexandria strongly imply that Alexander chose a largely undeveloped site.

Nevertheless, this need not be an objection to the other aspects of the theory, because, as has been discussed, it is virtually certain that Alexander's original entombment took place at Memphis. The circumstantial evidence favours the idea that the sarcophagus was left at Memphis, possibly at the Serapeum, when Nectanebo fled into exile. For Memphis was the de facto capital of the 30th

---

[24] John Marlowe, *The Golden Age of Alexandria*, 1971, Chapter 13, "Vicisti Galileae", pp.264-78. Athanasius returned to Alexandria after the death of Julian the Apostate in AD363 and remained there until his death in AD373; see also Haas, *Alexandria in Late Antiquity*, Appendix.
[25] Barbara Tkaczow, *Topography of Ancient Alexandria (An Archaeological Map)*, Warsaw 1993, Item 25 in the Catalogue of Sites.
[26] A.J.B. Wace, "The Sarcophagus of Alexander the Great," *Farouk I University, Bulletin of the Faculty of Arts* 4, 1948, pp. 1-11; Wace also refuted a 19th century misapprehension that the cartouches on the sarcophagus were those of Nectanebo I and affirmed the now undisputed fact that they refer to Nectanebo II.
[27] Diodorus Siculus 16.51.
[28] Stoneman (translator), *The Greek Alexander Romance*, 1.1-12.
[29] Strabo 17.1.6; Stoneman (translator), *The Greek Alexander Romance*, 1.31.

The Mysteries of the Mosques

Dynasty pharaohs, whose tombs remain undiscovered; whereas the contemporaneous cemetery and monuments at the Serapeum are suspiciously reminiscent of a Late Period royal funerary complex.

Fraser has observed, "The presence of this mighty sarcophagus in Alexandria is surprising."[30] In fact, it is well established that the Ptolemies transported large numbers of sphinxes, obelisks and similar Pharaonic architectural embellishments to Alexandria. Most, including, for example, Cleopatra's Needles, were robbed from the Egyptian city of Heliopolis, which had fallen into ruin before the Ptolemaic era.[31] However, the only culturally feasible use for a pharaoh's sarcophagus in ancient Egypt would have been the entombment of a king. Indeed, it is likely that its exploitation for any lesser purpose would have been considered sacrilegious by the native Egyptians.[32] It is therefore difficult to imagine that anyone would anciently have gone to the considerable trouble and expense of moving the sarcophagus from Memphis to Alexandria, unless it was their intention to use it for a pharaonic sepulcher. But the Ptolemies all had the opportunity to arrange for carefully customized sarcophagi for themselves. The sole scenario that seems to make sense of the conundrum is to suppose that the tradition concerning this relic is essentially true. It is uniquely Ptolemy Soter who discovered a sudden need for a kingly sarcophagus in 321BC. If Soter had therefore used Nectanebo's empty sarcophagus for Alexander's corpse in the Memphite tomb, then it would subsequently have been transported to Alexandria with Alexander's body by Philadelphus, thus neatly solving the mystery of how it came to rest for millennia in a city, which was not founded until at least a dozen years after it was sculpted.

Regarding the sarcophagus, Fraser concludes, "I do not think it can seriously be maintained that Soter or Philadelphus would have buried the Founder in this manner." Ostensibly this seems reasonable, since it seems extraordinary that Ptolemy should have placed Alexander's remains within a vessel emblazoned with Nectanebo's cartouches. However, a close analysis of the political context of the Memphite entombment reveals that this view is not tenable. At that time Ptolemy was avidly seeking to ingratiate himself with the native Egyptians in order to help in cementing his power base. For example, in the "Satrap Stele" of 311BC he firmly links himself with an Egyptian leader called Khabbash (or Khababash), who seems to have led an insurrection against the hated Persians in about 338-335BC.[33] Furthermore, Ptolemy's son, Philadelphus, is actually

---

[30] P.M. Fraser, *Ptolemaic Alexandria*, Note 86 to Chapter 1.
[31] Jean-Yves Empereur, *Alexandria Rediscovered*, Chapter 6.
[32] The recent suggestion by Nicholas Saunders, *Alexander's Tomb*, pp. 196-198, that one of the early Ptolemies had drilled the holes in the sides of the sarcophagus to transform it into a public fountain to grace the streets of Alexandria is preposterous, because these apertures are punched crudely and arbitrarily through the hieroglyphic text of the *Amduat* - it is equivalent to proposing that the Pope might perforate the text of an antique bible, then display his handiwork in the Vatican Museum.
[33] Alan K. Bowman, *Egypt after the Pharaohs*, British Museum Press, 1986, Chapter 2.

attested to have used an obelisk quarried by Nectanebo for a shrine to his sister-wife, Arsinoë.[34] In these circumstances the association of Alexander's tomb with the last native pharaoh may well have seemed an astute political ploy, especially since it simultaneously circumvented the need for a considerable financial outlay and a delay of several years in order for a fresh sarcophagus to be fashioned.

To recapitulate: the attribution of the sarcophagus to Nectanebo II indicates that it would have been available to Ptolemy in an unused state, when he entombed Alexander at Memphis. It explains how the sarcophagus reached Alexandria and why a group of Greek statues guarded the entrance to the Nectanebo II temple at the Serapeum (Figures 3.7 to 3.9). If we should suppose its association with Alexander's tomb in Alexandria to be a forgery, then the perpetrators were either incredibly fortunate or remarkably sophisticated in their choice of this particular sarcophagus. If the latter, then they needed to be able to read the pharaoh's name in its cartouches, yet hieroglyphics died out at the end of the 4th century AD very shortly after Alexander's Alexandrian tomb was destroyed. This would tend to date the forgery to within a few generations of the existence of the original, but at such an early date Alexandrian records and recollections should still have been sufficiently fresh to expose such a deception. Furthermore, the hypothetical forgers would also have had to arrange the clues at the Nectanebo II temple at Saqqara, which led Dorothy Thompson independently to locate Alexander's first tomb near the semicicle of Greek statues in 1988.[35] This is virtually inconceivable.

It is also vanishingly improbable that later tomb forgers in Alexandria should serendipitously have utilized a sarcophagus with such tantalizing links with Alexander's original Memphite tomb. These considerations combine to compel us to conclude that the vacant Nectanebo sarcophagus really was adopted by Ptolemy to house Alexander's corpse (see also my article published in Greece & Rome in April 2002 and reproduced in Appendix B). An immediate corollary is that the funeral chamber beneath the destroyed Soma Mausoleum was pillaged in late antiquity, probably around the end of the fourth century AD. Most probably at that time too, the sarcophagus and the corpse parted company.

A further implication is that the semicircle of statues at the Serapeum guarded the entrance to the first tomb of Alexander, which was therefore located within the Nectanebo II temple. Returning to Mariette's detailed plan (Figure 7.7) it is apparent that, besides the temple proper, the entrance guarded by the statues also leads via a passage to a small side chamber (marked A). It is possible to fit the Nectanebo sarcophagus within this chamber in the area to the east of its entrance (as indicated), leaving space for a votive sculpture in its western end. Furthermore, there are some hints in the plan of the temple that the side

---

[34] Pliny, *Natural History* 36.14.67.
[35] Dorothy Thompson, *Memphis after the Ptolemies*, 1988, p. 212.

chamber may have been appended subsequent to its original construction. To see this, consider the hypothetical symmetrical outline of the mudbrick (dark grey) drawn over the actual plan in the righthand side of Figure 7.7. This has been positioned such that the outer face of the original southern wall of the temple is placed where the fine masonry (light grey) of the façade ends. When this is done, we discover various intriguing coincidences between the actual wall faces and the hypothetical symmetrical wall faces. For instance, an interior face of the appended chamber coincides with the outer face of the southern wall of the symmetrical temple and one side of the passageway to the appended chamber coincides with its inner face. It is particularly striking that this hypothesis explains various curiosities of the groundplan excavated by Mariette. Notice, for example, the darker grey mudbrick extends less far behind the light grey façade on the south side than on the north side in Mariette's plan, but that in the hypothetical unmodified building this discrepancy did not exist.

It is also pertinent that Mariette shows a side-entrance to the temple at the corner of the southern wall (B in Fig. 7.7). This too was guarded by sculptures: in this instance four lions in the Greek style (2 in Fig. 7.7). Similar lions were a symbol of the Macedonian monarchy and are a prominent feature of the tombs of the Macedonian magnates of the Hellenistic world: e.g. the Lion Tombs of Knidos, Amphipolis and Gerdek Kaya and the Lion of Hamadan.[36] Most significantly of all, we hear from Diodorus that two such lions had guarded the entrance to Alexander's catafalque (Figure 3.1).[37] Clearly the chamber appended to the Nectanebo temple at the Serapeum is an excellent candidate for the specific location of Alexander's first tomb (see also my article in Appendix C).

One other feature of Mariette's plan merits comment. A processional way or *dromos* ran due westwards from the Nectanebo temple to the entrance to the subterranean Bull Galleries of the Serapeum. It was the key axis of the entire Serapeum complex. But notice that Mariette uncovered an entranceway (E in Figure 7.7) on the opposite side of the Nectanebo temple to the *dromos*, yet precisely aligned with it and matching the width of the steps of the temple. If an archaeologist were seeking corroborative evidence for 30th Dynasty royal tombs at the Serapeum, then the area to the east of E should be a high priority target. Mariette was distracted by his discovery of the Bull Galleries and so he never completed the excavation of the foundations behind E.

The use of the Nectanebo II sarcophagus for Alexander's tomb is also consistent with the newly identified comment by Libanius referring to Alexander's corpse having been exhibited in Alexandria in about AD390. The authenticity of the sarcophagus requires that it should have been exhumed from beneath the Soma Mausoleum or its ruins at some point and that it was attributed to Alexander. This step is necessary in order that the sarcophagus

---

[36] Janos Fedak, *Monumental Tombs of the Hellenistic Age*, Toronto, 1990, pp.76-78 & 100.
[37] Diodorus 18.27.1.

The Quest for the Tomb of Alexander by Andrew Chugg

should have found its way into the courtyard of the Attarine Mosque, whilst retaining its association with Alexander. The Libanius reference suggests that the sarcophagus was recovered prior to the final outlawing of paganism in AD391. It sets up the rioting and turmoil that broke out in Alexandria in that year as the most likely occasion for the final disappearance of Alexander's corpse, especially since John Chrysostom and Theodoret both claimed that Alexander's tomb had been lost by the early fifth century.

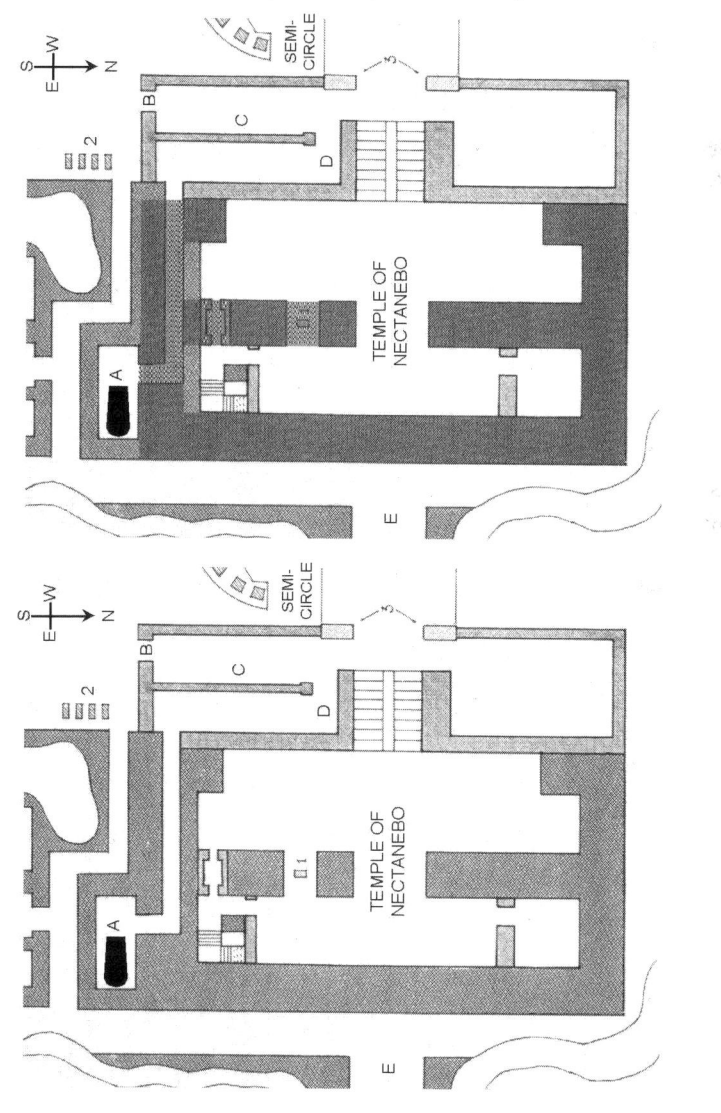

Figure 7.7. Auguste Mariette's detailed plan of the Serapeum – detail of the Nectanebo temple and its hypothetical original groundplan (cf. Figure 3.9)

The Mysteries of the Mosques

Although it is not always recognized today, the people of the ancient world believed Alexander to be an authentic god. In Egypt the pharaoh was always considered to be a deity, but even Greek states, such as Athens and Sparta, awarded Alexander divine honours, whilst he still lived. His successors portrayed the King with divine attributes on their coinage and even as late as the 4th century AD the ordinary folk would wear these medallions as holy charms. There are even reports that the Roman Senate formally elected Alexander as the 13th member of the pantheon of the Olympian gods.

Consequently, his remains were sacred pagan relics. Butler provides a fascinating illustration of the kind of fate that was typically suffered by pagan religious artefacts in fourth century Alexandria, when the Christians seized power. He quotes the Coptic Synaxary and Eutychius to show that the Christian Patriarch of Alexandria under the emperor Constantine - coincidentally also named Alexander - wished to abolish a pagan feast day and destroy an associated statue of Saturn, to which the Alexandrians traditionally offered sacrifices. However, resistance from the populace persuaded him to compromise by retaining the festival as a Christian celebration and by fashioning a cross from the bronze of the statue. We also hear that the Caesareum temple became the Christian cathedral of the city in the mid-fourth century.[38] Popular sentiment often favoured the adaptation and absorption of the pagan legacy in the service of Christianity, in preference to the wanton destruction occasionally perpetrated by the fanatics. This perspective illustrates that those who insist that the Christian authorities must inevitably have destroyed or discarded Alexander's remains are overstating the case.

*   *   *   *   *   *   *   *

Another traditional site for the Soma Mausoleum in Alexandria has gripped the imaginations of successive generations of tomb-hunters even more tenaciously than the story of the sarcophagus in the Attarine Mosque, but perhaps with less justification. This is the Mosque of Nabi Daniel in the modern Nabi Daniel Street (Figure 7.8 & map location in Figure 7.9), which is often marked, rather speculatively, on plans of the ancient city as the "Street of the Soma". Nabi is the Arabic word for a prophet, but the Arab legend of the Prophet Daniel, although probably having its origins in the Old Testament story, differs considerably from the Christian account. It has been traced back to at least the 9th century AD via two Islamic astronomers: Mohammed Ibn Kathir el Farghani and Abou Ma'shar. Their story is faintly relevant, because it has some elements that seem to have been inspired by Alexander's career. In particular, their Daniel was promised victory over all Asia and he acquired support from the Egyptians, founded Alexandria and was buried in a golden sarcophagus in the city, which

---

[38] A. Butler, *The Arab Invasion of Egypt & the Last 30 Years of the Roman Dominion*, Oxford, 1902, p.374 (note); *The Coptic Synaxary*, for 12 Ba'ûnah; Eutychius in J.-P. Migne, *Patrologia Graeca* 111, col. 1005.

The Quest for the Tomb of Alexander by Andrew Chugg

was subsequently stolen by the Jews to mint coins and replaced with a stone casket.

Figure 7.8. The Nabi Daniel Mosque as built in 1823 in an engraving by Rouargue from a drawing of c.1837 by Bartlett (author's collection)

Notwithstanding this traditional basis for the dedication of the mosque, some Islamic scholars have suggested that its name actually derives from a certain Sheikh Mohammed Daniel of Mosul, who lived in Alexandria in the 15th century.[39] He is said to have made the mosque, supposedly previously known as the Mosque of Alexander, into a centre of religious teaching and himself to have been buried within it. The contention of these scholars is that confusion between the Sheikh and the eponymous prophet resulted in the modern designation of the building. This has all the reassuringly homely logic of Kipling's *Just So Stories*.

In fact, the present mosque seems to have been built under the auspices of Mohammed Ali in 1823. However, there are two empty tombs in a subterranean vault under the mosque, which local tradition attributes to the Prophet Daniel and a legendary religious storyteller called Sidi Lokman. This basement appears to be of earlier date than the overlying building. Furthermore, a Russian monk, Vassili Grigorovich Barskij, visited Alexandria in 1727 and 1730 and he identified a small shrine in his plan of the city, which has been proposed as a precursor of the Nabi Daniel Mosque, but other evidence from more accurate maps belies the existence of a substantial building on the exact site in the eighteenth century. However, the ruinous building with a small minaret at the extreme left of Figure 7.8 seems to be an older religious complex located

---

[39] P.M. Fraser, *Ptolemaic Alexandria*, Section 1 of Note 86 to Chapter 1.

The Mysteries of the Mosques

around 100m west of the Nabi Daniel Mosque. It is probably to be identified with the shrine in the Barskij map.

Ambrose Schilizzi, who was a dragoman at the Russian Consulate in Alexandria in the middle of the 19th century, claimed to have gone down into the vault beneath the mosque in 1850, whilst escorting some European travellers.[40] He descended into a narrow and dark subterranean passage and came to a worm-eaten wooden door. Peering through the cracks of the planks he glimpsed a body seated on a throne or somehow raised up in a crystal or glass cage. Its head was crowned with a golden diadem. All around lay papyrus scrolls and books. Schilizzi sought to investigate further, but was dragged away by one of the monks of the mosque.

This exotic tale conflates details from Strabo (for the the crystal sarcophagus), Suetonius (for the diadem left by Augustus) and Dio Cassius (on the secret books gathered by Septimius Severus). However, it is almost certain that papyrus would have perished over such a long period, given Alexandria's dank climate and the fact that capillary action tends to draw dampness upwards through the soil from the water table. No ancient papyri have ever been found in Alexandria.[41] It would appear that Schilizzi was well read among the ancient sources, but his account is quite certainly a shameless hoax.

The Nabi Daniel tradition seems first to have been given written form by Mahmoud Bey. In his book published in Copenhagen in 1872,[42] whilst conceding that this location for Alexander's tomb derives from a purely oral tradition (i.e. hearsay), he nevertheless sought to build on the theory with several further lines of argument (with comments in *italics*):-

a) The site reconciles the statement of Strabo, that the Soma was part of the Royal Quarter, and the description of Achilles Tatius, that the "place called after Alexander" lay at a central crossroads on the Canopic Way. *However, according to Mahmoud Bey's own map the Nabi Daniel Mosque is distant from the principal crossroads, is set well back from Canopic Way and seems too distant from the main palace district readily to be assigned to the Royal Quarter.*

b) The adjacent hill, Kom el-Dikka (from which the view of Figure 7.8 was drawn), means the mosque is on rising ground, which can help to preserve a corpse from the effects of sources of dampness. *But this hill is now known to have been an artificial mound of pottery industry waste underlain by Roman ruins.*

---

[40] Evaristo Breccia, *Alexandrea ad Aegyptum*, 1922, p. 99; A.M. de Zogheb, *Etudes sur l'ancienne Alexandrie*, Paris, 1909, p.170.
[41] E.G. Turner, *Greek Papyri*, Oxford, 1968, p. 43 states that, 'The site of Alexandria has provided no papyri.'
[42] Mahmoud Bey, *Mémoire sur l'antique Alexandrie, ses faubourgs et environs découverts...*, Copenhagen, 1872, Chapter 2, pp. 50-51.

c) Bones dating back to pagan times were found buried in the vicinity of the mosque and a small subterranean tomb chamber with a damaged marble statue was discovered at the foot of the mound on which the mosque is constructed. *Nonetheless, more recent archaeological investigations have shown that none of the nearby inhumations is older than the Christian period.*[43]

d) The Prophet Daniel died long before Alexandria was founded, so he could not have been buried in the city, and he spent nearly all his life in captivity in Babylon. Maybe over time the people confused Alexander with this better-known prophet. *Mahmoud does not actually say so, but he seems to imply that the fact that Alexander also had an association with Babylon may have contributed to the supposed error.*

e) The particular foothill of Kom el-Dikka on which the mosque is built is known as Kom el-Demas, which means the "hill of the bodies" in Arabic, so there is a continuity in the name of the spot, since it was called the Soma (i.e. "body" in Greek). *But, of course, the name could also refer to the two tombs in the crypt of the mosque. Although Mahmoud does not actually mention it, there is also a rather fantastical story in the Alexandrian Synaxary of the erection of a church dedicated to Elias and John on a site called Dimas-Demas, which Breccia states is identical with Kom el-Demas.*[44] *During the clearance of the site a treasure of golden ornaments of the time of Alexander was discovered. However, Vassilios Christides has recently disputed whether "demas" can bear this interpretation in this context and there is anyway no definite connection with the Soma in any of this.*[45]

In addition, de Zogheb tells of a visit by Mahmoud Bey to the vaults beneath the Nabi Daniel Mosque.[46] He entered a large chamber with an arched roof on the ground level of the ancient town. From this paved crypt, inclined corridors ran out in four directions. They were, however, too lengthy and dilapidated for him to survey them properly. He was subsequently forbidden to return and the entrances to the passages were walled up.

De Zogheb also quotes a letter from Yacub Artin Pacha written early in the 20th century attesting to the traditional association of the mosque with the site of Alexander's tomb: *For as long as I can recall, I remember the mosque of Nabi Daniel, and its memory is indissolubly linked in my mind with the name of Alexander the Great; as I have always been told that it contained the tomb of the Macedonian and I also believe that in 1850 this was the general belief in Alexandria.*[47]

---

[43] Jean-Yves Empereur, *Alexandria Rediscovered*, p. 149.
[44] Evaristo Breccia, *Alexandrea ad Aegyptum*, 1922, p. 99.
[45] Vassilios Christides, "The Tomb of Alexander the Great in Arabic Sources" in *Studies in Honour of Clifford Edmund Bosworth, Part I, Hunter of the East*, edited by Ian Richard Netton, 2000, p. 168.
[46] A.M. de Zogheb, *Etudes sur l'ancienne Alexandrie*, Paris, 1909, pp.171-172.
[47] P. Fraser, *Ptolemaic Alexandria*, Section 1 of Note 86 to Chapter 1.

The Mysteries of the Mosques

In 1879 a mason working in the basement of the Nabi Daniel Mosque accidentally broke through into the vaulted chamber. The Cheih of the mosque accompanied him in a brief exploration of an inclined passage. They were able to discern granite monuments with an angular summit, but the Cheih then insisted that they return. The entrance was subsequently walled up and the mason was asked not to reveal the incident.[48]

Inspired by the evocative legend fostered by Mahmoud Bey and de Zogheb, a long succession of archaeologists has excavated in the vicinity of the Nabi Daniel Mosque and across the nearby hill of Kom el-Dikka starting with Hogarth at the end of the 19th century.[49] Even before Hogarth, Schliemann, the famous discoverer of Troy, had failed even to acquire the requisite permit to dig at the site, which had fuelled the rumour of a conspiracy to conceal the tomb.[50] Breccia, who actually excavated in the vault beneath the mosque, found nothing that could be considered antique down to the foundations of the building.[51] Adriani found sections of a Roman street 30 feet beneath Kom el-Dikka and still lower at the level of the water table he uncovered some Ptolemaic wall foundations.[52] More recently in the 1960's, a team of Polish excavators clarified the probable nature of the "passages" discovered beneath the mosque in the 19th century. They confirmed that the building lies above ancient cisterns on two levels, which were fed by artificial water channels.[53] They were also responsible for excavating away the entire hill, discovering only modest Late Roman structures beneath it.

We may reasonably conclude that the excavations have been sufficiently extensive as virtually to rule out the possibility of the Soma having been located beneath the Nabi Daniel Mosque or the nearby hill. It would also appear doubtful, whether the legendary association between this building and the Soma is really any older than the middle of the 19th century. Sadly perhaps, this, the most romantic of the candidate sites for Alexander's tomb, is now among those parts of ancient Alexandria that can safely be excluded from further investigation.

Nonetheless, such mythology is self-perpetuating, quite independent of the restraints of truth and evidence. Many popular guides to Egypt and Alexandria still confidently assert that the Nabi Daniel Mosque overlies the site of the Soma. Even academic archaeologists are not immune to its allure: applications

---

[48] Zogheb, *Etudes sur l'ancienne Alexandrie*, 1909, p.173.
[49] D.G. Hogarth and E.F. Benson, *Egypt Exploration Fund* 1895, pp. 1-33.
[50] Leo Deuel, *The Memoirs of Heinrich Schliemann*, Hutchinson, 1978.
[51] P. Fraser, *Ptolemaic Alexandria*, Note 88 to Chapter 1.
[52] P. Fraser, *Ptolemaic Alexandria*, Note 90 to Chapter 1.
[53] P. Fraser, *Ptolemaic Alexandria*, Note 88 to Chapter 1; M. Rodziewicz, *Les habitations romaines tardives d'Alexandrie*, Centre d'archéologie méditerranéenne de l'Académie Polonaise des Sciences, Warsaw, 1984.

for permits to dig for Alexander's tomb around this mosque were still being received throughout the 1990's.[54]

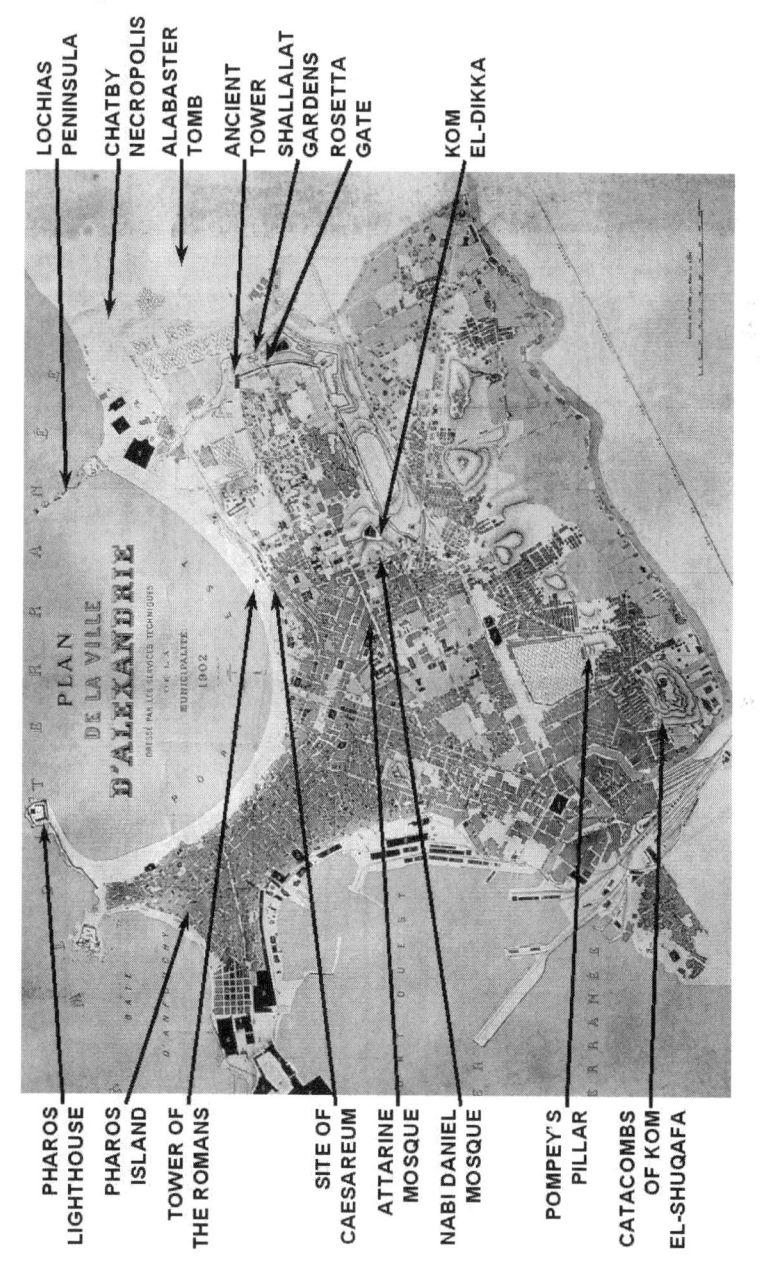

Figure 7.9. Plan of Alexandria in 1902 showing locations of ancient sites

---

[54] Jean-Yves Empereur, *Alexandria Rediscovered*, p. 149.

8. The Astronomer's Chart

*As when it happeneth that some lovely town
Unto a barbarous besieger falls,
Who there by sword and flame himself instals,
And, cruel, it in tears and blood doth drown;
Her beauty spoiled, her citizens made thralls,
His spite yet so cannot her all throw down,
But that some statue, arch, fane of renown
Yet lurks unmaimed within her weeping walls:
So, after all the spoil, disgrace, and wrack,
That time, the world and death could bring combined,
Amidst that mass of ruins they did make,
Safe and all scarless yet remains my mind:
   From this so high transcending rapture springs,
   That I, all else defaced, not envy kings.*

Sonnet XXIV, William Drummond of Hawthornden, 1623

The population of ancient Alexandria probably peaked at around half a million in the first century BC.[1] A larger number than this would have been difficult to accommodate within the known extent of the Ptolemaic city, because the evidence implies that Alexandria lacked high density accommodation such as imperial Rome's multi-storey tenement blocks, the so-called *insulae*. Evidence from ancient papyri suggests a slow decline throughout the Roman period, though probably punctuated by wild swings in consequence of various wars, plagues and natural disasters.[2] By the 4th century AD the figure was probably around 180,000, whilst the vicissitudes of the early 7th century make it seem likely that the "40,000 tributary Jews" mentioned by the Arab general, 'Amr, is actually a loose reference to the total population remaining in the city. In the 9th century the Arab historian Ibn Abdel Hakim gave various estimates of the population at the time of the Arab conquest in the range of hundreds of thousands, but 'Amr would have been in a better position to know the truth. The relative areas of the Ptolemaic and Arab cities, as defined by the circuits of their respective defensive walls, suggests a 9th century population probably below 200,000.[3] Alexandria was languishing ever more deeply in the shadow of the new capital at Cairo and was extensively quarried to recycle luxurious architectural materials to such a degree that by the time of the map of Braun and Hogenberg (mid-sixteenth century) there were huge vacant areas even

---

[1] Diodorus, 18.52.6, gives 300,000 free citizens, which leads to a total around half a million when slaves are added in.
[2] Christopher Haas, *Alexandria in Late Antiquity*, Chapter 3.
[3] For a more detailed survey of the often contradictory evidence on the population of ancient Alexandria see Diana Delia, "The Population of Roman Alexandria", *Transactions of the American Philological Association* 118, 1988, pp. 275-292.

The Quest for the Tomb of Alexander by Andrew Chugg

within the Tulunid walls. Also by this time, the Heptastadion Causeway, which connected the island of Pharos with the mainland, had silted up, producing a broad, flat isthmus between the harbours.

As the old Arab city had suffered irreparable damage from the ravages of time and the stone robbers, the Ottomans, who took over the rule of Egypt from the Mamelukes in 1517, found it expedient to found the town afresh on the virgin soil of the isthmus.[4] This process was already well underway by the time of the excellent map by Razaud dating to 1687 (Figure 8.1).[5] Only a minority of the inhabitants still dwelt within the ancient wall perimeter in villages concentrated near its principal gates. The new town on the isthmus now dominated the port.

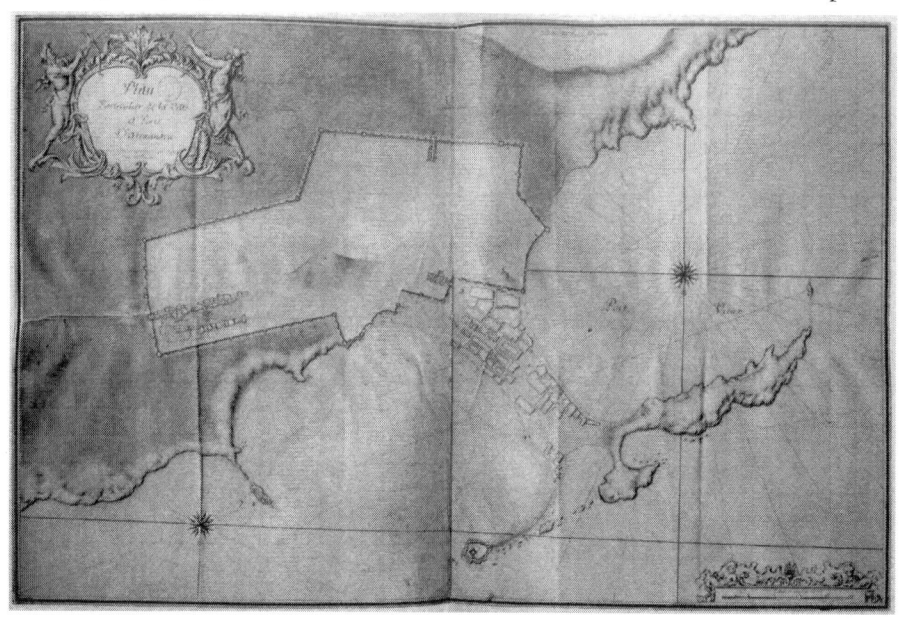

Figure 8.1. The Razaud map of Alexandria in 1687

By the time the French arrived with Napoleon's expedition in 1798 the transition was largely complete and Alexandria had reached the nadir of her fortunes. The map made at this time by Napoleon's Engineers from his Army of the Orient is shown in Figure 8.2. The old, walled Arab city was largely deserted and even the new town on the isthmus only accommodated some five or six thousand inhabitants.[6] In 1806 the residents were estimated to number 6000, but in the 1820's Mohammed Ali began to revitalise the port and the population started to rise rapidly: 12,000 in 1821; 52,000 in 1835; 200,000 in

---

[4] Jean-Yves Empereur, *Alexandria Rediscovered*, Note 2.
[5] Gaston Jondet, *Atlas Historique de la Villes et des Ports d'Alexandrie*, Cairo, 1921, Planche VIII; the Razaud map seems to have formed the basis of several important 18th century French plans of Alexandria, such as those by d'Anville (1766), Savary (1785) & Cassas (1785).
[6] Evaristo Breccia, *Alexandrea ad Aegyptum*, 1922, p. 30.

155

The Astronomer's Chart

1868; and 317,000 in the census of 1897. In about 1920 the figure surpassed the Ptolemaic peak of half a million and by 1960 it had reached thrice that number.[7] In parallel, the urbanised area expanded beyond the confines of the isthmus and spilt inexorably across the ruin fields, obliterating or sealing over the great bulk of the archaeological remains as it spread.

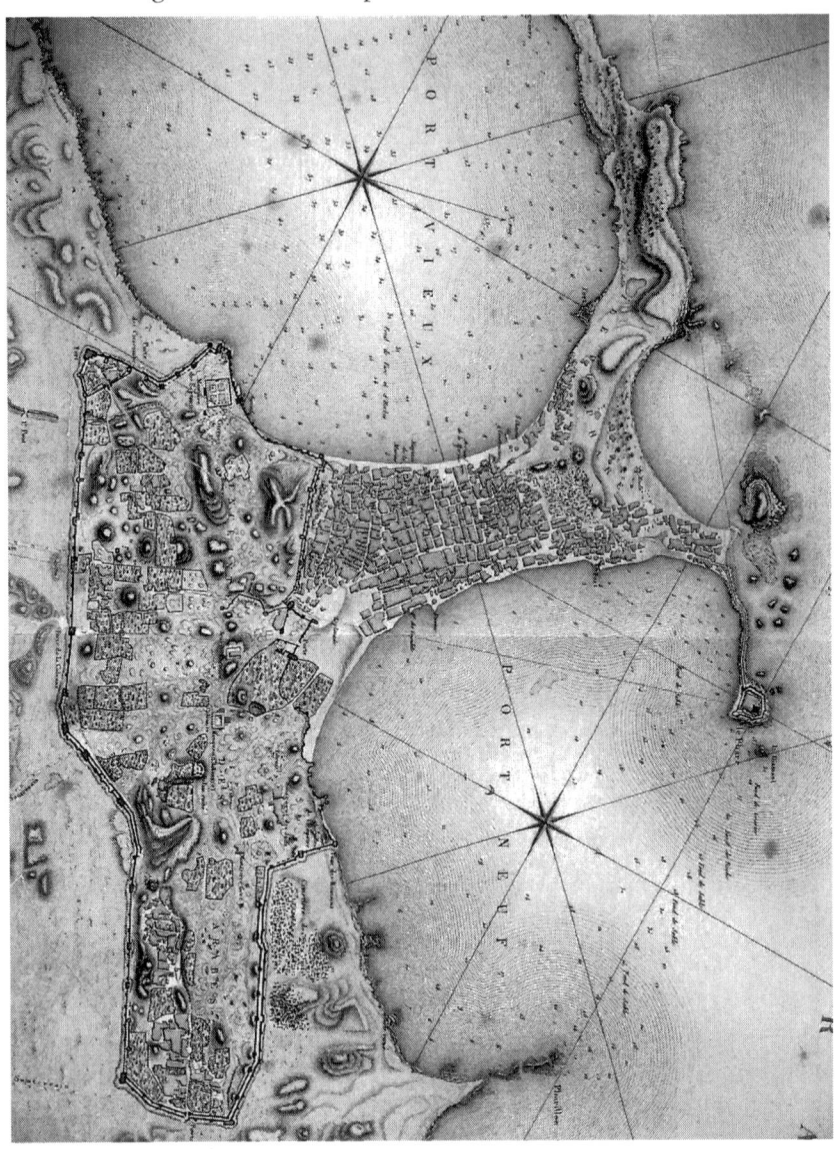

Figure 8.2. The magnificent plan of Alexandria in 1798 from Napoleon's *Description de l'Egypte*, Planche 84 in Vol. 2 of *Etat Moderne* (author's collection)

---

[7] M. F. Awad, *La revue de l'Occident Musulman et de la Méditerranée* 46, 1987, p. 4.

The Quest for the Tomb of Alexander by Andrew Chugg

The names of the great buildings and monuments of ancient Alexandria were well known in Europe, especially in the wake of the Renaissance, during which the ancient Greek and Latin writers had once again become widely read. It was a natural consequence that European visitors to the port should seek to identify the famous sites among the scattered and anonymous ruins. One of the earliest attempts actually to map the layout of ancient Alexandria was made by the French traveller Bonamy in 1731.[8] His technique involved locating likely looking spots among the shifting sands and toppled pillars, principally inspired by the description of the ancient city given by Strabo. Unfortunately, his plan (Figure 8.3) is of little practical value, since it incorporates many demonstrable errors: such as placing Pompey's Pillar and the Serapeum on the wrong side of Canopic Way. However, it serves to illustrate the point that only careful excavations stood any significant chance of solving the riddles of the ruins.

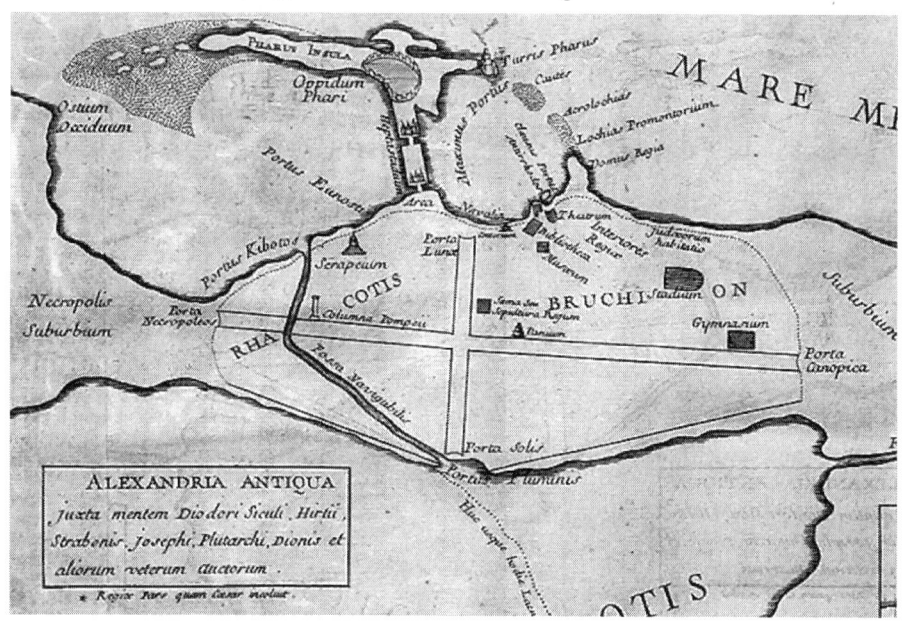

Figure 8.3. Reconstruction of ancient Alexandria published by Bonamy in 1731 (author's collection)

Scientific archaeology arrived in the eastern Mediterranean with the advent of the French School at Athens in 1846, closely followed by the German Archaeological Institute, the British School and others. However, these august institutions largely ignored Alexandria during the brief window of a few decades duration between their inception and the disappearance of the ruin field beneath the sprawling modern city. Nevertheless, it chanced that the topography of

---

[8] M. Bonamy, "Description de la Ville d'Alexandrie, telle qu'elle estoit du temps de Strabon," *Histoire de l'Académie des Inscriptions et Belles Lettres*, Tome 9, 1736, pp. 416-432; Bonamy's site for the *Soma seu Sepultura Regum* just north of the crossroads was probably the Attarine mosque.

The Astronomer's Chart

ancient Alexandria was rescued from the oblivion of urbanisation by the unlikely figure of Mahmoud Bey, the Court Astronomer to the Khedive Ismaïl, then ruler of Egypt.[9] Equally improbably, his investigations were prompted by the literary ambitions of the Emperor of France.

In the early 1860's Napoleon III conceived an ambition to compose a history of his hero, Julius Caesar. He was the nephew of Napoleon Bonaparte and, after becoming President of the French Republic in 1848, he followed in his family tradition by proclaiming himself emperor in 1852. Among the key problems that Napoleon hoped to address in this biography was the detailed explication of Caesar's Alexandrine War. To this end he asked his friend the Khedive as a personal favour to furnish him with a plan of the layout of ancient Alexandria.[10] Ismaïl Pacha was naturally delighted to have an opportunity to be of service to so powerful and potentially useful an ally. Fortunately for us, in 1865 he appointed an extremely competent and thorough member of his staff to undertake the requisite research.

Mahmoud Bey held the title *El-Falaki*, literally "the Astronomer", but this was merely the traditional epithet for an official operating in a scientific or technical capacity at an Ottoman court. He was actually an engineer and cartographer by training. He had been sent to study in Paris at the Ecole des Arts et Métiers for seven years in his youth by the Viceroy Mohammed Ali as part of a modernisation program. The high quality of this training is amply attested by the principal outcome of his investigations: a superbly detailed and accurate chart showing the walls and street-plan of ancient Alexandria.

Mahmoud Bey's map (Figure 4.2) also reflects the generous allocation of resources to this project by the Khedive. Several hundred excavations were undertaken across the undeveloped areas of the ruin field by two hundred workers, yielding a great wealth of information concerning the line of the defensive walls and the spacing and orientation of the street grid. Despite El-Falaki's lack of any archaeological training and his consequent inability reliably to assess the date of many of his discoveries, there is little reason broadly to doubt his version of the city's layout insofar as it is based on excavations and measurements.[11] It is only where he relied instead on local rumours and traditions, as with his location of the Soma beneath the Nabi Daniel Mosque, that his conclusions grow dubious.

*   *   *   *   *   *   *   *

---

[9] Except where otherwise indicated, the details concerning Mahmoud Bey El-Falaki's work in this chapter come from his book, *Memoire sur L'Antique Alexandrie…*, published in Copenhagen in 1872 together with (in some copies) an important reconstructed map of the ancient city. Of particular interest is Chapter 1: "Murs d'enceinte et rues de l'antique ville d'Alexandrie."
[10] Jean-Yves Empereur, *Alexandria Rediscovered*, Chapter 1, p. 25.
[11] The general accuracy of Mahmoud's work has been confirmed by more recent archaeology and is analysed in some detail by Jean-Luc Arnaud, "Nouvelles Données sur la Topographie d'Alexandrie Antique," *BCH* 121, 1997, pp. 721-737.

The Quest for the Tomb of Alexander by Andrew Chugg

The exact course of the Ptolemaic walls of Alexandria remains to some extent in dispute. However, there are good reasons to believe that Mahmoud Bey's version is not far from the truth. The Astronomer and his team found stone foundations five metres wide running along the shore just east of the Lochias peninsula (point A on his map). He describes them as comprising rubble stones fixed with a mortar of lime and ground brick. After a few hundred metres (at point B) these foundations became buried beneath loose rubble to a depth of 3 or 4 metres. Mahmoud relates that he spoke to a person who had been involved in the demolition of this section of the wall in order to provide building material for the expanding modern city. He traced the foundations beneath the rubble for 2 kilometres (to point C), where they descended beneath the modern water table. This corroborates the view that these foundations were ancient: most of Ptolemaic Alexandria is known to have subsided by around 4 metres relative to sea level since its construction: therefore some of the ancient catacombs as well as the ancient wall foundations have consequently become inundated in their lower courses as they have sunk beneath the level of freshwater seepage.[12]

The stone robbers furnished further testimony of the existence of foundations of the same type near a small mosque at the end of a tongue of rubble (point D). However, in the southern sections of the wall's course, the presence of modern houses and their gardens prohibited continuous excavations. Mahmoud resorted to searching for the foundations by seeking their intersections with eight paths running southwards across their general east-west line. In five cases he was successful in locating large tracts of masonry also 5 metres wide (points E to I), but with mortar of a slightly different composition than in the north-eastern sector. He also noted that ancient building foundations were to be found everywhere he looked on the north side of these remains at a depth of 3 or 4 metres, but they were entirely absent on the southern side. From the Serapeum to the port of Eunostos excavation was rendered completely impractical by modern development, but the Astronomer was able to infer the line of the wall from the condition of the soil and the general topography. He seems to have been influenced by Strabo's description, which suggests that the western perimeter lay only a short distance beyond the canal, known as the *Kalish*, which flows from the Canopic branch of the Nile.[13]

Mahmoud supposed the section along the sea front to have taken the form of a quay. Under the guidance of local fishermen, he used a boat on a flat calm day to search the seabed from the Lochias peninsula to the Caesareum. He discovered foundations 2 to 3 metres below the surface of the water (points A, b, c, d, e, f, g, h, i, k and l in Figure 4.2). In the remaining stretch across the isthmus, he based his plan on knowledge of discoveries made during the construction of the foundations of modern houses some years beforehand

---

[12] P. Fraser, *Ptolemaic Alexandria*, Chapter 1 and Note 32 thereto.
[13] Strabo, *Geography* 17.1.

(points m and n) and upon superficial inspection of the soil. Clearly, this was a meticulous investigation, the results of which merit credence.

But how does the location of the perimeter wall help us in locating the Soma Mausoleum? The key issue is the extent of the ancient city to the east of the Lochias peninsula, because of the implications for the whereabouts of the centre of the Ptolemaic capital, where Alexander's tomb is said to have lain. It has been argued that the ancient necropolis of Hadra and also that at Chatby might be expected to lie just outside the Ptolemaic walls. This is mainly because Roman law prohibited burials within the walls of towns, although projecting Roman practice backwards onto the Hellenistic culture of the Ptolemies is invalid: for example, the Mausoleum at Halicarnassus lay at the centre of that city. In fact the Hadra and Chatby cemeteries actually lie just inside the eastern stretch of Mahmoud Bey's walls. Furthermore, there is an impressively fine fragment of a major Ptolemaic wall lying a couple of hundred metres north of the eastern Rosetta Gate in the Tulunid walls, still to be found in the northern section of the modern Shallalat (waterfall) Gardens (see Figure 8.4).

The blocks of limestone in the oldest parts of this fragment are crammed with shell fossils and the largest stones are over a metre wide, although they vary in size and proportions. They have a distinctive band of drafting around their edges, but the remainder of the face of each was left rough-cut. The Tower of the Romans in Alexandria was faced with the same style of blocks, including the bands of drafting (see Figure 6.3). Such blocks are particularly to be found in the context of high status early-Hellenistic architecture. Pertinent examples elsewhere include the blocks lining the Lion Tomb at Knidos and the original base blocks of another Lion Tomb from Amphipolis in Macedonia. Both most probably date to around the end of the fourth century BC and are best associated with Alexander's immediate Successors.[14]

The Shallalat wall fragment has led some to speculate that the early Ptolemaic city might have ended there over 1500m to the west of Mahmoud's eastern wall line. Against these considerations, however, there is a strong implication in the testimony of Josephus dating from the early Roman period that the Jewish Quarter, known as Delta and comprising up to a fifth of the entire city, lay entirely to the east of the Lochias Peninsula.[15] Josephus also writes that the Jews were granted a district within Alexandria by Alexander himself[16] and Tacitus tells us that the walls of Alexandria were constructed by Ptolemy Soter,[17] whilst Ammianus states, "Alexandria herself, not gradually like other cities, but at her

---

[14] Janos Fedak, *Monumental Tombs of the Hellenistic Age*, Toronto, 1990, pp. 76-78 and Figs. 87 & 91 on the dates of the Lion Tombs at Knidos and Amphipolis and illustrating the bands of drafting.
[15] Josephus, *Contra Apion* 2.33.
[16] Josephus, *Contra Apion* 2.36, but it is doubtful whether any Jews actually arrived so early, although the Delta Quarter was probably established by the end of Soter's reign; Josephus, *The Jewish War* 2.487 attributes the gift to the Diadochi.
[17] Tacitus, *Histories* 4.83

very origin, attained her wide extent."[18] Additionally, Mahmoud Bey's walls agree well with the accounts of the nine ancient writers, who give dimensions for the ancient city (see Table 8.1). Excepting Diodorus' value, which probably includes suburbs, there is a good level of agreement for the east-west extent of the city at around 30 Alexandrian stades with a north-south width of about 10 stades at the centre and 8 at the extremities. If Mahmoud's version of the city is approximated as a rectangle, then it has a perimeter of about 80 stades, but if the sinuosities of the wall are followed, then the circuit increases to about 96 stades. Taking into account the fact that the length of the stade seems to have varied between about 145m and 185m at different places and times, there is a reasonable degree of consistency between Mahmoud's plan and the ancient authorities.

Pococke, who visited Alexandria in 1737-8, also saw wall foundations not far from those described by Mahmoud:-

The old walls of the city seem to have been built on the height, which extends from Cape Lochias towards the east, the remains of a grand gateway being to be seen in the road to Rosetto at this high ground; and the foundations of the walls may from thence be traced to the canal.[19]

Pococke's height seems to be the low ridge a few hundred metres inside Mahmoud's location for the Canopic Gate in the ancient walls. Thus Pococke's observations suggest a marginally shorter east-west dimension for the ancient city. Of course, it is entirely possible that the eastern walls were established in different lines in different eras within the thousand-year history of Graeco-Roman Alexandria.

---

[18] Ammianus Marcellinus, *Res Gestae* 22.16.15.
[19] Pococke, *Description of the East*, Vol. 1, 1743, p.3.

The Astronomer's Chart

Figure 8.4. Surviving northeastern tower of the Tulunid walls, which appears to be Ptolemaic or early Roman in origin (photo by the author)

Judith McKenzie has argued that the faint grid marked on a map of Alexandria made by Henry Salt, the British consul and later Belzoni's sponsor, in 1806 (Figure 8.5) represented extant traces of Mahmoud's street plan.[20] Her case is bolstered by a significant amount of agreement between Mahmoud's street grid and Salt's traces: notably every third of Salt's tracks coincides with one of Mahmoud's major streets. Presumably, Salt viewed the ruin field from an eminence at dawn or dusk, when the Sun's shadows were long enough to make the subtle alignments manifest. The Salt map tends to support Pococke's version of the location of the easternmost gateway. It also appears that Salt recognized the special significance of the north-south avenue marked as R1 on Mahmoud's plan: he shows a sort of gap in his grid, perhaps hinting at the line of an ancient canal in the path of the ancient subterranean aquaduct that runs beside the track of R1. In this way Salt lends implicit support to Mahmoud Bey in his designation of the intersection of R1 with Canopic Way (L1) as the central crossroads of ancient Alexandria. A variant version of Mahmoud's plan published in a German journal in 1872 (Figure 8.6) indicated that Mahmoud's team discovered especially large numbers of fallen columns along his streets R1 and L1.[21]

---

[20] Judith McKenzie, "Alexandria and the Origins of Baroque Architecture," *Alexandria and Alexandrianism*, Getty Museum, 1996, p.111; the Salt map appeared in G. Valentia, *Voyages and Travels to India, Ceylon, the Red Sea, Abyssinia and Egypt in the Years 1802 – 1806*, Vol. 4, London, 1811.

[21] H. Kiepert, "Zur Topographie der alten Alexandria: Nach Mahmud Begs Entdeckungen," *Zeitschrift der Gesellschaft für Erdkunde zu Berlin*, Vol. 7, 1872, pp. 337-349, pl. 5 (map facing p. 384).

The Quest for the Tomb of Alexander by Andrew Chugg

One additional piece of evidence on the eastern line of the ancient walls takes the form of a detailed panoramic view of Alexandria from the east, which was published in 1803 in the context of an account of the campaign of the British army against Napoleon's expeditionary force in Egypt.[22] This engraving is reproduced in Figure 8.7. The view is taken from a drawing, which must have been made at the time of the Battle of Alexandria in 1801 by an artist standing in the vicinity of the compass rose in Figure 8.5 and looking west towards the French lines and the city behind them. The ruined walls in the middle distance in the left and centre of the view are located approximately at the line of Mahmoud's eastern wall. Furthermore, these ruins incorporate a large archway in the approximate line of the road from Alexandria to Rosetta, which appears to be consistent with an ancient gateway. Perhaps these are also the ruins described by Pococke and he simply wrote a little loosely in describing their relationship with the rising ground immediately behind them.

A final line of argument in the Astronomer's favour is the population figure given by Diodorus of "300,000 free citizens", which implies a total approaching half a million, when slaves are included. The population density is very uncertain, but what scant evidence there is from archaeology reveals relatively low-density housing: perhaps ~200 persons per hectare.[23] This suggests that the populace could barely be accommodated by Mahmoud's city of around 1000 hectares, let alone a smaller area.

---

[22] Plate 25 in *Journal of The Late Campaign in Egypt: Including Descriptions of that Country and of Gibraltar, Minorca, Malta, Marmorice and Macri*, by Thomas Walsh, and published by T. Cadell and W. Davies, London, 1803.
[23] Christopher Haas, *Alexandria in Late Antiquity*, Chapter 3, p. 46; Jean-Yves Empereur, *Alexandria Rediscovered*, Chapter 3, p. 61.

The Astronomer's Chart

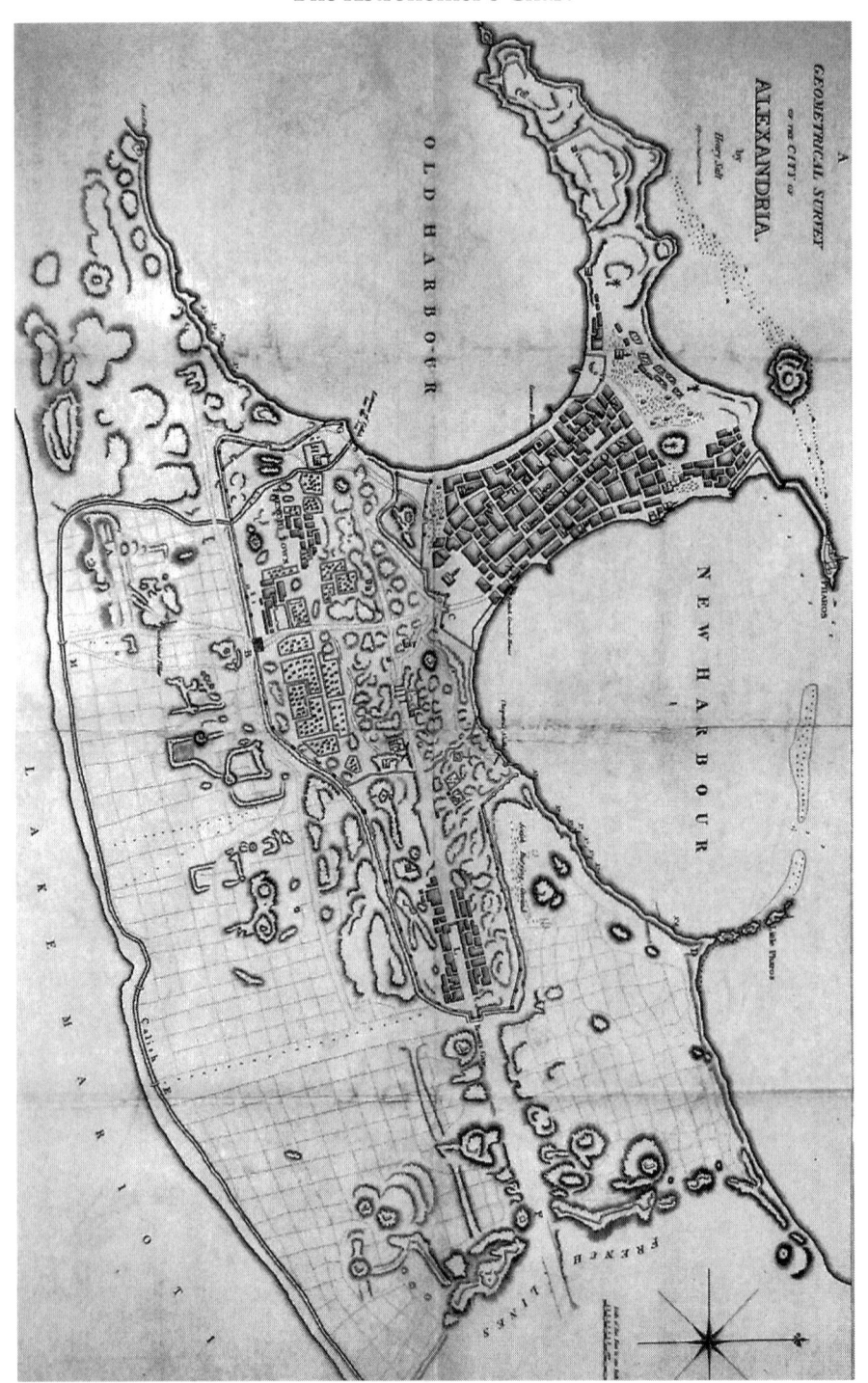

Figure 8.5. The map of Alexandria drawn by Henry Salt in 1806 (author's collection)

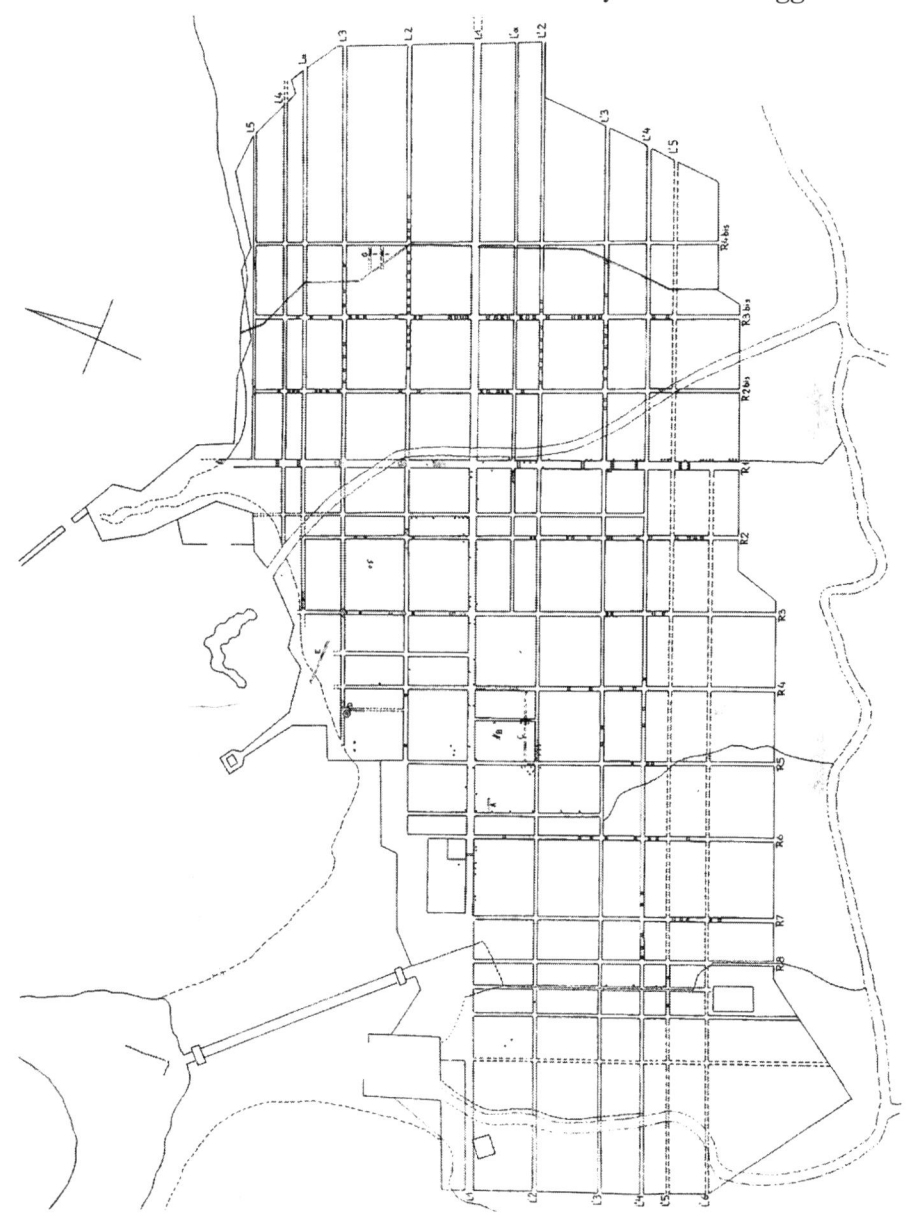

The Quest for the Tomb of Alexander by Andrew Chugg

Figure 8.6. Kiepert's version of Mahmoud Bey's plan of Alexandria with column finds marked by dots and road excavations indicated by crossbars

The Astronomer's survey of the ancient street grid was even more extensive than his investigation of the circuit of the defensive walls. The specific locations where Mahmoud's team excavated the ancient paving stones of the road surfaces are marked by double crossbars on the version of Mahmoud's plan given in Figure 8.6. He identified the surviving road, which passed by the

The Astronomer's Chart

Attarine Mosque and ran straight on through the eastern Rosetta Gate of the Arab city with Canopic Way, the principal longitudinal highway of ancient Alexandria. Six excavations were undertaken to confirm this hypothesis. One in front of the mosque, another 10 metres west of the gate and four more over a half kilometre stretch east of the gate. Further east the remains had been destroyed, probably when Mohammed Ali had renovated the road in the early 19th century. Mahmoud discovered paving stones of black or greyish stone, which were 20cm thick and from 30cm to 50cm in length and breadth. The paving was well preserved at the first, third, fourth and fifth excavation sites. It was 14 metres wide and lay 2.5 to 3 metres beneath the soil inside the Arab city, but at a depth of only 1.5 metres outside the Tulunid walls. Mahmoud also cited the evidence of large pieces of masonry and broken columns discovered whilst workmen were laying the foundations of modern houses along this road. Earlier illustrations from the late 18th century by Louis-François Cassas and Luigi Mayer show six columns still standing (Figures 8.8 & 8.9).[24]

Figure 8.7. Walsh's view of the eastern approaches to Alexandria in the context of the Battle of Alexandria in 1801 (author's collection)

On his plan of the city the Astronomer referenced Canopic Way as longitudinal street L1. He made further excavations in the lines of 3 further longitudinal avenues north of Canopic Way (L2, L3, L4) and 3 more to the south (L'2, L'3, L'4). He also found superficial traces of two more in the southern margins of the city, but he marked them with dashed lines to distinguish the fact that he

---

[24] Planche 35 in the Antiquités V section of the *Description de l'Egypte*, Paris, 1829 and maps of Alexandria in the same work show only the the three columns immediately opposite the Attarine Mosque; similarly the map by Henry Salt dating to 1806.

The Quest for the Tomb of Alexander by Andrew Chugg

made no attempt to excavate down to their paving stones. The paving stones formed a band 7 metres wide, wherever they were sufficiently well-preserved for the street width to be measured. Furthermore, Mahmoud noted that these streets recurred at a standard interval of about 278 metres in the north-south direction.

Figure 8.8. Engraving from a drawing of 1785 by L-F Cassas looking eastwards down Canopic Way past the Attarine Mosque (author's collection)

Figure 8.9. Aquatinted engraving from a drawing of ~1792 by Luigi Mayer looking eastwards down Canopic Way past the Attarine Mosque (author's collection)

167

The Astronomer's Chart

Exactly at right angles to the longitudinal avenues, Mahmoud discovered 11 major transverse roads and fainter traces of a twelfth at a regular east-west spacing of 330 metres from one another. His excavations also revealed evidence of five intermediate north-south streets. He inferred that the 330m interval probably represented 2 stades of 165 metres each. In the Greek measurement system a stade comprises 6 plethrons, so this hypothesis had the further attraction of making the standard spacing of the longitudinal avenues (278m) equal to almost exactly 10 plethrons (275m). The transverse road running from the Lochias peninsula down through the central declivity was found to be double the width of the others, matching the breadth of Canopic Way at 14 metres. However, it was split into two carriageways of equal width separated by a metre wide band of earth. The eastern lane was paved as elsewhere, but its pair had a surface composed of lime, earth, small pebbles and bits of rubble stone. A subterranean aqueduct ran parallel on its eastern side, whilst a sewer ran along its western edge. Mahmoud labelled this principal transverse route R1, with those to the east of it being designated R2^{bis}, R3^{bis} and R4^{bis} and those to the west R2, R3… R8, the last being the main approach road to the Serapeum temple from Canopic Way.

Strabo described the two principal streets of Alexandria as intersecting at right angles and being over a plethron wide (~30 metres). Although El-Falaki's paving was only half this width, the streets he labelled L1 and R1 were nevertheless over twice as wide as any other he excavated, so they are very likely to be Strabo's main thoroughfares.[25] The street surfaces uncovered by Mahmoud seem to have been Late Roman in date and therefore reflect the situation several centuries after Strabo wrote. They lay at a depth of just 2 or 3 metres, whereas the oldest levels are often found to lie 7 to 10 metres below the modern street level and close to the water table. The Astronomer himself observed that the pavings he had discovered could not have been original, early Ptolemaic, since they were underlain by at least a metre of older debris. Intriguingly, he also noted that these sub-strata were thicker towards the northeastern districts, which he attributed to destruction by warfare in the second half of the third century AD, but the tsunami of AD365 might have had similar consequences.

Did the original Ptolemaic street layout of Alexandria have a different orientation to the Roman roads excavated by Mahmoud? The evidence provided by more modern excavations seems to uphold the validity of the Astronomer's grid back to the origins of the metropolis, subject to a few minor

---

[25] The interpretation of R1 remains in dispute. F Noack, "Neue Untersuchungen in Alexandrien," *Mittheilungen des Kaiserlich Deutschen Archäologischen Instituts, Athenische Abtheilung* 25, 1900, p. 215-279, reports his own excavations on R1, which he found difficult completely to reconcile with Mahmoud's account, but he also concludes, "The reliability of little Mahmoud's street plan has in general been verified by our excavations."

qualifications.[26] For example, three sections of the transverse street labelled R4 were excavated in the 20th century, scattered along over a kilometre of its length and Adriani has investigated the longitudinal road L2.[27] Although one district with streets on a different alignment has been uncovered, it is confined to a sub-region of the palace area.[28] A team of geophysicists has recently shown that the Heptastadion causeway was aligned with Mahmoud's transverse street R9 (dashed in Fig. 8.6), so the Astronomer's oblique orientation for this link must now be rejected.[29] Nonetheless, Mahmoud emerges today relatively unscathed from the torrent of criticism unleashed upon him by scholars such as Hogarth:-

Anyone, however, who attempts to write a topographical memoir on the city will have to appraise, and, I think, condemn in the main, the work of Ismail's Court Astronomer. Mahmud Bey had, it is true, facilities in 1870 which exist no longer in 1895: not only was an autocratic Khedive behind him, but the site was far more open.... Mahmud Bey had had, however, no sort of training for the work he was set to do; not only did he not know any classical language, but I am given to understand that this was his first essay in excavation.[30]

Not only did this exhibit the worst kind of intellectual arrogance, but it was also thoroughly mistaken: Hogarth even got the year of Mahmoud's investigations wrong.

*   *   *   *   *   *   *   *

If the broad accuracy of Mahmoud Bey's map is accepted and the extrapolation of the Roman layout back to the Ptolemaic era is considered legitimate, then there are several implications for the location of the Soma. Most obviously, the map precisely locates the central crossroads of ancient Alexandria, which seems to be the site best favoured by the ancient sources for the Soma Mausoleum. In addition, however, both the large size of Mahmoud's city and the near coincidence of its central crossroads with the later eastern Rosetta Gate are also significant.

The vastness of the area encompassed within the perimeter circuit of Mahmoud's ancient walls suggests that the Royal Quarter, which Strabo described as constituting between a quarter and a third of the entire city, must have been proportionately enormous.[31] Strabo specifies that the Royal Palaces

---

[26] For a good up-to-date survey of the evidence see Judith Mckenzie, "Glimpsing Alexandria from Archaeological Evidence," *JRA* 2003, pp. 35-63.
[27] Jean-Yves Empereur, *Alexandria Rediscovered*, Chapter 3, pp. 56-7; excavations have discovered remains of R4 at the Rio Cinema (Adriani), Kom el-Dikka (Polish mission) and at the site of the Diana Theatre; Christopher Haas, *Alexandria in Late Antiquity*, Chapter 2, p. 30.
[28] M. Rodziewicz, "Ptolemaic street directions in Basilea," *Alessandria e il mondo ellenistico romano*, Congrès Alexandrie, 1992, published in Rome, 1995, pp. 227-35.
[29] Albert Hesse *et al.*, "L'Heptastadium d'Alexandrie (Égypte)," in Jean-Yves Empereur (ed.), *Alexandrina* 2 (Études Alexandrines 6, Cairo 2002), pp.191-273.
[30] D.G. Hogarth and E.F. Benson, "Report of Prospects of Research in Alexandria," *Egypt Exploration Fund* 1895, p. 17.
[31] Strabo, *Geography* 17.1.8; Strabo states a quarter or even a third of the *circuit* of the city – maybe he is referring to the angle subtended by this district at the city's centre.

were located on the Lochias peninsula and extended along the front of the Great Harbour about as far as Mahmoud's Timonium, beyond which lay the Caesareum, the Emporium and associated commercial districts. To the east of Lochias, the Royal District was bounded and confined by Delta, the Jewish Quarter.[32] These tight eastern and western boundaries require that Strabo's Royal Quarter must have extended a long way to the south of Lochias, probably even southwards beyond Canopic Way, in order even to approach a quarter of the city's total area. The location of the Soma near the main crossroads is therefore entirely consistent with its being a part of the Royal Quarter as defined by Strabo. Strabo himself confutes those who have argued that the location of the Soma within his Royal Quarter places it on or near the eastern shore of the Great Harbour.

The association of the crossroads with the Rosetta Gate recalls Ibn Abdel Hakim's record of a Mosque of Dulkarnein (i.e. Alexander) situated adjacent to the gate of 9th century Alexandria.[33] It also prompts the question of why Sultan Ahmed Ibn Tulun chose to encompass the ancient crossroads within his defensive circuit? Might the nearby fragment of a Ptolemaic wall (Figure 8.4), the only stretch which survives anywhere in the city today, betoken more ancient walls already surrounding the vicinity of the ancient crossroads before Ibn Tulun's era?

*   *   *   *   *   *   *   *

The main rival to the Astronomer's central crossroads as a candidate for the heart of the ancient city is the intersection of Mahmoud's transverse street R5 with Canopic Way about 1.5km further west.[34] This substitution of R5 for R1 as the principal transverse highway remains common in published plans even today.[35] Curiously, this theory also seems to have its origins in Mahmoud Bey's work, for it was he more than any other who transformed a mixture of legend and local gossip into a serious argument that the Soma lay beneath the Nabi Daniel Mosque. This building lies on street R5 not far south of Canopic Way and the reasoning runs that, if the Soma lay at the centre of town, therefore the centre of town must be adjacent to the supposed site of the Soma. Such was the line adopted by Evaristo Breccia in his influential works published in the first half of the 20th century. It is a stupendous irony of this subject that some later commentators have used Breccia's location of the centre of ancient Alexandria near R5 to support the candidature of the Nabi Daniel Mosque as the site of the Soma Mausoleum: of course this reasoning is perfectly circular. Whereas it is true that the centre of gravity of Alexandria drifted westwards late in the Roman

---

[32] Josephus, *Contra Apion* 2.33, places Delta near the Royal Palaces on a harbourless stretch of the coast.
[33] P.M. Fraser, *Ptolemaic Alexandria*, Chapter 1, Note 86, Section 1.
[34] G. Botti (on rather eccentric grounds) placed the crossroads at the intersection of R2 with L'3.
[35] E.g. Christopher Haas, *Alexandria in Late Antiquity*, p. 2.

The Quest for the Tomb of Alexander by Andrew Chugg

period, there seems to be no tenable basis for the Nabi Daniel Mosque as the site of the Soma.

In this chapter we have worked through complex and abstruse evidence from archaeological investigations and antique maps and engravings in considering how they can be reconciled with the ancient testimony. The totality of this evidence virtually compels the conclusion that Mahmoud Bey and Henry Salt were correct, when they independently attributed special significance to the intersection of R1 and L1: in all probability it is the site of the central crossroads of ancient Alexandria as described by Strabo.

Table 8.1. Sources for the dimensions of ancient Alexandria

Author	Reference	Era	Length	Breadth	Circuit
Diodorus Siculus	17.52	Mid 1st century BC	40 stades	-	-
Strabo	17.1.8	~25BC	30 stades	7 or 8 stades	-
Philo	In Flaccum 92	1st half of 1st century AD	-	10 stades	-
Curtius	4.8.2	~AD50	-	-	80 stades
Josephus	Bell. Jud. 2.16.4	2nd half of 1st century AD	30 stades	10 stades	-
Pliny the Elder	5.11	AD77	-	-	15 Roman miles
Pseudo-Callisthenes	1.31.10 Jul. Var.	3rd century AD	-	16 stades & 395 feet	-
Stephanus Byzantinus	Alexandreia	Early 6th century AD	34 stades	8 stades	110 stades
Michael bar Elias*	Chronicle v, ch. 3	Late 12th century (~3rd century original?)	14987 feet (4.57km or 27.7 Alex stades?)	-	-
Mahmoud Bey	L'Antique Alexandrie	1865	31 Alex stades	10 Alex stades	96 Alex stades

Alexandrian stade = 165m

Typical Greek stade = 180m

Roman stade (Pliny) = 148m

Roman mile = 1480m

*See P.M. Fraser, "A Syriac Notitia Urbis Alexandrinae," *Journal of Egyptian Archaeology* 37

9. Alexander's City

Softly sweet, in Lydian measures,
Soon he soothed his soul to pleasures:
War, he sung, is toil and trouble;
Honour, but an empty bubble;
Never ending, still beginning,
Fighting still, and still destroying:
If the world be worth thy winning,
Think, O think it worth enjoying…
Now strike the golden lyre again;
A louder yet, and yet a louder strain.
Break his bands of sleep asunder,
And rouse him, like a rattling peal of thunder
Hark, hark! the horrid sound
Has raised up his head;
As awaked from the dead,
And amazed, he stares around…

Excerpts from *Alexander's Feast* by John Dryden

Sadly, the search for the Soma has acquired a faint aura of disrepute in academic circles, not just on account of the rogues' gallery of fraudsters, charlatans and crackpots who have dabbled in the subject, but also because of the otherwise distinguished scholars who have sacrificed their reputations on the altar of Alexander's tomb.[1] Heinrich Schliemann, the famous excavator of Troy and Mycenae, visited Alexandria in 1888 with the specific objective of finding the tomb. Having declared his infallible conviction that its remains lay beneath the Nabi Daniel Mosque, his plans to quarry the vicinity were nevertheless frustrated by the local religious authorities, who refused point-blank to grant him permission to dig on their land.[2] Subsequently, in the 20th century the Italian archaeologist, Evaristo Breccia, who was a distinguished Director of the Graeco-Roman Museum in Alexandria between 1904-1932, also embraced the folklore surrounding the Nabi Daniel Mosque with similarly misplaced enthusiasm:-

But in any case we may consider it as established that the Sema, and consequently also the Mausoleums of the Ptolemies, were near the Mosque Nabi Danial.[3]

---

[1] E.g. P.M. Fraser, *Ptolemaic Alexandria*, p. 16, "The actual location of the 'tomb of Alexander' has been much debated, but… the unending search for it, rather than for the Mausoleum of the Ptolemies, must be regarded as misdirected and pointless. Nevertheless a brief account of the mixture of legend and surmise is necessary…"
[2] Leo Deuel, *The Memoirs of Heinrich Schliemann*, Hutchinson, 1978.
[3] Evaristo Breccia, *Alexandrea ad Aegyptum*, 1922, p. 99.

The Quest for the Tomb of Alexander by Andrew Chugg

These eminent archaeologists were bedazzled by an old misconception, which caused the Nabi Daniel Mosque incorrectly to be linked with the sixteenth century account of the tomb of Alexander by Marmol, who was in fact very probably referring to the shrine at the Attarine Mosque. This came about, because Marmol also mentioned a Church of St Mark in the city, where the body of the saint himself was supposed to have lain. Although Marmol's own account did not in any way associate the church with the tomb, Bruce, writing in 1790, mistakenly quoted him as saying that the tomb lay near the church.[4] By the late 19th century this Church of St Mark had ceased to exist, but there was a new Coptic Church of St Mark about 300 hundred metres northwest of the Nabi Daniel Mosque. It was assumed that the new church stood on the foundations of the old, thus forging the missing link between the sixteenth century accounts and the Nabi Daniel Mosque.[5] In fact Braun and Hogenberg's 16th century map of Alexandria depicts a stone just inside the *Porte du Caire* (Cairo Gate) of the city, beneath which the body of St Mark was believed to have been discovered and there is a church-like building drawn beside the spot (Figure 9.1). Especially since both the map legend and Marmol mention the Venetians, who had kidnapped St Mark's supposed remains in AD828, it seems probable that it was actually this building just within the portal that was later known as the Rosetta Gate that Marmol was describing.[6] We will have cause to revisit this site for the tomb of St Mark in ensuing chapters.

*   *   *   *   *   *   *   *   *

Other more or less dubious theories concerning the location of the Soma abound. One of the most blatant forgeries was perpetrated by Joannides in 1893.[7] He discovered a Ptolemaic necropolis at Chatby, east of the Lochias peninsula (Figure 7.9), as was reported in the Egyptian Gazette of 20th June 1893:-

Mr. Joannides asserts that he has discovered the tombs of Alexander the Great and of Cleopatra. The former is at a depth of 16 metres from the surface and the latter is at a depth of 12 metres. He says the doors of the tombs are of bronze on which there are inscriptions in Greek and that the name of the occupant of the tomb is sculptured over the doorway. The bronze is eaten through in parts and with the aid of magnesium light, Mr. Joannides says that he was able to distinguish marble sarcophagi that had feet like lions' feet. He also says that he saw something like parchments or skins in these vaults. This is only part of what Mr. Joannides asserts to be in the vaults in question for it appears he found much jewellery and

---

[4] Bruce, *Travels*, I, 1790, p. 13, "Marmol… says he saw it [Alexander's tomb] in the year 1546. It was, according to him, a small house in form of a chapel, in the middle of the city, near the church of St. Mark, and was called Escander."
[5] See P.M. Fraser, *Ptolemaic Alexandria*, Section 1 of Note 86 to Chapter 1, who provides a lucid explanation of the confusion.
[6] The Latin legend on the Braun & Hogenberg map appears to read, *Sub hoc lapide corpus S Marci inventum et Venetia est delatum*, which could be translated, "Beneath this stone the body of St Mark was discovered and was carried away to Venice."
[7] P.M. Fraser, "Some Alexandrian Forgeries," *Proceedings of the British Academy* 47, 1962, p.243, n.2.

Alexander's City

some beautiful Greek vases. This differs very much from the statements of the Conservator of the Alexandria Museum but we feel it our duty to our readers to place before them the statement of the original discoverer of these antiquities. In due time we shall know the real truth of the affair.

In recent decades the most famous graduate of the eccentric school of tomb-hunters was the dauntless Stelios Koumoutsos, a waiter in L'Élite café-bar in Alexandria, who used to fritter away his carefully hoarded tips in financing a long series of ineffectual and frequently unauthorised excavations across the city. He picked locations that were underwater in antiquity on at least two occasions and the official dossier kept by the Egyptian authorities contains 322 permit applications and excavation reports dating from 1956, when he commenced his fruitless endeavours.[8]

Figure 9.1. Detail of the map of 1575 by Braun & Hogenberg showing the place within the *Porte du Caire* (Rosetta Gate) where St Mark's corpse had been found beneath a stone and carried away by the Venetians (cf. Figure 7.2)

Koumoutsos was also the proud owner of the so-called *Alexander Book*, a leaf from which is shown in Figure 9.2. It depicts various temple buildings in a Greek style, lining a highway and plastered with crude Greek legends enlivened by the odd Coptic character and the evocative appellations "Alexander" and "King Ptolemy". P. M. Fraser, a well-known expert on ancient Alexandria, was

---

[8] Jean-Yves Empereur, *Alexandria Rediscovered*, Chapter 8, p. 148.

The Quest for the Tomb of Alexander by Andrew Chugg

shown this book by Koumoutsos in June 1961.[9] He immediately recognised that the legends mainly comprised poor quality reproductions of two genuine inscriptions, which were kept in the Graeco-Roman Museum. Furthermore, another poor quality stone forgery based on one of these inscriptions was known to exist. Fraser also discovered that the two genuine inscriptions had been acquired by the museum in 1912 after having been found near one another close to the village of Abu el Matamir on the western edge of the Nile Delta. He therefore reasoned that the forgeries had probably all been made in a workshop in the village in about 1912, on the grounds that it was most unlikely that their perpetrator would have chosen that particular pairing of inscriptions, whilst they lay among countless others in the museum. He was, however, convinced that Koumoutsos was entirely innocent of any complicity in the fraud, but was instead a credulous victim. Indeed, he writes that he felt too sorry for the waiter to disabuse him of his fantasies. Koumoutsos died in 1991, but he is still fondly remembered in Alexandria as one of the city's most colourful characters.

Figure 9.2. A leaf from the forgery known as the *Alexander Book*

---

[9] P.M. Fraser, "Some Alexandrian Forgeries," *Proceedings of the British Academy* 47, 1962, pp.243-50.

Alexander's City

Koumoutsos' torch was kept ablaze in the 1990's by a colourful lady called Liana Souvaltzis, who undertook a series of widely publicised excavations at the Siwa Oasis commencing in 1989. The object of her enthusiastic investigations was a putative tomb of Alexander at a small Doric Greek temple of Ptolemaic date in the spot called *El Maraqi Bilad El Rum*. The structure was described whilst it still stood by Frederic Cailliaud (1822-4), Heinrich Minutoli (1826) and Gerhard Rohlfs (1869). Its interior has an unusual plan, comprising five chambers, arranged one behind the other.[10] The Egyptian authorities ordered the suspension of the excavations in October 1996 due to lack of credible evidence in support of any of Souvaltzis' claims.

Experts are understandably dismissive of her conclusions, but it is important to be clear as to why her assertions are considered so dubious. Firstly, the best dating evidence for the temple suggests it was constructed at least a century after Alexander's death, when his body certainly lay at Alexandria. Secondly, the inscriptions discovered at the site provide evidence that it was dedicated to the goddess Isis rather than to Alexander. Thirdly, claims that other inscriptions found there refer to the poisoning theory of Alexander's death appear to be demonstrably attributable to gross mistranslations according to reputable experts. Fourthly, the "rays" sculpted onto stone fragments, which Souvaltzis identified as parts of a Macedonian star symbol, were misaligned with one another. Finally, Souvaltzis' anecdotal evidence gleaned from the local people and their use of star designs in their clothing cannot be accepted as constituting material indications for a tomb of Alexander.[11] It is only to be expected that Alexander's visit and the ensuing three centuries of Ptolemaic rule should have left some traces at the Siwa Oasis and have influenced the legends and traditions of its denizens.

Curtius, Diodorus and Justin all mention Alexander's last wish that his body should be taken to Ammon, which might mean Siwa, although Lucian and the *Liber de Morte* say only that Alexander commanded that his corpse should be transported to Egypt. Diodorus and Justin go on record that the Macedonians initially *planned* to deliver the corpse to the Temple of Ammon. It is nevertheless virtually impossible, given the mass of contrary evidence, that Alexander actually was buried at Siwa. The Parian Marble, Pausanias, Curtius and the Alexander Romance all record an initial entombment at Memphis. Strabo, Diodorus, Zenobius, Dio Cassius, Suetonius, Lucan, Herodian, Libanius and others all confirm its subsequent relocation to Alexandria. There is no ancient testimony that disputes this. Only Justin leaves his readers to suppose that Alexander's corpse might really have been transported to the Temple of Ammon, since he simply fails to record the change of plan. It is characteristic of Justin's epitome to introduce confusion on points of detail: for example, he speaks of *King* Arrhidaeus being commissioned to convey Alexander's corpse to

---

[10] Robert S. Bianchi, "Hunting Alexander's Tomb," *Archaeology*, July-August 1993.
[11] Tony Spawforth, *Alexander: The God King*, UK television broadcast, BBC2, 20:25, 18/5/1996.

The Quest for the Tomb of Alexander by Andrew Chugg

the Temple of Ammon, whereas we know from Diodorus that the task was assigned to a Macedonian commander of the same name.[12] Despite the fact that Justin himself seems to have believed that Siwa was the intended destination, the matter is ambiguous, because there were shrines to Ammon in virtually all the cities of Ptolemaic Egypt. The main cult center for Ammon was always located at Thebes and there is even evidence for a Ptolemaic temple dedicated to Ammon at Memphis, which was still the capital when Ptolemy Soter brought Alexander's body thither in 321BC.[13] Having gone to considerable trouble to secure the corpse of the King, it is unlikely Ptolemy would have considered sending it to a remote oasis, sequestered from civilisation by hundreds of miles of blistering desert and vulnerable to a seaborne raid by his enemies.

Nonetheless, it should be conceded that the relocation of Alexander's body to Siwa by pagans in the fourth or fifth centuries AD is not an altogether impossible scenario. It is conceivable that Alexander's remaining worshippers might thus have sought to protect his remains from the ravages of Christian fanaticism. However, this is pure speculation and there are anyway a hundred other equally probable places, to which the corpse might have been dispatched: to Palmyra by Zenobia; or to Augila, where Procopius mentions the continuing worship of Alexander in the 6th century AD; or to Thebes, which was the centre of Ammon's cult; or to Ethiopia, a traditional haven for Egyptian exiles; or to Macedon, Alexander's homeland; or to Rome, the imperial capital; or further north in Italy... The list could be extended indefinitely. In the absence of any record of its removal or of any evidence of its presence elsewhere that bore any scrutiny, we should have to conclude that Alexander's body more probably remained at Alexandria.

*   *   *   *   *   *   *   *

Perhaps the only serious candidate for a tomb of Alexander to emerge in the 20th century is the "Alabaster Tomb" situated in the Terra Santa section of the Latin Cemeteries around 600 metres northwest of the central crossroads of ancient Alexandria (Figures 7.9 & 9.3). It was first published by Breccia who discovered it in tumbled pieces in 1907,[14] but its reconstruction in 1936 and later attribution as the antechamber of a possible tomb of Alexander rely on the work and opinions of Achille Adriani, who succeeded Breccia as the Director of the Graeco-Roman Museum in Alexandria in 1932.[15] It comprises monumental blocks of rosy alabaster, which are cut perfectly flat on their interior faces,

---

[12] Justin 13.4.6.
[13] A Memphite *Imensthotieion* (Temple of Ammon & Thoth) is mentioned in pLondon 1.50 (= UPZ 116): C. Préaux, *L'Economie Royale des Lagides,* New York, 1939, p. 299; A. Deleage, *Etudes Papyrologiques* 2, 1934, p. 85.
[14] Evaristo Breccia, *Rapport du Musée Gréco-Romain* 1907, p.7.
[15] Nicola Bonacasa, "Un Inedito di Achille Adriani Sulla Tomba di Alessandro," *Studi Miscellanei – Seminario di Archaeologia e Storia dell'Arte... dell'Universita di Roma*, Vol. 28, 1991, pp. 3-19; Achille Adriani (posthumously edited by Bonacasa), *La Tomba di Alessandro*, L'Erma di Bretschneider, Rome, 2000.

Alexander's City

revealing the beautiful natural veining of the stone, which resembles the growth rings of wood. However, in contrast, the external faces are only roughly cut, which is suggestive of their having been covered over by earth, as would have been the case were this one of the chambers within a traditional Macedonian tumulus tomb. The simple moulding over the surviving entranceway has parallels in other Ptolemaic period tombs in Alexandria (e.g. Moustafa Pacha Tomb 2), which provides firm evidence for a Ptolemaic date. Adriani has also argued that the relative proximity of its site to the central crossroads of ancient Alexandria is consistent with the central location of the Soma suggested by the ancient writers, but a cursory glance at the map (Figure 7.9) shows that this is overstated.

Figure 9.3. The Alabaster Tomb: possibly the antechamber of a tumulus tomb of Alexander in Alexandria according to Achille Adriani (sketch by the author)

In support of Adriani's hypothesis parallels may be drawn with the Royal Tombs at Vergina in Macedonia, including that probably belonging to Alexander's father, since they also consisted of man-made stone chambers covered over by substantial mounds of earth. Furthermore, the Alabaster Tomb is undeniably part of a monument of the very highest quality and magnificence: for example, its polished alabaster interior faces are imitated with paintwork in other major Ptolemaic tombs found in Alexandria.[16] Nevertheless, there is no

---

[16] For example in the Necropolis of Moustafa Pasha and the Necropolis of Anfushi: see Achille Adriani, *La Tomba di Alessandro*, Rome, 2000, Plates 20-22.

specific evidence to link it with Alexander, whereas there were very many other individuals, who died within its date range and were of sufficient status to merit such a grand sepulcher: for instance, members of the royal family and certain top officials and generals. Neither is its location easy to reconcile with the inference from Achilles Tatius, Zenobius and Strabo that Alexander's tomb was close to the central crossroads of the ancient city.

Supposing that the Alabaster Tomb was indeed part of a tomb of Alexander, then it is more likely to have been his first Alexandrian tomb constructed by Ptolemy Philadelphus, rather than the Soma Mausoleum built by Ptolemy Philopator. Firstly, Macedonian influence in tomb design is likely to have been more pronounced under the earliest Ptolemies. Secondly, an earth tumulus fits ill with Lucan's description of the Soma as a monumentally tall mausoleum surmounted by a pyramid and the "splendid temple" mentioned by Ammianus Marcellinus.[17] Thirdly, it is not necessary to suppose that the first tomb was on the same site as Philopator's Soma Mausoleum.

If the first Alexandrian tomb of Alexander was a Macedonian style tumulus, and the very existence of the Alabaster Tomb bolsters this idea, then the Paneum, described by Strabo as a large, conical, artificial hill near the middle of the city, could be a good candidate.[18] It is in fact possible that the tumulus over the Alabaster Tomb was the Paneum, since the location of the latter is not precisely known and it is anyway not entirely certain that the Alabaster Tomb always stood in the same spot in which its slabs were excavated.

* * * * * * * * *

Clearly, the question of the location of the Soma Mausoleum built by Philopator is complex and difficult. The ancient testimony is enigmatic and the archaeological information is fragmentary and susceptible to a variety of interpretations. Nevertheless, I believe that the question can be answered quite specifically. This is because it appears that there is a unique sensible hypothesis, which fits all the evidence simultaneously. Furthermore, this same theory seems to be helpful in explaining various other mysteries concerning ancient Alexandria, which have previously been considered unrelated to the problem of Alexander's tomb. I first published this hypothesis in the American Journal of Ancient History in 2003 in a paper reproduced in Appendix D. What follows is an updated and extended version of the same arguments.

The accounts of Strabo and Diodorus describe the Soma as a walled enclosure or *temenos*, whilst Achilles Tatius and Zenobius locate it in the middle of the city, probably straddling or adjacent to the central crossroads. If Mahmoud Bey is correct in placing this crossroads at the intersection with Canopic Way of the principal street running south from the Lochias peninsula, then the Soma

---

[17] Ammianus Marcellinus, *Res Gestae* 22.11.7; Zenobius, *Proverbia* 3.94, describes the construction of a "memorial house," which does not sound at all like a description of a tumulus tomb.
[18] Strabo 17.1.10.

enclosure will have been contiguous with the Royal Palaces, which is consistent with Strabo's description of the Soma being part of an extended Royal Quarter. But what would this enclosure have looked like? How large might it have been? Diodorus, who certainly saw it when he visited Alexandria in ~50BC, says it was "worthy of the glory of Alexander in size and construction", so he must have considered it immense.[19] It is possible to form some conception of what this might mean by considering some *temenos* structures in other cities, especially those which might have inspired Alexander, the early Ptolemies and their architects.

The Mausoleum at Halicarnassus stood in a walled enclosure measuring 100 x 240 metres.[20] Reconstructions suggest its walls were at least 5 metres high. Halicarnassus was besieged by Alexander for some months in 333 BC and formed part of the Ptolemaic empire in the 3rd century BC. There are some striking parallels with Alexandria. Not only did the Mausoleum lie at the centre of ancient Halicarnassus, but also the royal palace was located on a promontory next to the harbour, rather like a smaller version of the Lochias peninsula. It would seem unlikely, that the Soma enclosure, built for a far more important king in a much larger city, was smaller than the *temenos* of the Mausoleum of Mausolus.

The layout of Memphis would, naturally, have been an even more immediate influence upon Alexandria's architects and their patrons. It was dominated by two vast, quadrilateral temple enclosures, both nearly 500 metres square (Figure 3.5). Various highways ran straight through them, entering and exiting via gates in opposite walls, as is indicated in the archaeological map of the more southerly of these *temenos* structures (Figure 9.4), which accommodated the temple-complex of Ptah.[21] If the builders of the Soma drew any inspiration from the sacred precincts at Memphis and especially if they harboured any ambitions to rival them, then the Alexandrian enclosure may well have been hundreds of metres square.

The interesting aspect of the notion that the Soma enclosure may have been very extensive is that it resolves several incongruities in the evidence concerning ancient Alexandria. Firstly, Achilles Tatius has a rather curious description of walking westwards down Canopic Way through an "open" part of the city, then entering into a "second city", named after Alexander, where he sees the central crossroads lined with magnificent colonnades.[22] If the Soma enclosure were very large and encompassed the central crossroads, then this suddenly makes perfect sense, because the "second city" then *becomes* the Soma enclosure. It

---

[19] Diodorus Siculus 17.52.6 (for his visit) & 18.28 (for his description of the *temenos* of Alexander).
[20] Kristian Jeppesen, "Tot Operum Opus, Ergebnisse der Dänischen Forschungen zum Maussolleion von Halikarnass seit 1966," *Jahrbuch des Deutschen Archäologischen Instituts* 107, 1992. pp. 59-102.
[21] David Jeffreys, *The Survey of Memphis*, Egypt Exploration Society, London, 1985, Figure 63.
[22] Achilles Tatius, *Clitophon and Leucippe* 5.1; refer to Chapter 4 for a full translation of this passage.

would thus be the walls of the Soma enclosure, rather than the defences of the city, that Caesar failed to stop to admire on his way to visit Alexander's tomb in Lucan's *Pharsalia*.[23]

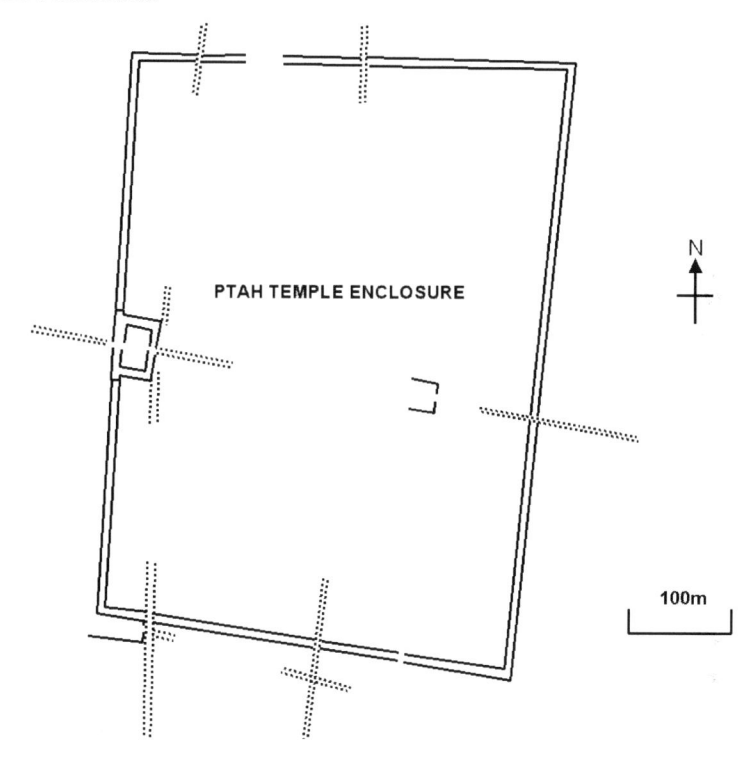

Figure 9.4. The *temenos* of Ptah at Memphis, perhaps the inspiration for the Soma enclosure in Alexandria.

There is intriguing testimony, which may corroborate Achilles Tatius, dating from some five centuries after his time. A passage from the Arab writer Suyuti (or Sujuti), where he quotes the 9th Century Islamic scholar, Ibn Abdel Hakim, has long puzzled historians of Alexandria:-

"Alexandria consists of three towns, one beside the other, each surrounded by its own wall. All three are enclosed by an outer, fortified wall."[24]

There is now a way of understanding this enigmatic report, if the Soma enclosure were the first town, the Serapeum enclosure a second and the rest of the city lying between them were the third town.

The power of the hypothesis that the Soma enclosure was very large to elucidate the topographical mysteries of ancient Alexandria is further illustrated by the

---

[23] Lucan, *Pharsalia* 10.14-20, e.g. translated by J.D. Duff, Loeb Classical Library.
[24] Quoted by Alfred Butler, *The Arab Invasion of Egypt...*, Ch. XXIV and by Evaristo Breccia, *Alexandrea ad Aegyptum*, p. 70; the latter errs in stating that Hakim was quoting Sujuti.

possibility that the Soma enclosure and the Alpha Quarter were one and the same. Achilles Tatius describes a place at the central crossroads that was named after Alexander and which is associated with the Soma due to Zenobius' statement that Alexander's tomb lay at the center of Alexandria. Similarly, Pseudo-Callisthenes says that the Alpha Quarter was named after Alexander.[25] Once it is conceived that the two regions were comparable in size, then the conclusion that they are variant names for the same district becomes clear. The obvious objection would be Strabo's inclusion of the Soma in the Royal Quarter. However, he fails to mention the traditional sub-division of the city into five quarters at all, so he may, as a foreigner, simply be partitioning it according to logic rather than tradition. The Beta Quarter may not have extended much beyond the area Strabo calls the "inner palaces", which also seems to coincide with the district that was called the Bruchium in the Roman era (i.e. the eastern coastline of the Great Harbour and the Lochias Promontory). But Strabo evidently combined the Alpha and Beta Quarters in defining his Royal District of *Basileion*, which explains how he could truthfully assert that it constituted approaching a third of the urban area of the city.

Another ostensibly paradoxical piece of evidence is the existence of a substantial fragment of a Ptolemaic wall of superlative quality two hundred metres north of the site of the eastern Rosetta Gate of the medieval city in the modern Shallalat Gardens, which in turn lay just a few tens of metres east of Mahmoud Bey's location for the central crossroads.[26] It has proven difficult to make sense of this fragment in the context of the defensive walls of Alexandria, for it is located near the centre of the ancient city. By virtue of the magnificent quality of its masonry and the fact that it lies close to the ancient city's principal north-south thoroughfare, it must surely delineate the boundary of some very high status area of the metropolis. Our new perspective should lead us to suspect that it is the last remaining portion of the enclosure wall of the Soma.

The rest of the ruins of the Tulunid wall circuit were substantially remodeled and refortified in the 1820's, but subsequently demolished in the late 19th century. However, these walls and especially their massive towers were magnificently recorded in the Description de l'Egypte by Napoleon's coterie of *savants* (Figure 9.5). Their map of the city (Figure 8.2 with detail of the eastern part of the city in Figure 9.6) clearly indicates the double nature of most of the wall circuit, which had until then survived particularly well in its eastern sectors.[27] There are some good reasons to believe that the inner and outer rings were not coeval constructions and that the outer circuit may in fact be late

---

[25] Stoneman (translator), *The Greek Alexander Romance* 1.32.
[26] The surviving wall is identified as Hellenistic (Ptolemaic) by Jean-Yves Empereur, *Alexandria Rediscovered*, Chapter 3, pp. 51-3; there is one other surviving medieval tower ~300m to the south.
[27] Galice Bey undertook a massive program of reconstruction of the medieval wall circuit in 1826 at the behest of the Viceroy Mohammed Ali, so later maps differ in many details from the undisturbed version in the Description de l'Egypte.

The Quest for the Tomb of Alexander by Andrew Chugg

Roman or in parts even earlier. Firstly, we have seen that the population in the late Roman period had shrunk to the point where some reduction in the wall perimeter would have been a natural development. Secondly, the surviving fragment in the Shallalat Gardens appears to be typically Ptolemaic both in its style and the type of stone used, though it was later incorporated in the medieval walls. Thirdly, some of the illustrations of the walls in the Description de l'Egypte depict stonework, which looks more typically ancient, rather than Arab, in style: for example, having semicircular rather than pointed arches. The outer portal of the Rosetta Gate also appears to have been ancient as depicted in an aquatint from a sketch by Luigi Mayer from about 1792 (Figure 9.7). The pillars to either side sported Corinthian capitals and the stone of the frame has a pink coloration in the original aquatint (rear cover), which indicates the polished pink granite that was widely used in the public architecture of ancient Alexandria: fragments of another ancient, rectangular portal in pink granite are displayed at Pompey's Pillar (site of Serapeum) in modern Alexandria. Furthermore, the statue niche in the wall beside the gate must be ancient, since the public representation of human figures is banned by religious doctrine in Islamic art. An exterior view of the Rosetta Gate was drawn by Louis-François Cassas during his visit in 1785 (Figure 9.8).

Figure 9.5. Contrasting styles in views of the "medieval" walls and towers of Alexandria from the Description de l'Egypte, Pl. 89, Etat Moderne II (author's collection)

Examining the Napoleonic map in more detail (Figure 9.6), a curious little zig-zag is marked in the course of the outer wall precisely where Mahmoud Bey's ancient street R3 would have intersected this wall on the northern side. Given this coincidence, this zig-zag may be a vestige of a gateway in the outer wall, yet it is not echoed by the inner wall. Furthermore, Pococke, who paced around the walls in 1737 made some pertinent observations:-

The outer walls around the old city are very beautifully built of hewn stone, and seem to be antient (sic); all the arches being true, and the workmanship very good... The inner walls of

Alexander's City

the old city, which seem to be of the middle ages, are much stronger and higher than the others and defended by large high towers.[28]

Pococke is amply corroborated by the map published by Louis-François Cassas (Figure 9.9), which labels the eastern walls with the legends: *anciennes murailles elevées en differents temps* and *tours construites avec d'anciens debris*, which translate, "ancient walls raised in different eras" and "towers built with ancient debris".

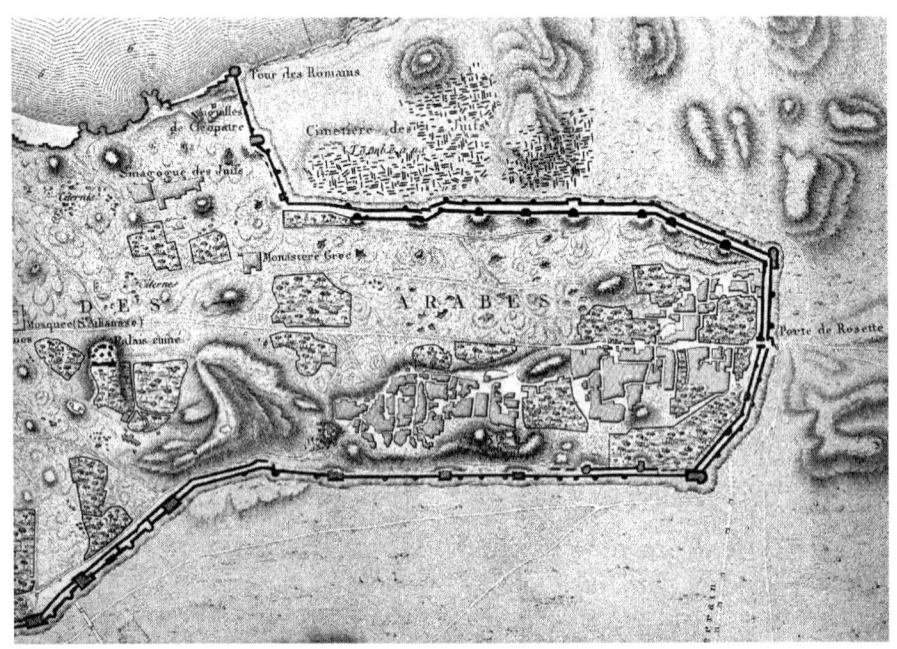

Figure 9.6. Detail of the general plan of Alexandria from the Description de l'Egypte, Planche 84, Etat Moderne II (author's collection)

Finally, Hogarth observed in 1895 that the fosse associated with the Tulunid walls (Figure 9.10) running beside Mahmoud Bey's street L2 in their eastern sector had "been cut to a depth of about 15 feet", and showed "no indications of having pierced large buildings". This strongly indicates that the line of the Tulunid walls in this sector was far more ancient than the Arab period, since it is certain that the ancient city existed on both sides of these walls.[29]

---

[28] Pococke, *Description of the East*, 1743, Vol. 1, pp.3-4; Louis-François Cassas visited Alexandria twice in 1785 and drew his views and map of the town, published in *Voyage pittoresque de la Syrie, de la Phénicie, de la Palestine et de la Basse Egypte*, Paris, 1799.

[29] D.G. Hogarth, "Report on Prospects for Research in Alexandria," *Egypt Exploration Fund*, 1894-5, p. 8. In a later section dealing with his investigations south of Canopic Way (p. 13) Hogarth adds, "Some fragments of Roman brick-work project from the sides of fosse, belonging evidently to a building entirely ruined." However, this was an isolated exception to the general rule. Hogarth evidently investigated the entire 2km section of this ditch between the Tower of the Romans and the SE corner of the Arab city (as marked on his accompanying map) and found just this single instance of Roman brickwork. Such brickwork could easily be explained as the remains

The Quest for the Tomb of Alexander by Andrew Chugg

Figure 9.7. Aquatinted engraving of the Rosetta Gate from a sketch of ~1792 by Luigi Mayer, published in London by R. Bowyer on 1st May 1801 (author's collection)

Figure 9.8. Exterior view of the Rosetta Gate in 1785 based on a drawing by L-F Cassas (author's collection)

of a bridge or other structure built across an existing ditch, so it has no significance for the general theory that the wall line is older than the Arab period.

Alexander's City

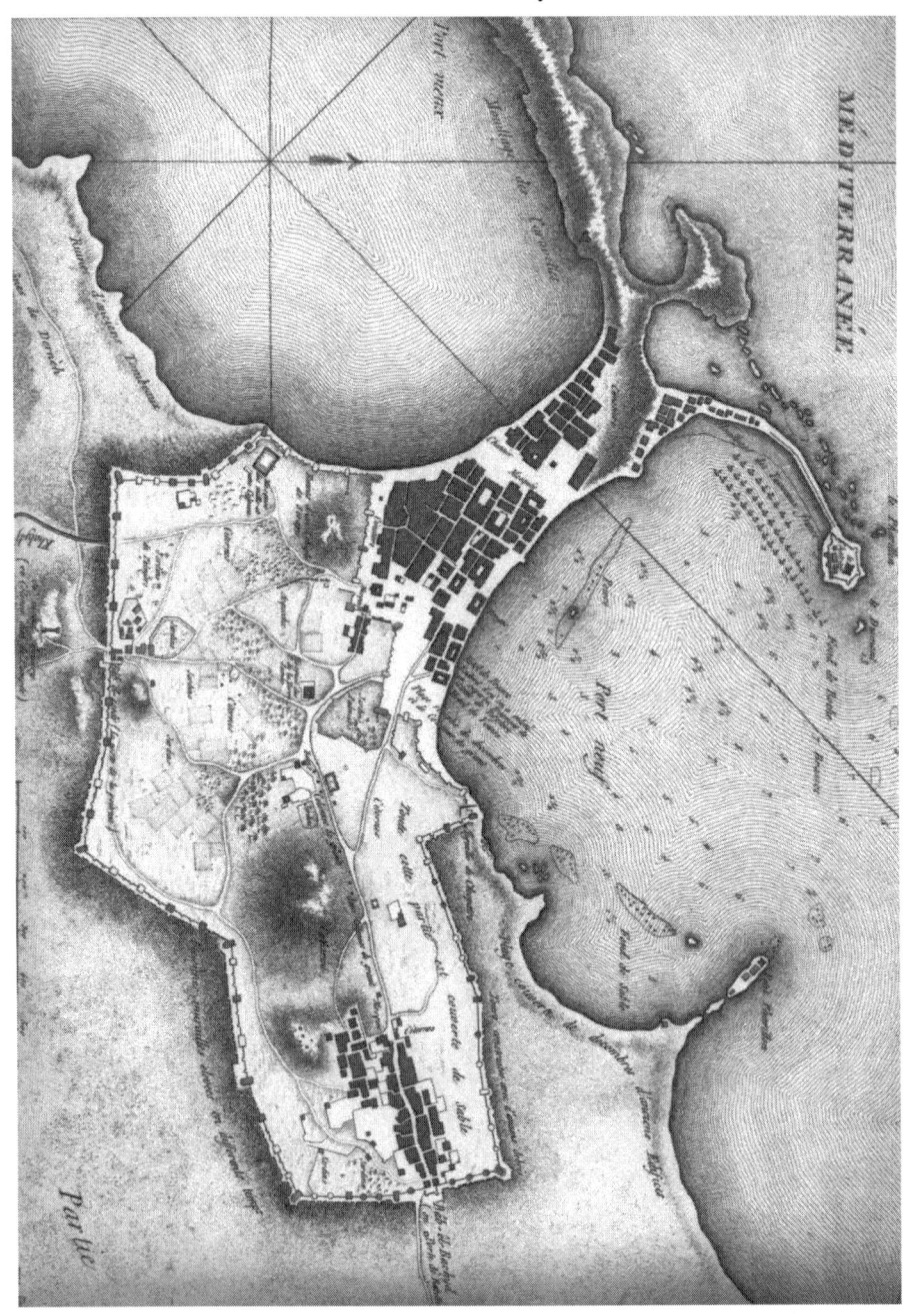

Figure 9.9. Map of Alexandria in 1785 by L-F Cassas – the outline of the city appears to have been based on the d'Anville map of 1866, which in turn followed the 1687 plan of Razaud shown in Figure 8.1, but Cassas introduced refinements (author's collection)

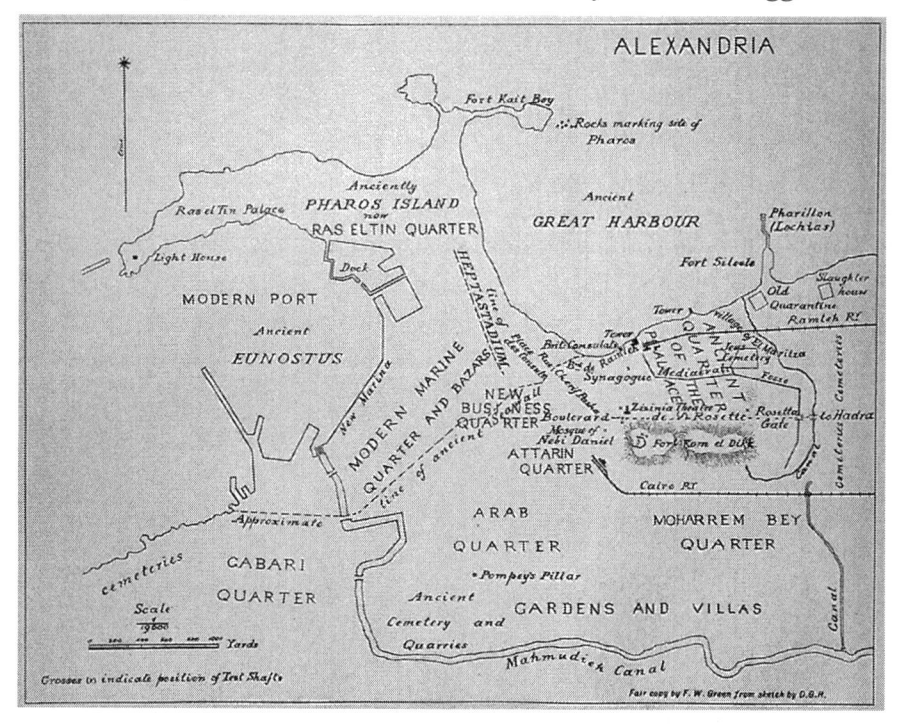

The Quest for the Tomb of Alexander by Andrew Chugg

Figure 9.10. Plan of Alexandria in 1895 by D.G. Hogarth showing the "Mediaeval Fosse" which still marked the course of the demolished walls

It may also be relevant that Mahmoud Bey shows the southern and eastern sectors of the medieval walls coinciding with the ancient street grid to a notable degree (Figure 4.2). In fact, the whole eastern section of these walls from Mahmoud's street R1 west to R3 encloses an area about 600 metres by 800 metres on three sides. It would seem probable that the late Roman (and subsequently the Arab) walls here incorporated the remnants of the enclosure wall of the *temenos* of the Soma.

A New Plan of Ancient Alexandria with the Soma shown in this location is given in Figure 9.11. Notice that the missing western stretches of its walls are defined so as to make them symmetrical with the eastern side. This has the special merit of explaining the short, oblique deviation in the medieval walls on their northern side in the vicinity of the zigzag that we have identified as a possible vestige of an ancient gateway.

Scant excavation has ever been undertaken within the proposed area of the Soma enclosure. However, Hogarth found traces of "a massive structure" just north of Canopic Way near its intersection with the transverse street labelled R2 at the heart of the area.[30] It is also interesting that the only ancient sculpted head

---

[30] D.G. Hogarth, *Egypt Exploration Fund*, 1894-5, p. 8.

of Alexander with a precise provenance within Alexandria was discovered at the intersection of R1 with L2 inside the proposed *temenos* of the Soma.[31] Furthermore, Mahmoud Bey provides the following tantalizing description of finds within the area in the early to mid 19th century:-

In fact, the excavations which were made by Gallis Bey[32] (and those which were executed later) discovered some enormous foundation walls on Canopic Way on the west side between the two transverse streets R1 and R2 together with a great number of fallen columns. Beside Canopic Way and R1 we ourselves have discovered several of them beneath the rubble: one can still today see some overthrown in the area around the first bastion. The extent of these monumental foundations is greater than 150 metres on each side. In conclusion, everything on this site shows us that this was the finest monument in the city of Alexandria…

Naturally, the Soma Mausoleum will have been among the finest and most impressive buildings in ancient Alexandria.

*   *   *   *   *   *   *   *   *

It is interesting to note that several sources describe the shape of ancient Alexandria as resembling a chlamys, a type of short Greek cloak.[33] However, this shape is superficially difficult to recognise in the form of the ancient city reconstructed in the plans of Mahmoud Bey and Henry Salt. Yet a fair approximation to the outline of a chlamys is provided by the proposed plan of the Soma enclosure in Fig. 9.11. A possibility is that this enclosure is in fact the city as it was originally founded by Alexander, for it is almost inconceivable that his foundation was as large as the later city revealed by Mahmoud Bey's excavations. Strabo actually uses the term *peribolos* to describe Alexander's Alexandria just two sections prior to his description of the Soma enclosure using the same word.[34] As we have seen in the chapter on *The Capital of Memory* (above), one way of translating Strabo's mention of the Soma would be to infer that he was indeed attempting to indicate that the Soma enclosure was simply the region within the original boundary wall of Alexander's foundation. This hypothesis also explains why the wall line of the Soma enclosure would have dated back to the origin of the city, as suggested by Hogarth's inspection revealing an absence of cut-through foundations within its perimeter ditch. Presumably a memory that the early city had the shape of a chlamys became so fixed in Alexandrian tradition that it continued to be repeated, even after the booming expansion of the city's bounds had rendered the comparison obsolete.

*   *   *   *   *   *   *   *   *

---

[31] Barbara Tkaczow, *Topography of Ancient Alexandria (An Archaeological Map)*, Warsaw 1993, Object 19, p. 193.
[32] This was Galice Bey, during his reconstruction of the Tulunid defences in 1826.
[33] Strabo, *Geography* 17.1.8; Plutarch, *Alexander* 26.5; Diodorus 17.52.3; Pliny, *Natural History* 5.11.62 where it is specifically a "Macedonian chlamys"; cf. F.B. Tarbell, "The Form of the Chlamys," *Classical Philology* I, 1906, pp. 283-9.
[34] Strabo, *Geography* 17.1.6 & 17.1.8.

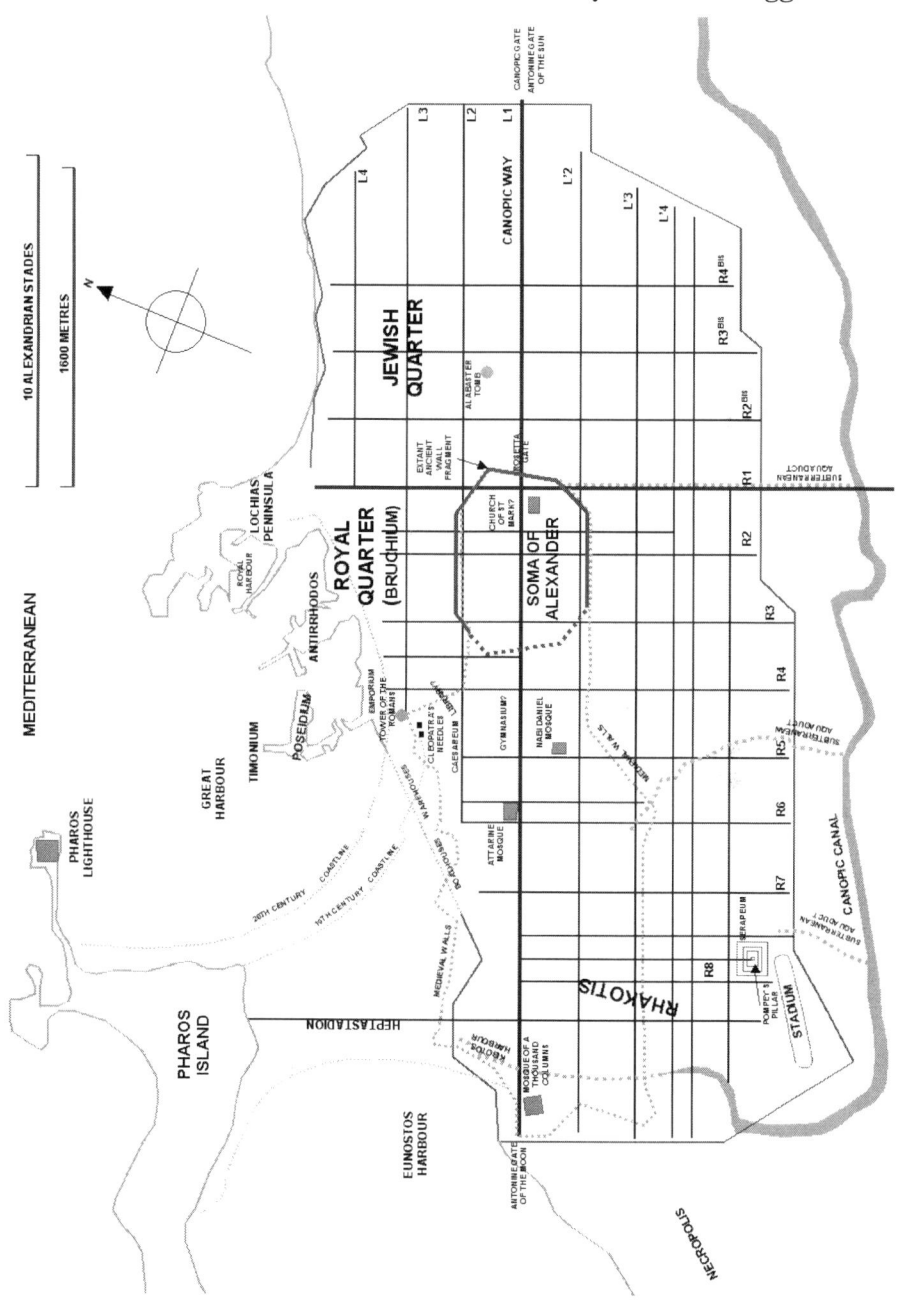

The Quest for the Tomb of Alexander by Andrew Chugg

Figure 9.11. A New Plan of Ancient Alexandria as proposed by the author

In the course of narrating this curious history a variety of conjectures have been put forward concerning Alexander's death and his several tombs. At this juncture, it will be convenient to recapitulate the key points, prior to proceeding

Alexander's City

to the climax of our account, in which a yet more controversial hypothesis will be enunciated and explored. The following inferences are significant because they specifically identify where both the Memphite tomb and the Alexandrian Soma are probably to be found. Equally importantly they imply the possibility of defining practicable archaeological tests by which the sites might be firmly attributed.

1) Alexander the Great probably died of cerebral malaria due to infection by the falciparum malarial parasite when bitten by mosquitoes during a boating trip among the marshes south of Babylon about four weeks before his death.

2) Alexander was entombed at Memphis in 321 BC, where he remained for at least several decades. This tomb was probably located at the Nectanebo II temple in the Serapeum complex at Saqqara. Ptolemy probably commissioned a cult statue of Alexander for this tomb. In this sculpture Alexander wore an elephant scalp and the ram's horns of Ammon. Ptolemy used the same design in his original series of silver tetradrachm coins first issued from about 320BC. The entrance of the Nectanebo II temple was guarded by a group of Greek statues of philosophers and poets dating to the reign of the first Ptolemy, which should be interpreted as part of the embellishment of the tomb. The side-chamber seemingly appended to the Nectanebo temple is an excellent candidate for having accommodated the sarcophagus containing Alexander's body.

3) The sarcophagus sculpted for the tomb of the pharaoh Nectanebo II and now in the British Museum has a much better claim to having been used for Alexander's body than has previously been recognised. If this claim is true, then the Nectanebo temple at the Serapeum in North Saqqara was almost certainly the site of Alexander's first tomb in Egypt.

4) The famous tomb of Alexander at Alexandria was built around 215BC by Ptolemy Philopator. It lay in a mausoleum within an enclosure known as the Soma and its architecture was probably modelled on that of the Mausoleum at Halicarnassus. It was tall and splendid with a pyramidal roof probably supported by an elevated peristyle. There was a subterranean funeral chamber beneath the building, which was sealed by the emperor Septimius Severus and probably re-sealed by his son, the emperor Caracalla, who was the last known visitor to the chamber in AD215.

5) The mausoleum building overlying the funeral chamber was destroyed with high probability in the century between AD262 and AD365. The revolt of Aemilianus, the Palmyran wars between Zenobia and Aurelian, the uprising of Firmus and the sack of the city by Diocletian remain suspects for the cause of its destruction, but the most likely culprit was the earthquake and tsunami which struck Alexandria in

The Quest for the Tomb of Alexander by Andrew Chugg

AD365. The collapsed masonry might have protected the burial chamber and its contents from immediate rediscovery. Nevertheless, the vault must surely have been excavated in the late 4th century, since Libanius states that Alexander's body was on display in the city in about AD390 and because the empty sarcophagus made for Nectanebo II, but traditionally associated with Alexander's tomb, evidently remained on public display until the arrival of Napoleon's expedition in Alexandria in 1798.

6) The Soma was located in a walled sacred precinct (a *temenos* or *peribolos*) in the shape of a chlamys and with dimensions of the order of 800 x 600 metres, which encompassed the central crossroads south of the Lochias Peninsula and straddled Canopic Way. The surviving Ptolemaic wall fragment in the Shallalat Gardens and the ancient Rosetta Gate drawn by Mayer in the 1780's were probably parts of the *temenos* enclosure of the Soma and it is likely that the entire eastern sector of the medieval walls of Alexandria was established in the same line as the walls of the Soma enclosure.

There are those who regard the hunt for the Soma as sufficiently hopeless, that they see no point in its active pursuit. They plead the supposed paucity of the evidence and the idea that there are many more accessible objectives for archaeological funding in the Egyptian context.[35] Yet I have shown that there exist in fact a great number of relevant clues from multifarious sources, perhaps lacking only a sufficiently inspired decipherment. Furthermore, it is the very inaccessibility of the most interesting sites, sealed deep beneath a modern metropolis, which permits some lingering optimism regarding the preservation of the foundations of the Soma Mausoleum. Perhaps a more credible explanation for the reluctance of some to become involved in the search is that it is intrinsically risky to do so, for on this subject there has always been a better chance of being proved wrong than right. Nevertheless, others will undoubtedly consider that the magnitude of the prize is a sufficient incentive to pursue even so elusive a goal.

Maybe the last word on the hunt for the Soma should be left to the protagonist of the epic theatrical production that was ancient Alexandria:-

Toil and risk are the price of glory, but it is a lovely thing to live with courage and die leaving an everlasting fame.

Alexander the Great, *Address at the Beas*[36]

---

[35] E.g. D.G. Hogarth, *Egypt Exploration Fund*, 1894-5.
[36] Arrian, *Anabasis* 5.26.4.

10. Famous Alexandrian Mummies

Hamlet: *To what base use we may return, Horatio! Why may not imagination trace the noble dust of Alexander, till he find it stopping a bung-hole?*
Horatio: *'Twere to consider too curiously, to consider so.*
Hamlet: *No, faith, not a jot; but to follow him thither with modesty enough, and likelihood to lead it: as thus; Alexander died, Alexander was buried, Alexander returneth into dust; the dust is earth; of earth we make loam; and why of that loam, whereto he was converted, might they not stop a beer-barrel?*

William Shakespeare, Hamlet, Act V, Scene I

The ultimate question in the quest for Alexander's tomb must be the fate of his actual body. The evidence suggests that we should be especially interested in any already ancient mummified corpses, which appeared within the immediate vicinity of Mahmoud Bey's central crossroads of Alexandria at the end of the 4th century AD. These might be deemed stringent criteria, yet it transpires that there exists a unique set of human remains, which appears to satisfy them.

According to various Christian sources, the earliest being Clement of Alexandria in about AD200, the church in Alexandria was founded by St Mark the Evangelist in the mid-first century AD.[1] In the Late Roman period a Church and Tomb of St Mark became one of the key religious sites in the city.[2] The oldest reliable historical reference to the tomb itself is found in the Lausiac History of Palladius, who wrote in the early 5th century AD of a pilgrimage "to the Martyrion of Mark at Alexandria," which took place at the end of the 4th century, but additionally St Jerome was the first to mention that St Mark was buried in Alexandria, thus implying the tomb, in AD392.[3] Although the second half of a Passio of St Peter claims to describe a tomb of St Mark in Alexandria in AD311, William Telfer has shown that this part of the manuscript was the invention of a 6th century hagiographer, who seems to have been inspired by the most influential Christian account of the Evangelist's career, the Acts of St Mark.[4] This is an apocryphal account of the martyrdom and entombment of the saint, which may well have been composed in Alexandria in the late 4th century.

---

[1] Morton Smith, *Clement of Alexandria and a Secret Gospel of Mark*, Harvard University Press, 1973; Eusebius, *Ecclesiastical History*, 2.16; Birger A. Pearson, "Earliest Christianity in Egypt: Some Observations," *The Roots of Egyptian Christianity*, edited by Birger Pearson and James Goehring, Philadelphia, 1986, pp.132-159.
[2] M. Chaîne, "L'Église de Saint-Marc à Alexandrie," *Revue de l'Orient Chrétien*, Vol. 24, 1924, pp.372-386.
[3] Palladius, *Lausiac History*, Section 45 on *Philoromus of Galatia*; St Jerome, *De viris illustribus* 8 written in Bethlehem in AD392 (as noted within the work by its author) mentions that St Mark died in the 8th year of Nero and was buried in Alexandria.
[4] William Telfer, "St Peter of Alexandria and Arius," *Analecta Bollandiana* 67, 1949, pp.117-130; Richard Adalbert Lipsius, *Die Apokryphen Apostelgeschichten Und Apostellegenden* 2/2:338-39, Braunschweig, 1883-90.

The Quest for the Tomb of Alexander by Andrew Chugg

According to these Acts, the pagans attempted to burn St Mark's body, but a miraculous storm intervened and doused the flames allowing the Christians to snatch back the corpse and convey it to their church beside the sea in a district of Alexandria called Boukolia. The oldest versions of the Acts mention that the Christians subsequently entombed the body in an eminent location in the east of the city. Later writers have often assumed that the location of St Mark's tomb was at the site of the church in Boukolia, which they consequently infer to have occupied the site of the Late Roman Church of St Mark, said by other ancient sources to have housed St Mark's tomb. Hence they place the Martyrion of St Mark by the sea to the east of Lochias.[5] However, the original Acts did not provide any grounds for making such a connection.[6] An alternative Christian tradition in Dorotheus, Eutychius and the Chronicon Paschale states that St Mark's body actually was burnt. For example, Dorotheus of Tyre observes:-

It is said that the Apostle St Mark was led from the place called Boukolou to that referred to by the name of Angelion and he was burnt there.[7]

Dorotheus is a late 3rd to early 4th century Christian figure, which suggests that the tradition of the cremated corpse is older than the tradition that the body was miraculously preserved from attempted incineration, all versions of which seem to stem from the Acts. It may consequently be suspected that the miracle in the Acts was contrived at the end of the 4th century to explain a newly fabricated tomb of the saint.

In AD828 there transpired the most remarkable event in the history of the Church of St Mark: the abduction of the saint's remains by the Venetians, which is known in Italy as the *Translazione*. A pair of Venetian merchant captains, Buono, Tribune of Malamocco, and Rustico of Torcello, sailed their vessels into the port of Alexandria, where they visited the Church of St Mark the Evangelist. The Alexandrian clergy were said at that time to be concerned for the safety of their most sacred relics, especially the corpse of the Evangelist, due to the antagonistic rule of their Islamic governors. Some accounts suggest that the Arabs were appropriating rich stones from the church to construct a palace. The Venetians persuaded (or bribed) the guardians of the remains to allow them to be taken away. One version of the legend explains that the shroud was slit up the back and the corpse of St Claudian, which was close at hand, was substituted for that of St Mark in order to conceal the theft. The Evangelist's remains were then carried down to the waiting ships in a large basket. The

---

[5] Such a line is taken by various modern authorities, e.g. Christopher Haas, *Alexandria in Late Antiquity*, John Hopkins University Press, 1997, pp. 213, 271-2, 341 and map on p. 2; so too Evaristo Breccia, *Alexandrea ad Aegyptum*, 1922, map in pocket inside back flap.

[6] J-P Migne (ed.), *Patrologia Graeca*, Vol. 115, cols. 163-170; Getatchew Haile, "A New Ethiopic Version of the Acts of St Mark," *Analecta Bollandiana* 99, 1981, pp.117-34; Severus, *History of the Patriarchs*, ed. & tr. B. Evetts in *Patrologia Orientalis*, Vol. 1, 1904, pp.135-148.

[7] See J-P Migne (ed.), *Patrologia Graeca*, 86, col. 59, note, which cites the *Synopsis of the Apostles* by Dorotheus of Tyre; *Chronicon Paschale* 252, in *Patrologia Graeca* 92, cols. 608-609; Eutychius 336 in *Patrologia Graeca* 111, col. 983.

aroma of the embalming spices was so overpowering as to arouse the suspicions of the local authorities, but covering the remains with pork, anathema to Moslems, foiled an inspection by port officials. The inspectors fled with cries of "Kanzir! Kanzir!" (Pig). The body was then wrapped in canvas and hoisted up to the yardarm. A visitation from St Mark's ghost subsequently saved the ship from some peril, either a reef or a storm, in the course of the journey back to Venice.[8]

This story is preserved in a set of mosaics in the Basilica of St Mark in Venice (Figure 10.1) dated by Gardner Wilkinson to the late 11th century on the grounds that they are an original feature, although they may not have been completed until some time in the 12th century.[9] They cover the interior of the arch between the presbytery and the *Capella di San Clemente*. It is interesting that these representations depict the saint's body with intact flesh and beard, rather than as a skeleton, despite his having been dead for centuries at the *Translazione*. Is this mere artistic convention or does it hint at a mummified corpse? The *Translazione* has also been related by several early Venetian chroniclers, such as Martino da Canale in *La Cronique des Veniciens* dating to 1275, who asserts that the aroma of the corpse was so strong that, "If all the spices of the world had been gathered together in Alexandria, they could not have so perfumed the city." P. Daru adds that the corpse was sealed in linen.[10]

The evidence of special interest for our story is the short legend in the Braun and Hogenberg map of Alexandria, which identifies the location of a stone just inside the Cairo Gate of Alexandria, later known as the Rosetta Gate, beneath which the Venetians are stated to have discovered St Mark's body (Figure 9.1).[11]

There is a mention of St Mark's church lying close by a gate on the eastern side of the city in the Chronicle of John of Nikiu (circa AD670) in the context of an account of a battle in ~AD609:-

And Nicetas opened the second gate, which was close to the church of St Mark the Evangelist, and he issued forth with his barbarian auxiliaries, and they went in pursuit of the fleeing troops and put some of them to the sword....[12]

The association of St Mark with a gateway of Alexandria at this time is also supported by a 7th century ivory from the city (now in the Louvre), which depicts the Evangelist enthroned before a monumental gateway and surrounded by his successors as Patriarch.

---

[8] John Julius Norwich, *Venice: the Rise to Empire*, Allen Lane, London, 1977, pp.52-3.
[9] Gardner Wilkinson, "On an early mosaic in St Mark's [Venice] representing the removal of the body of the evangelist to Venice," *Journal of the British Archaeological Association* 7, 1851, p.258; Otto Demus, *The Mosaic Decoration of San Marco Venice*, University of Chicago Press, 1988, pp.28-38.
[10] P. Daru, *Histoire de Venise*, 3rd edition, Tome 1, Paris, 1826, p.56.
[11] Georg Braun and Frans Hogenberg, *Civitates Orbis Terrarum*, Cologne, 1572; F.L. Norden, *Voyage d'Egypte et de Nubie*, Paris, 1755, *Carte Particuliére de la Vieille et de la Nouvelle Aléxandrie, et des Ports*, Tab. I, appears to identify the Attarine Mosque as St Mark's, but this must be an error.
[12] John of Nikiu, *Chronicle* 108.8-9.

The Quest for the Tomb of Alexander by Andrew Chugg

·MARCVM FVRANTVR·KANZIRHIVOCIFERANTVR·

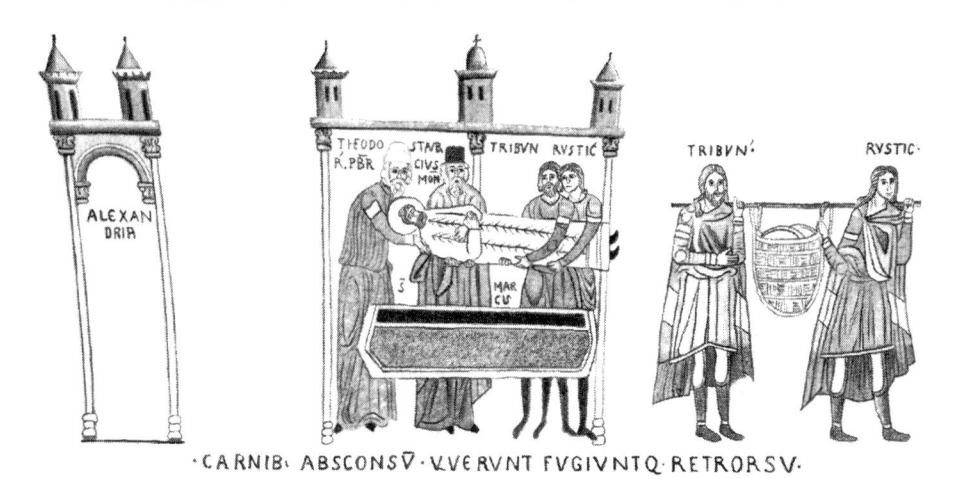

·CARNIB· ABSCONSV·VVERVNT FVGIVNTQ·RETRORSV·

Figure 10.1. A mosaic of the 12th century on an arching vault in the Basilica di San Marco depicting Buono the tribune and Rustico receiving the corpse of St Mark from Theodorus the presbyter and Staurcius the monk in Alexandria; they carry the body off in a basket concealed beneath pork (sketch by the author)

There survives an account of a pilgrimage to Alexandria by a certain Arculfus in about AD680, which seems also to locate the Church of St Mark just inside the gate on the main route to Cairo:-

Item de parte Aegipti aduentantibus et urbem intrantibus Alexandrinam (alexandriam) ab aquilonali [propinquo] latere occurrit grandis ecclesia structurae, in qua Marcus euangelista in terra humatus iacet; cuius sepulchrum ante altare in orientali eiusdem quadrangulae loco ecclesiae memoria superposita marmoreis lapidibus constructa monstratur.[13]

"Approaching from the direction of Egypt as one enters the city of Alexandria on (almost) the north side a large church presents itself, in which Mark the Evangelist lies buried in the ground. His tomb is on view before the altar in the east end of this square church and a memorial to him has been built of marble stones on top of it."

The Latin presents some ambiguities, preserved in the translation, especially concerning whether Arculfus approached Alexandria from the north or alternatively saw the church on his north side on entering the city. It is feasible that he thought he was entering Alexandria from the north, even though the Mediterranean shore lies on the northern side. The Rosetta Gate faced twenty degrees north of east and we know from other clues in the text indicating the date and time of Arculfus' arrival that the morning sun, by which he would have

---

[13] Adamnan, *de locis sanctis* 2.30.25, where *alexandriam* is an alternative and *propinquo* an addition in a second manuscript (B); J.H. Bernard (trans.), *Expliciunt peregrinations totius terre sancta, Guide-Book to Palestine*, Palestine Pilgrim Text Society, London, 1894, vi, p.33.

195

defined east, may have been about fifty degrees south of due east at the hour of his entry into Alexandria.

Around a century after Arculfus (circa AD750-800) Epiphanius the Monk confirmed the continuing presence of the remains:-

To the west, four days away, is the city of Alexandria. There Saint Mark the Apostle and Evangelist lies buried...[14]

In about AD1369 Guillaume de Machaut composed a poetical work in medieval French entitled *La Prise d'Alexandrie*, which relates the capture and temporary occupation of Alexandria by the King of Cyprus in AD1365. Several passages, when read together, demonstrate conclusively that the Gate of St Mark was then an alternative name for the Cairo/Rosetta Gate.[15] In lines 3182-4 we have:-

Saint Marc est la porte nommée,	This gate is called St Mark's,
Et pluseurs, qui nommer la veulent,	And some, who wished to name it,
La porte dou Poivre l'appellent.	They called it the Pepper Gate.

Then in lines 3214-7:-

En Alexandre a une rue	In Alexandria is a street
Qu'on claimme la rue dou Poivre.	Known as the Pepper Street.
Des autres forment se desoivre,	It differs much from the others
Car c'est la grant rue, à droit dire.	For it's the main street, rightly speaking.

Also in lines 3002-4:-

Ceste porte estoit appellé	This gate was called
La porte dou Poivre, & s'estoit	The Pepper Gate, and it was
Li chemins qui au Quaire aloit.	The road that led to Cairo.

Bernard, a French monk who visited Alexandria in about AD870, verified the abduction of the corpse by the Venetians, but also attested that the Church of St Mark lay close by a monastery dedicated to St Mark, which was located just *outside* the eastern Cairo/Rosetta/St Mark/Pepper Gate:-

Haec Alexandria mari adjacet, in qua praedicans sanctus Marcus Evangelium, gessit pontificale officium. Extra cujus portam orientalem est monasterium praedicti sancti, in quo sunt monachi apud ecclesiam, in qua prius ipse requievit. Venientes vero Venetii navigio tulerunt furtim corpus a custode ejus, et deportarunt ad suam insulam.[16]

"This Alexandria, in which St Mark the Evangelist preached and bore the Patriarchal office, is adjacent to the sea. Outside its eastern gate is the monastery of the saint, in which there are monks close by the church, in which

---

[14] Epiphanius the Monk, *Description of Palestine* 5 in *Patrologia Graeca*, Vol. 120, col. 266.
[15] Guillaume de Machaut, *La Prise d'Alixandre*, 1369, trans. R. Barton Palmer, Routledge, New York and London, 2002.
[16] Bernardus Monachus Francus, *Itinerarium 6, Patrologia Latina* Vol 121.

The Quest for the Tomb of Alexander by Andrew Chugg

he himself formerly lay at rest. But the Venetians coming by sea secretly took his body into their keeping, and bore it away to their own island."

The earliest surviving map of Alexandria was drawn by Ugo Comminelli in 1472. It too depicts some kind of religious establishment dedicated to St Mark outside the eastern gate (marked *sā marci* in the lower left of Figure 10.2).[17] Nevertheless, Bernard's testimony does not exclude the possibility that the Church lay just within the gate, whilst the associated monastery lay just outside the city walls, so the location for the Church specified by the Braun and Hogenberg map can be reconciled with Bernard and thereby with Ugo Comminelli.

A range of late medieval visitors to Alexandria mention the existence of a Church of St Mark without specifying its location beyond indicating that it lay within the circuit of the medieval walls. Those known to me include Fra Niccolo of Poggibonsi in 1349; Anselme Adorno in 1470; Hans Thucher in 1480; Félix Fabri in 1483; Francesco Suriano in 1503; Martin Baumgarten in 1507, who importantly mentions that St Marks was in a different place to the other churches; Jean Thenaud and Zaccaria Pagani in 1512.

Leo Africanus seems to have been among the last eyewitnesses of the ancient church of St Mark in Alexandria. He included a mention of it at the time of his visits to the city in around 1517:-

At this present there are amongst the ancient inhabitants of Alexandria many Christians called Jacobites [i.e. Copts], being all of them artizans and merchants: these Jacobites have a church of their own to resort unto, wherein the body of S. Mark the Evangelist lay in times past interred, which hath since been privily stolne by the Venetians, & carried unto Venice. And the said Jacobites pay tribute unto the Governor of Cairo.[18]

Leo's St Mark's in 1517 is particularly likely to be the small church-like building next to the site of the discovery of St Mark's corpse just inside the Cairo/Rosetta Gate of medieval Alexandria in Braun and Hogenberg's map, because the latter was based on contemporaneous information from the early 1530's. This may not have been the original Late Roman church, because there is evidence that the building was damaged or destroyed and rebuilt several times during its long history, but each successive establishment may well have shared the same site.[19] If so and if our cartographers from Cologne are to be believed,

---

[17] Gaston Jondet, *Atlas historique de la ville et des ports d'Alexandrie*, Mémoires de la Société Sultanieh de Géographie 2, Cairo, 1921, Map 1; but Melchien 1699 labels Lochias buildings "St George".
[18] Leo Africanus (ed. Ramusio, *Descrizione dell'Africa*, 1550), trans. John Pory AD1600, *Description of Africa*, Vol. 3, Hakluyt Society 94, London, 1896, p.864.
[19] For example, the Church of St Mark is said to have been damaged by fire when 'Amr recaptured Alexandria following the Revolt of Manuel in AD646 (e.g. Butler, *The Arab Conquest of Egypt*, p.475), then restored variously under the Patriarch Agathon (AD661-677) according to Makrizi or by the Patriarch John III (AD677-686) according to Severus' *History of the Patriarchs* and also the Chronicle of Peter ibn Rahib or even during the episcopate of the Patriarch Isaac (AD686-689) according to the *Coptic Synaxary*.

Famous Alexandrian Mummies

then the tomb of St Mark was located very close to Mahmoud Bey's central crossroads of ancient Alexandria, which, as we have seen, was also the likely location of Alexander's mausoleum.

Figure 10.2. The plan of Alexandria by Ugo Comminelli daing from 1472

Accounts by subsequent 16th and early 17th century travellers such as Marmol in 1546 mainly echo Leo's words on the Church of St Mark in Alexandria: it would appear that they used Leo's work as their model. An exception is Pierre Belon, who passed through Alexandria on a diplomatic mission in 1547, but he is vague and ambiguous: *and in fact there are some Caloieres, Jacobites and Greeks who have a dwelling there for the Patriarchate with their Church, in the place where anciently was*

The Quest for the Tomb of Alexander by Andrew Chugg

the corpse of St Mark, before the Venetians stole it to take it to Venice. Aside from which the Catholics and the Jews also similarly have their Churches there.[20]

It is not until the account of Cornelius de Bruyn's visit in 1681 that we read more specific information:

The present town of Alexandria is mostly empty and deserted, but has a few inhabited areas. Here the Church of St Mark, occupied by the Coptic Christians, is still present. It was once a large church, but is now a small, round chapel. Still displayed within the chapel is a part of the former stairs together with a piece of the pulpit where the Evangelist Mark preached… Within this church the body of St Mark, the first Patriarch of Alexandria, lay at rest behind the altar from the year AD64 until some Venetian merchants on their way back from the Holy Land removed the remains to Venice.[21]

In the eighteenth century the evidence for a Church of St Mark in Alexandria is elusive. The Norden map of Alexandria drawn in 1737 appears absurdly to label the location of the Attarine Mosque with the legend "St Marc".[22] However, the locations of three Christian foundations within the medieval enclosure of Alexandria are reasonably well established by the maps of Pococke and Napoleon's expedition. Firstly, there was a "Latin" Christian monastery about 300m west of the Attarine Mosque just north of Canopic Way. Secondly, a "Greek" monastery with a dedication to St Catherine & St George stood opposite to Kom el-Dikka on the northern side of Canopic Way; Kom el-Dikka itself is labeled *Butte Sainte Catherine* in the d'Anville and Cassas maps (Figure 9.9). Finally, the building adjoining the *Sinagogue des Juifs* on its eastern side in the map from the Description de l'Egypte (Figure 9.6) is called a "Coptic convent" by Pococke. It is not impossible that it had a dedication to St Mark, though specific testimony is hard to find. There is difficulty in equating it with the small, round chapel visited by Cornelius de Bruyn, since it appears as a single-storey rectilinear structure in 18th century drawings and engravings. Its location was only ~150m south of Cleopatra's Needles, so part of its site may actually have fallen within the bounds of the Caesareum temple complex of ancient Alexandria. In the Late Roman period the Christian authorities took over the Caesareum (a.k.a. Sebasteum). It stood at the centre of the Great Harbour with Cleopatra's Needles guarding its entrance. It was very grand, so the Christians

---

[20] Pierre Belon du Mans, *Voyage en Egypte*, 1553, edition of Serge Sauneron, IFAO, 1970 - Alexandria is covered across pp.91b-97a.
[21] Cornelius de Bruyn, *Reizen van Cornelis de Bruyn door de vermaardste Deelen van Klein Asia*, 1698, p.239.
[22] F.L. Norden, *Voyage d'Egypte et de Nubie*, Paris, 1755, *Carte Particuliére de la Vieille et de la Nouvelle Aléxandrie, et des Ports*, Tab. I & *Vue de la Vieille Aléxandrie*, Tab. VI – it is difficult given the location he identifies to avoid the conclusion that Norden is confusing the Attarine Mosque with St Mark's church, although the view in Plate VI does not actually show the minaret and the possibility remains that he is making a very inaccurate reference to the Coptic convent noted by Pococke at about the same date.

made it their cathedral.[23] Hence it is sometimes confused with the Church of St Mark by medieval sources.[24] It was ultimately razed by a fire in the early 10th century.[25] The modern Coptic Cathedral of St Mark in Alexandria seems to be close to the site of the Coptic convent identified by Pococke, although the Coptic and Jewish religious establishments appear mysteriously to have swapped sites in the 19th century.[26]

This completes our analysis of the history of St Mark's tomb in Alexandria. It is a subtle matter to distinguish the true site of this shrine from the several decoy establishments in and around the city, which may at various times have been associated with St Mark. Nevertheless, it seems firmly established that the Rosetta Gate was generally known as the Gate of St Mark from the Late Roman period through to the Cypriot raid in 1365. The church of St Mark was closely associated with this Gate by the pilgrims Arculfus and Bernard the Monk. The Acts of St Mark itself states that the Evangelist's tomb was created in an illustrious eastern district of Alexandria. It is the location just inside the Rosetta Gate as specified by the Braun & Hogenberg map that best fits this evidence. This leads to the conclusion that St Mark's tomb not only replaced Alexander's Mausoleum as the holiest shrine in Alexandria, but it was also located at virtually the same spot within the city.

Furthermore, it is now possible to see that there is also a coincidence in time between the disappearance of Alexander's body and the appearance of St Mark's shrine. Libanius states that Alexander's corpse was on display in Alexandria just before the outlawing of paganism in AD391, but it is never heard of again, whereas St Mark's tomb first appeared at about the end of the 4th century AD. Especially in the light of these coincidences, we may reasonably wonder whether some late 4th century patriarch or high officer of the Alexandrian church recognised an opportunity through a small act of deception both to preserve the corpse of the city's founder from the most fanatical of his own followers and to furnish Christianity with a potent relic to encourage the devotion of the faithful? There are precedents demonstrating that the church authorities in 4th century Alexandria were in the habit of adapting pagan relics to Christian purposes: for example, a bronze idol of Saturn in the Caesareum was melted down to cast a cross by the Patriarch Alexander in the time of

---

[23] A. Butler, *The Arab Invasion of Egypt & the Last 30 Years of the Roman Dominion*, Oxford, 1902, pp.372-5.
[24] A building called the Kamsija, which had been built by Cleopatra and which burnt down in AD912, must be the Caesareum, but it is nevertheless associated with the Church of St Mark by various Coptic and Arab sources according to M. Chaîne, *L'Église de Saint-Marc à Alexandrie*, Revue de l'Orient Chrétien, Vol 24, 1924, pp.372-386.
[25] In AD912 according to Neroutsos Bey, *L'Ancienne Alexandrie*, Paris, 1888, p.14.
[26] Neroutsos Bey, *L'Ancienne Alexandrie*, Paris, 1888, p.69 therefore supposes the Coptic Cathedral to lie on the site of the ancient Church of St Mark.

The Quest for the Tomb of Alexander by Andrew Chugg

Constantine and the Caesareum itself became a Christian cathedral.[27] Might a similar metamorphosis have been contrived in the case of Alexander's mummy? There are after all hints that the putative corpse of St Mark was mummified and steeped in rich spices just like that of Alexander, whereas we have seen that a credible and early Christian tradition insists that St Mark's body was cremated by the pagans in Alexandria in the 1st century AD.

*   *   *   *   *   *   *   *

What of the history of St Mark's remains after they reached Venice? A Church of St Mark appears to have been established to host the Venetian tomb of the Evangelist within a short period of the arrival of his corpse in the city.[28] It was damaged by a fire that swept through several districts of Venice in August AD976, but was speedily repaired by the Doge Pietro Orseolo. In AD1063 the surging power and wealth of Venice enabled the Republic to fund the construction of a more glorious Basilica di San Marco, the same building as continues today to grace the Piazza di San Marco at the heart of the city (Figure 10.3). There is a curious legend that St Mark's mummy was somehow mislaid by the Venetians in the context of the reconstruction of the Basilica in the late 11th century. However, following a period of prayer and fasting, it was miraculously rediscovered when one of the saint's arms was seen to emerge from a pillar, indicating the location of his inhumation.[29] Tintoretto has illustrated the incident in a well-known painting, but the historical accuracy of the tale is questionable. Associating miracles with medieval Christian relics was good for the business of their shrines, since it helped to encourage pilgrimages. It was the equivalent of a modern marketing campaign; hence there were solid financial incentives for minor incidents to be talked up into supernatural dramas.

We know that the body of St Mark was lodged in a new tomb in the crypt of the Basilica on 8th October 1094 under the Doge Vitale Falier, because a lead plaque with an inscription to this effect was found in the tomb on the occasion of a subsequent relocation.

From AD1094 until the early 19th century St Mark's corpse rested peacefully in its new tomb in the crypt of the Basilica at a point lying almost directly beneath the high altar in the presbytery above.[30] In 1811 there was perceived to be a rising risk to the remains in the crypt due to increasingly frequent flooding episodes. Furthermore, there was a desire to make the sacred relics more accessible to the faithful, so the decision was taken to relocate St Mark's tomb to lie within the entablement of the high altar itself on the main floor of the

---

[27] A.J. Butler, *The Arab Conquest of Egypt and the Last Thirty Years of the Roman Dominion*, 2nd edition revised by P.M. Fraser, OUP, [1902] 1978, footnote to Chapter 24, "Alexandria at the Conquest".
[28] Ferdinando Forlati, *La Basilica di San Marco Attraverso I Suoi Restauri*, Trieste, 1975, Ch. II, *Il Primo S. Marco*, pp. 45-70.
[29] Ettore Vio, *St Mark's Basilica in Venice*, Thames & Hudson, London, 2000, p.19.
[30] With the proviso that in a recent episode of the BBC Antiques Roadshow TV programme a relic of St Mark with an 18th century "certificate of authenticy" from Venice was shown.

Famous Alexandrian Mummies

Basilica. The marble sarcophagus of the saint is now visible behind a grill and visitors are encouraged to process on a route that encircles his remains.

Figure 10.3. View of the Basilica di San Marco from the gallery of the Campanile (photo by the author)

Of vital interest to our story is the fact that the only documented investigation of the remains of St Mark the Evangelist that is known and published took place in 1811 on the occasion of the mini-*translazione* between crypt and altar. The transfer was witnessed by Leonardo Conte Manin, who wrote an account of the history of St Mark's tomb, entitled *Memorie storico-critiche intorno la vita, translazione, e invenzioni di san Marco evangelista principale protettore di Venezia* (Historical Monograph concerning the Life, Transferral and Rediscovery of St Mark the Evangelist, Patron Saint of Venice). It was first published in Venice in 1815 and a second edition appeared in 1835.

Manin's treatise establishes that the remains recovered in 1811 are very probably those brought to Venice from Alexandria in Egypt in AD828 by two Venetian merchant-adventurers (i.e. the *Translazione*). That it is an historical fact rather than a mere myth is strongly supported by the fact that the removal of the remains is reported by contemporaneous Alexandrian sources, such as Bernard the Monk, as well as in the Venetian chronicles and mosaics. Manin also records the evidence of the lead tablet, found accompanying the remains, which

The Quest for the Tomb of Alexander by Andrew Chugg

commemorated their installation in the crypt, when the current Basilica was constructed in AD1094.

Nevertheless, the ultimate identity of the corpse is brought into question by the arguments presented earlier in this chapter, most of which were originally put forward in 2004.[31] These recent suspicions regarding the authenticity of the remains are a first reason for considering a fresh investigation of the corpse at the present time. A second motivation is that newly developed forensic techniques have recently reached such a high level of sophistication and accuracy that there is now a strong probability that the question of the identity of the corpse could finally be resolved. Furthermore, the potentially crucial historical information bound up in the remains might thereby be extracted and rescued for posterity.

In support of this objective, let us first consider the scant details of the remains of St Mark recorded by Leonardo Manin in his aforementioned book. It is especially important to draw attention to the very limited nature of Manin's information. No illustration of the remains was provided. Manin did not even record the dimensions and weights; nor did he catalogue the remains in any sense, so we still have no exact knowledge of the contents of the tomb.

The most important description of the remains in Manin's book seems to that given on pages 24-25, detailing the opening of the coffin on 9th May 1811. A transcription of the original text and a translation are given below:-

Io non mi tratterro a descriver queste minutamente, ma dirò solo, che si vide un capo co'suoi denti fornito, le ossa principali che formano lo scheletro di un uomo, affatto scarnate e disseccate, oltre a molti pezzetti già polverizzati e molta cenere. La cassa era internamente foderata di un manto rosso, e le sante reliquie erano di altro tessuto coperte di un colore più chiaro, e di una solidità maggiore del velo, il quale e dall'umido e dal tempo erasi alle sante ossa attaccato, e di esse quasi un involto formava. Per antico rito e per cristiano costume, come asserisce monsignor Fontanini nella dissertazione sul corpo di s. Agostino, soleansi di veli i santi corpi ricoprire, che chiamansi brandea, sudaria, oraria.

"I won't dwell upon describing them in detail, but I'll confine myself to saying that those present saw a head furnished with its teeth, the principal bones which form the skeleton of a man, completely bare and dry, besides many little bits already pulverised/smashed and many ashes. The chest was internally lined by a red mantle, and the holy relics were covered by another hand-weave of a lighter colour and of a greater solidity than veil/shroud, the which was by the humidity and by the time become adhered to the saintly bones, almost forming a parcel. According to antique rites and by Christian custom, as is asserted by Mr Fontanini in his dissertation on the body of St Augustine, they were in the habit of re-covering the corpses of saints with veils/shrouds, which they would call *brandea, sudaria, oraria.*"

---

[31] A.M. Chugg, "Alexander's Final Resting Place," *History Today*, Vol. 54(7), July 2004, pp. 17-23; A.M. Chugg, *The Lost Tomb of Alexander the Great*, London, October 2004.

Famous Alexandrian Mummies

The reportedly decayed state of the remains reflects the dank conditions in the crypt, which is subject to continual flooding. Clearly, the intact state of the skull and principal bones is inconsistent with these remains ever having been cremated. The mention of "ashes" (*cenere*) merely means crumbled organic remains. There is no imputation of burning in the context of human remains. Rather, Manin's observation that parts of the skeleton were stuck to cloth wrappings is consistent with the theory that he was describing a perished mummy.

There are also a few further mentions at later points in the book, which are quoted for completeness below.

Page 42, second paragraph:-

… e attentamente si è estratto il sacro corpo consistente nel Cranio e varie ossa, …

"… and attentively extracted the sacred corpse consisting of a Cranium and various bones…"

Page 45, second paragraph (re-interment beneath the high altar on 30th September 1811):-

… si è aperta la cassa stessa e si è osservato il sacro corpo consistente nel teschio, ossia cranio, ed ossa in parte di uno schelatro già riposte fra bombace. Nella cassa medesima si sono rinchiuse due scatole contenenti delle ceneri prodotte dale ossa e dai veli sfacellati.

"… he himself opened the same chest and he observed the sacred corpse consisting of a skull, cranial bones, and partial bones of one skeleton already put back between cotton. In the same casket were shut up two tins/boxes containing ashes produced from the bones and from perished shrouds…"

Manin's book also presents some key information concerning other relics found together with the remains of St Mark. For example on pages 26-27 it describes the box illustrated in Figure 10.4:-

On the left, near the place of the Evangelist's head, a round wooden box was found, with a lid in the shape of a cyma reversa (S-shaped moulding in classical architecture) minutely decorated with drawings, but plain and unadorned in its other parts. This box contained some relics wrapped in a silk cloth, more substantial than the others, and, scattered among them, there were ancient silver coins. At first sight it was thought that these relics were some specially precious part of the sacred body itself that time had reduced to dust, of a colour partly ashen-grey and partly dark blood-red; the presence of the coins seemed to show that this was true, and that this part of the sacred body, whichever it was, had been made an object of special devotion. But when the box was more thoroughly observed, some words could be seen in its middle, which, read and examined by signor Counsellor Cavalier Abbot Morelli, late royal librarian, were interpreted by him as ΑΓΙΟΣ ΑΝΤΟΝΙΟΣ, that is sanctus Antonius (Saint Anthony). Since this saint was particularly famous in Egypt, one could infer that the relics contained in the case belonged to him and had been directly transferred from Egypt together with Saint Mark's and that this wooden vase too, whatever it was, had come from Alexandria. This argument was disputed by some malevolent people, who took this discovery

The Quest for the Tomb of Alexander by Andrew Chugg

as a pretext for discrediting the others, and claimed that it was very difficult to reconcile the idea of Saint Mark with what the box suggested.

Saint Anthony was the 4th century AD founder of monasticism in Egypt. The likelihood that the partially obliterated lettering is Greek certainly supports the connection with Alexandria, where it was the principal tongue spoken under the Roman and Byzantine Empires. These details from Manin's book further alleviate the concern that the body currently beneath the altar of San Marco is not that brought from Alexandria in AD828, aroused by the alleged difficulty in tracking down the place of its interment back in the 11th century and the still earlier fire of AD976.

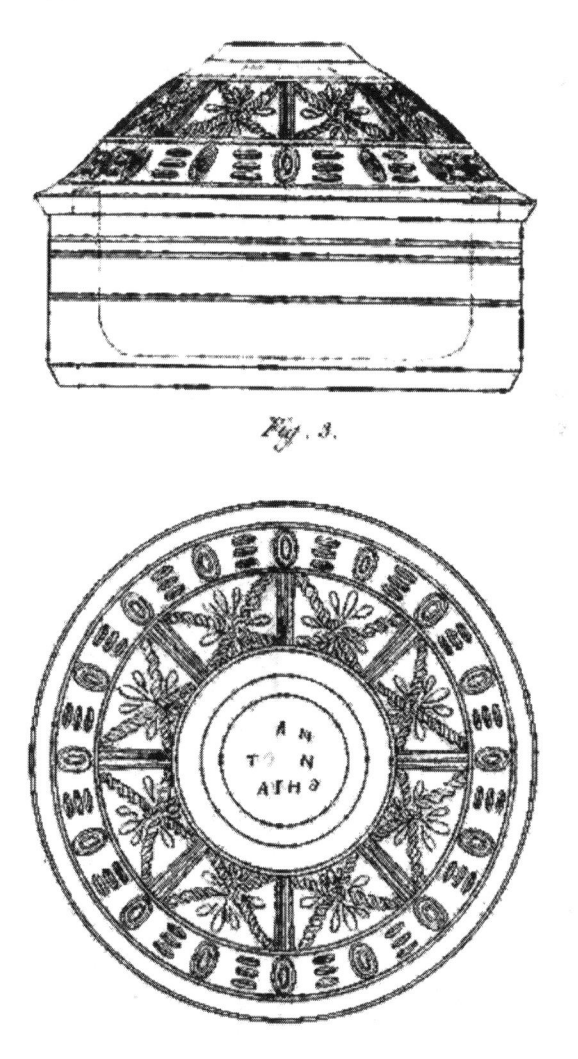

Figure 10.4. Illustration of a box found with the remains of St Mark (Figure 3 in Plate 5 of Manin's book – 1835 edition from the author's collection)

205

Famous Alexandrian Mummies

There may have been one or two inspections of the remains, whilst accommodated by the new marble sarcophagus within the altar. In 2006 *Marco Evangelista: L'Enigma delle Reliquie* by Gianni Vianello was published in Naples. It deals with many matters concerning the relics of St Mark, but its information on post-1811 inspections of the remains within the altar is confined to part of footnote 26 on page 103:

Si ricorda di una ricognizione del patriarca Monico del 1834 e di un'altra, recente, del 24.11.1957, essendo patriarca di Venezia Angelo Roncalli.

"One recalls an inspection under the patriarch Monico in 1834 and another, recently, on 24.11.1957, the patriarch of Venice being Angelo Roncalli."

However, Gianni Vianello subsequently clarified in email correspondence with the author that the inspection of 1957, though mooted, was thwarted before it could be perpetrated. Neither do any details of the inspection of 1834 seem to be available, so nothing may yet be added to Manin's exceedingly spare account.

* * * * * * * * *

In principle, it should be a straightforward matter to determine the age and provenance of the remains, which continue to reside beneath the altar in the Basilica.[32] The following lists identify some of the tests which are now feasible. Many of them have only recently been perfected, due to great advances in forensic archaeology over the last few decades. The exact range of tests to be performed in an investigation would be a matter for further deliberation and negotiation. The tests have been divided into two categories. The first category includes non-invasive tests that it should be possible to perform without moving the remains and without taking samples from the remains. There is an excellent chance that mere inspection of the remains would decide between the alternative identities. The second category would probably require that small samples were taken from among the remains or that the remains were temporarily removed to a laboratory.

Category 1, visual examination and inspection

a) Examination of the remains by an expert should permit confirmation of sex and approximate age at the time of death; it should be possible to determine the original type of preservation of the corpse.

b) Photographs would record appearance and dimensions: the remains should be catalogued against the photos with weights.

---

[32] In June 1968 a small piece of bone from Venice attributed to St Mark was returned to Egypt by order of Pope Paul VI and was received by the Patriarch Kyrillos VI of Alexandria; it is now kept in a new cathedral in Cairo, since the seat of the Patriarch was transferred to Cairo in the 11th century; however, the rest of the body of the saint still rests in its marble sarcophagus within the entablement of the high altar of the Venetian Basilica.

The Quest for the Tomb of Alexander by Andrew Chugg

c) Skeletal marks/scars: the issue of skeletal marks, especially evidence of healed wounds, could be highly significant, because two of Alexander's many wounds (listed in Table 10.1) are specifically stated to have caused bone damage. Firstly, Alexander's fibula and/or tibia in one of his lower legs is stated to have been badly damaged when the army was en route to Samarkand in ~328BC. Secondly the arrow which pierced Alexander's chest in the siege of the Mallian town in India in 325BC is said by the majority of sources to have lodged in the chest bone (perhaps in the sternum). Clearly, healed bone damage or its absence in these locations could furnish a strong indication of whether the remains are likely to be Alexander.

d) Facial reconstruction is feasible assuming the skull is intact as is indicated by Manin. This might be based on photos taken from multiple angles or there exist safe laser beam or Computer Aided Tomography (CAT) scanning systems which can record 3D object in detail: for example, Tutankhamun's face was recently reconstructed from CAT scans of his skull by independent groups (one of which was ignorant of the origin of the data) and the results were recognisable from one another. For purposes of comparison there survive numerous authentic portraits of Alexander.[33]

Category 2, advanced test techniques

a) Radiocarbon (Carbon-14) dating: radioactive carbon generated by cosmic rays is absorbed by living things in a constant proportion relative to stable carbon-12, whilst they are alive, but decays away at a steady rate, after they die; by measuring the ratio of radiocarbon to ordinary carbon in an uncontaminated part of the remains, it is feasible to date the time of death to within ~50 years; clearly a date in the second half of the first century AD would strongly support the identification of the remains as St Mark; any other date would suggest a forgery. In particular, Alexander's remains should give a date in the latter part of the 4th century BC, quite distinct from the date range for St Mark. Note however that contamination by more recently deceased organic material would give an erroneously young age for the remains. It will therefore be important to extract samples from parts of the skeleton (e.g. cores of large bones) which are unlikely to have experienced interim contamination. Normal precautions would include arranging for samples to be analysed by several independent laboratories and to include some unidentified control samples of similar material and appearance, but of known dates, for cross-calibration purposes.

b) Strontium tooth-enamel isotopes: certain measurable isotopic ratios in parts of remains (e.g. strontium and oxygen isotope ratios in tooth-enamel) can reveal in which regions or climates the deceased lived his life.

c) DNA testing: it may be possible to decipher some of the DNA of the deceased; this would be a rich source of information on the ethnicity and place

---

[33] See in general Andrew Stewart, *Faces of Power: Alexander's Image & Hellenistic Politics*, University of California, 1993.

of origin of the deceased; it might even be possible to identify related individuals alive today. Despite the fact that the remains of various of Alexander's relatives (son, father/half-brother) found at Vergina (ancient Aegae) in Macedonia have been cremated, there is nevertheless still a possibility of extracting some DNA sequences from them. There has recently been some limited success in extracting DNA data from cremated remains.[34]

d) spores/pollens etc, perhaps trapped in the wrappings; these may provide clues on places or regions in which the remains have been stored for long periods.

e) The weave, material and dye of the wrappings may provide important clues.

The technical case for an independent, scientific investigation would therefore appear to be overwhelming. In all likelihood it would resolve many of the uncertainties and might well establish the true identity of the deceased. Supposing the corpse is actually that of St Mark, then it is desirable to conduct the investigation as soon as possible in order to remove the uncertainty. If the body is that of someone other than St Mark, then it is best that the tests should be performed as soon as possible in order that the faithful are not deceived for any longer than is necessary: anyone who seeks to postpone the inspection risks being seen as being complicit in the deception. Since mere inspection of the remains may suffice, it is virtually inevitable that the truth will eventually be known. In this context it should be obvious that lifting the lid on this mystery would be in the best interests of all parties.

'It is a consummation devoutly to be wished,' for, as a reviewer once told me, the story of Alexander's tomb without a body is like Hamlet without the Prince.... 'The rest is silence.'

---

[34] E.g. D.J. & C.H. Sweet, "DNA Analysis of Dental Pulp to Link Incinerated Remains of Homicide Victim to Crime Scene," *J. Forensic Sci.* March 1995, 40(2), pp.310-4; N. von Wurmb-Schwark, A. Ringleb, M. Gebuhr, E. Simeoni, "Genetic Analysis of Modern and Historical Burned Human Remains," *Anthropol. Anz.* March 2005, 63(1), pp.1-12.

The Quest for the Tomb of Alexander by Andrew Chugg

Table 10.1. Wounds of Alexander (skeletal damage in bold)

Nature of Wound	Location	References
Head wound by stone	Among Illyrians	Plut. Mor. 327A
Cudgel wound to neck	Among Illyrians	Plut. Mor. 327A
Dagger cut to head or helmet cleft through to scalp by sword/scimitar (Arrian: helmet protection was effective, though part was sheared off – Diodorus: scalp wound was slight)	Battle of Granicus	Plut. Mor. 327A, 341B, Plut. A 16, Arrian 1.15.7, Diod. 17.20
Thigh pierced by sword/dagger (Chares said by Darius)	Battle of Issus	Plut. Mor. 327A, 341C, Plut. A 20
Attempted assassination – dagger cut(?)	Siege of Gaza	Curtius 4.6.16, Hegesias
Shoulder dislocated when wounded by a missile or catapult bolt or arrow driven through shield and corselet	Siege of Gaza	Plut. Mor. 327A, 341B, Plut. A 25, Arrian 2.27.2, Curtius 4.6.17-18
Arrow strikes ankle (corrupt?) – wound to leg by a stone (Curtius)	Siege of Gaza	Plut. Mor. 327A, Curtius 4.6.23-24
Stone struck neck and dimmed his sight for many days	Somewhere in Hyrcania	Plut. Mor. 341B
Leg bone split open by an arrow: "shin was so torn by an arrow that by the force of the blow the larger bone was broken and extruded" Plutarch, Moralia 341B – "struck by an arrow below the knee so that splinters of the larger bone came out" Plutarch, Alexander 45.3 – "arrow... left its point fixed in the middle of his leg" Curtius – "shot right through his leg by an arrow and part of his fibula bone was broken" Arrian	**On the way to Maracanda (Samarkand)**	**Plut. Mor. 327A, 341B, Plut. A 45.3, Arrian 3.30.11, Curtius 7.6.3**
Arrow to shoulder (minor according to Arrian, since breastplate prevented full penetration)	Among Aspasians	Plut. Mor. 327B, Arrian 4.23.3, Curtius 8.10.6
Arrow(?) to leg	Among Gandridae	Plut. Mor. 327B
Ankle wound by Indian arrow (Ichor quote), Wound to Alexander's left leg/shin by an arrow shot from the wall of Massaga (Metz Epitome)	Among Assacenians	Plut. Mor. 341B, Metz Epitome 40
3ft arrow pierced breast plate and sank deep into breast ("penetrated the bones of his breast and was lodged there... iron point four fingers wide and five long... lodged in bony part of breast in front of the heart") and struck on neck from behind by a cudgel (according to Aristobulus) and wounded through helmet by an axe (Arrian cites Ptolemy for air and blood bubbling from wound indicating lung perforation, but Ptolemy also states he was not present)	Among Mallians	Plut. Mor. 327B, 341C, 344C-D, 345A, Plut. A 63.6, Arrian 6.9.10, Diod. 17.99.3, Curtius 9.5.9-32, Strabo 15.1.33

11. The Sword in the Stone

Τῆι γὰρ Μακεδόνων εὐψυχείαι πρέπον ἐστὶν ἐν μὲν ταῖς πράξεσι τὰ ἀπὸ τῶν ὅπλων, ἐν δὲ ταῖς ψυχαῖς τὰ ἀπὸ τῆς εὐγνωμοσύνης μαρτυρεῖσθαι, ἵνα τὰ μὲν τρόπαια κηρύσσηι τὴν τοῦ σώματος ἀρετήν, τὰ δὲ δόγματα μαρτυρῆι τὴν τῆς ψυχῆς εὐγένειαν.

It is fitting for the Macedonian spirit to bear witness to exploits with arms in fighting, and to fairness of the soul, so that trophies may proclaim the valour of the body, but opinions may testify to the soul's nobility.

FrGrHist 2.153 F4 = Freiburg Papyrus 7-8 (2nd century AD)

All the known circumstances in Alexandria at the end of the 4th century AD are closely consistent with the possibility that the deified pagan mummy of the city's founder was reclassified as the sacred Christian mummy of the founder of the Alexandrian Church shortly after pagan worship became illegal in AD391. It may indeed have been sufficient for the perpetrator merely to assert to his flock that the remains of *the* Founder were actually the remains of the *Founder*, thus allowing his fellow Christians to deceive themselves. Alexander was officially known as the Founder (*Ktistes*) in ancient Alexandria and it seems that 4th century Christians referred to St Mark in similar terms.[1]

In general, the argument presented so far could reasonably be described as relying on circumstantial evidence. It merely shows that there is a significant possibility that the substitution occurred. Whereas this should be sufficient to justify an investigation seeking definitive information, the circumstantial nature of this evidence leaves open other possibilities for the origins of the corpse, which are equally significant. They include the possibility that the corpse is genuinely that of St Mark.

However, there is one independent discovery of ancient archaeological material in the context of the Basilica di San Marco in Venice, which may be connected with our story. The matter is still under investigation, but if it should be possible to establish a connection between this find and the nearby remains of St Mark, then we would have a cardinal piece of evidence associating the body with a high status Macedonian tomb of the Hellenistic Period.

The object in question first sprang out at me half a decade ago as I leafed casually through the pages of a book describing work on the fabric of the Basilica di San Marco by the former *proto* Ferdinando Forlati, who was responsible for the care, maintenance and restoration of the building and its

---

[1] P.M. Fraser, *Ptolemaic Alexandria*, Oxford, 1972, p.212 and notes for Alexander as *Ktistes* in Alexandria; Eusebius, *Ecclesiastical History* 2.16.1 for St Mark as founder of the Church in Alexandria.

The Quest for the Tomb of Alexander by Andrew Chugg

contents between 1948-1972. I was startled to discover photos of a large block of stone with a sculpted relief that was instantly recognizable as a Macedonian shield bearing the classic starburst device.[2] The accompanying text noted that it had been found just metres from the original site of St Mark's tomb in the crypt. I briefly recorded this find and noted a possible association with the tomb in my book published in 2004.[3] However, the mystery surrounding this monolith has considerably broadened and deepened in the meantime, such that a far more detailed account of it is now required.

The discovery had originally been reported by Forlati in a short notice published in Arte Veneta in 1963.[4] During restoration works this block of limestone masonry, described by Forlati as "part of a Roman funerary monument", had been found embedded in the oldest part of the foundations: specifically, the foundations of the main apse, the lower courses of which date back to the original 9th century Church of St Mark. A diagram adapted from Forlati's original section showing the block *in situ* in the lower courses of the foundations of the apse is given in Figure 11.1. A complete plan of the foundations and cross-section of the Basilica di San Marco are shown in Figures 11.2a and 11.2b respectively. Forlati's investigations revealed that the original 9th century San Marco had been constructed on the parts of the foundations shown in solid black in this plan.[5] Virtually the entirety of the foundations of the main apse can be seen to be common to the original and current Basilicas. The 11th century tomb of St Mark was located directly beneath the high altar within the crypt. It can be seen in Figure 11.2a that the arc of the apse lay at an approximate radius of 8m from the high altar, so the starburst shield block long lay at a similar distance from the the tomb of St Mark.

The stone bears a high relief sculpture of an ancient shield with a central starburst emblem accompanied by a lance and a badly damaged pair of greaves. Although the carved objects are sparsely distributed over the faces of the block, in keeping with the early Hellenistic style, the quality of the piece is readily perceived by noticing that more than 10cm of hard limestone has been carved away across almost the entire main face simply in order to give the shield its militarily correct degree of convexity.

A photo of the block as it is currently displayed in the Cloister of St Apollonia just across the canal running behind the Basilica di San Marco is shown in Figure 11.3. It has approximate maximal dimensions 138x118x40cm and must therefore weigh around one and a half metric tonnes. The shield has a diameter

---

[2] Ferdinando Forlati, *La Basilica di San Marco Attraverso I Suoi Restauri*, Trieste, 1975, p.82 and diagram on p.63.
[3] A.M. Chugg, *The Lost Tomb of Alexander the Great*, London, 2004, p. 267 and Figure 9.4.
[4] Ferdinando Forlati, "Ritrovamenti a San Marco: 1. Un monumento funerario romano," *Arte Veneta* XVII, 1963, pp.222-3.
[5] Ferdinando Forlati, *La Basilica di San Marco Attraverso I Suoi Restauri*, Trieste, 1975, p.48 for the foundations of the original Basilica and p.63 for the original site of the starburst shield block.

The Sword in the Stone

of just under 70cm and is therefore about life-size: it is particularly close to the size and shape of the Macedonian phalangite shield, which was a little smaller than the standard hoplite version (~95cm) and lacked its broad lip.[6] Forlati originally described the shield emblem as a "wheel", but there are distinct gaps between the ends of the "spokes" and both the "hub" and the "rim", so it is not mechanically viable as a wheel. A ribbon or belt hung over a round peg or nail with tassels at its ends decorates the lefthand side of the block and a slightly indistinct object intersects this ribbon diagonally (Figure 11.4). Careful examination confirms that this object is a sword of the single-edged type called a *kopis* by the Greeks. All authorities agree upon this interpretation of the side-panel, despite the abrasion of most of its original surface.

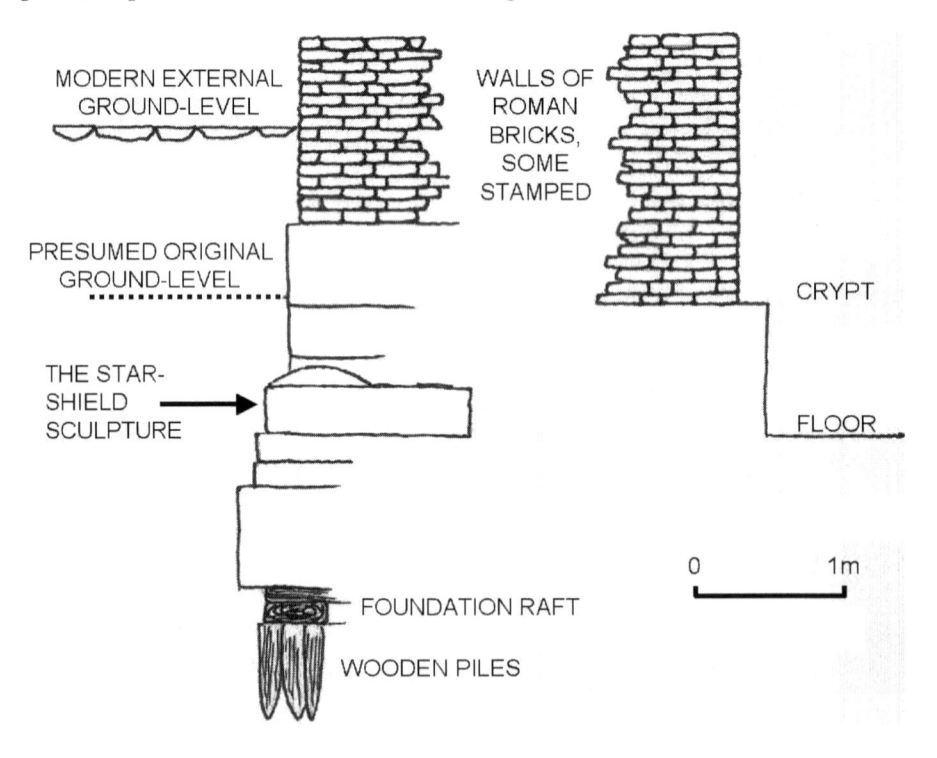

Figure 11.1. Section through the wall of the main apse of the Basilica di San Marco showing the star-shield sculpture *in situ* (drawn by the author from a diagram by Forlati)

It is known that the Macedonian army deployed rather similar weaponry in the early Hellenistic Period and the tombs of high status warriors were commonly decorated with such armaments. Such decoration recalls battlefield trophies: displays of the armaments and panoplies of the defeated enemy. An extraordinarily close parallel to the Venetian starburst shield sculpture is

---

[6] Minor M. Markle, "A Shield Monument from Veria and the Chronology of the Macedonian Shield," *Hesperia* 68.2, 1999, pp.219-254.

The Quest for the Tomb of Alexander by Andrew Chugg

depicted in a mural in the tomb of Lyson & Kallikles (Figure 11.5), which dates to the 2nd century BC and is located between between Beroia and Edessa in Macedon itself. This beautifully preserved mural, a rare survival from antiquity, has a similar round shield with an 8-pointed starburst device as its centrepiece, but it also has a *kopis* sword suspended diagonally from a tasselled belt on its left-hand side. Furthermore, there is a pair of greaves beneath the shield, which amplify the resounding echoes of the decoration of the sculpture from the Basilica di San Marco.

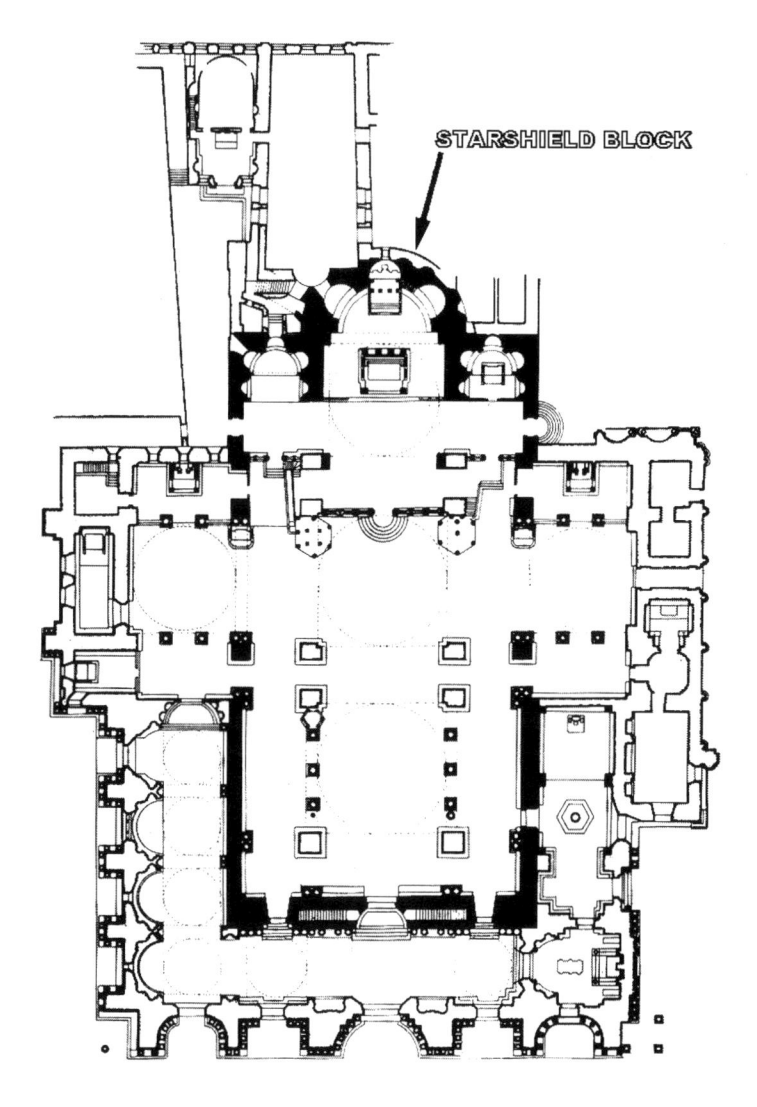

Figure 11.2a. Plan of the Basilica di San Marco with the original 9th century foundations in solid black (drawn by the author from a diagram by Forlati)

The Sword in the Stone

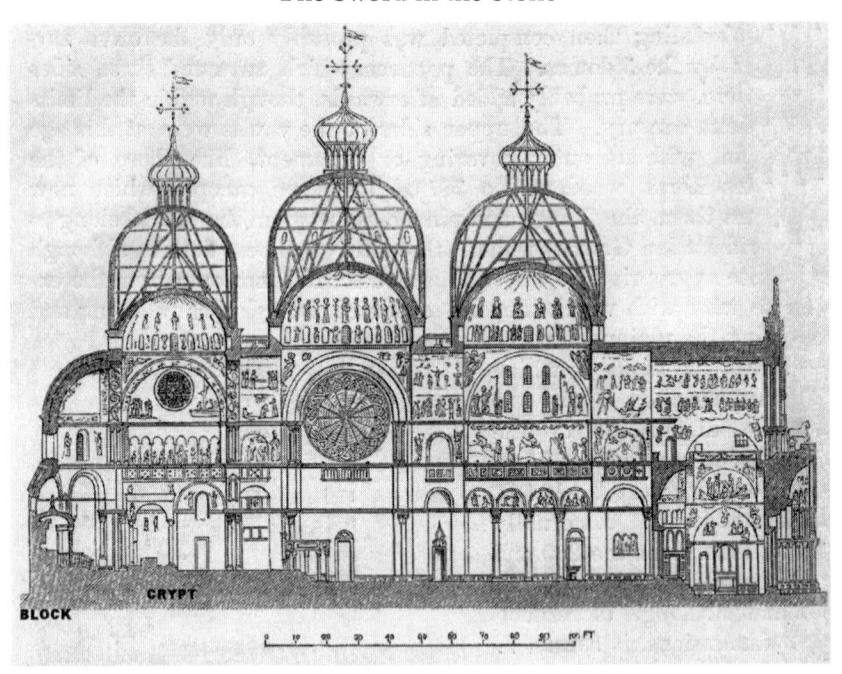

Figure 11.2b. Section through the Basilica di San Marco indicating the locations of the crypt (beneath the Altar) and the starshield block

Another example of a starburst shield accompanies a man and woman of royal Macedonian status in a Roman fresco from Boscoreale near Pompeii.[7] Further examples of this shield are borne by Macedonian warriors in a frieze from the Hellenstic tomb found at Aghios Athanasios (~20km west of Thessaloniki) in 1994 and half of the bronze starburst boss of an actual Macedonian shield (perhaps attributable to Demetrius Poliorcetes) has been uncovered at the Sanctuary of Olympian Zeus at Dion, where it had been deposited as a dedicatory offering.[8] More generally, the starburst symbol resembles the Star of Macedon, which was the special symbol of Alexander's family. The Star of Macedon is famously represented on the lid of the gold larnax from Tomb II in the Macedonian royal cemetery at Vergina (ancient Aegae).[9] The symbol has a particularly widespread association with Alexander, being, for example, the main motif of a pebble mosaic excavated at Ai Khanoum, a city founded by

---

[7] Illustrated in M.B. Sakellariou (editor), *Macedonia*, Greek Lands in History series, Ekdotike Athenon, Athens, 1988, p.145.
[8] Demetrios Pandermalis, *Alexander the Great: Treasures from an Epic Era of Hellenism*, Exhibition Catalogue, Onasis Cultural Center, New York, December 2004 – April 2005: Maria Tsimbidou-Avloniti, "The Macedonian Tomb at Aghios Athanasios, Thessalonike", pp. 149-151; Polyxeni Adam-Veleni, "Arms and Warfare Techniques of the Macedonians", Item 5 on p. 55.
[9] Manolis Andronicos, *Vergina*, Athens, 1984, p.178.

The Quest for the Tomb of Alexander by Andrew Chugg

Alexander in Afghanistan.[10] It also occurs on dichalkon coins from Alexandria minted in the Antonine period. Though the Venetian sculpted starburst has additional small roundels at the ray points, there are already some hints of this feature in the stars on various small gold discs also found in the Vergina tomb (Figure 11.6) as well as in the aforementioned mosaic at Ai Khanoum.

Figure 11.3. The star-shield sculpture as currently displayed in the Cloister of St Apollonia in Venice (photo by the author)

---

[10] Illustrated in Robin Lane Fox, *The Search for Alexander*, Little Brown Books, Boston & Toronto, 1980, p.95.

The Sword in the Stone

Figure 11.4. The *kopis* sword slung diagonally from a belt on the side panel of the star-shield sculpture (photo by the author)

The *kopis* suspended diagonally from a tasselled belt has numerous further parallels among funerary monuments from the Hellenistic Greek world: e.g. versions from the 3rd century BC were found in the necropolis at Byzantion.[11] Real examples of Macedonian swords of this type have been displayed in recent exhibitions of Macedonian arms found in archaeological contexts.[12]

On 18th September 2006 I gave a presentation on the connections between Alexander's tomb and Venice at the *Eroi, Eroismi, Eroizzazioni* conference at the

---

[11] Nezih Firatli & Louis Robert, *Les Stèles Funéraire de Byzance Gréco-Romain*, Paris, 1964, items 36 & 189.
[12] Demetrios Pandermalis, *Alexander the Great: Treasures from an Epic Era of Hellenism*, Exhibition Catalogue, Onasis Cultural Center, New York, December 2004 – April 2005: Polyxeni Adam-Veleni, "Arms and Warfare Techniques of the Macedonians", Items 8 & 9 on p. 57.

The Quest for the Tomb of Alexander by Andrew Chugg

Palazzo del Bo in the Università degli Studi di Padova in Italy (Figure 11.7).[13] At its end, prof. Monica Centanni of the Dipartimento di Storia dell'Architettura in the Università Iuav di Venezia suggested that stone tests had recently been performed upon the starburst shield fragment, which indicate that it is fashioned of Pietra Aurisina, a type of beige marble quarried locally just northwest of Trieste. Afterwards, I requested confirmatory details of the test results on the stone, but no technical data from the testing was published before the time of writing the first edition of this book in 2007.

Figure 11.5. Mural of the 2nd century BC in the tomb of Lyson & Kallikles in Macedonia (sketch by the author)

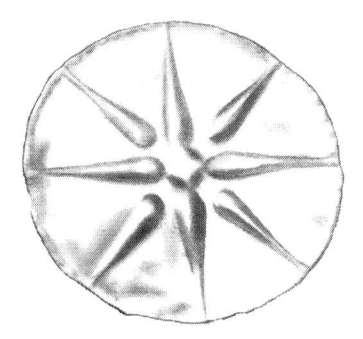

Figure 11.6. Macedonian royal starburst on a small gold disc found in Tomb II at Vergina (sketch by the author)

---

[13] My presentation at 16:30 was entitled "Famous Alexandrian Mummies: the Adventures in Death of Alexander the Great and St. Mark the Evangelist"; the conference was organised by Alessandra Coppola of the Dipartimento di Scienze del Mondo Antico of the Università degli Studi di Padova on 18th-19th September 2006; the Proceedings are expected to be published soon.

217

The Sword in the Stone

Figure 11.7. Statement by Monica Centanni (far left) at the *Eroi* Conference in the Palazzo del Bo on 18th September 2006 with the author second from the right (author's photo)

Subsequently, however, (and in time for the first edition of this book) Alessandra Coppola was able to elicit some clarification of the matter from Dr. Prof. Lorenzo Lazzarini of the Laboratorio di Analisi dei Materiali Antichi at the Istituto Universitario di Architettura di Venezia, who actually conducted the stone analysis of the starburst shield sculpture on behalf of Monica Centanni. His information took the form of the following email:

Sì, ho eseguito io lo studio petrografico di un campione della stele, su richiesta della collega Monica Centanni. Il risultato indica senza alcuna ombra di dubbio che la stele è stata scolpita nella Pietra di Aurisina, un calcare che ancora si estrae nella località omonima in provincia di Trieste. Naturalmente non so risponderle per ciò che riguarda la datazione del manufatto, sul quale come sa, sta lavorando un gruppo di ricerca che fa capo a Monica.[14]

"Yes, I performed the petrographic investigation of a specimen from the stele, at the request of our colleague Monica Centanni. The results indicate without any shadow of doubt that the stele has been sculpted from Pietra di Aurisina, a limestone still extracted from the eponymous locality in the Province of Trieste. Naturally, I cannot respond with regard to dating the manufacture, on which as is known, a research group is working headed by Monica."

* * * * * * * *

In March of 2007 the pendulum swung back again, when Alessandra Coppola discovered a highly topical reference to the starburst shield sculptural fragment

---

[14] This email was sent in response to a direct enquiry and forwarded to the author by Alessandra Coppola on 23/3/07.

The Quest for the Tomb of Alexander by Andrew Chugg

in a study of ancient sculptural depictions of armaments written by Eugenio Polito and published in 1998.[15] Polito's date of publication means that he wrote before I began my research on Alexander's tomb, so he can have had no inkling of the possibility that the corpse of St Mark is actually the famous Macedonian, when he composed the following comments on the starburst shield relief:

Un frammento adespoto pertinente ad un monumento funerario con motivi analoghi è conservato oggi a Venezia, ma proviene sicuramente dal mondo ellenistico (n. 46): vi compaiono uno scudo macedone con al centro il motivo astrale, una copia di schinieri ed una lunga lancia (sarissa?), e sul lato minore il resto di una spada appesa obliquamente ad un chiodo tramite il balteo; il blocco doveva appartenere ad un grande monumento collocabile genericamente fra il III e gli inizi del II secolo a.C.

"An unattributed fragment relating to a funerary monument with analogous motifs is today conserved in Venice, but definitely derives from the Hellenistic world (see note 46): it features a Macedonian shield with a star motif at its centre, a pair of greaves and a long lance (a sarissa?) and on the smallest side the remains of a sword hung obliquely by means of a nail and a leather shoulder-slung sword-strap; the block must have belonged to a large monument that may generically be placed between the 3rd and the beginning of the 2nd century BC."

In his note 46 Polito adds:

Venezia, Museo del Chiostro di S. Apollonia, dal pavimento della Basilica di San Marco. Calcare non cristallino... La provenienza dal Mediterraneo orientale è resa verosimile dal confronto con i numerosi blocchi con inscrizioni giunti a Venezia, come il nostro pezzo, verosimilmente come zavorra di navi.

"Venice, Museum of the Cloister of St Apollonia, from the floor of the Basilica di San Marco. Non-crystalline limestone... The provenance from the eastern Mediterranean is confirmed by comparison with the numerous blocks, which have joint registration at Venice as our piece, probably brought as ship's ballast."

Polito evidently concluded that the sculpture is Macedonian in character and that the fragment probably derives from the eastern Mediterranean, both of which points are difficult to reconcile with it having been sculpted from a block of Pietra di Aurisina. However, Polito's observations are perfectly consistent with the possibility that the block was brought from Alexandria, perhaps at the same time as the putative corpse of St Mark.

Polito's dating of the sculpture to the 3rd or early second centuries BC is intriguing, since, for example, the Soma Mausoleum of Alexander in Alexandria was constructed about 215BC at the centre of his range.

---

[15] Eugenio Polito, *Fulgentibus armis: Introduzione allo studio dei fregi d'armi antichi*, L'Erma di Bretschneider, Roma, 1998, p.79 & p.99 (note 46).

The Sword in the Stone

If Polito is correct in his suggestion that the lance might be a sarissa, then this further underlines the Macedonian character of the block's decoration. Although he does not state his reasoning, there is a strong argument for this identification of the weapon from the specifics of the sculptural arrangement on the block. Its sculptor was especially careful to fit elements of his design precisely onto the edges and into the corners of the piece: both the shield and the sword touch upon the original lefthand edge of its main face and the shield touches at the midpoint of that edge. The sculptor was evidently motivated to maintain a strong symmetry in his design. The spearpoint of the lance is similarly precisely extended to the very limit of the upper lefthand corner of the main face, then slants down at a moderate angle towards the place where the original lower righthand corner of the block must have been, except that the righthand side of the original block is unfortunately roughly broken away and now entirely missing. In the light of the symmetry elsewhere, it is reasonable to infer that the other end of the lance was tightly fitted into the lower righthand corner. If so, then the original length of the lance and the width of the block may be reconstructed as shown in Figure 11.8.[16] This gives a width for the block that was originally about 2.5x its height and a length for the lance of about 3.15m. Since we have noted that the sculpture appears to be lifesize, the lance is too long to be an ordinary spear. It is also at the lower limit of the length range for a Macedonian infantry sarissa. However, it is the perfect length for a Macedonian cavalry sarissa or xyston, which Alexander himself is depicted wielding in the Battle of Issus in the Alexander Mosaic from Pompeii (now in the Naples Museum and believed to be based on an early Hellenistic painting).

The resultant size of the block happens coincidentally to give it integer dimensions in units of the common Egyptian foot (29.86 cm) or Roman foot (29.26cm): i.e. 4 x 10 feet to within about a centimeter.

Sarissas became enormously deprecated after the Battle of Pydna in 168BC, when their use by the Macedonian phalanx proved notably ineffectual against the Roman legionaries. So these considerations make it particularly difficult to date the starshield block much later than that engagement.

---

[16] Recent attempts to reconstruct the width of the block by fitting it to a monument with standard integer dimensions in Roman feet are unconvincing, because they fail to result in the opposite end of the lance fitting into the diagonally opposite corner of the block's face: see Maddalena Bassani & Giulio Testori, "La stella di Alessandro il Grande nel chiostro di Sant'Apollonia: due ipotesi di restituzione di un monumento onorario romano", *Engramma* 95, December 2011.

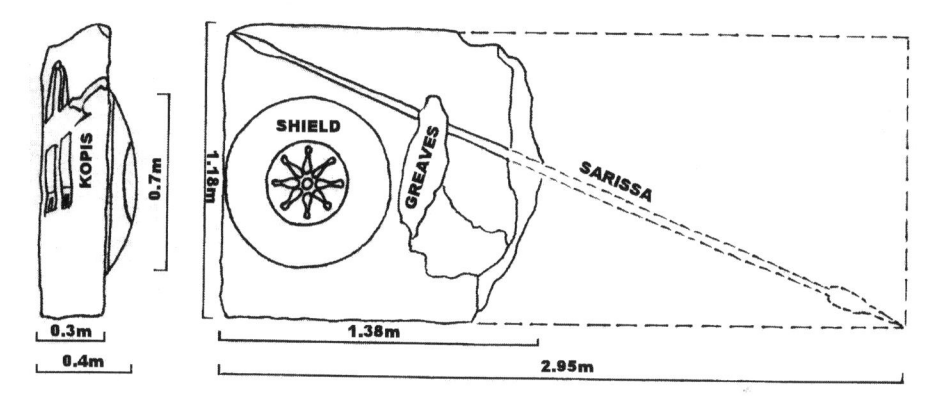

The Quest for the Tomb of Alexander by Andrew Chugg

Figure 11.8. Reconstruction of the starshield block on the basis of sarissa symmetry.

Overall Polito's insights are highly apposite and it is only necessary to differ with him on his suggestion that the block might have been shipped as ballast, because it is really too bulky and massive for this to have been the sole purpose of its transport halfway across the Mediterranean. The Venetians went to great trouble to move it to their ship and to manipulate it, so as to load it onboard. It would have been far more convenient to use the same weight of smaller stones or even to break up this stone. If they brought it back intact from so far away, it must have been because it had special significance for them. One possible reason for such significance would be that they had found it in the Church of St Mark in Alexandria, perhaps in close association with St Mark's tomb.

*　　*　　*　　*　　*　　*　　*　　*

The archaeological evaluation of the starburst shield block published a decade ago by Eugenio Polito is highly consistent with an origin in Hellenistic Alexandria. It is sharply at odds with the reported interpretation of the stone tests. To address this conundrum, it is important to learn more of the respective characteristics of the Alexandrian and Aurisina limestones. In particular we need to be able to specify clear tests to distinguish between the alternatives. Ideally, such tests should be performed blind with the incorporation of calibration samples of the actual Alexandrian and Aurisina limestones by several independent laboratories.

Regarding the limestone from the close vicinity of Alexandria, the following is a summary of several emails to the author from Professor James Harrell of the University of Toledo, who is an expert on ancient quarries in Egypt:

The limestone quarried near Alexandria, and copiously used in its construction, is actually a very poor quality stone. It is white to commonly pale yellow in color, and is very grainy, porous and soft. It was used simply because it was the only building stone available within 150 km of Alexandria. I am not familiar with Pietra Aurisina, but if this is a proper sculptural medium then it must be a very different kind of limestone. So far as I know, the first sculptural stones imported into Egypt date to the 1st century AD. Up until then only the native Egyptian sculptural stones were used. The Alexandrian stone is rather peculiar and is fairly easy to distinguish from all other white sculptural stones because it has a "clastic" texture. When a clean surface is viewed with a strong magnifying glass, you will see that the rock is made up of sand-size calcitic grains, both ooliths (nearly spherical grains with concentric layering) and coated shell fragments. Nearly all white sculptural stones have a "crystalline" texture (i.e., interlocking crystals - this is what makes them good sculptural stones), and are either metamorphic marble or recrystallized limestone. A similar limestone was quarried anciently on Crete, but otherwise the Alexandrian limestone is fairly unique.[17]

Below is reproduced a technical description of limestone quarried near Alexandria including quarry locations from Professor James Harrell's website:

ALEXANDRIA FORMATION (Pleistocene)

Calcarenite limestone: fine-grained, occasionally silty/sandy (quartzose), friable, highly porous packstones to mainly grainstones (calcarenites) with mostly nonskeletal carbonate grains (especially ooliths and coated grains) [0-5 % dolomite].

Mediterranean Coast: 1. numerous quarries on both sides of Mallahet Mariut marsh near Alexandria: between Abu Sir [30d 56.8m N, 29d 30.0m E] and Burg el-Arab [30d 55.0m N, 29d 32.7m E] villages to the SW and Mex village [31d 9.25m N, 29d 50.6m E] to the NE (Pt-R)[18]

Regarding Pietra di Aurisina, I have found a reference to detailed investigations of ten Roman gravestones of the Republican era from Aquileia that were shown to be made from this stone.[19] Specifically, the researchers found that all the gravestones had been extracted from the upper beds of the Roman Quarry near Aurisina, which they noted had been exploited since the 2nd century BC. They performed measurements of the ratio of strontium-87 to strontium-86 in the marine carbonates from their samples to show that all but one had been quarried from early Campanian beds formed 81 to 82 million years ago in the Late Cretaceous era. Given Eugenio Polito's early dating of the decoration of the starburst shield sculpture, we should expect it too to have been extracted from the upper layers of the Roman Quarry, if it is indeed Pietra Aurisina. Hence a test would be to show that its stone gives a strontium isotope ratio in the approximate range 0.707425 to 0.70755, which encompasses all the gravestones.

---

[17] From emails of 23-27/3/07 from Professor James Harrell, University of Toledo to the author; Professor Harrell has also recommended the following reference on the Alexandrian limestone: N.M. Shukri, G. Philip & R. Said, "The geology of the Mediterranean coast between Rosetta and Bardia, Part II: Pleistocene sediments, geomorphology, and microfacies," *Bulletin de l'Institut d'Égypte* 1956, v. 37, n.2, pp.295-433.

[18] http://www.eeescience.utoledo.edu/Faculty/Harrell/Egypt/AGRG_Home.html

[19] L. Maritan, C. Mazzoli, E. Melis, "A Multidisciplinary Approach To The Characterization Of Roman Gravestones From Aquileia (Udine, Italy)," *Archaeometry* 45.3, 2003, pp.363-374; the authors are from the Department of Mineralogy and Petrology, University of Padua.

The Quest for the Tomb of Alexander by Andrew Chugg

The article on the gravestones also appears to state that the Pietra di Aurisina limestone from the Roman Quarry was crystalline, e.g. on page 367: "All of the studied archaeological samples are texturally and palaeontologically homogeneous on the basis of microscope observations. They have organogenic, clastic and crystalline texture, sometimes with interstitial micrite." This would seem to be at odds with Eugenio Polito's description of the starburst shield block as "non crystalline limestone". However, Professor Harrell has cautioned (23/10/07) that Pietra Aurisina "is a partially recrystallized limestone and so could be described as either a fossiliferous limestone or, because of the partial recrystallization, a crystalline limestone."

* * * * * * * * *

Even as this chapter was originally being drafted in October 2007, new information emerged, when Professor Harrell kindly took advantage of a meeting in Jordan with Lorenzo Lazzarini to enquire about the latter's tests on the starburst shield block. It seems that analysis of the fossils in the stone has played a large part in the formulation of Lorenzo Lazzarini's conclusion regarding its origin. In particular, the stone contains fossils of a type of ancient mollusc, a sort of clam, known as a rudist.

After the appearance of the first edition of this book, Lazzarini authored a short article on the results of his examination of stone samples from the starshield sculpture, which was published in an Italian web journal called Engramma.[20] The technical details are confined to a few lines in this article, which essentially confirms that the block consists of a fairly standard type of limestone with the presence of small rudist and other bivalve fossils being the most distinctive feature of this material. Lazzarini notes that this matches limestone from the Roman Aurisina Quarry near Trieste, and then concludes that "we can reasonably assume" that the stone originated from that quarry. However, scientifically speaking, such an assumption may only be made, if there is no alternative source of matching stone elsewhere. Yet in this case it transpires that not only are there numerous other potential sources of similar stone, but at least one such source is as close to Alexandria in Egypt as Trieste is to Venice in Italy.

Rudists are a type of marine heterodont bivalve (resembling modern clams) that evolved in the Jurassic era, then became extremely common in the Cretaceous, but disappeared 65 million years ago in the K-T extinction event at the end of the Cretaceous era. Hence it is immediately clear from the presence of rudists that the starshield stone was most likely laid down in the Cretaceous era and cannot be derived from the very young limestone beds of the quarries in the immediate vicinity of Alexandria. Nevertheless, a wide variety of stone types from elsewhere in Egypt were used for sculptures and inscriptions in Ptolemaic

---

[20] Lorenzo Lazzarini, "Il dato materiale: natura e origine della pietra della lastra di S. Apollonia", *Engramma* 70, March 2009.

The Sword in the Stone

Alexandria, evidently quarried from a correspondingly wide-ranging set of locations.[21] This prompts the question of whether there are any sources of Cretaceous rudist-rich whitish limestone near Alexandria in Egypt, which might be confused with the Aurisina limestone? The straightforward answer is that there are at least two sites of such stone at a similar distance from Alexandria as the Aurisina quarry is from Venice (70 miles). Firstly, there are thick limestone beds in northern Sinai (Rizan Aneiza and Gebel Raghawi) dating to the Upper Aptian to Albian periods in the Early Cretaceous, which contain numerous rudist fossils.[22] But more significantly, there are outcrops of Turonian period limestone with a partially crystalline texture in rudist dominated beds from the Late Cretaceous era at Abu Roash to the west of Cairo, just south of the Canopic Branch of the Nile.[23] Indeed, this is among the closest better quality sources of limestone encountered on journeying southeast from Alexandria via the Nile waterways. This Egyptian limestone actually overlaps the Aurisina limestone in age and lies just 100 miles southeast of Alexandria.

In particular these strata cover the site of the pyramid of Radjedef (Djedefra) at Abu Roash and limestone from a nearby ancient (Old Kingdom) quarry was used for the core blocks of this vast structure. However, a great part of the pyramid itself was quarried away in ancient times. Although the predominant surviving evidence is for exploitation in the Roman period from the 1st century BC onwards, there are also some indications of Ptolemaic activity. Firstly, a beam of Lebanese cedar wood, which yielded a radiocarbon (Carbon-14) date in the range 355 BC to 95 BC, was found within the shaft used to construct the vault of the tomb-chamber beneath the pyramid.[24] Secondly, Michel Valloggia has discovered a Ptolemaic forge at the site dating (according to ceramic evidence) to between the 4th and the first half of the 3rd century BC.[25] Since the Abu Roash limestone was created in the same ancient ocean and at the same time as Pietra di Aurisina, it exhibits a rather similar fossil mix (rudists and other bivalves). Extremely careful petrological characterisations of the two rock types will be required to distinguish confidently between them. As Professor Harrell has commented in an email to the author on 25th October 2007: "Somebody will have to do a comparative study of the Trieste and Abu Roash limestones as well as the limestone relief from St. Mark's to settle the issue."

Another pertinent line of enquiry should now be to check whether any of the hundred or so limestone sculptural fragments from Ptolemaic Alexandria contain rudist fossils: most are in the Graeco-Roman Museum.

---

[21] See the catalogue of Ptolemaic sculptures and inscriptions from Alexandria in Barbara Tkaczow, *Topography of Ancient Alexandria (An Archaeological Map)*, Warsaw, 1993, pp.182-229.
[22] Thomas Steuber & Martina Bachmann, "Upper Aptian-albian Rudist Bivalves from Northern Sinai, Egypt," *Palaeontology* 45(4), June 2002, pp.725-749.
[23] Ahmed Sadek M. Mansour, "Diagenesis of Upper Cretaceous Rudist Bivalves, Abu Roash Area, Egypt: A Petrographic Study," *Geologia Croatica*, 57/1, Zagreb 2004, pp.55-66.
[24] Michel Valloggia, *Au Coeur d'une Pyramide*, Musée Romain Lausanne-Vidy, 2001, p. 62.
[25] Email to the author from Michel Valloggia, 18th November 2007.

The Quest for the Tomb of Alexander by Andrew Chugg

The connection between the starshield block and Alexandria is already supported by the discovery of a Hellenistic tomb in the Gabbari district of the Egyptian city, which contained sculpted funerary reliefs closely paralleling the style and forms of weaponry depicted on the starshield block. The principal documentation of this discovery made in 1953 is to be found in Achille Adriani's majestic tome: Repertorio D'Arte Dell'Egitto Greco-Romano, Serie C, I-II, Item 120 on page 172 & Tavola 85. There are arms either side of a false door in the wall opposite the entrance: to the left, a sword slung diagonally, a pair of greaves and a helm; to the right, a Macedonian corselet very similar to those depicted in the murals of the tomb of Lyson & Kallikles in Macedonia, and on the wall to the right, a Greek hoplite shield with a pair of spears running diagonally beneath it. In *Fulgentibus Armis* Eugenio Polito reviews this find immediately before his description of the starshield block and concludes that it dates to no later than the beginning of the 2nd century BC.[26]

* * * * * * * *

The Italian researchers associated with the University of Venice (Università Iuav di Venezia) and other Venetian institutions have published a range of articles in the online journal Engramma on the subject of the starshield block since the publication of the first edition of this book. They have generally taken the stone testing results as excluding any possible origin for the block other than the Roman Aurisina Quarry, which, as I have explained, constitutes a misrepresentation of the nature of the stone testing evidence. On this basis, they (specifically Monica Centanni) originally argued at the time of the Eroi conference in 2006 that the block reflected a 1st century BC style of sculpture that was local to the Venice region, but their more recent articles have abandoned any attempt to refute the unambiguously Macedonian nature of the piece and the associations of its symbology with Alexander the Great.[27] (In fact they now proclaim with more certainty than I myself that the symbol on the shield is the "Star of Alexander the Great".) Now instead they have resorted to proposing that a Republican Roman bigwig (they have speculatively named C. Asinius Pollio on the basis of no evidence whatsoever) perpetrated an exact copy of a Macedonian high status funerary monument in his home region in the later first century BC on account of having been sufficiently impressed by prototypes that he had encountered in Egypt or other parts of the Hellenistic World. Whereas it is not unknown for Roman art to be closely inspired by Greek prototypes, exact copies of Greek monuments with no sign of any Roman style or technique (to the extent that they fool a modern expert like

---

[26] Eugenio Polito, *Fulgentibus armis: Introduzione allo studio dei fregi d'armi antichi*, L'Erma di Bretschneider, Roma, 1998, p. 78-79.
[27] Maddalena Bassani, "Esempi archeologici per un'ipotesi interpretativa della lastra di S. Apollonia", *Engramma* 70, March 2009; Maddalena Bassani & Giulio Testori, "La stella di Alessandro il Grande nel chiostro di Sant'Apollonia: due ipotesi di restituzione di un monumento onorario romano", *Engramma* 95, December 2011.

The Sword in the Stone

Eugenio Polito into thinking that they are original Greek works) are at least very rare and maybe vanishingly so. Consequently, it will be transparent to any reasonable reader that this is not an explanation that should be given much credence, if there is any chance at all that the block is older and was imported to Venice from the eastern Mediterranean. As we have seen, there remains in actuality a strong possibility of it having been imported from Alexandria in particular after careful consideration of all the available evidence (including the stone testing). The simple fact is that the form and symbolism of the sculpture on the starshield block constitutes much stronger and more specific evidence than the stone testing. Anyone who thinks otherwise has been bedazzled by science.

* * * * * * * *

If the stone should be confirmed to be Pietra Aurisina, preferably through independent analysis with full publication of data, then the probability of a direct connection between the starburst shield sculpture and the *Translazione* would be diminished. However, it would remain possible that the Venetians incorporated this particular fragment in the foundations of San Marco, because they had seen something similar in the context of St Mark's tomb in Alexandria or else had copied a sculpture that they had seen in Alexandria.

Conversely, if it were determined that the block was quarried in the vicinity of Egypt, then there would be a strong possibility that it had been brought from Alexandria in AD828 together with the putative corpse of St Mark. This would tangibly connect the corpse with a high status Macedonian mausoleum constructed in Alexandria between the 3rd to early 2nd century BC. Given also that the starburst symbol was particularly the badge of Alexander's family rather than of the Ptolemies, the Soma Mausoleum would be by far the most likely source for the starburst shield block. Therefore we would have a tangible connection between St Mark's remains and those of Alexander, which should surely focus minds more sharply on the need to investigate the corpse itself.

In conclusion, it should be stressed that the finely balanced nature of the opposing strands of evidence and profound significance of the outcome means that confirmatory testing needs to be performed in a proper scientific fashion, if all parties are to be convinced by the results. By this I mean that tests on both samples of the stone and control samples from other limestone blocks should be undertaken by several independent laboratories in a double-blind fashion. The process should be administered by a co-ordinating panel incorporating representatives of the interested parties. As an initial step, existing stone test data should be published in more detail (including photos), such that it may be subjected to peer review and the informed criticism of interested parties.

Is there anyone who finds any of this unreasonable? I hope not, for the truth is sometimes elusive and needs to be coaxed forth. Certainly, he who can extract the essence of the sword in the stone will be deserving of a great prize.

12. Exequies

EMPEROR: *Then, Doctor Faustus, mark what I shall say.*
As I was sometime solitary set
Within my closet, sundry thoughts arose
About the honour of mine ancestors,
How they had won by prowess such exploits,
Got such riches, subdu'd so many kingdoms,
As we that do succeed, or they that shall
Hereafter possess our throne, shall,
I fear me, ne'er attain to that degree
Of high renown and great authority:
Amongst which kings is Alexander the Great,
Chief spectacle of the world's pre-eminence,
The bright shining of whose glorious acts
Lightens the world with his reflecting beams,
As when I hear but motion made of him,
It grieves my soul I never saw the man:
If, therefore, thou, by cunning of thine art,
Canst raise this man from hollow vaults below,
Where lies entomb'd this famous conqueror,
And bring with him his beauteous paramour,
Both in their right shapes, gesture, and attire
They us'd to wear during their time of life,
Thou shalt both satisfy my just desire,
And give me cause to praise thee whilst I live.

FAUSTUS: *My gracious lord, I am ready to accomplish your request,*
So far forth as by art and power of my spirit I am able to perform.

The Tragical History of Doctor Faustus by *Christopher Marlowe*[1]

There have been sporadic excavations throughout the 20th century at numerous sites within the walls of the ancient city, yet the exact locations of most of the major buildings of Ptolemaic Alexandria have still not been established. In particular, the centre of the city either side of Canopic Way, which is said to have contained the Gymnasium, the tribunal (*dicasterion*), the groves and the artificial mound of the Paneum as well as the Soma, remains an open question, for which I have proposed novel answers that beg to be tested through archaeology. Around 140 investigations have previously been targeted at discovering Alexander's tomb without revealing any identifiable trace, but scarcely any of these excavations have been made at the locations highlighted by my research.

---

[1] From Scene 10 in the 1604 A Text of *Dr Faustus*.

Exequies

In the 1990's some demanding archaeology was performed by divers in the Great Harbour yielding spectacular finds. In the sea around the base of the Qait Bey fortress, which is known to have been built on the site of the Pharos lighthouse, a team led by Jean-Yves Empereur has discovered nearly three thousand large blocks of ancient masonry and some statuary, including column fragments, obelisks and 26 sphinxes. Hieroglyphic inscriptions show that much of this material must have been transported to Alexandria from Heliopolis in order to decorate the Ptolemaic city. Most of this stonework may have been deposited across part of the harbour entrance by the Mameluke rulers in an attempt to make the city more readily defensible after a major raid by the King of Cyprus, Pierre de Lusignan, over two days in 1365. However, some pieces could be from the Pharos itself, cast into sea as the tower disintegrated during one of the medieval earthquakes. When this debris was observed in 1980 by a team of Italian film-makers, they considered it so impressive, that they published an article suggesting that Alexander's tomb had lain at the foot of the Pharos!

On the landward side of the harbour an area of submerged coastline in the vicinity of the ancient Royal Quarter has been investigated with similar success. A team led by Franck Goddio has mapped the sunken foundations of the ancient quays, previously glimpsed by Mahmoud Bey, in great detail. However, in their new interpretation Antirrhodos and the Timonium are interchanged relative to their locations in both Mahmoud's map and Strabo's eloquent description of the harbour front. In 1998 the wreck of a ship was found nearby with artefacts including rigging, ceramics, remains of food, shards of glass and jewellery. Radiocarbon dating on wood samples put the age of the ship at between 90BC and AD130. Further ancient wrecks have been discovered in the approaches to the harbour, but none of these discoveries has so far cast any light on the Soma problem.

In the city itself archaeology mainly proceeds as built-up sites become available between demolition and redevelopment. This is a slow and erratic means to rediscover the glories of the past, but much good work has been achieved. The archaeological institutes are so pressed for funding, that they are sometimes unable to exploit even all of these occasional opportunities. They have to some extent concentrated their efforts in particular districts in the hope of eventually building up a reasonably complete picture of a microcosm of the city. Although a fresh excavation has recently been undertaken by a Greek and Egyptian team in the Latin Cemeteries, relatively little attention has ever been paid to the areas immediately to the west of the Shallalat Gardens, which appear from the analysis presented here to be most relevant for the discovery of Alexander's tomb. It is in fact another of the virtues of the new theory that it explains exactly why 140 previous efforts have proven so fruitless.

If Alexandria's well-documented medieval walls (Figure 12.1) were built in the same line as the late Roman circuit, which had in turn incorporated the *temenos*

The Quest for the Tomb of Alexander by Andrew Chugg

of the Soma in their eastern sector, then this provides a new, fixed framework for interpreting the layout of the entire ancient city. It is now possible to suspect that the enclosure of the Soma was itself essentially the fossil of Alexander's original *peribolos* of Alexandria, adapted to serve as the sacred heart of a vastly expanded Ptolemaic metropolis. It is the final irony of this convoluted story that, in seeking an answer to the mystery of the Soma by investigating the plan of ancient Alexandria, we find that the location of the Soma enclosure may instead prove to be the key to understanding the rest of the city.

Figure 12.1. View of the medieval walls of Alexandria from the east in 1801 by Edward Orme (author's collection)

No theory or hypothesis has any great practical value unless it can be validated through testing. It is therefore important to be clear in specifying the types of testing which may most reasonably and effectively be applied to validate the various new theories put forward in this book:

a) Regarding the new hypothesis for the location of Alexander's Memphite tomb, it is recommended that the Nectanebo II temple at the Serapeum in Saqqara should be re-excavated; in particular the phases in the construction of this building should be identified and dated.

b) Regarding the theory concerning the location of the Soma enclosure in Alexandria, the easiest route to validation should be excavation to seek traces of the foundations of the western wall of the proposed *temenos* of the Soma, the existence of which is predicted by the theory; the optimal dig location would be the vicinity of the projection of the short oblique section of the northern branch of the medieval walls near its intersection with Mahmoud Bey's street R3.

c) More detailed confirmatory testing of the starburst shield sculpted limestone block in Venice should be commissioned to determine its true nature and origins.

d) Characterisation and testing of the putative remains of St Mark in the *Basilica di San Marco* in Venice should be performed to confirm their age and origins.

I first published the St Mark hypothesis for the fate of Alexander's corpse in my article in the July 2004 issue of History Today. Considerable media interest was generated by this novel theory, which culminated in my participation in a short debate hosted by the Today Programme on BBC Radio 4 on 18th June 2004, in which Robin Lane Fox appeared as my antagonist. The fascination exerted by the notion of such a brazen forgery was echoed in numerous press articles, which appeared all around the world.[2] Especially when I elaborated on the theory in my first book, *The Lost Tomb of Alexander the Great*, published by Periplus in London in October 2004, there were several enquiries from TV companies who were interested in funding testing of the remains of St Mark by independent experts. Various approaches to the authorities at the Basilica di San Marco in Venice eventually elicited a formal statement on 19th July 2005, which was issued on behalf of the Catholic Church:

I dati sul corpo di San Marco sono stati pubblicati nei volumi di Leonardo Manin, 'Memorie storico-critiche intorno la vita, translazione, e invenzioni di san Marco evangelista principale protettore di Venezia', Venezia 1815 e 1835. La Chiesa da allora ha ritenuto sufficienti le notizie e non intende procedere ad altre ricognizioni della tomba. Distinti saluti. Ettore Vio, Proto di San Marco

"The data on the body of St Mark have been published in the Leonardo Manin volumes, *Historical Monograph Concerning the Life, Transferral and Rediscovery of St Mark the Evangelist, Patron Saint of Venice*, Venice 1815 and 1835. The Church from then has considered this information as sufficient and does not intend to proceed to other investigations of the tomb. Best regards. Ettore Vio, Procurator of St Marks"

In the light of this somewhat complacent stance it is apposite to consider various points relating to its ultimate tenability. The combination of new issues regarding the authenticy of the remains with the newly perfected ability of advanced scientific techniques to solve the mystery of their identity will inevitably lead to serious questions being posed to the Church as custodians of the remains.

---

[2] E.g. "Does the tomb of St Mark in Venice really contain the bones of Alexander the Great?" by Jonathan Thompson & Nicholas Pyke, *Independent on Sunday*, 13th June 2004, p.15.

The Quest for the Tomb of Alexander by Andrew Chugg

It is usually agreed that the dead have a moral right to be identified. Most people agree that they would wish advanced scientific techniques to be used to identify their own remains in the event of any doubt following their death. For example, this argument was recently used to justify the application of sophisticated techniques to identify partially decomposed corpses following the tsunami in the Indian Ocean. As we have seen, there is now a good possibility that the remains of St Mark can be dated and their place of origin can be identified. Many other details relating to the identity of the corpse could also be revealed. Choosing to impede the identification of human remains, when a scientific resolution is feasible, is morally questionable.

The remains of St Mark embody much historically important information, which it is now possible to decipher by applying advanced scientific techniques. The custodians of such remains are usually deemed to have a duty to evoke such information insofar as the situation allows, thus making it available to enrich our comprehension of the past. Whilst this information lies undeciphered within the remains, it is under continuous threat. Firstly, the slow decay processes of time are continuously corrupting DNA information and causing increased contamination, which will reduce the accuracy of radiocarbon dating and other techniques. Secondly, whilst the information is encapsulated in a single location, it is vulnerable to a single point accident or catastrophe, such as fire or flood, the latter being a specially pressing issue in Venice. Once testing were performed, copies of the data could be distributed to many locations, rendering the historical information immune from further loss or deterioration. Anyone who impedes testing needs to consider whether their position will be defensible in the event of the subsequent destruction of the remains through some accident, attack or other calamity befalling them.

It should be practicable accurately to reconstruct the face of the deceased, since Manin asserted that the skull is present and intact. Facial reconstruction was recently performed by several independent teams for the skull of Tutankhamun. All of the reconstructions were recognisably similar, demonstrating that the technique is now reasonably reliable. If the remains are genuinely those of St Mark, there is likely to be great interest among the congregation of the faithful in seeing his face. We cannot know the true appearance of any other great Christian leader from the dawn of the Church. Yet no less interest would be excited by a reconstruction of the face of Alexander. This could be a unique opportunity.

* * * * * * * *

Some have supposed that my purpose is to secure my own access to the remains in order personally to conduct aggressive and damaging tests upon them. Nothing could be further from my intentions. It would be inappropriate, not only because I lack the specialist technical skills, but also because I could hardly qualify as an impartial investigator in the matter. What I would actually advocate is a thorough but sensitive investigation process, beginning with the least intrusive measures and performed by independent specialists and experts in accordance with the following general principles:

   a) The investigation could be funded by a TV company (or similar) in exchange for exclusive TV transmission rights
   b) All tests and analyses should be performed by third-party, independent experts and laboratories of high repute (e.g. Oxford Radiocarbon Accelerator Unit [ORAU])
   c) A technical report and datapack should be prepared and a copy should be presented to the Church
   d) A panel with Church members, relevant scientific and historical experts and representatives of other key interested parties should oversee the investigation

Precise details of the organisation of the testing would of course need to be decided through deliberation and discussion of the panel.

In the final analysis, opposing investigation of the remains is liable to prove to be an exercise in futility. Supposing the remains are a forgery, is it reasonable that the world should be kept perpetually in ignorance of the fraud? Supposing that the remains are genuinely those of St Mark, is it reasonable now that techniques exist to prove that they are authentic, that the world should be kept perpetually in doubt concerning the identity of the remains? If neither stance is reasonable, then testing should be permitted to proceed. It should also be borne in mind that the healed wound evidence may mean that merely lifting the lid of the sarcophagus will resolve the mystery.

To keep in touch with developments check regularly at the author's website dedicated to Alexander and the mysteries of his lost corpse and vanished mausoleum at www.alexanderstomb.com

Appendix A: The Journal of Alexander the Great

The following article by the author was first published in the Ancient History Bulletin (ISSN 0835-3638) 19.3-4, 2005, pp. 155-175.

Introduction

Several of the ancient sources on Alexander tell us that parts of their narratives are based upon a daily record or journal of his reign known as the Ephemerides. Controversy has raged for more than a century among scholars on the questions of the purpose and authenticity of this document, not least because its evidence is crucial in the matter of Alexander's death. All the while a pair of enigmas at the heart of the evidence have intrigued historians, for their resolution holds out the promise of determining the true nature of the Journal. It is the purpose of this account to propose solutions to these mysteries and to proceed to review the status of the Journal in the light of the new conjectures.

Diodotus of Erythrae

The first enigma concerns the authorship of the Ephemerides. It is a relatively uncontroversial orthodoxy, that Alexander maintained a secretariat, which compiled detailed and regular records of events during his reign. In particular, we have the testimony of Plutarch, Nepos and Arrian that Eumenes the son of Hieronymus[1] from Cardia served Philip II as his secretary for seven years until his assassination[2] and subsequently served Alexander as his Chief Secretary ἀρχιγραμματεύς or Royal Secretary γραμματεῖ τῷ βασιλικῷ.[3] Pseudo-Callisthenes also has ὑπομνηματογράφος.[4] We know that there were official papers that were specifically in Eumenes' keeping, because Plutarch tells us that Eumenes' tent burnt down at the time Alexander's expedition had reached the Indian Ocean and that Alexander's papers were destroyed in the blaze, so that the King had to write to his satraps and generals requesting copies.[5]

Eumenes of Cardia is named by Aelian as one among several sources[6] for a diary-like account of a succession of Alexander's drinking parties,[7] which

---

[1] Aelian, *Varia Historia* 12.43, suggests that Eumenes' father was a poor man who played music at funerals.
[2] Cornelius Nepos, *Eumenes* 1.4-6.
[3] Arrian, *Anabasis* 7.4.6.
[4] W. Kroll, *Historia Alexandri Magni (Pseudo-Callisthenes)* (Berlin 1926) 3.33.14.
[5] Plutarch, *Eumenes* 1-2.
[6] Aelian probably gave an additional name, which is seemingly corrupted to εκεινος; see E. Badian, "The Ring and the Book" in W. Will/J. Heinrichs (eds.), *Zu Alexander d. Gr., Festschrift G. Wirth zum 60. Geburtstag am 9.12.86* (Amsterdam 1987) 619-620 n. 8; A. B. Bosworth, *From Arrian to Alexander* (Oxford 1988) 171 n. 45.
[7] Aelian, *Varia Historia* 3.23.

The Journal of Alexander the Great

Bosworth has convincingly assigned to October 324 BC.[8] It is virtually certain that this summary is excerpted from the Ephemerides.[9] Unfortunately, Aelian in his surviving form only preserves the best-known writer correctly. There is a second name, but it seems corrupted in our text. However, more complete information on the authorship of the Journal is provided by Athenaeus, who makes reference to Alexander's "Ephemerides, written by Eumenes of Cardia and Diodotus of Erythrae."[10] Here then is confirmation that Alexander's secretary, whom we would naturally expect to have been involved in the compilation of the Ephemerides, was indeed recognised as one of its authors by our ancient sources. The only mystery arises from the existence of his co-author, Diodotus. Although Diodotus was subsequently the name of two Greek kings of Bactria, nobody of that name is known who was associated with Alexander, despite the fact that we have the names of many hundreds of men who accompanied Alexander's expedition gleaned from among our disparate sources.[11] Alexander historians have uniformly reported that, except for this single mention by Athenaeus, Diodotus is unknown.

It would be slightly strange, if Eumenes had granted anyone else from his own secretariat a co-authorship of the Journal, because it would implicitly have appeared that he was elevating one of his subordinates to be on a par with himself. Hammond has suggested that Diodotus might have been Eumenes' successor as Chief Secretary when the latter succeeded to Perdiccas' command of a regiment of the Companion Cavalry in 324 BC.[12] However, there is no reason to believe that an administrative position and a military command were mutually exclusive: Hephaistion's role as both the Chiliarch and a Hipparch is the most obvious counter-example. It is nowhere stated or implied that Eumenes gave up his administrative duties; rather Nepos indicates that Eumenes was Alexander's secretary for his entire reign of thirteen years and that his military command ran in parallel.[13] A more satisfactory explanation would therefore be for Diodotus to have been responsible for incorporating some type of complementary information or data in the Journal that was generated by a different branch of Alexander's staff. The most obvious type of additional information would have been survey data on the distance and direction of the

---

[8] Bosworth, *Arrian* (as in n. 6) 170-172; the account begins on the 5th of the Macedonian month *Dius*, which began at the autumnal equinox.
[9] It is one of the recognised fragments of the *Ephemerides* cited by F. Jacoby, *Die Fragmente der griechischen Historiker* II B (Berlin 1929) item 117.
[10] Athenaeus, *Deipnosophistae* 10.434B.
[11] E.g. H. Berve, *Das Alexanderreich auf prosopographischer Grundlage* II (Munich 1926): Diodotos is Berve 272; note that R. Lane Fox, *Alexander the Great* (London 1973) ch. 32, has suggested that the Diodotus mentioned in Isocrates, *Letter 4, To Antipater* written in about 340 BC, is a candidate – this man had been a pupil of Isocrates in Athens, had an adult, disabled son and had served potentates in Asia on unspecified missions, but his city is unknown.
[12] N. G. L. Hammond, "Alexander's Journal and Ring in his Last Days", *American Journal of Philology* 110 (1989) 157-158; Plutarch, *Eumenes* 1.2.
[13] Cornelius Nepos, *Eumenes* 1.

The Quest for the Tomb of Alexander by Andrew Chugg

daily march and the nature of the terrain when the army was on the move. The written-up versions of this survey information from Alexander's expedition are collectively known as the Stathmoi ("Stages"). Might Diodotus have been one of Alexander's surveyors, known as the bematists ("pacers", because they measured distances by counting paces)?

The elder Pliny names two of Alexander's bematists as Baeton and Diognetus.[14] The Greek-English Lexicon of Liddell & Scott (revised by Henry Stuart Jones) defines Diognetus as a (less common) synonym of Diogenes, meaning "sprung from Zeus" or Zeus-born.[15] The same work indicates that Diodotus is a synonym of Diosdotus, for which the translation is "given by Zeus". Evidently, the literal meaning of Diognetus is relatively similar to that of Diodotus.

Baeton wrote a lost work called "Stages in Alexander's Journey". Evidently, Diognetus wrote something equivalent, because Pliny cites both him and Baeton for distances between various stations on Alexander's route. However, Pliny appears to confirm that Diognetus wrote a separate work from Baeton, since he mentions them as distinct authorities on regions and nations and cites Diognetus alone as a source of information about trees.[16] Nowhere is the title of Diognetus' book specified.

There is one other reference to Diognetus in the ancient literature. Gaius Julius Hyginus (c. 64 BC – AD 17) was a Latin author, who was a native of Spain (or possibly Alexandria). He was a pupil of the famous Cornelius Alexander Polyhistor and a freedman of Augustus, by whom he was made superintendent of the Palatine library.[17] One of two works received under his name is a treatise usually called the Poetica Astronomica giving an elementary account of astronomy and myths associated with the stars, in the tradition of Eratosthenes. The style and basic mistakes suggest that it is an abridgement of part of the Genealogiae of Hyginus by an unknown grammarian of the second half of the 2nd century AD, who incorporated a work on mythology. In the Poetica Astronomica a story which tells of Venus and Cupid being confronted by Typhon on the banks of the Euphrates in Syria is attributed to "Diognetus of Erythrae".[18] It is likely that this is Alexander's bematist, in which case the information that he was a fellow-citizen of Diodotus from the small town of Erythrae on the Ionian coast is notable.

As well as the similarity in their meanings, the names Diognetus and Diodotus differ only in that γνη in the former is substituted by δο in the latter. For a group of N individuals, there are $(N^2-N)/2$ possible pairings. For any of more

---

[14] Pliny, *Natural History* 6.61.
[15] H. G. Liddell and R. Scott (revised and augmented by H. S. Jones), *A Greek-English Lexicon*, 9th Edition (Oxford 1996) s.v. Διόδοτος, Διόγνητος.
[16] Pliny, *Natural History* 1.5-6 and 1.12-13.
[17] Suetonius, *De Grammaticis* 20.
[18] Hyginus, *Poetica Astronomica* 2.30; Jacoby, *FGrH* (as in n. 9) 120 F2.

than 780 possible pairings among over 40 contemporary and near-contemporary writers on Alexander whose fragments have been listed by Jacoby, Diognetus and Diodotus have the most similar names with the single exception of the two writers called Marsyas, but the latter are from different cities.[19] Although some of the writers in Jacoby's Fragments share the same city (Callisthenes, Ephippus and Strattis of Olynthus or Chares and Potamon of Mitylene or Polycleitus and Medius of Larissa or Dorotheus and Anticleides of Athens), none of these have similar names. Among the much larger set of all the men who were associated with Alexander's expedition whose names are known (Berve has listed nearly 900 giving approaching 400,000 possible pairings) a few pairs may be identified who have the same name and the same city, but they are generally Macedonians, who were of course engaged by Alexander in particularly large numbers.[20] Diognetus and Diodotus appear to be the only named men from Erythrae who served with Alexander. Their identities are the most nearly matched of all the tens of known contemporary writers on Alexander, because they share the same city as well as having similar names. However, the coincidence is more striking than this, because they are also both members of a tiny subset of contemporary writers on Alexander: specifically those who were employed by Alexander himself to write records of his expedition. The only other known members of this group are: Callisthenes of Olynthus, Eumenes of Cardia and the other bematists, Baeton and Philonides of Crete. (Amyntas [Jacoby 122] and Archelaus [Jacoby 123] might also be included, but it is not clear from the Fragments that they were actually employed by Alexander). There are only 15 possible pairings within this sub-group, so it is statistically significant that it contains a pair whose identities match as closely as the closest pairing in the much larger group of all known contemporary writers on Alexander.

Diognetus is an author of the Stathmoi, whilst Diodotus is a co-author of the Ephemerides, but Hammond has previously argued on independent grounds that the Ephemerides and the official Stathmoi are merely two types of record within a single Royal Archive of Alexander's reign.[21] It is in fact possible that the official Stathmoi were simply a part of the Ephemerides, for they were certainly a part of Alexander's official daily records, whilst his expedition was on the move.

It would therefore seem reasonable to entertain the seemingly previously unnoticed possibility that Diodotus of Erythrae is in fact Diognetus of Erythrae, whose name has simply been corrupted in the Deipnosophistae of Athenaeus. This is especially credible, because the names of obscure individuals are particularly liable to corruption in ancient manuscripts, since there is generally a lack of contextual information to aid editors and transcribers in avoiding and

---

[19] Jacoby, *FGrH* (as in n. 9) 117-153.
[20] Berve, *Das Alexanderreich* (as in n. 11).
[21] N. G. L. Hammond, "The Royal Journal of Alexander", *Historia* 37 (1988) 139.

rectifying errors and defects. Furthermore, the main text of Athenaeus would appear to have come down to us via a single manuscript brought from Constantinople to Venice in 1423 by Aurispa,[22] which accentuates the risk of errors in this particular work: many have already been corrected by its modern editors. The ease with which this might happen is underlined by the occurrence of a similar error in a modern article that discusses Alexander's Journal, where Diodotus is given as Diodorus in one instance.[23]

It would seem to me more probable that one more name among many has suffered some corruption in the single manuscript mentioning Diodotus of Erythrae which has come down to us, than that Alexander employed two men from Erythrae with similar names among the small number of his staff who were responsible for writing up the daily records of his expedition. Others, such as palaeographers, may wish to comment further on the coincidence, but it is necessary to raise the matter in this article, because it relates closely to the greater issue of the authenticity of the Ephemerides.

Strattis of Olynthus

The second enigma concerns the authorship of an ancient commentary on Alexander's Ephemerides. The sole source for the existence and authorship of this lost work is an entry in the Suda Lexicon under the name of Strattis:

Στράττις, Ὀλύνθιος, ἱστορικός. Περὶ τῶν Ἀλεξάνδρου ἐφημερίδων βιβλία ε', Περὶ ποταμῶν καὶ κρηνῶν καὶ λιμνῶν, Περὶ τῆς Ἀλεξάνδρου τελευτῆς.

The orthodox translation is: "Strattis of Olynthus, Historian. On the Ephemerides of Alexander, five books; On Rivers, Springs and Lakes; On the Death of Alexander." This form of the entry has been authorised by Jacoby[24] and Ada Adler.[25] It seems generally to be accepted as the optimal distillation from the inferior manuscripts (deteriores), given that the most reliable manuscript (A) omitted Strattis of Olynthus, except for a marginal note in another hand, which in turn omitted the reference to the Ephemerides. Some historians of Alexander have used the manuscript difficulties to cast suspicion on the entry.[26] Furthermore, Pearson has argued that a translation "Five Books

---

[22] See C. B. Gulick (trans.), *Athenaeus: Deipnosophistae* (Harvard 1957-63) xvii-xviii (Introduction); apart from Aurispa's manuscript (the St Mark codex, A) and its derivatives, there are two important manuscripts of epitomes of the *Deipnosophistae* of Athenaeus from Paris (C) and Florence (E), of which a synthesis has been published by S. P. Peppink, *Athenaei Dipnosophistarum Epitome* (Leiden 1937), but these texts omit mention of Diodotus.
[23] A. B. Bosworth, "The Death of Alexander the Great: Rumour and Propaganda", *Classical Quarterly* 21 (1971) 119 (first line).
[24] Jacoby, *FGrH* (as in n. 9) 118.
[25] A. Adler (ed.), *Suidae Lexicon* (Leipzig 1928-35) sigma 1179.
[26] A. E. Samuel, "Alexander's Royal Journals", *Historia* 14 (1965) 7; Bosworth, *Arrian* (as in n. 6) 180-2.

The Journal of Alexander the Great

of Diaries about the Exploits of Alexander" is also viable.[27] Bosworth, Badian and Hammond have responded that this interpretation strains the Greek unreasonably, but Bosworth has also noted that small changes could make the Ephemerides entry refer to two works: five books of diaries and a separate account of Alexander's career.[28] Given, however, that we have several independent ancient references for the existence of Ephemerides of Alexander, Bosworth's alternative would also appear to be somewhat evasive of the obvious.

The more interesting aspect of this entry is the question of the identity of Strattis, for it is at least mildly surprising that the Suda alone should have communicated the existence of a writer who wrote such significant works in the generation after Alexander's death. He had probably composed his works by the early 3rd century BC, partly because the subject of Alexander's death was most topical in the immediate aftermath, but mainly because Olynthus was destroyed in 348 BC by Alexander's father, Philip II, and never refounded until the late Byzantine era after the Suda was compiled.[29] Consequently, citizenship of Olynthus rapidly became a rarity as the third century BC progressed.[30] This has inclined some to believe that Strattis' works were in fact later forgeries and that the name Strattis of Olynthus was an alias, which the forger chose in order to imply an earlier date for his writings. In particular, Pearson thought that Strattis' work was the forged source for the Ephemerides themselves as mentioned by ancient authors.[31] However, this opinion engenders more difficulties than it resolves. Supposing with Pearson that the Suda represented Strattis as the author of "Ephemerides about the Exploits of Alexander", why should Athenaeus and Aelian attribute the Ephemerides to Eumenes and "Diodotus"? Furthermore, Strattis is unambiguously credited with a work "On Rivers, Springs and Lakes". It is hardly likely that a forger would have composed an entire book on natural history simply to mask his tracks. It would seem, therefore, that the works of Strattis are unlikely to have been forgeries and were most probably written in the generation after Alexander's death.

---

[27] L. Pearson, "The Diary and the Letters of Alexander the Great", *Historia* 3 (1955) 437.
[28] Bosworth, *Arrian* (as in n. 6) 181; N. G. L. Hammond, *Three Historians of Alexander the Great* (Cambridge 1983) 171 n. 21, also observes that Pearson's alternative translation "is a very unlikely usage"; Badian, *Ring* (as in n. 6) 622, states "There is no question that it must mean 'About the *Ephemerides* of Alexander, Five Books'".
[29] C. A. Robinson, *The Ephemerides of Alexander's Expedition* (Providence 1932) 63.
[30] N. G. L. Hammond, "The Royal Journal of Alexander", *Historia* 37 (1988) 142 n. 40, observes that an early Ptolemaic papyrus lists a mercenary cavalryman known as "Aristokles of Olynthus": British Library Papyrus 573 (2) verso, documented by J. P. Mahaffy, *The Flinders Petrie Papyri* II (Dublin 1893) 115-117. The papyrus is dated to the "sixth year" of some early Ptolemaic king. Mahaffy asserts that this must be Euergetes, giving a date of ~240BC, but he appears to base this judgement solely on the style and form of the script. Mahaffy presumably overlooked the fact that the mention of Olynthus mitigates in favour of an earlier date, so it is not clear that we should exclude the reign of Philadelphus or even of Alexander IV.
[31] Pearson, *Diary* (as in n. 27) 439.

The Quest for the Tomb of Alexander by Andrew Chugg

Yet one feature of the entry for Strattis of Olynthus in the Suda is exceptionally mysterious. We are told that he wrote a work Περὶ τῆς Ἀλεξάνδρου τελευτῆς (On the Death of Alexander). However, there is another Olynthian called Ephippus who was, according to Athenaeus, the author of a book Περὶ τῆς Ἡφαιστίωνος καὶ Ἀλεξάνδρου τελευτῆς (On the Death of Hephaistion and Alexander).[32] Admittedly Athenaeus also gives a couple of variations on this title at other points in his text: Περὶ τῆς Ἀλεξάνδρου καὶ Ἡφαιστίωνος ταφῆς (On the Funeral of Alexander and Hephaistion)[33] and Περὶ τῆς Ἀλεξάνδρου καὶ Ἡφαιστίωνος μεταλλαγῆς (On the demise of Alexander and Hephaistion).[34] Nevertheless, the coincidence has led some to suggest that the account of Alexander's death might inadvertently have been transferred within the Suda from Ephippus to his fellow Olynthian, Strattis.[35] As already noted, that these authors were Olynthians makes for a double coincidence, since, as well as sharing the same home town, they were probably also contemporaries, writing on the same theme within the same period between Alexander's death and the early 3rd century BC.

Ephippus also seems once to have had an entry in the Suda. His name alone is still to be found there, but the rest of the entry listed against it has been shown to belong to Ephorus of Kyme.[36] It appears that the details of Ephippus' own entry have been discarded or possibly transferred to elsewhere within the Suda. There are some indications as to how to recognize Ephippus' missing entry. Pliny cites him as an authority on trees.[37] Pliny also includes some authors of accounts of Alexander's expedition, such as Callisthenes, Ptolemy and Onesicritus, among his references on trees. This is quite natural, for their works are known to have included long digressions on the natural history of the remote lands through which Alexander passed. For example, most of the surviving fragments of Onesicritus are parts of such digressions. However, it is a little unlikely that Ephippus' work on Alexander's death contained much of interest about trees, so perhaps we should expect to find a work which would have treated natural history subjects within Ephippus' missing entry. Interestingly, Strattis is credited with a work "On Rivers, Springs and Lakes", which might well have had something worthwhile to say on arboreal matters. Presumably the Ephemerides also incorporated many natural history observations, so a commentary upon it might also have been a source of

---

[32] Athenaeus, *Deipnosophistae* 12.537D.
[33] Athenaeus, *Deipnosophistae* 3.120D & 10.434A.
[34] Athenaeus, *Deipnosophistae* 4.146C.
[35] G. Sainte Croix, *Examen critique des anciens historiens d'Alexandre le Grand* (2nd edition, Paris 1810) 45; Robert Geier, *Alexandri Magni historiarum scriptores aetate suppares* (Leipzig 1844) 356-357; L. Pearson, *The Lost Histories of Alexander the Great* (New York 1960) 62 n. 5.
[36] Adler, *Lexicon* (as in n. 25) epsilon 3930; Pearson, *Histories* (as in n. 35) 62.
[37] Pliny, *Natural History* 1.12.13.

information on trees. Though this is only a minor coincidence, it is nevertheless worth noticing.

The fragments of Ephippus' account of the deaths of Alexander and Hephaistion as preserved in Athenaeus are notably rich in authentic details of events at Alexander's court in 324-3 BC. For example, he mentions the lobbying of Alexander by Gorgos the hoplophylax, seemingly at Ecbatana.[38] Inscriptional evidence confirms that Gorgos the son of Theodotus of Iasos was a real person who was granted Samian citizenship for his intercessions with Alexander on behalf of the islanders.[39] This and other minutiae remembered by Ephippus led E. Neuffer to suggest as long ago as 1929 that Ephippus may have had recourse to the Ephemerides in compiling his account of Alexander's death.[40] It is therefore intriguing that the elusive Strattis is also associated with the Ephemerides in that he wrote a detailed commentary upon them.

Evidently, all parts of the entry against Strattis of Olynthus in the Suda would appear to have connections with his compatriot Ephippus. This should be sufficient for us to suspect that the entry against Strattis is in fact the missing entry for Ephippus. However, it is not plausible that the name Ephippus could have been corrupted to Strattis, so what possible connection between the two names could have led to the Ephippus entry in the Suda being transferred to Strattis? There is an attractive solution to this conundrum, which makes the transfer seem particularly credible. In the Suda, the name and missing entry for Ephippus of Olynthus (Adler number: epsilon, 3930) is preceded by an entry for Ephippus of Athens (epsilon, 3929), a playwright of the Attic Middle Comedy, active between c. 375-340 BC. Similarly, the entry for Strattis of Olynthus (sigma, 1179) is preceded by that for Strattis of Athens (sigma, 1178), who was a playwright of the Attic Old Comedy, active in the 5th century BC. Thus the two names do indeed have a legitimate association with each other within the Suda Lexicon.

There are some further connections among the Ephippus and Strattis entries in the Suda. Strattis of Olynthus is credited with a book Περὶ ποταμῶν καὶ κρηνῶν καὶ λιμνῶν, whilst Strattis of Athens is the author of comic plays entitled Ποτάμιοι and Λημνομέδα according to Athenaeus.[41] However, Ποτάμιοι is the only play by Strattis, which is mentioned by Athenaeus, but not listed in the Suda, whereas Λημνομέδα appears as Λιμνομέδων in the Suda. Strattis of Athens also wrote a comedy entitled Μακεδόνες. A shared interest in rivers, lakes and Macedonians provides another hint as to why the

---

[38] Athenaeus, *Deipnosophistae* 12.537E-538B.
[39] Pearson, *Histories* (as in n. 35) 63-65, who cites W. Dittenberger (ed.), *Sylloge Inscriptionum Graecarum* (3rd edition, Leipzig 1921-4) 307 and 312.
[40] E. Neuffer, "Das Kostüm Alexanders des Grossen", *Diss. Giessen* (1929) 35; Pearson, *Histories* (as in n. 35) 65.
[41] Athenaeus, *Deipnosophistae* 7.299B, 7.327E, 11.473C.

The Quest for the Tomb of Alexander by Andrew Chugg

works of Ephippus of Olynthus might have been transferred to follow the entry of Strattis of Athens in the Suda.

It is known that the Suda took its information on the Attic comic playwrights from Athenaeus.[42] The Suda entry for Strattis of Athens actually states that information on his plays is taken from the second book of the Deipnosophistae by Athenaeus. Since Athenaeus is also our main source for the fragments of Ephippus of Olynthus, it is reasonable to suppose that the Suda's lost entry on him was also derived, at least in part, from the Deipnosophistae, though it might have been supplemented from other sources. If the Suda entry on Strattis of Olynthus is indeed the lost entry on Ephippus of Olynthus, then Athenaeus is a common source for all the Ephippus and Strattis entries in the Suda. This suggests the possibilities that the attribution of the works of Ephippus of Olynthus to Strattis might already have existed within the Suda compiler's manuscript of Athenaeus or have come about during the process of extracting information from Athenaeus preparatory to its incorporation in the Suda. It remains possible, that the whole of the Strattis of Olynthus entry came from the Suda compiler's manuscript of Athenaeus, because our surviving version of Athenaeus is known to be very incomplete.[43] The Deipnosophistae of Athenaeus is anyway a third connecting strand between the Ephippus and Strattis entries in the Suda.

The Suda is riddled with gross errors. Even within the Ephippus and Strattis entries we have seen that the works of Ephorus are attributed to Ephippus; also, Strattis of Athens is wrongly called a tragic rather than a comic poet and some of the titles of his plays have been corrupted: e.g. alternative titles of the same play are cited as different works. The Suda has clearly been subjected to some very careless processes of compilation, editing and transcription. It is not possible to determine precisely how the entry for Ephippus of Olynthus became assigned to Strattis of Olynthus, because there are many ways in which it might have happened. Nor is the argument one of proof, but rather of probability, based upon multiple parallels, associations and connections between these individuals and their entries. However, it may be helpful to outline a few ways in which the misattribution might have come about:-

a) The error occurred in a lost section of the Deipnosophistae: one of its editors or transcribers or possibly even Athenaeus himself became confused and wrote Strattis of Olynthus for Ephippus of Olynthus, because the comic playwrights Ephippus and Strattis of Athens were both extensively referenced in the same work and because both Strattis

---

[42] See C. B. Gulick (trans.), *Athenaeus: Deipnosophistae* (Harvard 1957-63) Introduction xv, note a.

[43] In our principal manuscript for the *Deipnosophistae*, the St Mark codex (A), books I and II and the first part of the third are missing, as is the last part of the final book XV and there are two lacunae in book XI. Some of these gaps have been partially filled using the two main epitome manuscripts from Paris (C) and Florence (E), but much material is altogether lost.

of Athens and Ephippus of Olynthus had produced works with titles relating to rivers, lakes and Macedonians.

b) The error occurred during the compilation of the Suda, perhaps being compounded by more than one person for the same reasons as in a), whilst entries were being extracted from the Deipnosophistae. If, for example, the list of works extracted from Athenaeus were organized alphabetically at any stage, then the Ποτάμιοι of Strattis of Athens could have immediately preceded the Περὶ ποταμῶν καὶ κρηνῶν καὶ λιμνῶν of Ephippus of Olynthus.

c) Strattis was a genuine pseudonym of Ephippus of Olynthus, used because Ephippus' works were politically dangerous and chosen because Strattis and Ephippus had both been famous comic playwrights in Athens in the decades before Ephippus of Olynthus wrote and also because both he and Strattis of Athens had authored works with titles relating to rivers, lakes and Macedonians.

Finally, I propose that Ἔφιππος is a plausible correction of ἐκεῖνός the corrupted second name cited by Aelian at the end of his fragment of the Ephemerides.[44] Although both names have seven letters and three syllables, begin with epsilon and have three other letters in common, they are still too distant to justify this correction on purely paleographic grounds. However, it may now be argued that Ephippus also fits the profile of the mysterious ἐκεῖνός in three other distinct ways. Firstly, Aelian indicates that ἐκεῖνός was another of the writers who told stories about Alexander's drinking habits in the same vein as Eumenes. We already know this to be true of Ephippus from the fragments of his book On the Death of Hephaistion and Alexander preserved by Athenaeus. Secondly, Bosworth has shown that the Aelian fragment describes events leading up to the death of Hephaistion and we know that Ephippus wrote an account of Hephaistion's demise. Thirdly, it is accepted that the Aelian fragment is ultimately derived from the Ephemerides and it has already been shown that Ephippus was probably the author of a commentary on the Ephemerides.

It is worthwhile, therefore, to reprise these multiple coincidences in summary:

a) Strattis and Ephippus were both citizens of Olynthus.

b) They were probably contemporaries writing in the generation after Alexander's death.

---

[44] Aelian, *Varia Historia* 3.23; note that Aelian uses an Athenian dating format, which came into use in the last quarter of the 4th century BC, whereas Plutarch, *Alexander* 76 uses the earlier Athenian format, which it replaced, in stating that he is citing the *Ephemerides* "word for word" (this is consistent with Aelian's source being an intermediary), see A. E. Samuel, *Greek & Roman Chronology* (Munich 1972) 60.

c) They both wrote books on the death of Alexander.

d) Ephippus is listed as an authority on trees by Pliny, whilst Strattis is credited with a work on a natural history theme ("On Rivers, Springs and Lakes") and a commentary upon the journal of Alexander's expedition, both of which are likely to have given interesting information on trees.

e) It has been independently argued by Neuffer that the fragments of Ephippus indicate familiarity with the Ephemerides, whereas Strattis wrote five books of commentaries on the Ephemerides.

f) Strattis and Ephippus of Olynthus are indirectly connected in the Suda by preceding entries for Strattis and Ephippus of Athens, who were comic playwrights of that city in successive generations and there are further connections between all these authors and the Deipnosophistae and between the works of Strattis of Athens and Strattis of Olynthus.

g) Ephippus is a plausible correction for the corrupted name of a second author who gave information on Alexander's drinking cited by Aelian at the end of his fragment of the Ephemerides.

One or two coincidences might readily be explained by chance, but seven imply an underlying connection. It is just conceivable that Strattis was an alias of Ephippus (as Plato was for Aristocles), but it is most likely that Ephippus' entry in the Suda has simply been transferred to Strattis, because of the association between the Athenian comic poets of the same names. As Bosworth has observed, "There are many demonstrable examples in the Suda where works are wrongly credited to authors."[45]

The Nature of the Ephemerides

Samuel has provided a detailed analysis of the meaning of the term Ephemerides with reference to a variety of ancient examples of its usage.[46] He notes that it is defined as a day-to-day record by the Suda Lexicon and he shows that most of the infrequent examples from papyri and the ancient literature are consistent with this definition. However, he further observes that Plutarch used the term to refer to Caesar's Commentaries, which are not regular daily records.[47] However, they are detailed, chronologically organised memoirs, often giving day-by-day accounts of campaigns, so it would seem pedantic to rule that this instance refutes the Suda definition. In particular, we should recall that Plutarch paired together his Lives of Caesar and Alexander, so it was convenient for his method of composing Parallel Lives that he should stretch a point by attributing sets of Ephemerides to both of them.

---

[45] Bosworth, *Arrian* (as in n. 6) 181.
[46] Samuel, *Journals* (as in n. 26) 1-3.
[47] Plutarch, *Caesar* 22.

The Journal of Alexander the Great

In addition to the mention in the Suda entry for Strattis, six fragments of the Ephemerides of Alexander may be identified with reasonable confidence:

a) Arrian on the death of Alexander (Anabasis 7.25.1-26.3)

b) Plutarch on the death of Alexander (Life of Alexander 76)

c) Aelian on Alexander's partying in Oct.-Nov. 324 BC (Varia Historia 3.23)

d) Athenaeus on Alexander's partying (10.434B)

e) Plutarch on Alexander hunting foxes and birds (Life of Alexander 23.3)

f) Plutarch, Moralia, Quaestiones Conviviales 1.6.1 (623E), stating that Philinus had used the Ephemerides to show that Alexander slept all day after parties

There are also a few other documents, which might be derived from the Ephemerides. Hammond has proposed that a papyrus on Alexander's Balkan campaign in 335 BC is a fragment of the commentary on the Ephemerides attributed to Strattis by the Suda,[48] but the evidence is merely circumstantial. A mention of Serapis in the story of the madman who sat on the throne in Plutarch's Life of Alexander echoes the appearance of Serapis in his Ephemerides fragment.[49] Hammond has associated the Hypomnemata (e.g. the "Last Plans"[50]) with the Ephemerides by suggesting that all such documents should be regarded as parts of a cohesive "Royal Archive".[51] It also remains possible that the Ephemerides are the undeclared source for numerous details in the surviving ancient histories of Alexander.

The Ephemerides fragments from Aelian, Athenaeus and Plutarch's Moralia all refer to Alexander's drinking habits. It would be attractive to suppose Aelian is quoting from Ephippus' book "On the Death of Hephaistion and Alexander", which in turn used the Ephemerides. This is especially attractive because Bosworth has shown that Aelian's fragment must date to the period immediately prior to Hephaistion's death. Furthermore, someone has clearly edited the extract to emphasise Alexander's drinking. Ephippus also highlighted Alexander's drinking and partying in his other fragments in Athenaeus. Ephippus presumably attributed his edited extract of the Ephemerides to Eumenes and this was preserved by Aelian. There is a strong possibility that Athenaeus also took his fragment of the Ephemerides from Ephippus, since he quotes from Ephippus on Alexander's drinking immediately before mentioning the Ephemerides on the identical topic:

---

[48] N. G. L. Hammond, "A Papyrus Commentary on Alexander's Balkan Campaign", *Journal of Greek, Roman and Byzantine Studies* 28 (1987) 331-347.
[49] Plutarch, *Alexander* 73.3-4.
[50] Diodorus 18.4.2.
[51] Hammond, *Journal* (as in n. 30) 131.

The Quest for the Tomb of Alexander by Andrew Chugg

"Proteas of Macedon, also, drank a very great deal, as Ephippus says in his work *On the Funeral of Alexander and Hephaistion*, and enjoyed a sturdy physique throughout his life, although he was completely devoted to the practice of drinking. Alexander, for example, once called for a six-quart cup and after a drink proposed the health of Proteas. He took the cup, and when he had sung the king's praises he drank, to the applause of everybody. A little while afterwards Proteas demanded the same cup, and again drinking, pledged the king. Alexander took it and pulled at it bravely, but could not hold out; on the contrary, he sank back on his cushion and let the cup drop from his hands. As a result, he fell ill and died, because, as Ephippus says, Dionysus was angry with him for besieging his native city, Thebes. Alexander also drank a very great deal, so that after the spree he would sleep continuously for two days and two nights. This is revealed in his Ephemerides, written by Eumenes of Cardia and Diodotus of Erythrae."[52]

Indirect transmission via Ephippus is another possible explanation for the authorship of Diognetus having become corrupted to Diodotus in this extract from Athenaeus. Plutarch probably knew the Ephemerides directly, but he is quoting Philinus when he mentions them as a source for Alexander's drinking habits. It would seem possible that Philinus had read Ephippus. Alternatively, φιλῖνος is a corruption of Ἔφιππος for the names are not too different for this to be feasible (both 7 letters and 3 syllables, with 4 letters in common) and Samuel has observed that the phraseology attributed to Philinus by Plutarch almost duplicates that in the Aelian fragment.[53] Nevertheless, this is venturesome and only a minor possibility without more evidence.

The co-authorship of the Ephemerides by Diognetus the bematist shows a more systematic aspect of the compilation of this record. It suggests that Alexander's official version of the Stathmoi ("Stages" of Alexander's marches) were incorporated within his Ephemerides. The existence of such official Stathmoi is attested by a passage from Strabo: "Patrocles says that those who campaigned with Alexander inquired cursorily (viz. into distances) in each case, but he Alexander made (them) accurate, since the entire territory was written up for him by those who were most experienced. The written up (account) was given to him [Alexander or Patrocles?], he says, later by Xenocles, the treasurer."[54] Patrocles was employed by Seleucus Nicator and afterwards by Antiochus I. In a second corrupt passage Strabo mentions that Eratosthenes had written that he was drawing together reports from many who dealt with the Stathmoi and that some of them lacked a title.[55] This may indicate that

---

[52] Athenaeus, *Deipnosophistae* 10.434A-B.
[53] Samuel, *Journals* (as in n. 26) 4.
[54] Strabo, *Geography* 2.1.6; the translation is by Hammond and is closely argued in differing from the Loeb and others – see Hammond, *Journal* (as in n. 30) 137-138.
[55] Strabo, *Geography* 2.1.23.

The Journal of Alexander the Great

Eratosthenes reviewed the Ephemerides and other accounts of the Stathmoi[56] for geographical information, but found some of them poorly documented. Bosworth has written that "nothing suggests that [Eumenes] published [the Journal] as an official extract from the archives",[57] but the presence of Stathmoi within the Ephemerides would in fact be suggestive of an official record.

It would indeed be surprising if a daily record of Alexander's expedition had omitted mention of the distance and direction of the day's march together with a description of the landscapes that were encountered. However, some might object that the incorporation of the Stathmoi within the Ephemerides would imply a document so lengthy as to be unpublishable. Nevertheless, prolixity does not seem to have been a great impediment to the publication of ancient texts. Among the ancient references for this article, both the Deipnosophistae of Athenaeus and Strabo's Geography are around half a million words long and Plutarch's Moralia (c. a million words) and the Natural History of Pliny are longer still. But it is not necessary to believe that the published version of the Ephemerides was as long as this, since all but the last two years of the work may have been destroyed in the fire that consumed Eumenes' tent in India. None of the surviving fragments of the Ephemerides need antedate India.

The Authenticity of the Ephemerides

Are our fragments of the Ephemerides genuine or were they forged? The question is important, because two of the fragments provide our most detailed account of Alexander's fatal illness in June 323 BC, whilst others offer the most authoritative descriptions of the King's drinking habits. Furnished with the new insights that Diodotus was probably Diognetus and that Strattis is likely to have been Ephippus, it is apposite to re-examine the issue of the integrity of the Ephemerides as a whole and of those few extracts, which have come down to us.

There is little real dispute that royal papers having the general nature of the Ephemerides were created by Alexander's secretariat. Hammond has cited a range of literary evidence for the existence of royal papers for Macedonian kings starting with Alexander's father Philip II and extending through Antigonus III Doson to Philip V.[58] There are also mentions of similar documents kept by Ptolemy Philadelphus and the Roman strategoi in Egypt.[59] Critics have therefore tended to confine themselves to the proposition that our fragments of the Ephemerides are forgeries that have displaced or been substituted for genuine originals. Nevertheless, these sceptics speak with discordant voices, tending to contradict one another as to the exact nature of the supposed deception.

---

[56] For example, Baeton, another of Alexander's bematists, is stated by Athenaeus, *Deipnosophistae* 10.442B, to have authored a work on *Stages in Alexander's Journey*.
[57] Bosworth, *Arrian* (as in n. 6) 179 n. 89.
[58] Hammond, *Journal* (as in n. 30) 130.

The Quest for the Tomb of Alexander by Andrew Chugg

It has long been recognised that the entry against Strattis of Olynthus in the Suda is potentially a serious embarrassment for anyone wishing to dispute the authenticity of the Ephemerides. As we have seen, the citizenship attributed to Strattis makes it seem likely that his five-book commentary on the Ephemerides was written in the generation following Alexander's death. Hammond has argued that it would have been difficult for a forger of the Ephemerides even to deceive Arrian and Plutarch, who wrote four centuries after the events.[60] I would not go so far, but it would be surprising if a contemporary writer could have been fooled into composing an enormously detailed work based on forged diaries of Alexander, since he must have been surrounded by men who had participated in Alexander's campaigns. Furthermore, if Strattis is actually Ephippus, then he had himself very probably taken part in Alexander's expedition. Most of the details from the Ephemerides in our surviving fragments relate to matters that would have been familiar to Alexander's companions and courtiers and many of these events would have been known in the ranks of the army as well, so lies would easily have been detected. It would be similarly preposterous to suppose that "Strattis" was complicit in the forgery, because his commentary would then have been a pointless and wasted effort. The advocates of forgery have therefore felt compelled to attack the credibility of the Strattis entry in various ways. For example, Lionel Pearson, in his original attack upon the authenticity of the Ephemerides, conceded that if Strattis had written a commentary upon them, then they "would have to be based on the authentic text, because at such an early date a forgery would readily have been detected."[61] It follows that any argument which demonstrates that the details in the Suda are essentially valid is tantamount to proving the authenticity of the Ephemerides themselves, even in the eyes of the doubters.

The line of attack adopted by Pearson was to suggest that Strattis' commentary on the Ephemerides was actually a fictitious work entitled, "Five books of Diaries about the Exploits of Alexander". He argued that this fictitious diary called for a faked author's name, i.e. "Strattis", and was itself the source for our fragments of the Ephemerides. As we have seen, Hammond, Badian and Bosworth have agreed that Pearson's translation of the title strains the Greek unreasonably, though Bosworth has nevertheless perpetuated the idea that Strattis' works were fictions.[62] However, the attribution of the Suda entry to Ephippus shows clearly for the first time that Pearson's assault on the authenticity of the Ephemerides was entirely misconceived, since Ephippus was certainly not a fictitious person, but rather a real author who wrote genuine historical works shortly after Alexander's death. In particular, Arrian mentions an Ephippus who was an overseer of mercenaries for Alexander in Egypt and who was either a Chalcidean or a son of Chalchideus. Either way, this man is an

---

[59] U. Wilcken, "Hypomnematismoi", *Philologus* 53 (1894) 84-126.
[60] Hammond, *Historians* (as in n. 28) 6; Hammond, *Journal* (as in n. 30) 140.
[61] Pearson, *Diary* (as in n. 27) 437.
[62] Bosworth, *Arrian* (as in n. 6) 180-182.

excellent candidate for Ephippus of Olynthus, because Olynthus had been the leading city of the Chalcidean federation.[63] Pearson is in fact right to infer that such a person would be unlikely to put his own name to a fake diary.

In all probability Ephippus did indeed compose five books of commentaries on a published (i.e. transcribed and disseminated) version of Alexander's Ephemerides, which must therefore have been substantially genuine. It might still be argued by some that these genuine Ephemerides were subsequently superseded by fictitious versions. Hammond has posed the question, "Could one forge an Archive [i.e. the Ephemerides] and displace the official Archive with it?" His lengthy answer explores a wide range of scenarios, but shows that in every case the forger would encounter enormous difficulties.[64] Apart from these problems, the existence of the genuine commentary by Ephippus would have made acceptance of a significantly distorted version of the Ephemerides inconceivable. If genuine Ephemerides were ever published or disseminated in numerous copies, then it is very unlikely they could have been superseded or displaced by a subsequent forgery.

A number of other points have been raised concerning the authenticity of the Ephemerides, which need to be reviewed in the context of the new perspective. Both Arrian and Plutarch mention a vigil in the temple of Serapis in Babylon by a group of Alexander's Companions on the eve of his death, the report evidently being taken from the Ephemerides. However, on the best evidence the cult of Serapis was invented and developed by Ptolemy in Egypt after Alexander's death. This god's occurrence in the Ephemerides therefore seems anachronistic, so it has frequently been used to dispute the authenticity of the fragments.[65] Nevertheless, it is accepted that Serapis was derived by the fusion of Osiris with Apis and that this cult had been prominent at Memphis under the last native pharaoh, Nectanebo II, a decade before Alexander's conquest of Egypt. Bosworth has therefore suggested that an hypothetical Egyptian community at Babylon had founded a shrine of Osirapis in the metropolis prior to Alexander's death, which was adopted by Alexander's courtiers for their vigil.[66] But this is a double supposition and it seems unlikely that a minor back-street shrine would have been preferred over the great temples of the city in the circumstances. A manuscript corruption of the name of the Babylonian goddess Zarpanitum to Serapis has also been postulated, but Arrian and Plutarch are explicit that the deity was male and neither was Zarpanitum associated with healing,[67] whereas Serapis was recognised as a god of healing in Egypt.[68] Hammond has implausibly argued that Serapis was already a widespread cult

---

[63] Arrian, *Anabasis* 3.5.3.
[64] Hammond, *Journal* (as in n. 30) 135-136.
[65] E.g. Pearson, *Diary* (as in n. 27) 438-439.
[66] Bosworth, *Arrian* (as in n. 6) 169; Bosworth, *Death* (as in n. 23) 119-121.
[67] Bosworth, *Arrian* (as in n. 6) 168.
[68] P. M. Fraser, *Ptolemaic Alexandria* (Oxford 1972) Vol. I, 257.

The Quest for the Tomb of Alexander by Andrew Chugg

under Alexander.[69] The best explanation, however, is the simplest. The Greeks frequently encountered the pantheons of other cultures, but, rather than believe that these foreign gods were false, they preferred to suppose them to be disguised manifestations of their own deities. This habitual syncretism is most clearly expressed in the Greco-Roman and Greco-Egyptian pantheons, but it also applied more generally, as, for example, in the story of Alexander recognising a local god of the city of Nysa as a manifestation of Dionysus in India.[70] It would therefore have been quite natural for a transcriber of the *Ephemerides* in Alexandria to have replaced mentions of the Babylonian chief deity, the healing bull-god Bel-Marduk,[71] with the name of Serapis, the healing bull-god of his own city. He would not have considered that he had changed the god, but merely translated his name into the local theological dialect.[72]

The integrity of the *Ephemerides* has also been questioned by asking why they are not cited more widely and why the known extracts seem to be concentrated in the last year of Alexander's reign? Actually we have only two datable fragments: drinking parties just before the death of Hephaistion and events surrounding Alexander's final illness and death. Statistically, therefore, there is no great anomaly, because this might readily have come about by pure chance. However, Robinson has pointed out that Eumenes' papers were burnt in India, so it is possible that only the *Ephemerides* for the final two years of Alexander's reign survived intact. Furthermore, it seems that Diognetus listed survey information as well as Eumenes' copious details of sacrifices and the daily comings and goings of the King. The original was probably much more verbose than Arrian's extract on Alexander's death. It is therefore easy to comprehend that the *Ephemerides* would have been a very unwieldy source for an ancient historian, which provides sufficient explanation for the rarity of citations in the extant literature. A new perspective on these issues may now be offered by the influence of Ephippus' works as intermediate sources. We can now see that it is likely that Ephippus' book "On the Death of Hephaistion and Alexander" referenced the *Ephemerides* extensively and this work may have been the immediate source of the fragments in Aelian, Athenaeus and Plutarch's *Moralia*. Furthermore, it is probable that Arrian and Plutarch were aware of Ephippus' writings and were thus drawn to look to the *Ephemerides* as a source for Alexander's demise. However, it is likely that they consulted the *Ephemerides*

---

[69] Hammond, *Journal* (as in n. 30) 144.
[70] Arrian, *Anabasis* 5.1-3.
[71] Bel-Marduk was associated with healing in Babylon, see for example U. Wilcken (trans. G. C. Richards), *Alexander the Great* (New York & London 1967) 238.
[72] It should be added that Robert Koldewey, the excavator of Babylon, believed he had found a shrine to Ea, Marduk's father, on the north side of the temple of Marduk, the Esagila - see R. Koldewey, *The Excavations at Babylon* (London 1914) 204. Ea is believed to have been identified with Serapis in the Hellenistic period, so Koldewey thought this to be the shrine mentioned in the *Ephemerides*. However, the conclusion is the same: that the temple of Serapis is an Alexandrian syncretism for the temple of Marduk in the context of the *Ephemerides*.

The Journal of Alexander the Great

directly, because they do not show any sign of the antagonistic spin, which we find in the fragments of Ephippus.

Some historians have sought to argue that there are significant mismatches between Arrian's and Plutarch's summaries of Alexander's last days.[73] They choose pairs of events that occur in both accounts and show that they are separated by different numbers of days. However, these arguments rely implicitly on the assumption that neither of the events in the pair occurred more than once in the original version of the Journal. It has been shown elsewhere that, provided it is allowed that Alexander was moved to the diving pool more than once, then an exact match between the two accounts becomes feasible.[74] In fact there is virtually irrefutable internal evidence that Plutarch and Arrian are drawing on a common account. Apart from a general concordance of the events in both accounts (e.g. the Serapis vigil), they have unusual words in common, e.g. κολυμβήθρα (diving pool) and πεντακοσιάρχους (a particular and genuine rank of commander in the Macedonian army) and the phraseology is often strikingly similar. Other discrepancies are best explained as indications that our authors have summarised their extracts differently from an original perhaps as much as ten times as long as Arrian's version. For example, on the 3rd June Arrian says Alexander discussed the forthcoming Arabian expedition with Nearchus, whilst Plutarch says Nearchus told Alexander stories about his voyage in the Indian Ocean. Presumably, the Ephemerides themselves noted multiple topics of discussion at some length.

By whom were the Ephemerides published? Hammond reasserted Wilcken's old argument that Ptolemy obtained them with Alexander's corpse, but the case is overstated, because the Ephemerides could not have ceased to be a useful reference for Perdiccas as soon as Hammond believes.[75] It would be surprising if Eumenes had left such important papers in Babylon within months of Alexander's death. In fact, Hammond has further argued that Ptolemy made exclusive use of the Ephemerides in the generation after Alexander's death, because he "kept the Ephemerides under his own hand". He suggests that they only later became publicly available through the Library at Alexandria.[76] However, this is incorrect, if Ephippus of Olynthus used the Ephemerides for his works. Furthermore, Arrian implies that his extract from the Ephemerides concerning Alexander's death did not come from Ptolemy by concluding it with the comment that the subject "has been written up not far from this by

---

[73] Badian, *Ring* (as in n. 6) 615-617, argues that Plutarch and Arrian were using different versions of the *Ephemerides*; conversely, Robinson, *Ephemerides* (as in n. 29) 69-70, argues in detail that the accounts are essentially congruent.
[74] A. M. Chugg, *The Lost Tomb of Alexander the Great* (London 2004) 27-29, Table 1.2.
[75] Hammond, *Journal* (as in n. 30) 133-135; Wilcken, *Hypomnematismoi* (as in n. 59) 84-126; P. A. Brunt, *Arrian: History of Alexander and Indica*, I (Harvard 1976) xxiv-vi (Introduction), objects particularly to the idea that Ptolemy made special use of the Ephemerides.
[76] Hammond, *Ring* (as in n. 12) 155.

Aristobulus and Ptolemy".[77] Arrian lacks any explicit citation to indicate that Ptolemy ever used the Ephemerides as a source, despite the fact that Ptolemy was Arrian's most important source. Bosworth is likely to be correct in supposing that the Ephemerides were retained by Eumenes after Alexander's demise, so it is the Secretary himself who is most likely to have been responsible for their dissemination. His motive may have been to refute poisoning rumours that had begun to circulate. Bosworth, however, thinks that the Ephemerides were substantially re-edited and thereby falsified by Eumenes.[78] In particular, he suggests that Eumenes selected only those of Alexander's symptoms that were consistent with a malarial attack. However, this ignores the fact that one of the main reasons for thinking Alexander contracted malaria was that he had been boating in the marshes a week or two before falling ill, which is precisely consistent with the incubation period of falciparum malaria. It is impossible that Eumenes arranged this retrospectively. Furthermore, the stabbing pain, which Alexander felt in his back at the onset of his illness, was not reported by the Ephemerides, but this symptom is nevertheless consistent with falciparum malaria.[79] Bosworth's view was originally inspired by the suspicion that Eumenes was implicated in poisoning Alexander.[80] Most historians now accept that poisoning was unlikely and even Bosworth has backed away from his earlier advocacy of conspiracy.[81] Among the earliest and most elaborate versions of the story that Alexander was poisoned is a document known as the Liber de Morte, which has survived through being incorporated in both the Metz Epitome and the Alexander Romance. Heckel has made a strong case that this had its genesis as a propaganda pamphlet targeted against Antigonus and his allies by the faction of Polyperchon between the spring of 317 BC and the summer of 316 BC.[82] Interestingly, this document takes the trouble specifically to exculpate Eumenes (and several other potential allies of Polyperchon) from involvement in the plot, perhaps indicating that someone had previously implicated him. The Liber de Morte incorporates a last testament of Alexander, which is a blatant forgery, apparently penned by someone who was favourably disposed towards Rhodes. In summary, the Liber de Morte is politically motivated and thoroughly untrustworthy in its assertions concerning the cause of Alexander's death.

If there was no poison, then Eumenes had nothing to hide and there is no reason to think that he concealed evidence from the Ephemerides by judicious editing. The only other motive for tampering with the original work would have been to protect Alexander's reputation. Eumenes was no detractor of Alexander after his death: he once set up the King's regalia to preside over a council of the

---

[77] Arrian, *Anabasis* 7.26.3.
[78] Bosworth, *Arrian* (as in n. 6) 178-9, 182-4.
[79] Plutarch, *Alexander* 75.3.
[80] Bosworth, *Death* (as in n. 23) 122-3.
[81] A. B. Bosworth, *Conquest and Empire: The Reign of Alexander the Great* (Cambridge 1988) 171-3.
[82] W. Heckel, *The Last Days and Testament of Alexander the Great* (Stuttgart 1988) 1-81.

Diadochi.[83] However, the Ephemerides evidently gave reports, albeit in a neutral fashion, detailing Alexander's drinking and partying habits, which argues against any attempt at sanitisation. Clearly, an unedited version of the Ephemerides would best have served the purpose of refuting vicious rumours, so the original publication was probably virtually verbatim. However, that is no reason to dispute the fact that the fragments which have reached us are heavily summarised and edited by intermediaries, who were motivated by a desire to illustrate particular points.

The Journal extracts on Alexander's death happen incidentally to mention a few details of the topography of Babylon. Considerable knowledge of the layout of ancient Babylon was also gleaned independently from excavations by a German team led by Robert Koldewey in the early 20th century.[84] A plan based largely on Koldewey's work is shown in Figure 2.5. Alexander was established in the palace of Nebuchadnezzar (D). The Journal mentions Alexander sailing across the river to the gardens, which should probably be the famous Hanging Gardens (H), said elsewhere to be built on terraces beside the river. It can be seen that this accords well with Koldewey's Babylon, for the palace is adjacent to the river and there is an area of the city just outside the interior walls on the opposite bank of the river. The river's course runs a little further to the west today, so it may well have meandered across the proposed site of the Hanging Gardens in the interim. This would help to explain why no convincing archaeological trace of the Gardens has been found. The Journal mentions a diving pool in the Gardens, which fits the theory of modern reconstructors that a large reservoir would have been required at the foot of the terraces as the source of water for their irrigation. The Journal also mentions Alexander's officers having been asked to wait in the courtyard of the Palace, when his condition deteriorated sharply on the evening of the 6th June 323 BC. Koldewey found a large courtyard within the palace with the throne room on its southern flank. In general, though far from conclusive in itself, the topographical evidence is broadly supportive of the case for the authenticity of the Journal.

Other aspects of the Journal account of Alexander's death are surely consistent with authenticity. The longer version in Arrian especially features almost daily accounts of Alexander performing the sacrifices. Such bland details would seem superfluous in anything but a genuine document. Furthermore, it has been shown elsewhere that the medical case history presented by the Journal account is highly self-consistent with death through contracting some biological disease, most probably falciparum malaria.[85]

---

[83] Diodorus 18.60.4-18.61.3.
[84] Robert Koldewey, *Das Wieder Erstehende Babylon* (Leipzig 1913).
[85] Chugg, *Tomb* (as in n. 74) 1-31; D. W. Engels, "A Note on Alexander's Death", *Classical Philology* 73 (1978) 224-228.

Conclusions

It has been shown that the ancient evidence presents us with a strong case that Diognetus of Erythrae, one of Alexander's bematists, was a co-author of Alexander's Ephemerides. Furthermore, a very strong case has been presented that Ephippus of Olynthus, a contemporary of Alexander, was the author of a five-book commentary on Alexander's Ephemerides. It has also been demonstrated that these new insights lead us inexorably to the conclusion that the Ephemerides was an authentic document of Alexander's reign, authored by his secretariat. Alexander's Ephemerides entered public circulation in the generation after the King's death, perhaps as part of an effort by Eumenes to refute rumours of poisoning. Although the surviving fragments of the Ephemerides have been subjected to editing and transmission errors by intermediaries, sufficient remains of the account of Alexander's death to show that its manner was highly inconsistent with any credible form of poisoning. Rather the Ephemerides provides a classic case study of death through some feverish disease, most probably falciparum malaria.

Appendix B: The Sarcophagus of Alexander the Great?

The following article by the author was first published in the classics journal Greece & Rome (ISSN 0017-3835) 49.1, April 2002, pp. 8-26. This article is © 2002 Cambridge University Press, reproduced with permission.

Vivant Denon, Edward Daniel Clarke and the Tomb of Alexander

In 1798 Napoleon Bonaparte led a French expedition in the conquest of Egypt. His troops were landed on the beaches on the 1st and 2nd of July and the General speedily assaulted and captured nearby Alexandria. At that time the great Hellenistic city had shrunk to a population of barely 6000, most of whom lived on an isthmus of land that had been formed by the accumulation of sand and silt against the ancient Heptastadion causeway, which once joined the mainland with the sometime island of Pharos, now a peninsula. Behind this "new town" the circuit of the massive walls of the medieval old city was still largely complete, though ruinous in many places. The area they enclosed was, however, largely deserted except for a handful of ancient monuments and a few dilapidated mosques. Most prominent among the latter was a building on the north side of the principal street and close to the centre of the old city known as the Attarine Mosque (Mosquée de St Athanase, Figures 8.2 & 9.6). The French "savants" who accompanied Napoleon were especially fascinated by this mosque, which it was suggested had been built on the site of the late Roman church of St Athanasius, a famous 4th century Patriarch of the city: five of the twelve plates on Alexandria in the Antiquities section of their monumental record of the country, the Description de l'Egypte, show plans and views of this mosque and its contents. Vivant Denon, a leading scholar in the team, described these contents glowingly in his subsequent travelogue:-

In the court, plants which have grown into trees, have forced up the marble pavement. In the center of this court, a little octagon temple incloses a cistern of Egyptian workmanship, and incomparable beauty, both on account of its form, and of innumerable hieroglyphics with which it is covered, inside and out. This monument, which appears to be a sarcophagus of antient Egypt, may perhaps be illustrated by volumes of dissertations. It would require a month to draw all its parts.[1]

Napoleon's fleet was virtually annihilated by H Nelson in the Battle of the Nile whilst it lay at anchor in Aboukir Bay on 1st August. Napoleon later escaped back to France. However, the English were content to leave the French army marooned for several years until their eventual capitulation at Alexandria in

---

[1] Vivant Denon, *Travels in Upper and Lower Egypt*, (London, 1802); this is the English edition of the French original.

The Quest for the Tomb of Alexander by Andrew Chugg

1801. As a condition of the treaty of surrender the French were required to hand over the antiquities they had garnered in the interim. Chief among these were the Rosetta Stone and the 7 tonne sarcophagus (Figure 7.5) from the chapel in the courtyard of the Attarine Mosque (Figure 7.1). Lord Hutchinson, the English commander, arranged for Edward Daniel Clarke of Cambridge University to secure these relics. His account of the recovery of the sarcophagus in Alexandria was as follows:-

We had scarcely reached the house in which we were to reside, when a party of the merchants of the place, who had heard the nature of our errand, came to congratulate us on the capture of Alexandria, and to express their anxiety to serve the English. As soon as the room was clear of other visitors, speaking with great circumspection and in a low voice, they asked if our business in Alexandria related to the antiquities collected by the French? Upon being answered in the affirmative, and, in proof of it, the copy of the Rosetta Stone being produced, the principal of them said, "Does your Commander in Chief know that they have the Tomb of Alexander?" We desired them to describe it; upon which they said it was a beautiful green stone, *taken from the mosque of St Athanasius; which, among the inhabitants, had always borne that appellation. Our letter and instructions from Caïro evidently referred to the same monument. "It is the object," they continued, "of our present visit; and we will shew you where they have concealed it." They then related the measures used by the French; the extraordinary care they had observed to prevent any intelligence of it; the indignation shewn by the Mahometans at its removal; the veneration in which they held it; and the tradition familiar to all of them respecting its origin. I conversed afterwards with several of the Mahometans, both Arabs and Turks, on the same subject; not only those who were natives and inhabitants of the city, but also dervises and pilgrims; persons from Constantinople, Smyrna, and Aleppo, who had visited, or who resided in Alexandria; and they all agreed in one uniform tradition, namely, ITS BEING THE TOMB OF ISCANDER (Alexander), THE FOUNDER OF THE CITY OF ALEXANDRIA. We were then told it was in the hold of an hospital ship, in the inner harbour; and being provided with a boat, we there found it, half filled with filth, and covered with the rags of the sick people on board.*[2]

This excerpt is taken from Clarke's treatise entitled "The Tomb of Alexander", which he published in 1805 after he had brought the sarcophagus back to England, where it is still exhibited in the British Museum. In this book Clarke reproduced a drawing by Vivant Denon showing Moslem pilgrims worshipping the chapel containing the sarcophagus (Figure 7.6). He also discussed a large variety of ancient and modern accounts regarding Alexander's tomb in Alexandria, but he scarcely managed to add any further significant evidence to authenticate the use of the sarcophagus for Alexander's corpse. Nevertheless he did succeed in showing that this same relic had been worshipped in the Attarine

---

[2] E D Clarke, *The Tomb of Alexander, a dissertation on the sarcophagus from Alexandria and now in the British Museum* (Cambridge, 1805).

The Sarcophagus of Alexander the Great?

Mosque throughout the 18th century by quoting the accounts of earlier European visitors.[3]

Decipherment, Obscurity and an Abortive Resurrection

In 1822 J-F Champollion used the trilingual inscription on the Rosetta stone to decipher hieroglyphics. It soon became clear that the Alexandrian sarcophagus is inscribed with sections from the ancient Egyptian "Book of What is in the Underworld" liberally interspersed with the cartouches of the Pharaoh Nectanebo II, for whom it was undoubtedly made. Not surprisingly this revelation was seen as completely undermining the association of the sarcophagus with Alexander and most modern works have cited its attribution as a sufficient reason to dismiss the possibility of a connection with the Macedonian King. Nonetheless P M Fraser, perhaps the leading sceptic, has admitted that "the presence of this mighty sarcophagus in Alexandria is surprising".[4]

In the mid-twentieth century a solitary challenge was made to the sceptical orthodoxy. In 1948 AJB Wace published a flawed, but nevertheless intriguing, argument that the sarcophagus might have come from Alexander's tomb after all.[5] Essentially, his case rested on three pillars:-

a) Nectanebo II was the last Pharaoh of the 30th dynasty and the final native Pharaoh of Egypt. He was defeated by a Persian invasion in 343BC and according to Diodorus he eventually fled south to Ethiopia in about 341BC.[6] He probably died in exile, so it is unlikely that he ever occupied his sarcophagus. Apart from a native uprising in about 338-6BC, Persian rule continued for the next decade until Alexander's arrival in 332BC. It is likely that the sarcophagus still lay unused when Ptolemy brought Alexander's corpse back to Egypt in 321BC, since it would have been sacrilegious to entomb a lesser mortal in a pharaonic sarcophagus.

b) Nectanebo II has a prominent role in a legendary account of Alexander's career, now known as the "Alexander Romance" or sometimes "Pseudo-Callisthenes", since some manuscripts implausibly attributed it to Alexander's court historian Callisthenes. It appears to have been compiled in Alexandria in the 3rd century AD from an agglomeration of earlier stories about the King. The Romance tells how Nectanebo employed magical powers to take on the persona of

---

[3] Richard Pococke, *Description of the East* (London, 1743), vol. i, p. 4; A Van Egmont and John Heyman, *Travels through part of Europe, Asia Minor, ...* (London, 1759), vol. ii, p. 133; Eyles Irwin, *Series of Adventures*, i, (London, 1780), p. 367; CS Sonnini, *Travels in Upper and Lower Egypt* (London, 1800), vol. i, p. 67; W G Browne, *Travels in Africa, Egypt and Syria* (London, 1799), p. 6.
[4] P M Fraser, *Ptolemaic Alexandria* (Oxford, 1972), Section 2 of Note 86 to Chapter 1.
[5] AJB Wace, *The Sarcophagus of Alexander the Great, Farouk I University, Bulletin of the Faculty of Arts 4* (Alexandria,1948), pp. 1-11.
[6] Diodorus Siculus, 16.51.

The Quest for the Tomb of Alexander by Andrew Chugg

Ammon, thus seducing Olympias and fathering Alexander on her.[7] Scholars have been moved to try to explain what could have inspired such an extraordinary legend. For example, Philippe Derchain,[8] has suggested that the story was disseminated by the early Ptolemies to legitimise Macedonian rule in Egypt. However, Wace pointed out that the use of Nectanebo's sarcophagus for Alexander's body would have provided a conducive stimulus for the legend.

c) Finally, Wace proposed that an Egyptian town called Rhakotis, which had pre-existed on the site of Alexandria, had incorporated a major Pharaonic necropolis, which included the intended tomb of Nectanebo and contained his sarcophagus.

The first two of these points are well made and of some significance for the issue, but the argument falls down badly on the third. In the first place, there appears to be no real evidence for a major necropolis of the 30th Dynasty at Alexandria. Nor is there any persuasive archaeological evidence for a very significant Egyptian port on the site prior to Alexandria's foundation.[9] Conversely, there are reports by the ancient writers, which indicate that the site was occupied by nothing more than a few Egyptian fishing villages, when Alexander arrived.[10] Finally, there is overwhelming evidence that Alexander's initial entombment in Egypt was not located at Alexandria.

The Memphite Tomb of Alexander

Aelian, Strabo and Diodorus all state that Alexander was entombed at Alexandria when his body was diverted to Egypt by Ptolemy, but Pausanias, Curtius and the Alexander Romance indicate that the King was initially laid to rest at Memphis and only later moved to Alexandria.[11] In particular, Pausanias states explicitly that it was Ptolemy's son and successor, Philadelphus, who was responsible for the transfer to Alexandria. The question is decided in favour of a Memphite entombment by an entry on a Ptolemaic chronology sculpted on the island of Paros, whilst it was ruled by Philadelphus in 263-262BC. The

---

[7] Richard Stoneman (translator), *The Greek Alexander Romance* (London, 1991), Book I, Sections 1-12.
[8] Philippe Derchain (editor Pierre Grimal), *Hellenism and the Rise of Rome* (London, 1968), p.208.
[9] The remains of a sea wall to the north and west of the island of Pharos are sometimes identified as pharaonic, but their date is actually very uncertain.
[10] The main Alexander historians imply that the site was empty in speaking of the marking of the street plan with barley – Arrian, *Anabasis Alexandrou* 3.2; Diodorus, 17.52; Plutarch, *Life of Alexander*, 26; Curtius, 4.8.1-6; the *Alexander Romance* (probably compiled in Alexandria) speaks explicitly of twelve Egyptian villages on the site, stating that Rhakotis was the largest of them (Section 31 of Book I); Strabo, 17.1.6, states that Rhakotis had been a κώμη, which is an unwalled village or country town.
[11] Aelian, *Varia Historia* 12.64; Diodorus Siculus, 18.28.3; Strabo, *Geography* 17.1.8; Pausanias, 1.6.3; Curtius, 10.10.20; Richard Stoneman, *The Greek Alexander Romance* (London, 1991), Book III, 34.

The Sarcophagus of Alexander the Great?

Parian Marble[12] unambiguously asserts that "Alexander was laid to rest in Memphis" under the year 321-320BC. It also gives the year of Philadelphus' birth as 309-8BC, but makes no mention of any transfer to Alexandria up to the last surviving entries around 300BC. At the time it was sculpted, the body almost certainly lay at Alexandria, so the sculptor would have perplexed his intended readership had he omitted to mention a transfer prior to 300BC. It is therefore overwhelmingly probable that Pausanias' account is true and that the Memphite entombment lasted 30 or 40 years with the relocation eventually taking place around 290-280BC.[13]

Where then was Nectanebo's sarcophagus likely to have been when Alexander was "laid to rest at Memphis"? The location of his intended tomb is not known. However, under the 30th dynasty Memphis was the capital and it retained this status some years into the rule of Ptolemy, until it was eventually superseded by Alexandria. There is also a substantial 30th dynasty cemetery in the Memphite necropolis at Saqqara.[14] This cemetery is adjacent to the Avenue of Sphinxes (see Figure 3.6) leading from the sanctuary of the living Apis bull near Memphis in the Nile flood plain up into the Memphite Sarapieion complex.[15] Nectanebo added a temple to this complex and also to the Sacred Animal Necropolis adjoining the Sanctuary of the Mother Cows of the Apis Bulls.[16] He also inaugurated his reign by officiating at the funeral of the Apis bull at this sanctuary,[17] just as Alexander subsequently showed his respect for Egyptian sensibilities by sacrificing to the Apis.[18] Given the special significance of Apis bull worship for Nectanebo, it is possible he intended to associate his tomb with his Sarapieion temple.

Late Period pharaohs in general tended to be buried in tombs in the courtyards of major temple complexes, typically in a vault beneath a cult-chapel. Examples are the 26th dynasty tombs at Sais and those of the 29th dynasty at Mendes. This type of tomb was one element of a Late Period revival of Old Kingdom styles and traditions.[19] The Sarapieion has independently been a favourite candidate for the location of the Memphite tomb of Alexander, because it was the most prominent temple at Saqqara at this time and because the Ptolemies set up a

---

[12] Jacoby, FGrH 239.
[13] P M Fraser, *Ptolemaic Alexandria* (Oxford, 1972), has argued for an early transfer to Alexandria on the basis of Curtius' remark that the transfer took place "after a few years", but 30 or 40 years are few on a timescale of centuries, so the remark is really too vague to have any evidential value.
[14] E.g. Ian Shaw and Paul Nicholson, *The British Museum Dictionary of Ancient Egypt* (London, 1995), p.252 under 'Saqqara'.
[15] The sphinxes are believed to have been created under Nectanebo I; two others found at the entrance to the Nectanebo temple are attributed to Nectanebo II.
[16] Jean-Philippe Lauer, *Saqqara, The Royal Cemetery of Memphis, Excavations and Discoveries since 1850* (New York, 1976), p. 18 and p. 220.
[17] Nicolas Grimal, *A History of Ancient Egypt* (Oxford, English Paperback Edition 1994), p. 379.
[18] Arrian, *Anabasis Alexandrou* 3.1.4.
[19] B G Trigger, B J Kemp, D O'Connor and A B Lloyd, *Ancient Egypt: A Social History* (Cambridge, 1983), p.321.

rather incongruous semi-circle of eleven marble statues of Greek sages and poets before the entrance of the Nectanebo temple (Figures 3.7 & 3.8). Dorothy Thompson has speculated that they may have "guarded a shrine of some importance – the site once perhaps of Alexander's tomb".[20] If so, then the shrine almost certainly lay within the Nectanebo temple, as can be seen from Auguste Mariette's detailed plan (Figure 3.9).[21] Some authorities prefer to date these sculptures to the late 3rd century BC many decades after the transfer of Alexander's tomb.[22] However, the analysis of this group by J-P Lauer & Ch. Picard[23] suggested that the era of the first Ptolemy is most probable, mainly because one of the statues may be Demetrios of Phaleron,[24] the foremost philosopher at Ptolemy I's court, who was banished at the start of Philadelphus' reign.[25] It would therefore seem that a date contemporary with the Memphite tomb of Alexander is not impossible. For these reasons Memphis and more specifically the Sarapieion complex is the most likely location of the sarcophagus at the time Ptolemy entombed Alexander there.[26] An obvious explanation for the subsequent appearance of the sarcophagus in Alexandria is therefore that it accompanied Alexander's body, when Philadelphus brought it to his capital probably in the second decade of the 3rd century BC.

Among reputable authorities Fraser in particular has doubted whether Ptolemy would have considered using a sarcophagus made for Nectanebo and emblazoned with his cartouches for his Memphite tomb of Alexander.[27] However, there are several lines of argument which support the opposite view:-

    a) Ptolemy could hardly have made any open preparations for Alexander's tomb prior to his hijack of the catafalque in Syria, since such preparations might have alerted the Regent Perdiccas as to his intentions. He would therefore have been driven by circumstances to improvise a Memphite tomb from available material.

    b) Ptolemy was keen to ingratiate himself with the native Egyptians at the time he brought Alexander's body back to Egypt in order to bolster his position in the civil wars that were about to break out. There is a clear example of this policy at work in an inscription set up by Ptolemy and

---

[20] Dorothy Thompson, *Memphis after the Ptolemies* (Princeton, 1988), p.212.
[21] Ulrich Wilcken, 'Die griechischen Denkmäler vom Dromos des Serapeums von Memphis', *JDAI* 32, 1917, pp.149-203.
[22] E.g. F Matz, 'Review of J-P Lauer & Ch. Picard; Les statues Ptolémaiques du Sarapieion de Memphis', Gnomon, 29, pp. 84-93; Fraser, *Ptolemaic Alexandria*, Note 512 to Chapter 5, says an early date is not impossible, but prefers a later one, as does Dorothy Thompson in *Memphis after the Ptolemies*.
[23] J-P Lauer & Ch. Picard, *Les Statues Ptolémaiques du Sarapieion de Memphis* (Paris, 1955).
[24] So too Ulrich Wilcken, based on Demetrios' association with the foundation of the Sarapis cult and the herm of Sarapis on which this figure leans.
[25] Diogenes Laertius, *Demetrios* 5.76; Cicero, *Pro Rabirio Postumo* 23.
[26] Sebbenytos is a secondary possibility, since this was the native city of Nectanebo I, the founder of the 30th dynasty.
[27] P M Fraser, *Ptolemaic Alexandria* (Oxford, 1972), Section 2 of Note 86 to Chapter 1.

The Sarcophagus of Alexander the Great?

known as the Satrap Stele. In this case Ptolemy seeks to associate himself with the mysterious pseudo-pharaoh, Khabbash,[28] leader of the Egyptian rebellion against the Persians in about 338-336BC. Use of the sarcophagus of the preceding pharaoh for Alexander would potentially have helped to fix the association in the minds of the native population.

c) If a scholar such as Philippe Derchain has found it credible that Ptolemy should have spread a rumour that Nectanebo had been Alexander's father, then it is a much smaller step to believe Ptolemy would have used the vacant sarcophagus.

d) There is an enormous amount of literary and archaeological evidence that the Ptolemies were very active in the re-use of pharaonic material to embellish Alexandria and its temples and shrines. Large numbers of obelisks and sphinxes from Heliopolis have been found in the harbour area. Cleopatra's needles are obelisks from Heliopolis, which may have been brought to Alexandria by Cleopatra, but were set up by Augustus. Pliny has recorded that Philadelphus used an uninscribed obelisk quarried by Nectanebo in a shrine to his sister-wife Arsinoë.[29]

These observations strongly refute the idea that Ptolemy would have harboured any aesthetic, religious or cultural prejudices against using an empty pharaonic sarcophagus for Alexander.

It is possible that Ptolemy took over a tomb site prepared for Nectanebo together with his sarcophagus, either at the Sarapieion or elsewhere. As we have seen, a site associated with the Nectanebo temple in the Sarapieion complex has the attraction of directly connecting the sarcophagus with previously unrelated academic speculation concerning the location of the Memphite tomb of Alexander.

Alternatively, a site in Memphis proper remains feasible. In particular there are some hints of an association between Alexander's Memphite tomb and the god Ammon. For example, Alexander wore the ram's horns of Ammon on Ptolemy's elephant scalp tetradrachms and he is reported to have requested that his body should be taken to Ammon or the Temple of Ammon on his deathbed.[30] In fact an Imensthotieion or Temple of Ammon and Thoth (Sun and Moon gods respectively) is mentioned as being located in the Hellenion or

---

[28] E.g. "...The land in its full extent which had been given by the king, the lord of the two lands, the image of Tanen, chosen by Ptah, son of the Sun, Khabbash living forever, the donation thereof has been renewed by this great Viceroy of Egypt, Ptolemy, to the gods of Pe and Tep forever..."(311BC); see also Alan K Bowman, *Egypt after the Pharaohs* (London, softcover edition, 1986), Chapter 2, p.22.
[29] Pliny, *Natural History*, xxxvi.xiv.67.
[30] Curtius 10.5.4; Justin 12.15.7.

The Quest for the Tomb of Alexander by Andrew Chugg

Greek Quarter of Memphis,[31] so this provides another possible context for the Memphite tomb.

Leo Africanus and the Domus Alexandri Magni

Are there any records of the sarcophagus that associate it with Alexander's tomb prior to Napoleon's invasion of Egypt? The various eighteenth century travelogues, which mention the Attarine mosque and its contents, are muted on this point. However, there is a group of sixteenth and early seventeenth century accounts beginning with the Description of Africa by Leo Africanus, which report a tomb of Alexander in the city:-

It should not be omitted, that in the middle of the city amongst the ruins may be seen a little house in the form of a chapel, in which is a tomb much honoured by the Mahometans; since it is asserted that within it is kept the corpse of Alexander the Great, grand prophet and King, as may be read in the Koran. And many strangers come from distant lands to see and venerate this tomb, leaving at this spot great and frequent alms.[32]

Leo Africanus appears to have visited Alexandria several times between about 1515-1520. The Spanish traveller Marmol visited Alexandria in 1546 and appears to have plagiarised Leo's account: most notably they both use "casa" (i.e. house) for the tomb building in the oldest surviving manuscripts.[33] A very similar account was also given by George Sandys following his visit in 1610:-

There is yet to be seene a little Chappell: within, a tombe, much honoured and visited by the Mahometans, where they bestow their alms; supposing his [Alexander's] body to lie in that place: Himselfe reputed a great Prophet, and informed thereof by their Alcoran.[34]

Clearly these descriptions are highly reminiscent of the small building in the courtyard of the Attarine Mosque. However, this obvious inference has been obscured by a much later legend, which located the tomb beneath the Nabi Daniel Mosque half a kilometre away. This story may not be any older than about 1850 when a dragoman from the Russian embassy claimed to have seen Alexander's sarcophagus in an old Roman cistern, which lies beneath some Arab tombs in the basement of the mosque.[35] Extensive excavations in the 20th century have virtually proved this tale to be apocryphal.[36] Nevertheless, many authorities still cite Leo as a possible early reference to the Nabi Daniel tomb.

---

[31] British Museum Catalogue, Papyrus 50; Claire Préaux, *L'Économie Royale des Lagides* (Brussels, 1939), pp. 298-9.
[32] Leo Africanus, ed. Ramusio, *Descrizione dell'Africa* (Rome, 1550), f. 89r; Leo Africanus, trans. John Pory, ed. Dr Robert Brown, *Description of Africa* (London, 1896), vol. 3, 8th book.
[33] Perrot (translator into French), *L'Afrique de Marmol* (Paris, 1677), Tom. III, liv. xi, c. 14, p. 276.
[34] George Sandys, *Relation of a Journey begun in AD 1610* (London, 1617), p.112.
[35] Evaristo Breccia, *Alexandrea ad Aegyptum* (Bergamo, 1922), p. 99; A M de Zogheb, *Etudes sur l'ancienne Alexandrie* (Paris, 1909); this theory was first given written form by Mahmoud Bey, *Mémoire sur l'antique Alexandrie, ses faubourgs et environs découverts...* (Copenhagen, 1872).
[36] P Fraser, *Ptolemaic Alexandria*, (Oxford, 1972), Note 88 to Chapter 1; M Rodziewicz, *Les habitations romaines tardives d'Alexandrie, Centre d'archéologie mediterranéenne de l'Académie Polonaise des*

The Sarcophagus of Alexander the Great?

However, an important piece of evidence, which strongly suggests that Leo's tomb of Alexander was indeed the Attarine sarcophagus, appears until now to have been overlooked. At the exact centre of Braun & Hogenberg's lovely map of Alexandria[37] (Figure 7.2), which was engraved in about 1573, there is a small domed building beside the minaret of a mosque, which is labelled "Domus Alexandri Magni" or "House of Alexander the Great" in English (Figure 7.3). It is believed that Braun & Hogenberg obtained their information from a Cologne merchant by the name of Conrad von Lyskirchen. He in turn is supposed to have drawn either on older Portuguese plans or upon information obtained by Charles V's spies, who gathered cartographic data on southern Mediterranean ports for the Holy Roman Emperor in around 1530 preparatory to his abortive invasions of North Africa.[38] Certainly the internal evidence of the map would date it to the first half of the sixteenth century.[39] Although the topography is somewhat distorted in places and there are a few minor errors, such as transposing the names of the Pharos and the Pharillon, overall the map is quite authentic. In particular the Domus Alexandri Magni is correctly situated for the Attarine Mosque (cf. the Description de l'Egypte map in Figure 8.2). The Nabi Daniel mosque was built at the foot of a hill called Kom el-Dikka, which may be identified with the hillock halfway across the city from the Attarine Mosque in the top left of the Braun & Hogenberg view.

It is very likely that the Domus Alexandri Magni, Leo's Tomb of Alexander and the small domed building in the courtyard of the Attarine Mosque are one and the same. The traditional association of the Nectanebo sarcophagus with Alexander's tomb therefore dates back at least five centuries. It is probably much older still: in the 9th century Ibn Abdel Hakim recorded a Mosque of Dulkarnein (i.e. Alexander[40]) in Alexandria[41] and a century later Massoudi (943-

---

Sciences (Warsaw, 1984); the Nabi Daniel mosque was built in 1823 by Mohammad Ali over some older Arab tombs.

[37] George Braun and Frans Hogenberg, *Civitates Orbis Terrarum* (Cologne, 1572 –1618).

[38] Constantin van Lyskirchen was a Hanse merchant located in Cologne, where also Braun and Hogenberg worked. He supplied views of many towns in Asia and Africa to Braun and Hogenberg including Alexandria. Braun & Hogenberg may have used other sources as well. According to Oscar Norwich edited by Jeffery Stone, *Norwich's Maps of Africa, an illustrated and annotated carto-bibliography* (Norwich, Vermont, 1997), page 380: "in the Hanse merchant Constantin van Lyskirchen of Cologne the editors found a willing agent, who supplied views of the towns of India, Asia, Africa, and Persia never portrayed before." According to Norwich, "Lyskirchen obtained these views from the manuscript produced by an unknown Portuguese illustrator." He goes on to say that "apart from these Portuguese views, some of the African illustrations were taken from military plans concerned with the expeditions of the Emperor Charles V in 1535 and 1541 to Tunis and Algeria." Braun's & Hogenberg's plates subsequently passed to Jansson, so the Alexandria map was republished in his famous Atlas of 1619.

[39] It depicts Qaid Bey fortress, built in the 1480's, but shows few buildings on the Pharos isthmus, which started to be developed under the Ottomans in the late sixteenth century.

[40] Dulkarnein means the "two horned lord" in Arabic, which alludes to the representations of Alexander wearing a pair of ram's horns or bull's horns on the coins of his successors, especially the tetradrachms of Lysimachos; Alexander appears in this guise in Surah 18 of the Koran.

[41] P Fraser, *Ptolemaic Alexandria* (Oxford,1972), Section 1 of Note 86 to Chapter 1.

4 AD) mentioned the existence of a modest building called the "Tomb of the Prophet and King Eskender".[42]

The Church of St Athanasius

There is yet one other coincidence between the history of the Soma mausoleum of Alexander in Alexandria and the provenance of the Nectanebo sarcophagus. The Soma is last mentioned by Herodian,[43] who wrote in about AD240 concerning Caracalla's visit in AD215. Alexandria was peaceful until the early 260's, so it is very likely that the building survived at least until the later part of the 3rd century, when the city became embroiled in three successive civil wars. In the early 260's the Roman governor was acclaimed as a rival emperor by his troops in a rebellion that was bloodily extinguished following a siege of the fortified Bruchium quarter.[44] In the early 270's Aurelian subdued the city after a rebellion by Firmus, an Alexandrian supporter of Zenobia, the Queen of Palmyra. Finally, Diocletian crushed a major revolt in AD298 by capturing the city after a long siege and his troops indulged in an orgy of retribution.[45]

Strabo states that the Soma enclosure was part of the Ptolemaic Royal Quarter.[46] The Roman fortress called the Bruchium was formed when Caracalla walled in the region of the city that had previously contained the Royal Palaces. Consequently, Ammianus Marcellinus' statement that Aurelian laid waste to the Bruchium[47] has been cited as the most likely explanation for the destruction of the Soma. However, the issue is very unclear, since Strabo also says that his Royal Quarter constituted between a quarter and a third of the entire city, whereas the Roman Bruchium fortress was barely half that size.[48]

Ammianus also refers to a temple of the Genius of Alexandria in a passage describing the antagonism between the Patriarch Georgius and the Alexandrian mob in about AD361:-

And, among other matters, it was said that [Georgius] maliciously informed Constantius also of this, namely, that all the edifices standing on the soil of the said city [Alexandria] had been built by its founder, Alexander, at great public cost, and ought justly to be a source of profit to the treasury. To these evil deeds he added still another, which soon after drove him headlong to destruction. As he was returning from the emperor's court and passed by the splendid temple of the Genius [speciosum Genii templum], attended as usual by a large crowd, he turned his eyes straight at the temple, and said: "How long shall this tomb [sepulcrum] stand?" On hearing

---

[42] Maçoudi trans. C. Barbier de Meynard and Pavet de Courteille, *Les Prairies d'Or* (Paris, 1869), t. II, p.259.
[43] Herodian, 4.12 (and the Introduction to the Loeb edition by C R Whittaker).
[44] John Marlowe, *The Golden Age of Alexandria* (London, 1971), Chapter 10, p.220.
[45] Stephen Williams, *Diocletian and The Roman Recovery* (New York, 1985).
[46] Strabo, *Geography* 17.1.8.
[47] Ammianus Marcellinus, *Res Gestae* 22.16.15.
[48] The Bruchium seems to have been the area adjoining the eastern coastline of the Great Harbour that lay outside the medieval walls (see Figure 1).

The Sarcophagus of Alexander the Great?

this, many were struck as if by a thunderbolt, and fearing that he might try to overthrow that building also, they devised secret plots to destroy him in whatever way they could.[49]

D G Hogarth thought that this mention of a tomb of the Genius of Alexandria in a splendid temple might well refer to the Soma mausoleum.[50] However, P M Fraser has argued that it is the Agathos Daimon that is meant and that the use of the word 'sepulcrum' is rhetorical.[51] Alternatively, Christopher Haas[52] has claimed that it is the female personification of the Tyche of Alexandria that is meant. However, there appear to be explicit representations of Alexander in the guise of the Genius of Alexandria on several Alexandrian coin types of Hadrian,[53] which strengthens the view that Georgius is indeed referring to Alexander's Mausoleum. If so, this building survived until at least AD361. Given that John Chrysostom asserted that Alexander's tomb was 'unknown to his own people' a few decades later,[54] the most likely occasion of the destruction of the Soma Mausoleum was the earthquake and tidal wave, which devastated Alexandria in AD365.[55] The relevant point here is that Athanasius was Patriarch of Alexandria in AD365, which may help to explain how the sarcophagus ended up in a mosque on the site of a late Roman church dedicated to his memory.

Conclusions

The established fact that the sarcophagus was originally sculpted for Nectanebo II has for nearly two centuries been assumed to discredit the Alexandrian tradition that it had once contained Alexander's remains. However, as we have seen, this fact actually seems to place the sarcophagus in the right place at the right time in a vacant condition. It also connects the sarcophagus with a previously unrelated line of academic reasoning, which has associated the Nectanebo temple at the Sarapieion with the Memphite tomb of Alexander. It is therefore more properly recognised as the best single reason to believe in the authenticity of the tradition. Furthermore, the use of the sarcophagus for the Memphite tomb provides a straightforward explanation as to how it found its way to Alexandria. Even those who have doubted its authenticity have conceded that it is otherwise difficult to account for its presence there.

In addition it is now possible to make a strong case that it is this same sarcophagus housed within its own little chapel that Leo Africanus saw during

---

[49] Ammianus Marcellinus, *Res Gestae* 22.11.7.
[50] D G Hogarth, 'Report on Prospects for Research in Alexandria', *Egypt Exploration Fund* 1894-5, note 3 on p. 23.
[51] P M Fraser, *Ptolemaic Alexandria* (Oxford, 1972), note 84 to Ch. 1.
[52] Christopher Haas, *Alexandria in Late Antiquity* (Baltimore, 1997), p. 287.
[53] AM Chugg, 'An Unrecognised Representation of Alexander the Great on Hadrian's Egyptian Coinage', The Celator Journal, Vol. 15, No. 2 (February, 2001).
[54] John Chrysostom, *Homily XXVI on the second epistle of St Paul the Apostle to the Corinthians*, circa AD400.
[55] Ammianus Marcellinus, *Res Gestae*, 26.10.15-19; Sozomenus, *Ecclesiastical History*, 6.2.

his visits to Alexandria around 1517. This takes the tradition regarding the sarcophagus back at least five centuries and in all probability it is far older.

Starting from the premise that this tomb is a forgery, either the perpetrators were extraordinarily lucky in their choice of a pharaonic sarcophagus which really was available to Ptolemy, when he entombed Alexander at Memphis, or they were able to recognise that this was the sarcophagus made for Nectanebo. For the latter purpose, they probably needed to be able to read hieroglyphics. However, the latest hieroglyphic inscriptions date from the late 4th century AD.[56] Even from a sceptical stance it would therefore appear likely that the sarcophagus was associated with Alexander within a few centuries of the disappearance of the Soma Mausoleum.

The evidence presented in this article falls short of absolute proof (as do nearly all historical arguments). Nevertheless, there appears to be no substantive contrary evidence and the coincidences are sufficiently numerous and striking as to make it difficult to avoid the conclusion that this relic is in all probability the genuine sarcophagus of Alexander the Great.

---

[56] The last known hieroglyphic inscription, on the island of Philae, is dated to August 24th AD394. Presumably the closure of the temples by Theodosius following his decrees "contra paganos" of AD391 was the immediate cause of the disappearance of this form of writing.

Appendix C: A Candidate for the First Tomb of Alexander

Moves to publish the following article by the author were superseded by the publication of *The Lost Tomb of Alexander the Great* in 2004, so it has only previously appeared as a pdf download from the author's website at www.alexanderstomb.com.

Introduction

Alexander's achievements in life are a core feature of the classics curriculum, but there is scattered and fragmentary evidence to suggest that his influence in death over the politics and religion of later antiquity was equally momentous. For example, the Senate is said to have elected him the thirteenth member of the Pantheon.[1] However, much of the tangible evidence for the worship of Alexander has been lost. In particular, the centre of his cult was always associated with his mummified remains in Egypt and we hear of pilgrimages by Caesar, Octavian, Severus and Caracalla.[2] Yet none of the sites of his several tombs has ever been identified and some have despaired of ever finding them. However, fresh and hitherto unrecognised evidence is now emerging, which suggests that the problem may not be as intractable as it has seemed. The present article focuses upon a new candidate for the site of the first tomb at Memphis.

The Memphite Entombment

Some time around the winter of 322-321BC Ptolemy Soter perpetrated the hijacking of the catafalque of Alexander the Great, whilst it was progressing through Syria bound for Macedon.[3] He brought it back to Egypt and promptly arranged for the entombment of the corpse of his former king at Memphis, which was still the capital of the country at that time.[4] Some modern authorities have sought to argue that Alexander's tomb was transferred to Alexandria within the next few years, mainly in pursuit of an unproven and disputed theory

---

[1] Clement of Alexandria, Exhortation to the Greeks, Ch. X: "For these are they who have dared to deify men, describing Alexander of Macedon as the thirteenth god, though 'Babylon proved him mortal'"; St John Chrysostom, Bishop of Constantinople, Homily XXVI on the second epistle of St Paul the Apostle to the Corinthians: "Thus the Roman senate decreed Alexander to be the thirteenth God, for it possessed the privilege of electing and enrolling Gods"; Lucian, Dialogues of the Dead XIII: Diogenes to Alexander, "Some even added you to the twelve gods, built you temples, and sacrificed to you as the son of the serpent."

[2] Caesar: Lucan, *Pharsalia* 10, lines 14-20; Octavian: Suetonius, *Lives of the Caesars, Augustus* 2.18; Dio Cassius, *Roman History* 51.16.5; Severus: Dio Cassius, *Roman History (Epitome)* 76.13; Caracalla: Herodian, 4.8.6 to 4.9.3.

[3] Arrian, History of Events after Alexander, summarised by Photius, 92; see also Goralski 1989; Aelian, Varia Historia 12.64; Pausanias, 1.6.3.

[4] Pausanias, 1.6.3; Curtius, 10.10.20; Stoneman 1991, 3.34; Diodorus Siculus, 18.28.2-3.

that Alexandria became the capital as early as 320BC.[5] However, the historical evidence supports the view that the Memphite tomb existed for at least 30 years, for Pausanias states that its transfer was undertaken by Ptolemy's son Philadelphus.[6] Furthermore, Pausanias' account is significantly corroborated by the silence of the Parian Marble regarding the relocation.[7] This ancient chronology from Paros pays special attention to events concerning Ptolemy and Philadelphus, for the latter was the ruler of the island at the time it was sculpted in 263-262BC. In particular, it records the burial of Alexander at Memphis in 321BC and the birth of Philadelphus in 309-308BC, yet it fails to mention the transfer of Alexander's tomb up to its last surviving entries around 300BC. If the tomb had been transferred in the 4th century, then the Parian Marble should have mentioned the fact, else it would have conveyed a misleading impression that the tomb still lay at Memphis. This would have been a remarkable flaw in an inscription, which has otherwise proven highly authoritative. Hence it is reasonable to conclude that Alexander's body remained at Memphis until at least 290BC.[8] Most probably it was there until shortly after Philadelphus became sole ruler upon Ptolemy's death in 282BC. Having therefore established that Alexander's body probably lay at Memphis for about four decades, it is the purpose of this article to draw together a variety of strands of evidence in order to propose a candidate for its exact location.

The Sarcophagus of Nectanebo II

In the Summer of 1798 Napoleon invaded Egypt. In retrospect this is often regarded as the founding event for Egyptology as a serious science. Not only did the expedition's scholars gather the material for the magnificent and still crucially important *Description de l'Egypte*, but they also discovered the Rosetta Stone and had the wit to recognise its immense importance. What is less well remembered, however, is that at the time the greatest excitement was accorded to the discovery of an empty pharaonic sarcophagus in a chapel in the courtyard of the Attarine Mosque in Alexandria (Figure 7.1). This was for the very good reason that the local inhabitants confidently asserted that it had once held the remains of Alexander the Great.[9]

The British defeated the French at the Battle of Alexandria in 1801. Under the terms of the treaty of surrender, the French were required to hand over their

---

[5] Fraser 1972, note 79 to ch. 1, has argued for an early transfer to Alexandria on the basis of Curtius' remark that the transfer took place "after a few years", but 30 or 40 years are few on a timescale of centuries, so the remark is really too vague to have any evidential value. Fraser cross-references his note 28 to ch. 1, in which he outlines his argument against Welles, that Alexandria became the capital just a few years after Alexander's death. This would seem to have been an ulterior reason for arguing for an early transfer.
[6] Pausanias, 1.7.1.
[7] F. Jacoby, *FGrHist* 239, The Parian Marble.
[8] 290BC seems to be the earliest date for the institution of the Priesthood of Alexander; see Fraser 1972, p. 216 and note 215.
[9] E.D. Clarke, *The Tomb of Alexander*, Cambridge, 1805, pp.39-40.

A Candidate for the First Tomb of Alexander

collection of Egyptian antiquities, including the Rosetta Stone and the Alexandrian sarcophagus (Figure 7.5). The latter was tracked to its hiding place in the hold of a French hospital ship by the Cambridge scholar Edward Daniel Clarke, who subsequently arranged for its transport to the British Museum, where it is still exhibited today. Clarke also wrote a treatise entitled, "The Tomb of Alexander", in which he published his reasons for believing the attribution of the relic to the Macedonian king.[10]

Unfortunately, however, Clarke was able to contribute scant additional evidence for the attribution. Even more unfortunately, when Champollion deciphered hieroglyphics in 1822, it was soon realised that the sarcophagus bore the cartouches of a 30th dynasty pharaoh, originally identified as Nectanebo I (Nakhtnebef), but subsequently corrected to Nectanebo II (Nakhthorheb). Clarke's opponents, already outraged by the suggestion that the greatest of Greek kings had been buried in a mere Egyptian artefact rather than in some masterpiece of classical sculpture, now considered themselves wholly vindicated. An air of complacent scepticism enshrouded the sarcophagus, the legacy of which continues to taint the investigation of its provenance to this day.

A solitary and misconceived attempt to challenge the sceptical orthodoxy was made by Alan Wace in 1948.[11] He pointed out that Nectanebo II had fled from Egypt having been ousted by a Persian invasion begun in about 341BC.[12] Alexander in turn ejected the Persians in 332BC. Consequently, Nectanebo's sarcophagus and conceivably an associated tomb should have been available to Ptolemy in a vacant state, when he needed to inter Alexander in 321BC. Secondly, Wace noted that the role of Nectanebo II as Alexander's putative father in the Alexandrian Alexander Romance,[13] might potentially be explained by Ptolemy's use of Nectanebo's sarcophagus for Alexander's tomb. These points were well made, but Wace seems principally to have been motivated by a desire to support his precarious theory that Alexandria had already been the site of a major Egyptian city in the pharaonic period. He therefore proposed that Ptolemy had found the empty sarcophagus in a hypothetical 30th dynasty royal necropolis located at Alexandria. In this way he sought a combined explanation both for its use by Alexander and also for its otherwise surprising presence in Alexandria. However, the various ancient accounts of the foundation of Alexandria by Strabo, the Alexander historians and the Alexander Romance speak of a site comprising open countryside scattered with a few fishing villages, the largest of which was called Rhakotis.[14] If Rhakotis had been such a major

---

[10] Clarke 1805.
[11] Wace 1948, pp. 1-11.
[12] Diodorus Siculus, 16.51.
[13] Stoneman 1991, 1.1-14.
[14] The main Alexander historians imply that the site was empty in speaking of the marking of the street plan with barley – Arrian, Campaigns of Alexander 3.2; Diodorus, 17.52; Plutarch, Life of Alexander 26; Curtius, 4.8.1-6; the Greek Alexander Romance 1.31 (probably compiled in

town as Wace suggested, then it is very surprising that it left virtually no historical or archaeological trace. Perhaps, though, the greatest problem for Wace's theory lies in the evidence that Alexander's body initially rested at Memphis for at least three decades. Yet therein also lies its salvation, for from this perspective it makes more sense in every respect to assume that Ptolemy found and used the empty Nectanebo II sarcophagus at Memphis in 321BC.

None of the sites of the tombs of the three 30th dynasty pharaohs is currently established, though fragments of the sarcophagus of Nectanebo I have been found re-used in the walls of medieval buildings at Cairo[15] and both the sarcophagus and shabtis (statuettes made to act as servants for the dead in the afterlife) of Nectanebo II exist in museums.[16] Tombs of the 26th dynasty and the short-lived 28th dynasty are at Sais, whilst those of the 29th dynasty have recently been proven to lie at Mendes.[17] These locations seem to have been chosen, because they had been the ancestral seats of the founders of the respective dynasties. The founder of the 30th dynasty, Nectanebo I, is known to have hailed from Sebennytos in the Delta, so speculation has favoured this town as the location of his dynasty's royal cemetery, despite the lack of any corroborative archaeological or literary evidence (except, rather tenuously, that the sarcophagus of Udjashu, wife of Tjahapimu and mother of Nectanebo II, was found reused near Mansura in the northern Delta, and has been suggested as from Behbeit el-Hagar,[18] site of a temple of Isis, erected by Nectanebo II five miles north of Sebennytos). However, there are indications that Memphis was the capital under the 30th dynasty, which makes it a credible alternative location for the royal tombs.[19] Conversely, Alexandria/Rhakotis was neither the ancestral seat of the dynasty nor the capital, so it is an innately improbable site.

The Memphite Serapeum

It has been known since the very beginning of scientific excavation in Egypt that the 30th dynasty pharaohs were very active in the Memphite necropolis at Saqqara. Among the earliest and greatest archaeological discoveries were those made by Auguste Mariette. In particular, between 1850 and 1853 he relocated and excavated the Serapeum temple complex to the northwest of the step pyramid of Djoser (Figure 3.6).[20] Using Strabo as his guide, he exhumed a mile-

---

Alexandria) speaks explicitly of twelve Egyptian villages on the site, stating that Rhakotis was the largest of them; Strabo, 17.1.6, states that Rhakotis had been a κώμη, which is an unwalled village or country town.
[15] Dodson 2000, p.163.
[16] There is a complete shabti of Nectanebo II in Turin and some ten fragments also, but all unprovenanced, see Clayton 1994, pp. 204-5.
[17] Dodson 2000, pp. 160-163.
[18] C.C. Edgar & G. Maspero, "The Sarcophagus of an Unknown Queen," *ASAE 8*, 1907, 276-81.
[19] Memphis was probably the *administrative* capital throughout the Late Period (see Trigger 1983, pp. 332-333; Thompson 1988, p. 4). However, Sais and Mendes might be regarded as ceremonial capitals during the 26th and 29th dynasties respectively.
[20] Mariette 1882.

A Candidate for the First Tomb of Alexander

long avenue of sphinxes of Nectanebo I, which led from the Nile flood plain to the entrance pylon of the Serapeum. Especially towards the Serapeum end, cut into the banks to either side of the avenue, Mariette found high status tombs dating to the 30th Dynasty and the Graeco-Roman period (Figure C.1).[21] At the point where the avenue entered the complex by sharply deflecting to the south, Mariette discovered the ruins of a substantial temple to the east of the pylon, which contained sculpted reliefs of the pharaoh Nectanebo II in a posture of adoration before Osiris-Apis and Isis. Furthermore, he found a second temple of Nectanebo II at the opposite end of the first enclosure of the Serapeum and yet a third by this pharaoh, dedicated to the mother cows of the Apis bull, has been uncovered at the nearby Sacred Animal Necropolis. Evidently, the 30th dynasty lavished considerable efforts upon the necropolis of North Saqqara and the Serapeum complex was the focus for their attentions.

Figure C.1. Mariette's plan of his discoveries at North Saqqara from Choix des Monuments, Paris, 1856 (author's collection)

However, Nectanebo I and II were not alone in their embellishments of the Serapeum in this era. Their successors, the early Ptolemies, seem to have been responsible for the creation of a curious and ostensibly incongruous variety of sculptures in its precinct.[22] Most startling of all is the semicircle of eleven life-size Greek poets and sages (Figure 3.7), who appear placed to guard the main entrance to the temple of Nectanebo II. This is shown most clearly in a plan made by Mariette to detail his discoveries, but which went unregarded among his papers until 1939 (Figure 3.9).[23]

The semicircle has been dated to the reign of the first Ptolemy on the grounds that one of the statues (Figure 3.8) seems to represent Demetrios of Phaleron.[24] He was the leading philosopher at the court of Ptolemy I, but he was exiled to the countryside and subsequently compelled to commit suicide by Philadelphus, because he had supported a rival son in the struggle for the succession.[25] It would therefore seem likely that the semicircle is contemporaneous with the

---

[21] Mariette 1882, pp. 10-13; Dodson 2001, pp. 27-38.
[22] Wilcken 1917, pp.149-203; Lauer & Picard 1955.
[23] Lauer & Picard 1955, Plate 26.
[24] Lauer & Picard 1955, p. 87.
[25] Diogenes Laertius, *Demetrios* 5.76; Cicero, *Pro Rabirio Postumo* 23.

The Quest for the Tomb of Alexander by Andrew Chugg

Memphite tomb of Alexander. Furthermore, the semicircle is presided over by the central figure of Homer, Alexander's favourite poet.[26]

In fact Dorothy Thompson speculated that the semicircle had guarded the site of the Memphite tomb of Alexander in 1988,[27] though she believed the statues to post-date the tomb and she seems not to have been aware of the other connection between Alexander's tomb and Nectanebo II: i.e. the sarcophagus found in Alexandria. It is particularly this striking coincidence between two independent strands of evidence that underpins a persuasive case for the authenticity of the sarcophagus and the location of the first tomb.

The Temple of Nectanebo II

According to Mariette's detailed map of his excavations (Figure 3.9), it is apparent that the semicircle stands specifically beside the entrance to the temple of Nectanebo II. If, therefore, the poets guarded the tomb of Alexander, then we are directed within that entrance for its site. Apart from the floor of the temple itself, one other chamber is accessed via this entrance. This chamber is built into the southern flank of the temple (marked A in Figure 7.7) and is reached by a passage, which is prolonged as far as the southern side of the steps into the temple (D) by a dividing wall (C). Mariette's scale demonstrates that this chamber is of such a size (6m x 2.7m) as neatly to accommodate the sarcophagus of Nectanebo II to the east of its doorway as shown by the outline of the sarcophagus drawn to scale within the chamber in Figure 7.7.

There are other features of the chamber A that are suggestive of a tomb. The long entrance passage with bends seems to have been intended to produce a dark interior, which would have made most alternative uses awkward. The orientation and shape of the chamber implies an East-West orientation of the sarcophagus. Orientation was very important to the Ancient Egyptians. The East signified rebirth while the West signified the empire of the dead, so they saw the dead as departing into the West and an approximate East-West orientation of the burial chamber and/or the sarcophagus was common in royal tombs.

Mariette's plan shows a side entrance to the temple (B), just outside which he discovered a row of four Greek style lions (2). These sculptures appear to guard the side entrance in much the same way as the semicircle guards the main entrance. This is especially interesting, because lion sculptures are a prominent feature of the tombs and monuments of Alexander's Macedonian successors (e.g. the Lion Tombs of Knidos, Amphipolis and Gerdek Kaya and the Lion of Hamadan).[28] Furthermore, a pair of golden lions is known to have guarded the

---

[26] Plutarch, *Alexander* 8.2.
[27] Thompson 1988, p.212.
[28] Fedak 1990, pp.76-78 & 100.

entrance to the catafalque on which Alexander's body was borne from Babylon to Egypt (Figure 3.1).[29]

Mariette's account of the temple of Nectanebo II states that he found low relief carvings depicting Nectanebo II in a posture of adoration before a divinity, whom he identifies as Apis or Osiris-Apis.[30] However, Lauer notes that the sole fragment from the temple on display at the Louvre shows Nectanebo II adoring Isis, who would originally have been accompanied by Osiris.[31] Mariette also notes that where the walls of the temple were no more that 60cm to 70cm thick (light grey in Figure 3.9, i.e. the façade), they were made of finely dressed blocks of plain limestone. The thicker walls (2.95m and dark grey in Figure 3.9) were made of a core of large bricks mixed with vegetable matter with a covering of stone. Notably, branches of spiny acacia were embedded within the walls here and there (such logs were commonly used as cross-ties in Egyptian mud-brick architecture). Some of them bore two carefully carved cartouches of Nectanebo II. If the attached chamber was a tomb, then the temple itself should be interpreted as fulfilling the requisite role of the funerary offering chapel. Egyptians believed that they would appear before Osiris to be judged shortly after their demise, so the wall reliefs are not inconsistent with the offering chapel function.

The floor plan of the Nectanebo II temple is almost symmetrical about an East-West axis in the line of the dromos (the processional route to the bull galleries on the western side of the temple). However, it is noteworthy that the brickwork of the southern wall projects slightly beyond the fine masonry of the temple façade. If a southern brick wall be drawn in exactly to mirror the northern wall, such that the external face coincides with the end of the façade (as shown in Figure 7.7), then it is interesting to observe that its outer face coincides with the inner wall of the chamber A, whilst its interior face runs along the surface of the northern wall of the passage leading to chamber A. It is possible that this reflects the modus operandi of the architect, who may have drawn a symmetrical temple, then modified the southern flank to accommodate chamber A. However, it also suggests the possibility that chamber A was appended to an originally symmetrical Nectanebo II temple, some time subsequent to its construction. For instance, it would have been logical to construct a new end wall against the old one prior to its removal in order to maintain the support of the roof. The question might also be posed as to whether sufficient dressed stone might have been removed from the side of the steps (D), the doorway of the side entrance (B) and the area of the entrance to the passage to chamber A in order to construct the dividing wall (C) at the time of the hypothetical addition of chamber A? If chamber A was appended to the temple after its construction, then it is possible that it was added for the specific

---

[29] Diodorus Siculus, 18.27.1.
[30] Mariette 1882, pp.18-19.
[31] Lauer & Picard 1955, p.10.

The Quest for the Tomb of Alexander by Andrew Chugg

purpose of providing a tomb for Alexander. If it is original, then it is more likely that it was the intended tomb of Nectanebo II, taken over by Ptolemy to house Alexander's corpse.

Against the latter hypothesis it might be argued that the tomb would have broken with a precise royal tomb format, which had been current since the Tanis Pharaohs (21st Dynasty) and was followed until at least the 29th dynasty. In this scheme a subterranean tomb chamber was excavated beneath the offering chapel. Mariette mentions that he found and excavated tombs in pits beneath the paving of the Nectanebo II temple,[32] so perhaps a conventional tomb beneath the temple floor had been intended for Nectanebo II.

Conversely, chamber A was effectively subterranean. Its floor is a storey below that of the temple proper, which was itself built into a steep bank. This explains Mariette's cruciform outline indicating a tomb seemingly overlying the walls of the Nectanebo II complex just behind the temple (Figure 3.9) and why only the temple façade was constructed with dressed masonry. Chamber A might also be regarded as a close parallel to the tomb chambers, which Mariette found dug into the banks of the avenue of sphinxes nearby (Figure C.1).

There is a sketch by Barbot looking east along the dromos from near the entrance to the bull galleries towards the Nectanebo II temple (Figure C.2). The double flight of steps leading up to the entrance of the temple can just be discerned with the semicircle of statues to their right. The walls of the temple itself are drawn at varying heights indicating their ruinous condition at the point of excavation. The huge mound into which the temple was recessed looms behind the remains. In Mariette's plan (Figure 3.9) there are further walls built deeper into the mound beyond the eastern wall of the temple. There is a gap in these walls (marked E in Figure 7.7), which is in alignment with the dromos and the temple entrance. Did the eastern wall of the temple once have a gateway leading into the deeper parts of the complex within the mound? All these questions tend to emphasise the case for re-excavation of the area.

The Sarcophagus in Alexandria

Apart from Mariette's discoveries at the Memphite Serapeum there are several further pieces of evidence from Alexandria, which tend to support the authenticity of the sarcophagus. In the first place, it is now possible to show that the sarcophagus found in the Attarine Mosque is identical with the tomb of Alexander reported by several visitors to Alexandria in the 16th and early 17th centuries. Most importantly, Leo Africanus visited the port in around 1517 and subsequently described a "little house in the form of a chapel" which was honoured as the tomb of Alexander the Great.[33] It has been doubted whether this was the chapel in the courtyard of the mosque, mainly because of a mid-19th century hoax that the tomb lay beneath the Nabi Daniel Mosque several

---

[32] Mariette 1882, p. 19.
[33] Africanus 1550, f. 89r; Africanus 1896, vol. 3, 8th book.

A Candidate for the First Tomb of Alexander

hundred metres away at the foot of a hillock called Kom el-Dikka.[34] The Nabi Daniel legend seems to have been stimulated by a preposterous tale told by an amateur tourist guide called Ambrose Schilizzi in about 1850. Probably motivated by a desire to drum up business, he described glimpsing Alexander's corpse through cracks in a worm-eaten door whilst exploring passages beneath the Nabi Daniel Mosque. He described a corpse with a crown within a glass enclosure and papyrus scrolls strewn about the chamber. All these details are lifted straight from the accounts of ancient writers and were well known in Alexandria in the 19th century.[35] The most telling evidence of Schilizzi's mendacity is his mention of the scrolls, evidently inspired by Dio Cassius' account, which implies that Septimius Severus locked up some Egyptian books of magic lore in the tomb. However, papyri do not survive in Alexandria, because capillary action raises dampness from its high water table.[36]

Figure C.2. Sketch by Barbot of the view looking east up the dromos to the ruins of the Temple of Nectanebo II at the time of Mariette's excavation of the Memphite Serapeum

It turns out that there is direct evidence in a map of Alexandria by Braun & Hogenberg (Figures 7.2 & 7.3), which strongly connects Leo's tomb of Alexander with the Nectanebo II sarcophagus. This map was engraved in around 1573, but its information seems to date from the 1530's.[37] At its exact

---

[34] Breccia 1922, p. 99; A M de Zogheb 1909, p.170; this theory was first given written form by Mahmoud Bey 1872, pp.49-52.
[35] Crown left by Augustus, Suetonius, Augustus 18; glass sarcophagus, Strabo, 17.1.8; papyri, Dio Cassius, 76.13.2.
[36] See also p.282 below.
[37] Braun and Hogenberg 1572. Constantin van Lyskirchen, a Hanse merchant located in Cologne, supplied views of many towns in Asia and Africa to Braun and Hogenberg including Alexandria.

The Quest for the Tomb of Alexander by Andrew Chugg

centre beside the minaret of a mosque there is marked a small domed building with the legend *Domus Alexandri Magni* or House of Alexander the Great, which should clearly be identified with Leo's "little house". Its location is roughly correct for the Attarine Mosque (Figure 8.2), but it is half way across the city from Kom el-Dikka, which is the mound in the upper left quarter of the city in Braun & Hogenberg's plan.

It is therefore apparent that the attribution of the sarcophagus to Alexander goes back at least 5 centuries. In all probability it is far older, for there are Arab accounts which speak of a mosque or tomb of Alexander in his city in the 9th and 10th centuries.[38]

The Attarine Mosque, in which the sarcophagus was found, is said to have been named for the 4th century Alexandrian Patriarch Athanasius. It is believed that this mosque was originally constructed soon after the Arab conquest (but reconstructed in AD1084) on the site of a late fourth century (AD370) church dedicated to St Athanasius. It was finally destroyed in 1830 (the Attarine mosque in present day Alexandria was built of modern materials on an adjacent site in the later 19th century). Many of the architectural components of the eleventh century mosque, notably its pillars, appear to have had a Late Roman origin.[39] This is pertinent, because there is literary evidence, which suggests that AD365, when Athanasius was the reigning Patriarch, is the most likely date for the destruction of Alexander's tomb in Alexandria. In that year, Alexandria was struck by an earthquake and tidal wave, which lifted ships onto roofs and destroyed many great buildings according to Ammianus Marcellinus.[40] A few years earlier Ammianus had mentioned the "splendid temple of the Genius" of Alexandria and had quoted Georgius, another Patriarch, referring to this building as a sepulcher.[41] Hogarth thought this a reference to Alexander's tomb and indeed Alexander is the only possible Genius of Alexandria with a tomb in the city.[42] However, a few decades later St John Chrysostom was able to state in one of his homilies, that Alexander's tomb was by then "unknown to his own

---

Braun & Hogenberg may have used other sources as well. According to Norwich 1997, page 380: "in the Hanse merchant Constantin van Lyskirchen of Cologne the editors found a willing agent, who supplied views of the towns of India, Asia, Africa, and Persia never portrayed before." According to Norwich, "Lyskirchen obtained these views from the manuscript produced by an unknown Portuguese illustrator." He goes on to say that "apart from these Portuguese views, some of the African illustrations were taken from military plans concerned with the expeditions of the Emperor Charles V in 1535 and 1541 to Tunis and Algeria." Braun's & Hogenberg's plates subsequently passed to Jansson, so the Alexandria map was republished in his famous Atlas of 1619.

[38] Ibn Abdel Hakim recorded a Mosque of Dulkarnein (i.e. Alexander) in the 9th century; Maçoudi (Massoudi) mentions a tomb of the prophet and king Eskender in the 10th century.
[39] Tkaczow 1993, Attarine Mosque, entry 25 in the Catalogue of Sites, pp.78-79.
[40] Ammianus Marcellinus, *Res Gestae* 26.10.15-19; Sozomenus, *Ecclesiastical History* 6.2.
[41] Ammianus Marcellinus, *Res Gestae* 22.11.7.
[42] Hogarth 1894-5, note 3 on p. 23.

A Candidate for the First Tomb of Alexander

people", by which he seems to have meant the coeval pagans of Alexandria.[43] The calamity of AD365 is therefore the prime suspect for the cause of the destruction and disappearance of the Alexandrian tomb, so it is interesting that the sarcophagus should have been recovered from the site of a church built shortly afterwards in memory of Athanasius.

It should perhaps be mentioned that there has been speculation by Achille Adriani, mostly published posthumously by Nicola Bonacasa,[44] that the Alabaster Tomb in the modern Latin Cemeteries lying within the eastern district of ancient Alexandria is part of one of the Alexandrian tombs of Alexander. This appears to be the antechamber of a high status tumulus tomb of the Ptolemaic period, since lesser Ptolemaic tombs have marbling resembling its interior faces painted onto their walls. It was found in pieces by Evaristo Breccia in 1907, but was reconstructed in situ in 1936. However, nothing else at the site seems to be connected with it. Although there is nothing in the research for this article which necessarily contradicts Adriani's theory, it must be noted that there is an absence of evidence specifically connecting the Alabaster Tomb with Alexander and there were many other royal tombs in Ptolemaic Alexandria.

The Alexander Romance

The semi-legendary Graeco-Egyptian account of Alexander's career known as the Alexander Romance has survived in a wide variety of manuscripts in numerous ancient languages, but it seems originally to have been compiled in Alexandria in the third century AD from a medley of earlier tales. The oldest Greek manuscript and also the early, accurate and almost complete Armenian translation seem to preserve many authentic details of the topography of Roman Egypt, including a few hints regarding the location of the Memphite tomb.

The Greek Alexander Romance has:-

They gave Ptolemy the task of transporting the embalmed body to Memphis in a lead coffin. So Ptolemy placed the body on a wagon and began the journey from Babylon to Egypt. When the people of Memphis heard he was coming, they came out to meet the body of Alexander and escorted it to Memphis. But the chief priest of the temple in Memphis said, "Do not bury him here, but in the city he founded in Rhakotis. Wherever his body rests, that city will be constantly troubled and shaken with wars and battles."[45]

The hint here is that the first tomb might have been associated with a temple. Although there were numerous temples in Memphis and Saqqara, the Serapeum seems to have been the most significant in the Graeco-Roman period.

In the Armenian Alexander Romance, there is an extra clue:-

---

[43] John Chrysostom, Homily XXVI on the second epistle of St Paul the Apostle to the Corinthians, circa AD400.
[44] Bonacasa 1991; Adriani 2000.
[45] Stoneman 1991, 3.34.

The Quest for the Tomb of Alexander by Andrew Chugg

And when they reached Pellas [Pelusium?], the Memnians came forth with trumpeters to meet at the altars in their accustomed way. And they took [Alexander's body] to Memphis near Sesonchousis, the world-conquering demigod.[46]

Sesonchousis was the subject of another Graeco-Egyptian Romance in a similar vein to the Alexander Romance. He is believed to be loosely based on a conflation of the twelfth dynasty pharaohs, Senusret I and Senusret III.[47] Interestingly, the latter built his pyramid complex near Dahshur at the southern end of the Saqqara necropolis, though there is a paucity of evidence as to whether he ever occupied it. Consequently, the Romance might be correct in suggesting that Alexander's first tomb was "near Sesonchousis". It should also be mentioned that Sesonchousis appears several times in the Alexander Romance, usually in association with manifestations of Serapis.

Notably, the Alexander Romance has an oracle for Alexander from Serapis, *You, a callow young man, shall subdue all the races of barbarian nations; and then, by dying and yet not dying, you shall come to me. Then the city of Alexandria… is to be your grave.*[48] Coming to Serapis reads like a euphemism for dying and indeed Serapis is believed to have derived from Osiris-Apis, a manifestation of Osiris, lord of the afterlife. However, this pretended prophecy of Serapis would have had a double meaning, if, as has been suggested, Alexander's first tomb was located at the Memphite temple of Serapis.

Even in Arrian, the most authoritative ancient history of Alexander, the King is reported to have sacrificed to Apis when he reached Memphis.[49] The connection between Alexander and this deity is ultimately historical.

Conclusions

The sarcophagus found in Alexandria by Napoleon's expedition in 1798 is linked in a wide range of mutually independent ways with the tomb of Alexander the Great:-

a) The citizens of Alexandria declared it to be Alexander's tomb in 1798.

b) Leo Africanus and Braun & Hogenberg referred to it as Alexander's tomb in the 16th century.

c) The mosque in which it was found was built on the site of a church dedicated to Athanasius, who was the Patriarch of Alexandria at the most probable time of the disappearance of Alexander's tomb.

---

[46] Wolohojian 1969, 283, p.158.
[47] See the excellent editorial notes for *P Oxy 3319*, Addendum to 2466: Sesonchosis Romance (fragment); see also Ian Shaw & Paul Nicholson, *British Museum Dictionary of Ancient Egypt*, London, 1995, under "Senusret".
[48] Wolohojian 1969, 93; Sesonchousis repeats part of the same oracle at Wolohojian 1969, 249.
[49] Arrian, Campaigns of Alexander, 3.1.4.

A Candidate for the First Tomb of Alexander

d) The fact that the sarcophagus was made for Nectanebo II has the effect of making it available to Ptolemy in a vacant state when he entombed Alexander at Memphis.

e) Ptolemy erected a magnificent, life-size semicircle of Greek poets and philosophers to guard the entrance to the temple built by Nectanebo II at the Memphite Serapeum; the central sculpture represents Homer, Alexander's favourite author.

f) The presence of the sarcophagus in Alexandria is explained by Pausanias' statement that Philadelphus moved Alexander's tomb to Alexandria.

g) The use of the sarcophagus potentially explains the legendary connections between Nectanebo II and Alexander in the Alexander Romance.

h) The Alexander Romance provides hints that Alexander's first tomb was at the temple of Serapis at Memphis.

If the attribution of the sarcophagus to Alexander is a forgery, then the perpetrators were either incredibly fortunate in their choice of such a well-connected relic or they effected an astonishingly sophisticated deception and must have known that the sarcophagus had been made for Nectanebo II. For the latter purpose they needed to be able to read hieroglyphs, but this form of writing ceased to be used within a few generations of the disappearance of Alexander's tomb in Alexandria.[50] It is difficult to conceive of a motive for such an early and elaborate forgery and to understand how it could have succeeded within living memory of the existence of the original. It is still harder to see how the semicircle of statues guarding the temple of Nectanebo II at Memphis could have been arranged to fit the scheme. Clearly, anyone who seeks to doubt the authenticity of the sarcophagus is forced to argue that many unlikely things happened. Conversely, there is no evidence that contradicts its use for Alexander.

If the sarcophagus was genuinely used by Ptolemy to accommodate Alexander's corpse, then it points to a first tomb of Alexander at the temple of Nectanebo II in the Memphite Serapeum. It has been shown that a chamber appended to this temple is of a suitable size and form to have housed the sarcophagus. This chamber was accessed via the entrance to the Nectanebo II temple as well as through a side entrance, guarded by four Greek sculptures of lions. It is reasonable to conclude that this chamber is a prime (and currently unique) candidate for the first tomb of Alexander the Great.

---

[50] The last hieroglyphic inscription was made at Philae on August 24th AD394. The closure of the temples by Theodosius at that time was evidently the immediate cause of its rapid and complete disappearance. Even Demotic graffiti does not occur after the middle of the fifth century.

Appendix D: The Tomb of Alexander in Alexandria

The following article by the author was first published in the American Journal of Ancient History, New Series 1.2 (2002) [2003], pp. 75-108.

Abstract

It is evident from references in the ancient literature that the tomb of Alexander in Alexandria ranked high among the most famous sights of antiquity. Accounts of visits by Julius Caesar, Octavian, Severus and Caracalla have survived, whilst Antony and Cleopatra, Germanicus and Caligula, Vespasian and Titus and Hadrian and Antinous must all have seen it. Yet little more than its fame is known today. In particular, the scattered references regarding its appearance and its location within the city have been believed to be hopelessly vague and contradictory and archaeological investigations have been severely hampered by the spread of the modern city to seal over the ancient remains in the later 19th century. However, in this article new lines of evidence are combined with a synthesis of the ancient descriptions to show that the Mausoleum of Alexander, built by Ptolemy Philopator in about 215BC, probably had the general form of a family of Hellenistic funerary monuments inspired by the Mausoleum at Halicarnassus. It is argued that it lay near the centre of ancient Alexandria within a huge walled enclosure called the Soma of Alexander. Finally, it is demonstrated that all the evidence is in fact consistent with the hypothesis that three sides of this enclosure were incorporated into the eastern section of the walls of medieval Alexandria. These walls were eventually demolished in the early 1880's. But a short section of a massive wall of the Ptolemaic era remains standing 200m north of the site of the Eastern or Rosetta Gate of the medieval city in the modern Shallalat Gardens, and a magnificent ancient portal is depicted in an aquatinted engraving of the Rosetta Gate dating from the late 18th century.

The Historical Record

In the autumn of 322BC the catafalque of Alexander the Great left Babylon, ostensibly carrying the King's corpse towards the royal cemetery at Aegae in Macedon.[1] However, Arrhidaeus, the commander of its escort, was secretly in league with Ptolemy with the intention of diverting the cortege to Egypt,[2] probably in accordance with Alexander's final request.[3] On reaching Syria the

---

[1] PAUSANIAS, 1.6.3.
[2] ARRIAN, *History of Events after Alexander*, summarised by PHOTIUS, 92 (e.g. Photius, Bibliothèque, Tome II, with French translation by R Henry, Paris, 1960, p.20-33); see also W J GORALSKI, *Arrian's Events After Alexander*, in *AncW*, 19, 1989, p 81-108.
[3] JUSTIN, 12.15; CURTIUS, 10.5.4; LUCIAN, *Dialogues of the Dead* XIII.

The Tomb of Alexander in Alexandria

procession turned south through Damascus and was met by Ptolemy, who had brought an army to secure its acquisition.[4]

Perdiccas, the Regent, was wintering with the Grand Army in Pisidia when he received news of the hijack. He sent his associates Attalus and Polemon with a contingent of cavalry in hot pursuit. They may have clashed with Ptolemy's troops, but were unsuccessful in retrieving Alexander's body.[5] Consequently, in the spring of 321BC Perdiccas brought the Grand Army down into Egypt with the intention of punishing Ptolemy, but the Regent was assassinated by his own officers, having twice failed to force the crossing of the Nile with considerable loss of life.[6]

Ptolemy celebrated his victory with the formal entombment of Alexander at Memphis to the accompaniment of splendid funeral games.[7] Although he subsequently transferred his capital to Alexandria, the Memphite tomb was left undisturbed for thirty or forty years.[8] Eventually, Ptolemy's son and successor, Philadelphus, moved the body into a tomb in Alexandria.[9]

In about 215BC the fourth Ptolemy, called Philopator, constructed a magnificent new mausoleum in the centre of Alexandria, in which he placed both the corpse of Alexander and the remains of his own ancestors.[10] At the same time he incorporated the cult of the first Ptolemy and his wife Berenice under the priesthood of Alexander.[11]

In 89BC the tenth Ptolemy substituted a glass casing for Alexander's original coffin of hammered gold fitted to the body.[12] He used the gold to pay his mercenaries, but he so infuriated the Alexandrian mob that they expelled him within the year. He was soon drowned in a sea fight near Cyprus.[13]

---

[4] DIODORUS SICULUS, 18.28.2-3.
[5] AELIAN, *Varia Historia* 12.64.
[6] DIODORUS SICULUS, 18.33-37; ARRIAN in PHOTIUS 92 [n. 2]; JUSTIN, 13.8; CORNELIUS NEPOS, *Eumenes 3 and 5*; PAUSANIAS, 1.6.3; PLUTARCH,*Eumenes 8.2*; STRABO, 17.1.8.
[7] PAUSANIAS, 1.6.3; DIODORUS SICULUS, 18.28.2.
[8] PAUSANIAS, 1.6.3; CURTIUS, 10.10.20; R STONEMAN (trans.), *The Greek Alexander Romance*, London, 1991, 3.34; F JACOBY, *FGrHist* 239, *The Parian Marble*; P M FRASER, *Ptolemaic Alexandria*, Oxford, 1972, Note 79 to Chapter 1 on p.31-33 of vol. 2, has argued (without presenting any specific evidence) that the corpse was moved to Alexandria after just 2 or 3 years, but this is flatly contradicted by Pausanias, who is corroborated by the failure of the Parian Marble chronology to mention the transfer up to its latest entries circa 300BC, despite its having reported the burial at Memphis in 321BC.
[9] PAUSANIAS, 1.7.1.
[10] ZENOBIUS, *Proverbia* 3.94; this work, generally regarded as of Hadrianic date, is (according to Suidas) a collection of the "proverbs" of Didymus and Tarrhaeus: Didymus is presumably Arius Didymus, the Alexandrian scholar who accompanied Octavian on his visit to Alexander's tomb (PLUTARCH, *Antony 80*) – its authority is therefore probably first rate.
[11] E BEVAN, *A History of Egypt under the Ptolemaic Dynasty*, London, 1927, p.231.
[12] DIODORUS SICULUS, 18.26.3.
[13] STRABO, *Geography* 17.1.8.

The Quest for the Tomb of Alexander by Andrew Chugg

Caesar visited the tomb in 48BC[14] and Octavian broke a piece of the nose off, whilst viewing the mummified corpse in 30BC.[15] Germanicus almost certainly paid his respects during his stay in Alexandria in AD19, possibly accompanied by his seven year old son Gaius Caligula.[16] Vespasian, his son Titus, and later Hadrian are also likely visitors. But the next explicit historical reference to an imperial visit records that in AD200 of Septimius Severus, who was appalled by the ease of access and therefore ordered that the burial chamber be sealed up.[17] Severus' son, Caracalla, became the last recorded visitor in AD215, leaving his cloak, belts and jewellery in honour of his hero.[18]

Some have argued that the tomb was destroyed in one of the several episodes of warfare in which Alexandria became embroiled in the later part of the 3rd century AD. However, there is a mention by Ammianus Marcellinus of a splendid temple and tomb of the Genius of Alexandria existing in AD361, which is probably a reference to Alexander's sepulcher.[19] If so, the mausoleum may well have been destroyed by the earthquake and tidal wave which devastated Alexandria in AD365,[20] since John Chrysostom claimed that the tomb was unknown to Alexander's own people in a sermon given some time around AD400.[21] Even if it survived that disaster, it is most unlikely to have eluded the depredations of the Christian mob following Theodosius' edicts against paganism in AD391.

The Mausoleum of Alexander

This study will focus on the second Alexandrian tomb built around 215BC, since there are no detailed historical references to the tomb built by Philadelphus. However, it is pertinent to note that the 'Alabaster Tomb' discovered in pieces in the Latin Cemeteries by Evaristo Breccia[22] in 1907 seems

---

[14] LUCAN, *Pharsalia* 10, lines 14-20.
[15] SUETONIUS, *Lives of the Caesars, Augustus* 2.18; DIO CASSIUS, *Roman History* 51.16.5.
[16] TACITUS, *Annals* 2.59-61; SUETONIUS, *Lives of the Caesars, Gaius Caligula* 4.10; Caligula later dressed up in Alexander's cuirass, presumably fetched from the Tomb - DIO CASSIUS, *Roman History* 59.17.3.
[17] DIO CASSIUS, *Roman History (Epitome)* 76.13.
[18] The visit is recounted by HERODIAN, 4.8.6 to 4.9.8 and by DIO CASSIUS, 78.2278.23, though only the former mentions the Soma visit. The visit is also mentioned by John of Antioch (7th century, reproduced in C Müllerus, Fragmenta Historicorum Graecorum, Paris, 1868, vol. 4, p. 590), but his account seems to have been derived from Herodian.
[19] AMMIANUS MARCELLINUS, *Res Gestae* 22.11.7.
[20] AMMIANUS MARCELLINUS, *Res Gestae* 26.10.15-19; SOZOMENUS, *Ecclesiastical History* 6.2.
[21] JOHN CHRYSOSTOM, *Homily XXVI on the second epistle of St Paul the Apostle to the Corinthians* (Patrologia Graeca, vol. 61. p. 581): " For, tell me, where is the tomb of Alexander? show it me and tell me the day on which he died... his tomb even his own people know not, but This Man's the very barbarians know." (trans. J H Parker, 1848) – In this context Alexander's "own people" would appear to mean the contemporary pagans of Alexandria.
[22] E BRECCIA, *Rapport du Musée Gréco-Romain*, Alexandria, 1907.

The Tomb of Alexander in Alexandria

to be the antechamber of a high status, early Ptolemaic, tumulus tomb related to Macedonian archetypes and Achille Adriani has argued that it may be Alexander's.[23] Nevertheless, there seems to be no specific evidence to link it with the King, despite recent re-excavations, and numerous other high status tombs must have been built in Alexandria in the early Ptolemaic era. In the unlikely event that it is Alexander's, then it is more probably the tomb built by Philadelphus than part of the mausoleum erected by Philopator, for an earlier date would better connect it with its Macedonian antecedents and (it will be argued) its location is too far east of the central crossroads of the ancient city. It is, however, worth observing in this connection that the artificial conical hill, called the Paneion by Strabo,[24] resembled a high status Macedonian tumulus tomb, such as those at Aegae.

Zenobius states simply that the tomb created by Philopator was a memorial building (μνῆμα οἰκοδομήσας) erected in the centre of Alexandria.[25] Fortunately, a more elaborate description has come down to us in two passages from the poet Lucan's epic of the Roman civil war, the Pharsalia:-

Cum tibi sacrato Macedon seruitur in antro

Et regem cineres extructo monte quiescant,

Cum Ptolemaeorum manes seriemque pudendam

Pyramides claudant indignaque Mausolea,...[26]

...Tum uoltu semper celante pauorem

Intrepidus superum sedes et templa uetusti

Numinis antiquas Macetum testantia uires

Circumit, et nulla captus dulcedine rerum,

Non auro cultuque deum, non moenibus urbis,

Effossum tumulis cupide descendit in antrum.

Illic Pellaei proles uaesana Philippi,...[27]

---

[23] N BONACASA, *Un Inedito di Achille Adriani Sulla Tomba di Alessandro* in *Studi Miscellanei, Seminario di Archaeologia e Storia dell Arte... dell Universita di Roma*, Vol. 28, Rome, 1991; A ADRIANI (ed. N BONACASA), *La Tomba di Alessandro*, Rome, 2000.
[24] STRABO, 17.1.10.
[25] ZENOBIUS, *Proverbia* 3.94.
[26] LUCAN, *Pharsalia* 8, 694-697;
'Though you preserve the Macedonian (Alexander) in a consecrated grotto
and the ashes of the kings rest beneath a loftily constructed edifice,
though the dead Ptolemies and their unworthy dynasty
are covered by unseemly pyramids and Mausoleums,...'
(trans. the author)
[27] LUCAN, *Pharsalia* 10, 14-20;
'Then, with looks that ever masked his fears,

The Quest for the Tomb of Alexander by Andrew Chugg

On analysing these words, written during the reign of Nero, a number of architectural details of the mausoleum of Alexander may be revealed. Lucan speaks of a grotto hewn out of the bedrock to form a chamber in which Alexander's body was preserved. Since Caesar **descended** into this chamber, it can hardly be doubted that it was subterranean. There is anyway a good practical reason to keep a mummified body below ground: the thermal insulation of the soil helps to maintain a cool ambient temperature in hot weather, hence aiding the preservation of the corpse.

Presumably the burial chamber lay beneath the mausoleum building, which is described as a loftily constructed edifice. The actual words, *extructo monte*, have sometimes misleadingly been translated as a 'man made mountain'. This is incorrect because *mons* translates equally as a crag or a tower of rock in classical Latin[28] and it was often used to indicate a tall, and massive building. In particular, there is no sense of a huge irregular conical pile with sloping sides, which is the dominant modern concept of a mountain. This is not a subtle distinction: to Lucan it would have been as natural to refer to the Canary Wharf tower as a mountain as to have termed the Great Pyramid at Giza mountainous. There is a good example of this usage in Cicero's oration Against Piso, where he describes a large country villa as a mountain: *ad hunc Tusculani montem exstruendem*.[29] It would be an engineering absurdity to imagine this villa built with sloping walls. It is anyway clear from the context that Cicero is merely emphasising the hugeness and tallness of the building. Lucan would, of course, have been familiar with the works of Cicero.

However, the most telling details come in the line, which states that the tombs of the kings were covered by pyramids and mausoleums. Given the Egyptian context, it is hardly surprising that many have jumped to the conclusion that Alexander's tomb must have imitated the pharaonic pyramids at Giza. This inference has been reinforced by the observation that Alexander's Last Plans had envisaged the erection of a mound comparable with the Great Pyramid over his father's grave at Aegae[30] and also by the fact that some small-scale pyramidal tombs are known from the period. The usual example is the

---

Undaunted, he [Julius Caesar] visited the temples of the gods and the ancient shrines
of divinity, which attest the former might of Macedon.
No thing of beauty attracted him,
neither the gold and ornaments of the gods, nor the city walls;
but in eager haste he went down into the grotto hewn out for a tomb.
There lies the mad son of Philip of Pella,...'
(trans. J. D. Duff, Loeb Classical Library, but with "vault" changed to the more literal "grotto")
[28] The Oxford Latin Dictionary gives, "A towering heap or mass... a huge rock or boulder" for *mons*.
[29] CICERO, *In Calpurnium Pisonem Oratio*, XXI.
[30] DIODORUS SICULUS, 18.4.5.

monument of Cestius at Rome, which probably dates from the reign of Augustus.[31]

Nevertheless, the literal sense of Lucan's words is that the tombs comprised a tall and massive mausoleum building having a pyramidal roof and constructed over a burial chamber. In fact this is one of the earliest uses of the word 'mausoleum' to describe a monumental tomb; early enough that a direct reference to the archetypal Mausoleum at Halicarnassus[32] (Figure 4.4) might be implied. Although this Wonder was almost completely destroyed by a medieval earthquake and stone-robbing by the Knights of St John, surviving descriptions make it clear that it was surmounted by a pyramidal roof. Like the tomb Lucan describes, it was built over an underground burial chamber (which is the only part that survives today) and was of course exceptionally massive and tall by ancient standards. Furthermore, at the time Philopator constructed the Soma Mausoleum in Alexandria, Halicarnassus was part of the Ptolemaic empire.[33]

But how authentic is Lucan's knowledge of Alexandria likely to have been? Suetonius mentions that the poet was at Athens when Nero summoned him back to Rome,[34] so it is conceivable that he had himself visited Alexandria. The sea crossing would have taken less than a week each way in good conditions[35] and it would have been useful research for the Pharsalia. However it is known that Lucan's uncle Seneca had seen Egypt,[36] so the poet's information was probably quite reliable, whether or not he was himself an eyewitness.

Two other ancient authors have provided hints of the architecture of the mausoleum. Suetonius refers to the burial chamber as a *penetrale* in describing how Alexander's corpse was brought out to be venerated by Octavian.[37] This translates as something like an inner sanctuary, but it also conveys a sense of 'the innermost or secret parts, depths, recesses',[38] so it would be particularly apt for a subterranean burial chamber accessed via a passage. Secondly, Ammianus Marcellinus mentions a tomb within a splendid temple of the Genius of Alexandria (*speciosum Genii templum*), which is a likely reference to Alexander's mausoleum.[39] This terminology is highly appropriate for a building related to

---

[31] D BORBONUS, in L Haselberger et al., *Mapping Augustan Rome*, JRA Supp. 50 (Portsmouth, RI 2002) p. 223.
[32] K JEPPESEN, *Tot Operum Opus, Ergebnisse der Dänischen Forschungen zum Maussolleion von Halikarnass seit 1966* in *JdI* 107, 1992, p. 59-102.
[33] E.g. A K BOWMAN, *Egypt after the Pharaohs*, London, 1986, Ch. 2, Fig. 2, p.28, map of Ptolemaic overseas possessions.
[34] SUETONIUS, *Lives of Illustrious Men, On Poets, Life of Lucan*.
[35] L CASSON, *Speed under Sail of Ancient Ships*, TAPhA 82 (1951) p. 136-148.
[36] H THIERSCH, *Die alexandrinische Königsnekropole*, *JdI* 25, 1910, p. 55-97 (p. 68-69 for the discussion of Lucan).
[37] SUETONIUS, *The Deified Augustus* 18.
[38] Oxford Latin Dictionary, s.v. penetrale.
[39] AMMIANUS MARCELLINUS, *Res Gestae* 22.11.7.

the Mausoleum of Halicarnassus, but rather less consistent with a simple pyramid.

It may also be added that there is a strong parallel between the context of the Mausoleum at Halicarnassus and that of Alexander's tomb, for both were situated at the geographical centre of a walled port city with a royal palace on a headland.

There exist a mere handful of ancient port scenes, which have been proposed as representations of Alexandria. The most widely published are probably the Roman lamps with depictions of the harbour of a large classical city often with fishermen and sometimes with a causeway built on arches, which resembles the Alexandrian Heptastadion. However, Donald Bailey has argued that some (especially those which seem to include a tall building with a pyramidal roof in their backgrounds) are forgeries and that others, though genuine, are based on Carthage and Ostia rather than Alexandria.[40] His arguments, which are founded in style and provenance, do not seem to be conclusive, but it has to be accepted that he has established a reasonable case against the Alexandrian hypothesis. A fragment of engraved glass from Roman Africa[41] and a mosaic from Toledo,[42] in which Alberto Balil has seen possible images of Alexander's tomb, have also to be regarded as doubtful.

Perhaps the least dubious candidate for a representation of the mausoleum is a tall tower with a pointed roof on the 4th century sarcophagus of Julius Philosyrius (Figure 4.7). The three-stage lighthouse depicted at the far right might seem conclusive evidence that this really is Alexandria, but this object hails from Ostia,[43] which is known to have had a lighthouse that resembled a smaller-scale Pharos. Nonetheless, the palm tree pictured at the extreme left appears on the same side of Alexandria in other undisputed representations of the city and the column at the centre could be Pompey's Pillar, erected by Diocletian at the close of the third century. Yet even this reasoning is relatively problematical. No truly convincing representation of Alexander's tomb has ever been recognised in surviving examples of ancient art.

Such a famous building as Alexander's mausoleum would be expected, however, to have spawned numerous lesser imitations, some of which should still exist today. At Alexandria itself almost nothing of the ancient city remains above ground: most of the stone was robbed in the medieval period. Even so, several Ptolemaic funerary monuments standing up to 3 metres tall with stepped bases

---

[40] D M BAILEY, *Alexandria, Carthage and Ostia* in *Alessandria e il mondo ellenistico-romano, Studi in onore di Achille Adriani*, 2, Rome, 1984, p. 265-272.
[41] A BALIL, *Una nueva representación de la tumba de Alejandro* in *ArchEspArq* 35, 1962, p.102-103; J FERRON and M PINARD, *Cahiers de Byrsa 8*, Paris, 1958-1959, p.103-109.
[42] A BALIL, *Monumentos Alejandrinos y Paisajes Egipcios en un Mosaico Romano de Toledo (España)* in *Alessandria e il Mondo Ellenistico-Romano, Studi in Onore di Achille Adriani* 3, Rome, 1984, p. 433-439.
[43] C PICARD, *Quelques représentations nouvelles du Phare d'Alexandrie* in *BCH* 76, 1952, p. 61-95 (specifically p. 91-92 on the sarcophagus of Julius Philosyrius).

The Tomb of Alexander in Alexandria

and stepped pyramidal top-sections (Figure 4.5) have been discovered in the Chatby necropolis at the NE corner of the ancient city.[44] The same basic form has also survived in numerous examples of monumental tombs of the Hellenistic and early Roman period, especially within the Ptolemaic empire and the adjacent territories of Syria, Ionia and North Africa. The N_{180} tomb at Cyrene (Figure 4.6 - left), the elegant mausoleums at Hermel and Kalat Fakra (Figure 4.6 – right) in Lebanon and the 'Tomb of Zachariah' in Jerusalem are all good examples. In fact this is the most common general type for high status tombs of the period in these areas, so it should still be the most probable form for Alexander's tomb even without Lucan's description.[45]

In summary, there are good reasons to trust the accuracy of Lucan's words, in which case there are only two possible models for the tomb built by Philopator: either a large (therefore solid) Egyptian-style pyramid in imitation of Old Kingdom practice or a tall and elegant temple structure echoing the magnificent Mausoleum at Halicarnassus. The Egyptian context, too literal a translation of the word *mons* and a simple lack of awareness of the aptness of the Mausoleum model have focussed most speculation upon the former. However, the latter form is actually far more probable, because:-

It fits the descriptions more precisely (explaining, for example, why Lucan insists upon 'Mausoleums **and** pyramids' and precisely why height and splendour were so significant).

It is a far more common form for monumental tombs of the Hellenistic age in the Eastern Mediterranean than a simple pyramid: no sizable pyramid is known for this period, whereas numerous lofty temple-tombs with pyramidal roofs still exist, especially within the Ptolemaic empire.

It is much easier to explain the sudden destruction and disappearance of a mausoleum than a solid pyramid due to warfare or natural forces.

The Soma of Alexander

There has been some understandable confusion between references to the mausoleum building and references to the huge walled enclosure within which it stood. This dichotomy derives from the ancient authors. The relatively early eyewitness accounts of Diodorus and Strabo refer to the entire enclosure as Alexander's tomb[46] and seem thereby to regard the enclosure as the most impressive feature, somehow surpassing Philopator's mausoleum in magnificence. Conversely, the later accounts of Suetonius, Zenobius, Dio

---

[44] A ADRIANI, *Repertorio d'Arte del'Egitto Greco-Romano, Serie C,* Palermo, 1963-1966, Vol. I-II, p.117-118, Plate 39.
[45] J FEDAK, *Monumental Tombs of the Hellenistic Age,* Toronto, 1990, p. 128, 142-144, 148-150.
[46] STRABO, 17.1.8; DIODORUS SICULUS, 18.28.2.

The Quest for the Tomb of Alexander by Andrew Chugg

Cassius and Herodian return the focus to the burial chamber and the actual mausoleum building.[47]

All the manuscripts of Strabo stated that the enclosure was called the Soma (i.e. the Body) and this name is confirmed by the older manuscripts of the Alexander Romance, which speak of a tomb in a sacred place called 'Body of Alexander'.[48] Since both Strabo and the redactor of the Alexander Romance lived in Alexandria whilst the tomb still existed, their accounts must be independent of one another on this point, so it is beyond reasonable doubt that this name is correct. The practice of changing Σῶμα to Σῆμα (i.e. the Tomb) as perpetrated by modern editors seems to have arisen because Zenobius, in referring explicitly to the mausoleum, specified that its name was the Σῆμα.[49] However, it is possible that this is a transcriptional error by some ancient copyist or else that the mausoleum really was called 'The Tomb', whilst its enclosure was called 'The Body'. Since it is relatively unlikely that anyone would have changed Σῆμα to Σῶμα and since the very fact that three ancient sources bother to specify the name suggests that it was distinctive rather than bland, there is no sound basis to doubt the fact that the enclosure was indeed called the Soma of Alexander.

That the Soma was a walled enclosure is explicit in Strabo's word περίβολος. That it was truly enormous and magnificent is clear from Diodorus' assertion that Ptolemy constructed a sacred precinct worthy of the glory of Alexander in size and construction:-

κατεσκεύασεν οὖν τέμενος κατὰ τὸ μέγεθος καὶ κατὰ τὴν κατασκευὴν τῆς Ἀλεξάνδρου δόξης ἄξιον

It is possible to gain some insight into the significance of this statement by considering contemporary parallels. The enclosure of the Mausoleum at Halicarnassus measured 105m by 242.5m. As the tomb of a far more important king in a much larger city, the Soma cannot reasonably have been smaller than this and should have been far larger. Memphis would have been an even more direct source of inspiration for Alexandria's architects, especially since its layout was dominated by two somewhat irregular quadrilateral temple enclosures,

---

[47] SUETONIUS, *Augustus* 18.1 *penetrali*; ZENOBIUS, Proverbia 3.94 μνῆμα οἰκοδομήσας; DIO CASSIUS 51.16.5 μνημεῖον; HERODIAN 4.8.6-7 μνῆμα.

[48] This is missing from the A manuscript of the Alexander Romance, but appears in the early and faithful Armenian version (A M WOLOHOJIAN (trans.), *The Romance of Alexander the Great by Pseudo-Callisthenes*, Columbia University Press, 1969); some later versions, such as the Syriac, change the name to the Tomb of Alexander, but this is just another example of the "correction" made by modern editors of Strabo.

[49] John Chrysostom also uses the word 'sema', but only in its ordinary sense and not as a name; conversely, Dio Cassius uses the word 'soma', but appears to mean the mummified corpse rather than the enclosure.

The Tomb of Alexander in Alexandria

which offer a close parallel to the descriptions of the Soma.[50] These enclosures were roughly 500m square (Figure 3.5) and were intersected almost at right-angles by several major streets of the city (Figure 9.4). This is the best model for the style and scale to be anticipated in the sacred precincts of Alexandria. Straightforward as this reasoning may seem, it nevertheless turns out to be a relatively novel perspective on the problem. Previous investigations have generally sought for the remains of a structure of much smaller dimensions with correspondingly little success.

Further support for a very large enclosure is provided by Achilles Tatius, who gives a description of Alexandria in his novel, *Clitophon and Leucippe*, which probably dates to the third century AD[51]:-

After a voyage lasting three days we arrived at Alexandria. I entered by the Sun Gate, as it is called, and was instantly struck by the splendid beauty of the city, which filled my eyes with delight. From the Sun Gate to the Moon Gate – these are the guardian divinities of the entrances – led a straight double row of columns, about the middle of which lies the open part of the town, and in it so many streets that walking in them you would fancy yourself abroad while still at home. Going a few stades further, I came to the place/district called after Alexander, where I saw a second/another town; the splendour of this was cut into squares, for there was a row of columns intersected by another as long at right angles.

The late seventh century writer John of Nikiu stated that Antoninus Pius had built the Sun Gate at the east and the Moon Gate at the west.[52] The road that ran between them was the principal street of ancient Alexandria and is usually known as Canopic Way. Strabo mentions a second major highway, which intersected Canopic Way at right angles at the centre of the city.[53] It is quite clear, therefore, that Achilles Tatius is imagining his characters entering Alexandria at the eastern gate and walking westwards along Canopic Way to a row of columns intersecting at right angles, presumably the central crossroads. However, he says this crossroads lay in another town, which was a place or district called after Alexander. By implication this second town was enclosed by walls, since he speaks initially of the open part of the town. This explicit association with Alexander, the location at the centre of the city (which agrees with Zenobius), its lying within an enclosure and the fact that the size was sufficient to be regarded as another town all point to this being the Soma.

Nor is this the only ancient reference to a district of Alexandria named after Alexander. The Alexander Romance, although in general a hopelessly garbled

---

[50] D, *The Survey of Memphis*, Egypt Exploration Society, London, 1985, Figures 60-63.
[51] ACHILLES TATIUS, *Clitophon and Leucippe* 5.1:' (trans. S Gaselee, Loeb Classical Library, except for substitution of "place/district" for "quarter" and coupling of "another" with "second" by the author).
[52] R H CHARLES (trans.), *The Chronicle of John, Coptic Bishop of Nikiu c.690 AD*, London, 1916, Ch. 74.6, p.56; see also A BUTLER, *The Arab Conquest of Egypt and the Last Thirty Years of the Roman Dominion*, 2nd ed. Oxford, 1902, Ch. XXIV, footnote 5 on p.369.
[53] STRABO, 17.1.8.

The Quest for the Tomb of Alexander by Andrew Chugg

and semi-legendary account of the King's career, is nevertheless recognised as good on Alexandrian topography in the Roman period, since it was very probably compiled by a third century resident of the city.[54] In particular the Romance mentions the division of the city into five quarters, A, B, Γ, Δ, E, a detail which is corroborated by Philo.[55] However, the Romance also tells us what the letters stood for and A was for Alexander.[56]

Furthermore, the concept of one or two large walled enclosures within Alexandria is strikingly confirmed by a comment attributed to the 9th century Arab writer, Ibn Abdel Hakim:-

Alexandria consists of three towns, one beside the other, each surrounded by its own wall. All three are enclosed by an outer, fortified wall.[57]

Nevertheless, all this would remain of casual interest were it not for the fact that there is also substantial tangible evidence from the modern era for a walled enclosure, on a slightly larger scale than those at Memphis, located in the vicinity of the centre of ancient Alexandria. In order to understand this evidence, it is first of all necessary to appreciate that archaeological investigations have substantially revealed the street plan of the ancient city and confirmed the testimony of ancient writers concerning its size and extent. Of central importance is the map compiled by Mahmoud Bey in 1865-66 on the basis of very extensive excavations carried out on the orders of the Khedive Ismail at the request of Napoleon III of France (Figure 4.2). The basis of the map is documented in an accompanying book.[58]

The location of the Soma on Mahmoud's map (off street R5) is based on the legend, current in the latter part of the 19th century and persisting in tourist guides to this day, that Alexander's tomb lay beneath the Nabi Daniel Mosque. There is no good reason to doubt that this belief was inspired by an interpreter (or dragoman) at the Russian embassy in Alexandria in 1850 called Ambrose Schilizzi. There are some medieval Arab tombs beneath the mosque, which was itself built by Mohammad Ali in 1823. Beneath them there is a large Roman

---

[54] P M FRASER, *Ptolemaic Alexandria*, Oxford, 1972, vol. 1, p. 4, states that, 'Whatever the author [of the Romance] has to tell us regarding the city, and particularly items of topography, must be examined with care, even with respect.'
[55] PHILO, *In Flaccum* 55.
[56] PSEUDO-CALLISTHENES, *The Romance of Alexander*, e.g. R STONEMAN (trans.), *The Greek Alexander Romance*, Book I, 32; Alpha (for Ἀλεξάνδρος = "Alexander"), Beta (for βασιλεύς = "king"), Gamma (for γένος = "descendant"), Delta (for Δίος = "Zeus") and Epsilon (for ἔκτισε πόλιν ἀείμνηστον = "founded an ever-memorable city"). P M FRASER, *Ptolemaic Alexandria*, Vol. 1, Ch. 1, p. 31, notes several mentions by ancient writers of an *Akra* or Citadel which lay adjacent to the palaces and which may also be a descriptive means of referring to the Soma Enclosure.
[57] Quoted by A BUTLER, *The Arab Invasion of Egypt*, Ch. XXIV, p.370; E BRECCIA, *Alexandrea ad Aegyptum*, Bergamo, 1922, p. 70: the latter seems to err in stating that Hakim was quoting Sujuti.
[58] MAHMOUD BEY EL-FALAKI, *L'Antique Alexandrie*, Copenhagen, 1872, p. 12-103.

The Tomb of Alexander in Alexandria

water cistern. Schilizzi said he saw the glass sarcophagus of Alexander through a chink in a decaying wooden door in the vicinity of this cistern.[59] Schilizzi's tale is now generally accepted to have been a fanciful lie. He often used to guide tourists around the town for additional income and seems to have thought this a good way to encourage business. We can be confident it was a lie, because he said that he saw papyri strewn around the coffin. This was inspired by the fact that Septimius Severus may have sealed up some books of Egyptian magic lore in the tomb when he visited it in AD200 (this is in Dio Cassius' account of Severus' visit, so Schilizzi could easily have heard or read of it). In the context of the damp atmosphere near a water cistern and close to the water table it is virtually impossible that papyri should have survived 1650 years, because of capillary action (no papyri have ever been found in Alexandria to my knowledge[60]). Unsurprisingly, numerous and extensive excavations in the vicinity of the Nabi Daniel mosque have failed to reveal the least trace of a monumental Ptolemaic entombment.[61]

Shortly after Mahmoud's investigations the modern city spread to seal over the ruin field, significantly curtailing the scope of subsequent investigations. However, except in a few limited instances, more recent archaeological investigation has tended to uphold the general accuracy of Mahmoud's work and his city matches the dimensions given by ancient writers more exactly than any other reconstruction.[62]

Of specific relevance to the issue of the location of the Soma enclosure is the identification of the central crossroads. The line of Canopic Way, the principal east-west axis, is incontrovertibly established (L1 on Mahmoud's map). But the identification of the main north-south boulevard remains in dispute, since

---

[59] The principal source on the Nabi Daniel legend is A M DE ZOGHEB, *Etudes sur l'Ancienne Alexandrie*, Paris, 1910, Chapter: *Le Tombeau de Alexandre le Grand*.
[60] E G TURNER, Greek Papyri, Oxford, 1968, p. 43 states that, 'The site of Alexandria has provided no papyri.'
[61] The area has been excavated by Mahmoud Bey, Evaristo Breccia, Achille Adriani and Rodziewicz' Polish team inter alia; see, for example, P FRASER, *Ptolemaic Alexandria*, Notes 88 and 90 to Chapter 1 on p. 41 of vol. 2 and M RODZIEWICZ, *Les habitations romaines tardives d'Alexandrie*, Centre d'Archéologie Mediterranéenne de l'Académie Polonaise des Sciences, Warsaw, 1984 (the entire book is an account of the complete excavation of Kom el-Dikka, the hill behind the Nabi Daniel mosque, which turned out to be a spoil heap from the Arab period glass and pottery industries concealing the ruins of Late Roman premises).
[62] On the accuracy of Mahmoud's map see especially J-L ARNAUD, *Nouvelles Données sur la Topographie d'Alexandrie Antique* in BCH 121, 1997, p. 721-737; on the dimensions of ancient Alexandria DIODORUS SICULUS, 17.52 gives 40 stades in length; STRABO, 17.1.8 gives 30 stades long by 7 or 8 in width; PHILO, *In Flaccum* 92 gives 10 stades wide; CURTIUS, 4.8.2 gives an 80 stade circumference; JOSEPHUS, *Bell. Jud.* 2.16.4 gives 30 stades long by 10 stades wide; PLINY THE ELDER, 5.11 gives a 15 Roman mile circumference; PSEUDO-CALLISTHENES, *Alexander Romance* (Latin version – i.31.10) gives 16 stades wide; STEPHANUS BYZANTINUS, under "*Alexandreia*" gives 34 stades long by 8 wide with a 110 stade circumference; Mahmoud Bey, *L'Antique Alexandrie*, p. 18-26, calculates 31 Alexandrian stades long by 10 wide with a 96 stade circumference.

Mahmoud's evidence for it being the street labelled R1 is not conclusive.[63] However, there is no persuasive evidence for any other street possessing this status[64] and R1 is reasonably central on Mahmoud's plan and it leads to the Royal Palaces on the Lochias Promontory at its northern end. As a working hypothesis it is reasonable to follow Mahmoud in supposing that the intersection of L1 with R1 was indeed the principal crossroads mentioned by Strabo and Achilles Tatius.

Strabo also states that the Soma enclosure was a part of the Royal District of the city,[65] which must mean that it was adjacent to the palaces, which ran from Lochias westwards about a third of the way to the Heptastadion. To discover the Soma we should therefore be looking for an enclosure around half a kilometre square which encompasses the R1 – L1 intersection and borders the palaces on its northern edge. It is gratifying to learn that we need look no further than Mahmoud's map to locate evidence of just such a structure, for Mahmoud marked in the precise course of the walls of medieval Alexandria, and in their eastern sector they form three sides of the sort of enclosure which we seek.

Arab sources and inscriptions[66] attribute the medieval walls of Alexandria to the ninth century Governor of Egypt, Sultan Ahmed Ibn Tulun, and there is no reason to doubt the basic truth of this testimony. A few fragments still exist, which are built of stone robbed from the ancient city. However, it is of course more than likely that Ibn Tulun incorporated sections of older walls in his scheme where practicable. That the eastern sections of the Tulunid walls do

---

[63] Mahmoud Bey, *L'Antique Alexandrie*, p.23, found R1 to be twice as wide as most of the other major streets, but he describes it as having had two carriageways with different surfaces; his identification may also have been influenced by the large numbers of columns he found lining the southern branch of R1 (shown in the version of Mahmoud's map published by H KIEPERT, *Zur Topographie der alten Alexandria: Nach Mahmud Begs Entdeckungen* in *Zeitschrift der Gesellschaft für Erdkunde zu Berlin 7*, 1872, p. 1-15); Mahmoud's identification has been disputed most notably by F NOACK, *Neue Untersuchungen in Alex.* in *Mittheilungen des Kaiserlich Deutschen Archaeologischen Instituts - Athenische Abtheilung*, 1900, p.215-279.

[64] Some modern maps have suggested R5, but this seems to rely on the spurious association of the Nabi Daniel mosque with Alexander's tomb; the source seems usually to be E BRECCIA, *Alexandrea ad Aegyptum*, Bergamo, 1922, p. 99, who in the words of J-Y EMPEREUR, *Alexandria Rediscovered*, London, 1998, p. 149, had 'lost his usual critical acumen' in accepting the 19th century Nabi Daniel legend. It is one of the numerous ironies of this subject that some modern writers have cited the identification of R5 being the principal transverse street as the conclusive reason to believe the Nabi Daniel legend, without realising that their argument is essentially circular.

[65] STRABO, 17.1.8, also mentions that this Royal District comprised between a quarter and a third of the entire city: a very large Soma enclosure south of the palaces is important in achieving this total size, because the palaces were hemmed in on the east and west by other districts of the city; e.g. JOSEPHUS, *Contra Apion* 2.33 places the Jewish Quarter (Delta) on the coast to the east of Lochias.

[66] J-Y EMPEREUR, *Alexandria Rediscovered*, London, 1998, p.49; H. DE VAUJANY, Recherches sur les Anciens Monuments Situé Sur le Grand-Port d'Alexandrie, Alexandria, 1888, Tour d'Ahmed Dite des Romains, p.80-82.

The Tomb of Alexander in Alexandria

indeed follow the line of an ancient walled enclosure is supported by numerous lines of evidence:-

a) The Tulunid walls respected the layout of the ancient city as can be seen in Mahmoud's plan, which indicates that the Tulunid fortifications ran along the line of the major ancient streets in their southern and eastern courses.

b) The ruins of the Tulunid walls were heavily modified in the 1820's and largely destroyed in the early 1880's, but Napoleon's scholars and engineers surveyed them and drew them with great accuracy for the Description de l'Egypte in 1798. In their plan of Alexandria[67] (Figure 8.2) it can be seen that these defences had a double circuit (i.e. an inner and outer wall), which was almost complete in the eastern sector at that time (Figure 9.6). Richard Pococke paced their entire length in 1737 and later commented particularly on the discrepancy in style between the inner and outer walls: 'The outer walls around the old city are very beautifully built of hewn stone, and seem to be antient (sic); all the arches being true, and the workmanship very good... The inner walls of the old city, which seem to be of the middle ages, are much stronger and higher than the others and defended by large high towers.'[68]

c) There is a curious zig-zag feature in a short oblique section of the outer Tulunid wall in the Napoleonic map at precisely the point where Mahmoud Bey's street R3 intersected it on the northern side (see Figures 4.2 and 9.6). Especially in view of its location this looks very much like a vestige of a gateway, but it is not echoed in the inner circuit. If newly constructed Arab walls had merely accommodated the passage of an ancient street, then the gateway should exist in both the inner and outer circuits. If it was only present in the outer wall, then the outer circuit would necessarily be more ancient than the inner.

d) The engravings of some of the towers of the Tulunid defences in three plates of the Description de l'Egypte[69] show a mixture of somewhat irregular stonework with pointed arches and stones of modest size contrasting with regular, precise masonry of massive blocks with semicircular arches (Figure 9.5). The latter closely matches the

---

[67] C L F PANCKOUCKE (publisher of 2nd edition), *Description de l'Egypte, Etat Moderne*, Paris, 1820-1829, plate 84 in Volume II. It should be noted that this is perhaps the only reliable plan of the walls of the old city; earlier surveys seem generally to have been imprecise, whilst Mohammed Ali's reconstruction of parts of the circuit in the early 19th century renders even Mahmoud Bey's plan questionable at the most detailed level. This reconstruction was performed in 1826 by Galice Bey (see J-Y EMPEREUR, *Alexandria Rediscovered*, p.50).

[68] R POCOCKE, *Description of the East*, London, 1743, vol. 1, p.3; his plan of Alexandria shows the double wall circuit complete on all but the seaward stretches.

[69] C L F PANCKOUCKE (publisher of 2nd edition), *Description de l'Egypte, Etat Moderne*, Paris, 1820-1829, plate 89 in Volume II.

architecture of the 'Tower of the Romans',[70] which lay at a corner of the fortifications at their eastern junction with the shore of the Great Harbour adjacent to Cleopatra's needles. This tower survived until the early 20th century and is generally accepted to have been of ancient construction.[71]

e) There exists an aquatinted engraving of the Rosetta Gate as a magnificent ancient portal flanked by columns with Corinthian capitals (Figure 9.7). It was made from a drawing by Luigi Mayer made between 1776-1792 on behalf of Sir Robert Ainslie during his embassy to Constantinople. It is dated 1801 and was published in 1804 in a collection of Views of Egypt,[72] but it has hitherto seemingly gone unnoticed in any topographical studies of ancient Alexandria. This may be because this gate is not depicted in the Description de l'Egypte, which might in turn indicate that it was destroyed during or prior to the arrival of Napoleon's expedition in 1798. It is noteworthy that this portal appears too decorative to qualify as a defensive structure (although some later attempt seems to have been made to defend it, judging by the arrow slits in the lower sections of wall abutting it). That its main blocks have in the aquatint a pink coloration (which is original) is also significant, because it is well-established that polished pink granite was used extensively in the public architecture of ancient Alexandria.[73] In short, the form, location and seeming antiquity of this gateway are absolutely consistent with its being one of the main entrances to an ancient enclosure. To explain it as military architecture or to date it after the Arab conquest would be difficult. Conversely, if an ancient origin is granted for this structure, then the case for an ancient origin for the whole of the eastern sector of the Tulunid walls becomes very strong.

f) A report made for the Egypt Exploration Fund on the subject of Alexandria by D G Hogarth in 1894-1895 provides an archaeological indication that the line of the Tulunid walls in the eastern sector is probably ancient. Although the walls themselves had been destroyed by

---

[70] C L F PANCKOUCKE (publisher of 2nd edition), *Description de l'Egypte, Etat Moderne*, Paris, 1820-1829, plate 35 in Volume V.
[71] J-Y EMPEREUR, *Alexandria Rediscovered*, London 1998, p.53.
[72] L MAYER, *Views in Egypt From the Original Drawings In The Possession of Sir Robert Ainslie, Taken During His Embassy To Constantinople*, Published by R Bowyer, London, 1804.
[73] Some excavated ancient columns of pink granite have been placed in the small Roman theatre/odium at Kom el-Dikka for inspection by visitors: they may be seen in a corner of a photo in J-Y EMPEREUR, *Alexandria Rediscovered*, London 1998, p.26. Pink columns along the line of Canopic Way near the Attarine Mosque are shown in another view by Luigi Mayer in Views in Egypt [n. 72]. The same columns are shown in Planche 35 of Vol. V of the Antiquités section of the Description de l'Egypte and in some other old engravings. Also D G HOGARTH, *Report on Prospects for Research in Alexandria* in *Egypt Exploration Fund, Report* 1894-1895, p. 1-28, mentions the discovery of 'a large granite column' near Canopic Way on p.6.

that time, the 5 metre deep ditch or fosse that ran in front of them still existed along a two kilometre stretch running from the Tower of the Romans to the south-east vertex (Figure 9.10). This ditch should have cut through ancient foundations, if the walls had been built on a new line in the 9th century, since it is certain that the ancient city existed on both sides of them. However, in the whole stretch the only foundations Hogarth[74] discovered were some Roman brickwork at one point just south of the Rosetta Gate.[75] Since a single such instance might readily be attributed to a bridge (or similar) across the ditch, the implication is that the line of the Tulunid defences in the eastern sector is likely to have been occupied by a wall from early in the Ptolemaic period.

g) A tangible piece of evidence for the ancient origins of the outer circuit is provided by a large fragment of a tower, which stood in the outer wall and which may still be seen today in the Shallalat Gardens around 200m north of the site of the Rosetta Gate. There is little doubt that it is of very early - probably Ptolemaic – construction[76] (Figure 8.4). Indeed its antiquity is so convincing that some have sought to make the eastern wall of the ancient city pass through it.[77] However, this solution involves ignoring the observations of ancient defensive walls much further to the east by Pococke and Mahmoud Bey and contradicting the dimensions of the city given independently by Diodorus, Strabo, Josephus and Stephanus Byzantinus.[78]

Little excavation has ever been undertaken within the proposed area of the Soma enclosure, but Hogarth found traces of a 'massive structure' just north of Canopic Way near its intersection with the transverse street labelled R2.[79] Furthermore, Mahmoud Bey gives a description of lavish finds in this vicinity in the early to mid 19th century:-

---

[74] D G HOGARTH, *Report on Prospects for Research in Alexandria* in *Egypt Exploration Fund, Report* 1894-1895, p. 8 & p.13.

[75] The Rosetta Gate was the principal eastern gate in the "medieval" walls. It lay at the point where Canopic Way passed through these walls. It is also sometimes called the Cairo Gate or the Arab East Gate.

[76] J-Y EMPEREUR, *Alexandria Rediscovered*, London 1998, p.51 & p.53.

[77] Such a map appears in E M FORSTER, *Alexandria, A History and a Guide*, Alexandria, 1922 (p. 106-107 at the beginning of Part II in the Doubleday edition, New York, 1961 and the Michael Haag edition, London, 1982).

[78] It might be added that the population figure of 300,000 free citizens (i.e. about half a million including slaves) given by DIODORUS SICULUS 17.52 is too large to be accommodated in a city much smaller than that given in Mahmoud's plan in the light of the archaeological evidence on the housing density. Furthermore, the argument that the city may have been smaller in the early Ptolemaic period has to discount AMMIANUS MARCELLINUS, 22.16.15, who says that Alexandria 'attained its wide extent at its origin' and TACITUS, *Histories* 4.83, who says that Ptolemy I built the walls.

[79] D G HOGARTH, *Report on Prospects for Research in Alexandria* in *Egypt Exploration Fund, Report* 1894-1895, p. 8.

The Quest for the Tomb of Alexander by Andrew Chugg

In fact, the excavations which were made by Gallis [=Galice] Bey (and those which were executed later) discovered some enormous foundation walls on Canopic Way on the west side between the two transverse streets R1 and R2 together with a great number of fallen columns. Beside Canopic Way and R1 we ourselves have discovered several of them beneath the rubble: one can still today see some overthrown in the area around the first bastion. The extent of these monumental foundations is greater than 150 metres on each side. In conclusion, everything on this site shows us that this was the finest monument in the city of Alexandria...[80]

Conclusions

In reviewing the history of the tomb of Alexander in Alexandria, it has been argued that Alexander's body was brought to the city in the first quarter of the 3rd century BC, whilst the famous mausoleum-tomb of the King was built by Ptolemy Philopator in around 215BC. The mausoleum was visited as a mark of respect for Alexander by numerous Roman princes prior to its eventual destruction, which was most probably consequent upon the earthquake and tidal wave of AD365.

It has also been shown that the literary and contextual evidence on the appearance of the mausoleum of Alexander in Alexandria strongly favours a design similar to that of the archetypal Mausoleum at Halicarnassus. That is to say, it was a relatively tall and large square or rectangular tower overlying a subterranean burial chamber and surmounted by a pyramidal roof.

Furthermore, this investigation leads us to a new solution for the location of Alexander's tomb, which is perhaps unique in simultaneously explaining all of the ancient evidence, which had previously been believed to be inconsistent and contradictory. It is also the first significantly to connect this ancient evidence with the remains of Alexandria as observed in the modern era.

Apparently one of the early Ptolemies, but possibly even Alexander himself, ordered the construction of an enormous sacred enclosure at the heart of ancient Alexandria, probably inspired by the two comparable temple enclosures at Memphis. This precinct encompassed the principal crossroads of the ancient city, stretching roughly from just north of the street labelled L2 by Mahmoud Bey to just south of the street labelled L'2 and from just west of R3 to just east of R1, altogether an area of about 600 x 800 metres (Figure 9.11). Alexander's Mausoleum, the Grand Altar of Alexander,[81] the tombs of the later Ptolemies and probably numerous other sacred and religious buildings were contained within this enclosure, which was properly known as the Soma of Alexander. Its splendid walls may have been the *moenia urbis* that Caesar failed to stop to admire in Lucan's Pharsalia. It was also considered the first (Alpha) of the five quarters of Alexandria and it is identical with the second/other city or place/district of Alexander mentioned by Achilles Tatius.

---

[80] MAHMOUD BEY EL-FALAKI, *L'Antique Alexandrie*, Copenhagen, 1872, p. 56-57 (extract translated from the French by the author).
[81] R STONEMAN (trans.), *The Greek Alexander Romance*, London, 1991, Book I, 33.

The Tomb of Alexander in Alexandria

Either late in the Roman era or early in the Arab period Alexandria shrank into its western districts due to depopulation. The superb and lofty masonry of the Soma enclosure wall was an obvious fallback line for the eastern defences of the city, so three sides of the enclosure became incorporated in the new fortifications, which were finalised by Ibn Tulun in the 9th century. Consequently the Soma wall lay largely intact until the early 19th century, when it was substantially modified by Galice Bey on behalf of Mohammed Ali. Nevertheless, much of it probably remained until the 1880's, when it was almost entirely destroyed during the spread of the modern city. However, a single fragment has fortuitously survived to the present day and may yet be viewed in the gardens near the site of the Rosetta Gate.

Bibliography

Ancient Sources

Achilles Tatius, Clitophon and Leucippe, S. Gaselee, Loeb, Harvard, 1917

Acts of St Mark, Patrologia Graeca, vol. 115, ed. J-P Migne, Paris, 1899

Adamantios, Physiognomonika

Adamnan, de locis sanctis, Denis Meehan (ed.), Scriptores Latini Hiberniae Vol. III, Dublin, 1958

Aelian, Varia Historia, N.G. Wilson, Loeb, Harvard, 1997

Ammianus Marcellinus, Res Gestae, John C. Rolfe, Loeb, Harvard, 1935-9

Arabic Synaxary of the Coptic Church, J. Forget, Corpus scriptorum christianorum orientalium, scriptores arabici, series tertia, tomus I et II, Louvain, 1905-26

Arrian, Anabasis Alexandri and Indica, P.A. Brunt, Loeb, Harvard, 1976 and 1983

Arrian, Epitome of the History of Events After Alexander, *Photius* 92, Photius Bibliothèque, vol. II, René Henry, Paris, 1960

Athenaeus, Deipnosophistae, (fragments of Ephippus, Nicobule and Callixinus), Charles Burton Gulick, Loeb, Harvard, 1927-41

Bernardus Monachus Francus, Itinerarium 6, Patrologia Latina, vol. 121, ed. J-P Migne, Paris, 1880

Caesar, The Civil Wars, A.G. Peskett, Loeb, Harvard, 1914

Caesar, The Alexandrine War (ghostwritten by Hirtius), A.G. Way, Loeb, Harvard, 1955

Chronicon Paschale, 252, columns 608-609 in Patrologia Graeca, vol. 92, ed. J-P Migne, Paris, 1865

Cicero, The Speech Against Piso, N.H. Watts, vol. 14, Loeb, Harvard, 1931

Cicero, Pro Rabirio Postumo, trans. N.H. Watts, vol. 14, Loeb, Harvard, 1931

Clement of Alexandria, Exhortation to the Greeks, G.W. Butterworth, Loeb, Harvard, 1919

Curtius, The History of Alexander, John C. Rolfe, Loeb, Harvard, 1946

Dio Cassius, Roman History, Earnest Cary, Loeb, Harvard, 1914-27

Diodorus Siculus, Library of History, (especially books 16 to 19): vol. VII, Charles L. Sherman, Loeb, Harvard, 1952; vol. VIII, C. Bradford Welles, Loeb, Harvard, 1963; vol. IX, Russel M. Geer, Loeb, Harvard, 1947

Diogenes Laertius, Lives of Eminent Philosophers: Zeno, Demetrios

Ephemerides, FrGrHist 2.117

Epiphanius Constantiensis, On Weights and Measures, columns 237-94, Patrologia Graeca, vol. 43, ed. J-P Migne, Paris, 1864

Bibliography

Epiphanius the Monk, Description of Palestine, columns 259-72 in Patrologia Graeca, vol. 120, ed. J-P Migne, Paris, 1880

Epitome de Caesaribus Sexti Aureli Victoris

Euripides, Andromeda

Eusebius, Ecclesiastical History, vol. 1, Kirsop Lake, Loeb, Harvard, 1926; vol. 2, J.E.L. Oulton, Loeb, Harvard, 1932

Eutychius, Patrologia Graeca, vol. 111, ed. J-P Migne, Paris, 1863

Hegesias, FrGrHist 2.142

Herodian, History of the Empire, Books 1 to 4, C.R. Whittaker, Loeb, Harvard, 1969

Homer, Iliad, trans. A.T. Murray, revised William F. Wyatt, Loeb, Harvard, 1999

St Jerome, De viris illustribus

John Chrysostom, Homilies on 2nd Corinthians, XXVI, columns 575-84, Patrologia Graeca, vol. 61, ed. J-P Migne, Paris, 1862; John Henry Parker, The Homilies of S. John Chrysostom Archbishop of Constantinople on the Second Epistle of St Paul the Apostle to the Corinthians, Oxford, 1848

John Chrysostom, Instructions to Catechumens (Ad Illum. Catech.)

John of Nikiu, Chronicle, Robert Henry Charles, Text and Translation Society 3, Amsterdam, reprint of London edition of 1916

Josephus, Jewish Antiquities, H. St J. Thackeray, R. Marcus, A. Wikgren, Loeb, Harvard, 1930-63;

Josephus, The Jewish War, H. St J. Thackeray, Loeb, Harvard, 1927-8;

Josephus, Contra Apion, H. St J. Thackeray, Loeb, Harvard, 1926

Justin, Epitome of the Philippic History of Pompeius Trogus, Books 11-12, J.C. Yardley and W. Heckel, Oxford, 1997; Justin, Cornelius Nepos and Eutropius, Rev. John Selby Watson, London, 1853

The Koran, Surah 18, The Cave, N.J. Dawood, London, 1956

Libanius, Oration XLIX, A.F. Norman, Selected Works II, Loeb, Harvard, 1977

Lucan, Pharsalia, J.D. Duff, Loeb, Harvard, 1928

Lucian, Dialogues of the Dead, XIII, vol. 7, M.D. MacLeod, Loeb, Harvard, 1961;

Lucian, Essay on How to Write History, vol. 6, K. Kilburn, Loeb, 1959

Metz Epitome & Liber de Morte, P.H. Thomas, Ed., Incerti Auctoris Epitoma Rerum Gestarum Alexandri Magni cum Libro de Morte Testamentoque Alexandri, Teubner, Leipzig 1966

Nepos, Eumenes; Justin, Cornelius Nepos and Eutropius, Rev. John Selby Watson, London, 1853

Palladius, Lausiac History, Robert T. Meyer, London, 1965

Pausanias, Description of Greece, vol. 1, W.H.S. Jones, Loeb, Harvard, 1918

Philo of Alexandria, In Flaccum, vol. 9, F.H. Colson, Loeb, Harvard, 1941

The Quest for the Tomb of Alexander by Andrew Chugg

Philo of Byzantium, Concerning the Seven Wonders

Pliny the Elder, Natural History, H. Rackham, W.H.S. Jones, D.E. Eichholz, Loeb, Harvard, 1938-62

Plutarch, Agesilaus, Lives vol. 5, B. Perrin, Loeb, Harvard, 1917

Plutarch, Alexander & Caesar, Lives vol. 7, B. Perrin, Loeb, Harvard, 1919

Plutarch, Eumenes, Lives vol. 8, B. Perrin, Loeb, Harvard, 1919

Plutarch, Demetrius, Antony & Pyrrhus, Lives vol. 9, B. Perrin, Loeb, Harvard, 1920

Plutarch, Moralia, vols. 3 and 4, Frank Cole Babbitt, Loeb, Harvard, 1931 and 1936

Polyaenus, Stratagems of War, trans. Peter Krentz & Everett L. Wheeler, Ares, Chicago, 1994

Polybius, The Histories, W.R. Paton, Loeb, Harvard, 1922-7

Procopius, On Buildings, H.B. Dewing and G. Downey, Loeb, Harvard, 1940

Pseudo-Callisthenes, Alexander Romance, e.g. Guilelmus Kroll, Historia Alexandri Magni, vol, 1, Weidmann, 1926

Claudius Ptolemy, Astronomical Canon

Rufinus, Ecclesiastical History

Severus, Bishop of Al-Ushmunain, History of the Patriarchs, B. Evetts, *Patrologia Orientalis* vol. 2, 4, Paris, 1907

Sibylline Oracles

Socrates Scholasticus, Ecclesiastical History, Patrologia Graeca, vol. 67, ed. J-P Migne, Paris, 1964; H. Wace and P. Schaff, A Select Library of Nicene and Post-Nicene Fathers of the Christian Church, vol. 2, Oxford and New York, 1891

Sozomenos, Ecclesiastical History, Patrologia Graeca, vol. 67, ed. J-P Migne, Paris, 1964; H. Wace and P. Schaff, A Select Library of Nicene and Post-Nicene Fathers of the Christian Church, vol. 2, Oxford and New York, 1891

Stephanus Byzantinus, Augustus Meineke, Stephani Byzantii, Ethnicorum, Berlin, 1849

Strabo, Geography, H.L. Jones, Loeb, Harvard, 1917-32

Suetonius, Lives of the Caesars: Caesar, Augustus, Gaius Caligula and Vespasian; Life of Lucan, J.C. Rolfe, Loeb, Harvard, 1913-14

Suidae Lexicon (a.k.a. The Suda), A. Adler (ed.), Leipzig, 1928-35

Tacitus, Histories, Clifford H. Moore, Loeb, Harvard, 1925-31;

Tacitus, Annals, John Jackson, Loeb, Harvard, 1931-7

Theocritus, Idyll XVII, Encomium to Ptolemy, J.M. Edmonds, Greek Bucolic Poets, Loeb, Harvard, 1919

Theodoret, Graecarum Affectionum Curatio, Patrologia Graeca vol. 83, J.-P. Migne, Paris, 1864

Vitruvius, De Architectura, Frank Granger, Loeb, Harvard, 1934

Bibliography

Zenobius, Proverbia, E.L. von Leutsch and F.G. Schneidewin (eds.), Corpus Paroemiographorum Graecorum, 1, Göttingen, 1839

Modern Sources

Achille Adriani (posthumously), *La Tomba di Alessandro*, L'Erma di Bretschneider, Rome, 2000

Achille Adriani, *Repertorio d'Arte dell'Egitto Greco-Romano*, Serie C, Vol. I-II, Palermo, 1963 & 1966

Leo Africanus, ed. Ramusio, *Descrizione dell'Africa*, 1550, trans. John Pory AD1600, *Description of Africa*, Vol. 3, Hakluyt Society 94, London, 1896

Manolis Andronicos, *Vergina*, Athens, 1984

Edward Anson, "Macedonia's Alleged Constitutionalism," *Classical Journal*, 80, 1985, 303-316

Edward Anson, "Early Hellenistic Chronology: The Cuneiform Evidence" in W. Heckel, L. Trittle & P. Wheatley (Editors), *Alexander's Empire: Formulation to Decay*, Regina Books, California, 2007, 193-198

Jean-Luc Arnaud, "Nouvelles Données sur la Topographie d'Alexandrie Antique," *BCH* 121, 1997, 721-737

Hutan Ashrafian, "The Death of Alexander the Great – A Spinal Twist of Fate," *Journal of the History of the Neurosciences*, Vol. 13, Issue 2, June 2004, 138-142

M.M. Austin, *The Hellenistic World from Alexander to the Roman Conquest*, Cambridge University Press, 1981

M.F. Awad, *La revue de l'Occident Musulman et de la Méditerranée* 46, 1987, 4

D.M. Bailey, "Alexandria, Carthage and Ostia," *Alessandria e il mondo ellenistico-romano, Studi in onore di Achille Adriani*, 2, Roma, 1984, 265-72

Alberto Balil, "Una nueva representación de la tumba de Alejandro," *Archivo. Españ. Arqueol.* 35, 1962, 102-3

Alberto Balil, "Monumentos Alejandrinos y Paisajes Egipcios en un Mosaico Romano de Toledo (España)," *Alessandria e il Mondo Ellenistico-Romano, Studi in Onore di Achille Adriani*, Vol. III, Roma, 1984, 433-9

Dr John Ball, *Egypt in the Classical Geographers*, Government Press, Cairo, 1942

Maddalena Bassani, "Esempi archeologici per un'ipotesi interpretativa della lastra di S. Apollonia", *Engramma* 70, March 2009

Maddalena Bassani & Giulio Testori, "La stella di Alessandro il Grande nel chiostro di Sant'Apollonia: due ipotesi di restituzione di un monumento onorario romano", *Engramma* 95, December 2011

Pierre Belon du Mans, *Voyage en Egypte*, 1553, edition of Serge Sauneron, IFAO, 1970

Gwen Benwell and Arthur Waugh, *Sea Enchantress: The Tale of The Mermaid and Her Kin*, Hutchison, London, 1961

The Quest for the Tomb of Alexander by Andrew Chugg

Maria Bergamo, "1962, Venezia: storia di un ritrovamento. Documenti, contesto storico e status quaestionis", *Engramma* 70, March 2009

Leif Bergson, *Der Griechische Alexanderroman Rezension β*, Uppsala, 1965

André Bernand, *Alexandrie la Grande*, Arthaud, Paris, 1966

J.H. Bernard trans., *Expliciunt peregrinations totius terre sancta, Guide-Book to Palestine*, Palestine Pilgrim Text Society, London, 1894, vi, 33

Edwyn Bevan, *A History of Egypt under the Ptolemaic Dynasty*, Methuen and Co, London, 1927

Robert S. Bianchi, "Hunting Alexander's Tomb," *Archaeology*, July/August 1993, 54-5

Tom Boiy, "Cuneiform Tablets & Aramaic Ostraca: Between the Low & High Chronologies of the Early Diadoch Period" in W. Heckel, L. Trittle & P. Wheatley (Editors), *Alexander's Empire: Formulation to Decay*, Regina Books, California, 2007, 199-208

Nicola Bonacasa, "Un Inedito di Achille Adriani Sulla Tomba di Alessandro," *Studi Miscellanei – Seminario di Archaeologia e Storia dell'Arte… dell Universita di Roma*, vol. 28, 1991, 5-19

M. Bonamy, "Description de la Ville d'Alexandrie, telle qu'elle estoit du temps de Strabon," *Histoire de l'Académie des Inscriptions et Belles Lettres*, Tome 9, 1736, 416-32

Osmund Bopearachchi & Philippe Flandrin, *Le Portrait d'Alexander le Grand*, 2005

A.B. Bosworth, "Alexander and Ammon", *Greece and the Eastern Mediterranean in Ancient History and Prehistory*, ed. K. H. Kinzl, Berlin 1977

A.B. Bosworth, *Alexander and the East: the Tragedy of Triumph*, OUP, 1996

A.B. Bosworth, *Conquest and Empire: The Reign of Alexander The Great*, CUP, 1988

A.B. Bosworth, "Heroic Honours in Syracuse" in *Crossroads of History: The Age of Alexander*, California, 2004

G. Botti, *Plan d'Alexandrie à l'époque Ptolémaïque*, Alexandria, 1898

Alan K. Bowman, *Egypt After the Pharaohs*, British Museum Press, London, 1986

Georg Braun & Frans Hogenberg, *Civitates Orbis Terrarum*, Cologne, 1572

Evaristo Breccia, *Rapport du Musée Gréco-Romain*, Alexandria, 1907

Evaristo Breccia, *Alexandrea ad Aegyptum*, Bergamo, 1922

Evaristo Breccia, "Alessandro Magno e la sua tomba", *La lettura: Rivista mensile del Corriere della Sera*, June 1930, Fascicolo 6, 523-528

Dale M. Brown (Series Editor), *Greece: Temples, Tombs and Treasures*, Time Life Books, Lost Civilizations Series, Richmond, 1994

W.G. Browne, *Travels in Africa, Egypt and Syria*, London, 1799

James Bruce, *Travels*, I, London, 1790

P.A. Brunt, *Arrian, Anabasis Alexandri and Indica*, vols. I and II, Loeb Classical Library, Harvard, 1976 and 1983

Bibliography

Cornelius de Bruyn, *Reizen van Cornelis de Bruyn door de vermaardste Deelen van Klein Asia*, 1698

E.A.W. Budge, *The History of Alexander the Great: Being the Syriac Version of the Pseudo Callisthenes*, Cambridge, 1889

E.A.W. Budge, *The Life and Exploits of Alexander the Great*, London, 1896

J.B. Bury, S.A. Cook and F.E. Adcock (eds.), *The Cambridge Ancient History: Volume VI; Macedon*, 401-301 BC, Cambridge, 1927

A.J. Butler, *The Arab Conquest of Egypt and the Last Thirty Years of the Roman Dominion*, 2nd edition revised by P M Fraser, OUP, [1902] 1978

Louis-François Cassas, *Voyage pittoresque de la Syrie, de la Phénicie, de la Palestine et de la Basse Egypte*, Paris, 1799

L. Casson, "Speed under Sail of Ancient Ships," *TAPhA* 82, 1951, 136-148

M. Chaîne, "L'Église de Saint-Marc à Alexandrie," *Revue de l'Orient Chrétien*, vol 24, 1924, 372-386

M. Chauveau, *L'Egypte au temps de Cléopâtre*, Daily Life Series, Hachette, Paris, 1997

Erik Christiansen, *The Roman Coins of Alexandria*, Aarhus University Press, 1988

Vassilios Christides, "The Tomb of Alexander the Great in Arabic Sources" in *Studies in Honour of Clifford Edmund Bosworth, Part I, Hunter of the East*, edited by Ian Richard Netton, 2000, 165-173

A.M. Chugg, "An Unrecognised Representation of Alexander the Great on Hadrian's Egyptian Coinage," *The Celator Journal*, Vol. 15, No. 2, February, 2001, 6-16

A.M. Chugg, "The Sarcophagus of Alexander the Great?" *Greece and Rome*, April 2002, 8-26

A.M. Chugg, "The Sarcophagus of Alexander the Great," *Minerva*, vol 13, No 5, Sept.-Oct. 2002, 33-6

A.M. Chugg, "The Tomb of Alexander the Great in Alexandria," *American Journal of Ancient History*, New Series 1.2, (2002) [2003], 75-108

A.M. Chugg, "A Double Entendre in the Alexandrian Bigas of Triptolemos," *The Celator Journal*, vol. 17, no. 8, August, 2003, 6-16

A.M. Chugg, "Alexander's Final Resting Place," *History Today*, July 2004, 17-23

A.M. Chugg, *The Lost Tomb of Alexander the Great*, London, October 2004

A.M. Chugg, "The Journal of Alexander the Great", *Ancient History Bulletin* 19.3-4 (2005) 155-175.

A.M. Chugg, "Is the Gold Porus Medallion a Lifetime Portrait of Alexander the Great?" *The Celator Journal*, vol. 21, no. 9, September 2007, 28-35

Amanda Claridge, *Oxford Archaeological Guide: Rome*, Oxford, 1998

E.D. Clarke, *The Tomb of Alexander, a dissertation on the sarcophagus from Alexandria and now in the British Museum*, Cambridge, 1805

The Quest for the Tomb of Alexander by Andrew Chugg

E.D. Clarke, *Letter addressed to the Gentlemen of the Bitish Museum by the Author of the Dissertation on the Alexandrian Sarcophagus*, Cambridge, 28th September 1807

E.D. Clarke, *Travels in Various Countries of Europe, Asia and Africa, Part 2: Greece, Egypt and the Holy Land*, Section 2 (Vol. 5), 4th Edition, 1817 (original preface dated 24th May, 1814)

P.D. Clarke and A. Bryceson (advisors), *The Medical Protection Society, Casebook (GP) no. 4*, London, 1994, 4-5

W. Clarysse and G. van der Veken, *The Eponymous Priests of Ptolemaic Egypt*, E J Brill, Leiden, 1983

N.L. Collins, "The Various Fathers of Ptolemy I" *Mnemosyne* 50.4, 1997, 436-476

Otto Cuntz, *Itineraria Romana*, Teubner, Rome, 1929

P. Daru, *Histoire de Venise*, 3rd edition, Tome 1, Paris, 1826

Christian Décobert and Jean-Yves Empereur (editors), *Alexandrie Médiévale 1*, Institut Français d'Archéologie Orientale, Cairo, 1998

A. Déléage, *Etudes Papyrologiques 2*, 1934

D. Delia, "The Population of Roman Alexandria," *TAPA* 118, 1988, 275-92

Otto Demus, *The Mosaic Decoration of San Marco Venice*, University of Chicago Press, 1988

Leo Deuel, *The Memoirs of Heinrich Schliemann*, Harper and Row, New York, 1977

Aidan Dodson, *After the Pyramids*, Rubicon Press, London, 2000

Boris Dreyer, "The Arrian Parchment in Gothenburg: New Digital Processing Methods & Initial Results" in W. Heckel, L. Trittle & P. Wheatley (Editors), *Alexander's Empire: Formulation to Decay*, Regina Books, California, 2007, 245-264

Jean-Yves Empereur, *Alexandria Rediscovered*, British Museum Press, London, 1998

Jean-Yves Empereur et al, *The Tombs of Alexander the Great (Hoi Taphoi tou Megalou Alexandrou)*, Hermeias, Athens, 1997

D.W. Engels, "A note on Alexander's death," *Classical Philology*, 73, 1978, 224-8

Andrew Erskine, "Life After Death: Alexandria and the Body of Alexander," *Greece and Rome*, Vol 49, No 2, October 2002, 163-179

Janos Fedak, *Monumental Tombs of the Hellenistic Age*, Toronto, 1990

Arthur Ferrill, *Caligula, Emperor of Rome*, Thames and Hudson, London and New York, 1991

J. Ferron and M. Pinard, "Un Fragment de Verre Gravé du Musée Lavigerie," *Cahiers de Byrsa* 8, 1958-9, 103-9

Nezih Firatli & Louis Robert, *Les Stèles Funéraire de Byzance Gréco-Romain*, Paris, 1964

Ferdinando Forlati, *La Basilica Di San Marco Attraverso I Suoi Restauri*, Trieste 1975

Robin Lane Fox, *Alexander the Great*, Allen Lane, London, 1973

Robin Lane Fox, *The Search for Alexander*, Little Brown Books, Boston & Toronto, 1980

P.M. Fraser, *Ptolemaic Alexandria*, OUP, 1972

Bibliography

P.M. Fraser, "Some Alexandrian Forgeries," *Proceedings of the British Academy*, 47, 1962, 243-50

P.M. Fraser, "A Syriac Notitia Urbis Alexandrinae," *J. Egyptian Archaeology*, 37, 1951, 103-8

Massimo Galli, Flavia Bernini and Gianguglielmo Zehender, "Alexander the Great and West Nile Virus Encephalitis [letter]", *Emerging Infectious Diseases*, Vol. 10, No. 7, July 2004

Russel M. Geer, *Diodorus Siculus*, vol. IX, Loeb Classical Library, Harvard, 1947

Edward Gibbon, *The Decline and Fall of the Roman Empire*, Vol. I, London, 1782 (revised 1845)

Franck Goddio et al, *Alexandria: The Submerged Royal Quarters*, Periplus, London, 1998

Walter J. Goralski, "Arrian's Events After Alexander," *Ancient World* 19, 1989

Michael Grant, *Cleopatra*, Weidenfeld and Nicolson, London, 1972

Nicolas Grimal, *A History of Ancient Egypt*, Blackwell, Oxford, 1994

Christopher Haas, *Alexandria in Late Antiquity*, John Hopkins University Press, Baltimore, 1997

Getatchew Haile, "A New Ethiopic Version of the Acts of St Mark," *Analecta Bollandiana* 99, 1981, 117-34

N.G.L. Hammond, *Alexander The Great*, Chatto and Windus, London, 1981

N.G.L. Hammond, *Philip of Macedon*, Duckworth, London, 1994

N.G.L. Hammond, *Three Historians of Alexander the Great*, CUP, 1983

Hans Hauben, "The First War of the Successors - Chronological and Historical Problems," *Ancient Society* 8, 1977, 85-120

Albert Hesse et al., "L'Heptastadium d'Alexandrie (Égypte)," in Jean-Yves Empereur (ed.), *Alexandrina* 2 (Études Alexandrines 6, Cairo 2002), 191-273

D.G. Hogarth and E.F. Benson, "Report on Prospects of Research in Alexandria," *Egypt Exploration Fund* 1895, 1-33

Silvia Hurter, "Review of Le Portrait d'Alexandre le Grand", *Swiss Numismatic Review*, Vol. 85, 2006, pp. 185-195

Dirk Husemann, *Mythos Alexandergrab*, Jan Thorbecke Verlag, Ostfildern, 2006

Anna Maria Bisi Ingrassia, "Influenze Alessandrine Sull'Arte Punica: Una Messa A Punto," *Alessandria e il mondo ellenistico-romano, Studi in onore di Achille Adriani*, 3, Rome, 1984, 835-42

Eyles Irwin, *A Series Of Adventures In The Course Of A Voyage Up The Red-Sea, On The Coasts Of Arabia And Egypt And Of A Route Through The Desarts Of Thebais Hither To Unknown To The European Traveller In The Year 1777*, I, London, 1780

F. Jacoby, *Die Fragmente der griechischen Historiker*, Berlin, 1923-30, Leiden, 1940-58

David Jeffreys, *The Survey of Memphis*, Egypt Exploration Society, London, 1985

The Quest for the Tomb of Alexander by Andrew Chugg

Kristian Jeppesen, "Tot Operum Opus, Ergebnisse der Dänischen Forschungen zum Maussolleion von Halikarnass seit 1966," *Jahrbuch des Deutschen Archäologischen Instituts*, Bd. 107, 1992, 59-102

Gaston Jondet, *Atlas historique de la ville et des ports d'Alexandrie*, Mémoires de la Société Sultanieh de Géographie 2, Cairo, 1921

H. Kiepert, "Zur Topographie der alten Alexandria: Nach Mahmud Begs Entdeckungen," *Zeitschrift der Gesellschaft für Erdkunde zu Berlin*, Vol. 7, 1872, 337-349

Robert Koldewey, *Das Wieder Erstehende Babylon*, Leipzig, 1913

Guilelmus Kroll, *Historia Alexandri Magni (Pseudo-Callisthenes)*, Weidmann, Germany, 1926

Royston Lambert, *Beloved and God*, Weidenfeld and Nicolson, London, 1984

J.-P. Lauer and C. Picard, *Les Statues Ptolémaiques du Sarapieion de Memphis*, Paris, 1955

Brian Lavery, *Nelson and The Nile*, Chatham Publishing, London, 1998

Lorenzo Lazzarini, "Il dato materiale: natura e origine della pietra della lastra di S. Apollonia", *Engramma* 70, March 2009

Richard Adalbert Lipsius, *Die Apokryphen Apostelgeschichten Und Apostellegenden*, 2/2:338-39, Braunschweig, 1883-90

Emile Littré, "On Alexander's Death," *Médecine et Médecins*, Paris, 1872, 406-415

Guillaume de Machaut, *La Prise d'Alixandre (~1369)*, trans. R. Barton Palmer, Routledge, New York and London, 2002

Mahmoud Bey El-Falaki, *Mémoire sur l'antique Alexandrie, ses faubourgs et environs découverts*, Copenhagen, 1872

Leonardo Conte Manin, *Memorie storico-critiche intorno la vita, translazione, e invenzioni di san Marco evangelista principale protettore di Venezia*, Venice, 1815 (second edition 1835)

Ahmed Sadek M. Mansour, "Diagenesis of Upper Cretaceous Rudist Bivalves, Abu Roash Area, Egypt: A Petrographic Study," *Geologia Croatica*, 57/1, Zagreb 2004, 55-66

Auguste Mariette, *Choix de Monuments et de Dessins du Sérapéum de Memphis*, Paris, 1856

Auguste Mariette (ed. Gaston Maspero), *Le Sérapéum de Memphis*, Paris, 1882

L. Maritan, C. Mazzoli, E. Melis, "A Multidisciplinary Approach To The Characterization Of Roman Gravestones From Aquileia (Udine, Italy)," *Archaeometry* 45.3, 2003, 363-374

Minor M. Markle, "A Shield Monument from Veria and the Chronology of the Macedonian Shield," *Hesperia* 68.2, 1999, 219-254

John Marlowe, *The Golden Age of Alexandria*, Gollancz, London, 1971

John S. Marr & Charles H. Calisher, "Alexander the Great and West Nile Virus Encephalitis", *Emerging Infectious Diseases*, Vol. 9, No. 12, December 2003, 1599-1603

Valerio Massimo Manfredi, *La Tomba di Alessandro: L'Enigma*, Mondadori, Milan, 2009

F. Matz, "Review of Lauer and Picard; Les Statues Ptolémaiques du Sarapieion de Memphis," *Gnomon*, 29, 1957, 84-93

Bibliography

Luigi Mayer, *Views in Egypt...*, R Bowyer, London, 1804

Judith McKenzie, "Alexandria and the Origins of Baroque Architecture," *Alexandria and Alexandrianism*, Getty Museum, Malibu, 1996

Judith Mckenzie, "Glimpsing Alexandria from Archaeological Evidence," *JRA* 2003, 35-63

Judith McKenzie, *The Architecture of Alexandria and Egypt: 300BC – AD700*, Yale University Press, Pelican History of Art, 2007

Otto Meinardus, *Christian Egypt Ancient and Modern*, 2nd edition, American University in Cairo Press, 1977 (NB. Chapter 3 on Relics of St Mark is not in the 1st edition)

M.W. Merrony, "The Graven Image in Early Islamic Floor Mosaics: Contradiction or Convention?" *Minerva* 15.1, 2004, 36-9

C. Barbier de Meynard et Pavet de Courteille (trans.) *al-Mas'udi, Les prairies d'or*, Imprimerie Imperiale, Paris, 1861-1917

R.D. Milns, *Alexander the Great*, Robert Hale, London, 1968

Orsolina Montevecchi, "Adriano e la fondazione di Antinoopolis," *Neronia IV, Alejandro Magno, modelo de los emperadores romanos*, Collection Latomus, Vol. 209, 1990, 183-195

Otto Mørkholm, *Early Hellenistic Coinage*, Cambridge, 1991

C. Müller, *Fragmenta Historicorum Graecorum*, Paris, 1868

T. Neroutsos Bey, *L'ancienne Alexandrie*, Paris, 1888

F. Noack, *Neue Untersuchungen in Alexandrien*, Mittheilungen des Kaiserlich Deutschen Archäologischen Instituts, Athenische Abtheilung XXV, 1900, 215-279

F.L. Norden, *Voyage d'Egypte et de Nubie*, Paris, 1755

John Julius Norwich, *Venice: the Rise to Empire*, Allen Lane, London, 1977

Oscar Norwich, *Norwich's Maps of Africa, an illustrated and annotated carto-bibliography*, edited by Jeffery Stone, Terra Nova Press, Norwich, Vermont, 1997

Joan Oates, *Babylon*, Thames and Hudson, London, 1979

John Maxwell O'Brien, *Alexander the Great: the Invisible Enemy*, Routledge, London and New York, 1992

David W. Oldach and Robert E. Richard, *A Mysterious Death*, The New England Journal of Medicine, June 11, 1998, Volume 338, Number 24

Demetrios Pandermalis, *Alexander the Great: Treasures from an Epic Era of Hellenism*, Exhibition Catalogue, Onasis Cultural Center, New York, December 2004 – April 2005

Birger A. Pearson, "Earliest Christianity in Egypt: Some Observations," *The Roots of Egyptian Christianity*, edited by Birger Pearson and James Goehring, Philadelphia, 1986, 132-159

Lionel Pearson, *The Lost Histories of Alexander the Great*, American Philological Association, New York and Oxford, 1960

Gratien Le Père, Saint-Genis, Vivant Denon etc., *Description de l'Egypte*, C.L.F. Panckoucke, Paris, 1829

The Quest for the Tomb of Alexander by Andrew Chugg

Nicolas Perrot (translator into French), *L'Afrique de Marmol*, Paris, 1667

Charles Picard, *Quelques représentations nouvelles du Phare d'Alexandrie*, BCH 76, 1952, 61-95

Richard Pococke, *Description of the East*, London, 1743-5

Eugenio Polito, *Fulgentibus armis: Introduzione allo studio dei fregi d'armi antichi*, L'Erma di Bretschneider, Roma, 1998

John Pory, *The History and Description of Africa written by Leo Africanus*, Hakluyt Society, London, 1896

Claire Préaux, *L'economie royale des Lagides*, New York, 1939

J.R. Rea, "A New Version of P.Yale inv. 299," *Zeitschrift für Papyrologie und Epigraphik* 27, 1977, 151-6

Mary Renault, *The Nature of Alexander*, Allen Lane, London, 1975

Katerina Rhomiopoulou, "An Outline of Macedonian History and Art" in *The Search for Alexander: an Exhibition*, New York Graphic Society, 1980

L. Richardson Jr., *A New Topographical Dictionary of Ancient Rome*, John Hopkins University Press, Baltimore, 1992

M. Rodziewicz, *Les habitations romaines tardives d'Alexandrie*, Centre d'archéologie mediterranéenne de l'Académie Polonaise des Sciences, Warsaw, 1984

M. Rodziewicz, *Ptolemaic street directions in Basilea*, Alessandria e il mondo ellenistico romano, Congrès Alexandrie, 1992, published in Rome, 1995, 227-35

John C. Rolfe, *Ammianus Marcellinus*, Vol. II, Loeb Classical Library, Harvard, 1937

M.B. Sakellariou (editor), *Macedonia*, Greek Lands in History series, Ekdotike Athenon, Athens, 1988

Robert Sallares, *Malaria and Rome*, OUP, 2002

A.E. Samuel, *Ptolemaic Chronology*, Munich, 1962

George Sandys, *Relation of a Journey begun in AD 1610*, London, 1617

Nicholas J. Saunders, *Alexander'sTomb*, New York, 2006

Fritz Schachermeyr, *Alexander der Grosse*, Vienna, 1973

David Shotter, *Augustus Caesar*, Routledge, London and New York, 1991

N.M. Shukri, G. Philip & R. Said, "The geology of the Mediterranean coast between Rosetta and Bardia, Part II: Pleistocene sediments, geomorphology, and microfacies," *Bulletin de l'Institut d'Égypte* 1956, v. 37, n.2, 295-433

Michael Radzivill Sierotka, *Hierosolymitana peregrinatio illustrissimi domini Nicolai Christopheri Radzivilli,…Ex idiomate Polonica in latinum linguam translate… Thorma trelere interprete*, Brunsbergae, 1601 [and Polish, Krakow, 1925]

Andreas Schmidt-Colinet, "Das Grab Alexanders d. Gr. In Memphis?", *The Problematics of Power: Eastern & Western Representation of Alexander the Great*, M. Bridges & J. Ch. Bürgel (eds.), Peter Lang, 1996, 87-90

D. Sly, *Philo's Alexandria*, Routledge, London, 1996, 44-7

Bibliography

Morton Smith, *Clement of Alexandria and a Secret Gospel of Mark*, Harvard University Press, 1973

C.S. Sonnini, *Travels in Upper and Lower Egypt*, vol. i, 67, edit. London, 1800

Tony Spawforth, *Alexander: The God King*, UK television program, BBC2, 20:25, 18/5/1996

Thomas Steuber & Martina Bachmann, "Upper Aptian-albian Rudist Bivalves from Northern Sinai, Egypt," Palaeontology 45(4), June 2002, 725-749

S.W. Stevenson, C. Roach Smith and F.W. Madden, *Dictionary of Roman Coins*, George Bell and Sons, London, 1889

Andrew Stewart, *Faces of Power: Alexander's Image and Hellenistic Politics*, California, 1993

Richard Stoneman (trans.), *The Greek Alexander Romance*, Penguin, London, 1991

Richard Stoneman, *Alexander the Great*, London, 1997

D.J. & C.H. Sweet, "DNA Analysis of Dental Pulp to Link Incinerated Remains of Homicide Victim to Crime Scene," *J. Forensic Sci.* March 1995, 40(2), 310-4

Moustafa Anouar Taher, "Les séismes á Alexandrie et la destruction du Phare" in *Alexandrie Médiévale* 1, ed. Christian Décobert and Jean-Yves Empereur, Institut Français d'Archéologie Orientale, 1998

F.B. Tarbell, "The Form of the Chlamys," *Classical Philology* I, 1906, 283-9

W.W. Tarn, "The Hellenistic Ruler Cult and the Daemon," *JHS*, 48, 1928, 206-19

W.W. Tarn, *Cambridge Ancient History, Vol. 6, Macedon 401-301 BC*, Cambridge, 1927

Lily Ross Taylor, "The Cult of Alexander at Alexandria," *Classical Philology*, 22, 1927, 162-9

William Telfer, "St Peter of Alexandria and Arius," *Analecta Bollandiana* 67, 1949, 117-130

H. Thiersch, "Die Alexandrinische Königsnecropole," *Jahrbuch d. K. D. Archaeol. Instituts* XXV, 1910, 55-97

Dorothy Thompson (formerly Crawford), *Memphis under the Ptolemies*, Princeton, 1988

Barbara Tkaczow, *Topography of Ancient Alexandria (An Archaeological Map)*, Warsaw, 1993

B.G. Trigger, B.J. Kemp, D.O'Connor and A.B. Lloyd, *Ancient Egypt: A Social History*, Cambridge, 1983

E.G. Turner, *Greek Papyri*, Oxford, 1980

G. Valentia, *Voyages and Travels to India, Ceylon, the Red Sea, Abyssinia and Egypt in the Years 1802 – 1806*, Vol. 4, London, 1811

Michel Valloggia, *Au Coeur d'une Pyramide*, Musée Romain Lausanne-Vidy, 2001

J.A. van Egmont and J. Heyman, *Travels Through Part of Europe, Asia Minor, the Islands of the Archipelago; Syria, Palestine, Egypt, Mount Sinai*, London, 1759

Marjorie Susan Venit, *Monumental Tombs of Ancient Alexandria: The Theater of the Dead*, Cambridge, 2002

The Quest for the Tomb of Alexander by Andrew Chugg

Gianni Vianello, *Marco Evangelista: L'Enigma delle Reliquie*, M. d'Auria Editore, Naples, 2006

Ettore Vio, *St Mark's Basilica in Venice*, Thames and Hudson, London, 2000

Dominique Vivant Denon, *Travels in Upper and Lower Egypt*, London, 1802

A.J.B. Wace, "The Sarcophagus of Alexander the Great," *Farouk I University, Bulletin of the Faculty of Arts*, 4, 1948, 1-11

Thomas Walsh, *Journal of The Late Campaign in Egypt: Including Descriptions of that Country and of Gibraltar, Minorca, Malta, Marmorice and Macri*, T.Cadell and W.Davies, London, 1803, Plate 25

C. Bradford Welles, *Diodorus Siculus*, Vol. VIII, Loeb Classical Library, Harvard, 1963

Pat Wheatley, "An Introduction to the Chronological Problems in Early Diadoch Sources and Scholarship" in W. Heckel, L. Trittle & P. Wheatley (Editors), *Alexander's Empire: Formulation to Decay*, Regina Books, California, 2007, 179-192

C.R. Whittaker, *Herodian*, vol. I, Loeb Classical Library, 1969

Ulrich Wilcken, "Hypomnematismoi," *Philologus*, 1894, 84-126

Ulrich Wilcken, "Die griechischen Denkmäler vom Dromos des Serapeums von Memphis," *JDAI* 32, 1917, 149-203

Gardner Wilkinson, "On an Early Mosaic in St Mark's…," *Journal of the British Archaeological Association*, vol. vii, 1851

Stephen Williams, *Diocletian and The Roman Recovery*, Routledge, London and New York, 1985

Stephen Williams and Gerard Friell, *Theodosius: The Empire At Bay*, B T Batsford, London, 1994

Albert Mugrdich Wolohojian, *The Romance of Alexander the Great by Pseudo-Callisthenes*, Columbia University Press, New York and London, 1969

Michael Wood, *In The Footsteps of Alexander The Great*, BBC Books, London, 1997

N. von Wurmb-Schwark, A. Ringleb, M. Gebuhr, E. Simeoni, "Genetic Analysis of Modern & Historical Burned Human Remains," *Anthropol. Anz.* March 2005, 63(1), 1-12

Orestes H. Zervos, "Early Tetradrachms of Ptolemy I," *ANS Museum Notes* 13, 1967, 1-16

A.M. de Zogheb, *Etudes sur l'ancienne Alexandrie*, Paris, 1909

Acknowledgements

I would like to express my particular gratitude to the following for their assistance in the research reported in this book:-

The staff of Bristol Central Library

The staff of Bristol University Arts and Social Sciences Library

David Jeffreys for his help concerning Memphis

Poul Pedersen of the Danish Halikarnassos Project

Pepe Peña of the University of Granada for a Spanish reference

Richard & Penelope Betz of Hemispheres Antique Maps and Prints for background on Braun & Hogenberg

Jean-Yves Empereur, Director of the Centre for Alexandrian Studies, for his encouragement

Mrs Gulgun Kazan of the British Institute of Archaeology at Ankara for providing an elusive reference

Sean Kingsley for his enthusiasm

Judith McKenzie for a new ancient reference

Mark Merrony for advice on mosaics and ancient city planning

Alessandra Coppola for her Eroi Conference and the discovery of Eugenio Polito

Reno Harboe-Sørensen for his translation of Cornelius de Bruyn

James Harrell for his mineralogical expertise in the ancient Egyptian context

Gianni Vianello for his photographic skills

Aidan Dodson and Michel Valloggia for advice on the pyramid at Abu Roash

Index

A

Abdalonymus............................ 44
Abercrombie........................... 139
Abou Ma'shar......................... 148
Aboukir.......................... 138, 254
Abu el Matamir 175
Abu Roash 224, 305
Achilles................... 15, 17, 41, 61
Achilles Tatius. 1, 73, 79, 80, 120, 150, 179, 180, 181, 182, 288, 291, 295, 297
Achilleus, Corrector of Egypt. 118
Actium 95
Acts of St Mark 192, 200
Adamantios....................... 30, 297
Adler, Ada 237, 239, 240, 299
Adorno, Anselme.................... 197
Adriani 4, 76, 85, 87, 89, 152, 169, 177, 178, 225, 276, 282, 285, 290, 300, 301, 304
Aegae 46, 47, 60, 62, 68, 102, 208, 214, 279, 282, 283
Aegean 4, 52, 82, 83, 112
Aegospotami............................ 17
Aelian 1, 2, 19, 28, 36, 40, 41, 47, 48, 49, 50, 51, 55, 62, 233, 238, 242, 243, 244, 245, 249, 257, 266, 297
Aemilianus, Marcus Julius 116, 190
Afghanistan 7, 215
Agathos Daimon........ iii, 123, 264
Agesilaus 25, 299
Aghios Athanasios................... 214
Agrippa............................. 95, 100
Agrippina............................... 100
Ahura-Mazda........................... 12
Ai Khanoum 214
Ainslie, Sir Robert 6, 293

Alabaster Tomb.. 4, 177, 178, 179, 276, 281
Alexander Book 174, 175
Alexander Helios 95
Alexander IV......... 42, 53, 69, 238
Alexander Mosaic 220
Alexander Romance... 1, 4, 12, 20, 24, 25, 26, 29, 30, 43, 46, 52, 54, 55, 57, 65, 66, 67, 73, 75, 77, 80, 112, 113, 143, 176, 182, 251, 256, 257, 268, 276, 277, 278, 280, 287, 288, 289, 290, 295, 299, 308
Alexander Sarcophagus 44, 45, 58, 105
Alexander the Patriarch.. 129, 143, 200
Alexander's Will 43
Alexandrea ad Aegyptum ...5, 150, 151, 155, 172, 181, 193, 261, 289, 291, 301
Alexandrine War 2, 158, 297
Al-Massoudi............ 133, 134, 262
aloe 25, 43
Alpha Quarter......................... 182
Amduat 141, 144
Ammianus Marcellinus....... 1, 117, 118, 119, 120, 122, 123, 124, 125, 160, 161, 179, 263, 264, 275, 281, 284, 297, 307
Ammon 17, 23, 31, 38, 40, 41, 42, 46, 51, 54, 56, 57, 58, 59, 60, 68, 69, 76, 128, 133, 176, 177, 190, 257, 260, 301
Ammonium 56, 129
Amphipolis.............. 146, 160, 271
Amr ibn al As.. 129, 130, 154, 197
Ancient History Bulletin ... 19, 233
Andronikos.............................. 46
Antigenes 51

Index

Antigonus..25, 52, 53, 54, 55, 251
Antigonus III 246
Antinoopolis 106, 107, 306
Antinous..104, 106, 107, 114, 279
Antioch...1, 3, 109, 113, 114, 123, 125, 126, 281
Antiochus I 245
Antipater 25, 26, 42, 50, 52, 53, 69, 234
Antirrhodos 73, 228
Antonine period 215
Antoninus Pius 79, 288
Apis 20, 63, 66, 248, 258, 270, 272, 277
Arabia 16, 22, 129, 304
Arabs130, 132, 139, 142, 193, 255
Arculfus 195, 196, 200
Aristander 47
Aristobulus...2, 17, 24, 28, 33, 36, 38, 209, 251
Aristotle 26, 30, 55, 64, 112
Armenia 95, 100
Armenian 1, 16, 20, 25, 43, 46, 54, 55, 65, 80, 112, 113, 276, 287
Arrhidaeus..39, 40, 42, 46, 48, 49, 50, 51, 53, 55, 68, 176, 279
Arrian2, 3, 4, 8, 12, 15, 19, 20, 21, 22, 24, 25, 26, 28, 30, 32, 34, 36, 37, 40, 41, 46, 48, 49, 50, 51, 55, 58, 63, 70, 191, 209, 233, 234, 237, 238, 243, 244, 246, 247, 248, 249, 250, 251, 252, 257, 258, 266, 268, 277, 279, 297, 301, 303, 304
Arsinoë 56, 75, 145, 260
Arte Veneta 211
Artemisia 83
Ashrafian 30, 300
Asia Minor 130, 256, 308
Athanasius 139, 142, 143, 254, 255, 263, 264, 275, 277
Athenaeus... 19, 20, 28, 31, 37, 58, 77, 234, 236, 237, 238, 239, 240, 241, 242, 244, 245, 246, 249, 297
Athens 3, 6, 17, 42, 69, 81, 95, 105, 148, 157, 214, 234, 236, 240, 241, 242, 243, 284, 300, 303, 307
Athribis 58
Attalus 23, 38, 48, 49, 68, 280
Attarine Mosque 134, 137, 139, 140, 141, 142, 143, 147, 148, 157, 166, 167, 173, 194, 199, 254, 255, 261, 262, 267, 273, 275, 293
Augila 128, 177
Augustus 2, 51, 78, 81, 82, 84, 97, 98, 100, 104, 107, 108, 123, 150, 235, 260, 266, 274, 281, 284, 287, 299, 307
Auletes 92
Aurelian 117, 118, 190, 263
Aurisina . 217, 218, 219, 221, 222, 223, 224, 225, 226
Avenue of Sphinxes 63, 258

B

Babylon iv, 7, 8, 9, 12, 13, 15, 17, 18, 19, 20, 21, 26, 27, 28, 29, 31, 32, 36, 39, 40, 41, 42, 46, 47, 48, 49, 52, 57, 62, 68, 90, 113, 130, 131, 151, 190, 248, 249, 250, 252, 266, 272, 276, 279, 305, 306
Bactria 7, 234
Badian, Ernst 20, 54, 233, 238, 247, 250
Baeton 235, 236, 246
Bailey 87, 285, 300
Balil 89, 285, 300
Barskij, Vassili Grigorovich .. 149, 150
Basileion 182
Basilica di San Marco.... 115, 194, 195, 201, 202, 203, 206, 210,

211, 212, 213, 219, 230, 303, 309
Bassani, Maddalena. 220, 225, 300
Baumgarten, Martin 197
BBC 201, 230, 309
Beas 7, 191
Belon 87, 198, 199, 300
Belzoni 162
Benghazi 128
Berenice 78, 280
Bergamo, Maria 301
Bernard 196, 197, 200, 202
Beroia 213
Bessus 7
Beta Quarter 182
Bevan 78, 301
biga 70, 71, 302
bivalve 223
Bodyguards 39, 40, 42, 68
Bonamy 157, 301
Boreium 128
Boscoreale 214
Bosworth, A. B. 17, 19, 30, 41, 133, 151, 233, 234, 237, 238, 242, 243, 244, 246, 247, 248, 251, 301, 302
Botti 5, 170, 301
Boukolia 193
Brahmins 34
Braun & Hogenberg 5, 87, 136, 137, 138, 141, 154, 173, 174, 194, 197, 200, 262, 274, 275, 277, 301, 310
Breccia. 5, 76, 150, 151, 152, 155, 170, 172, 177, 181, 193, 261, 274, 276, 281, 290, 301
British Museum 10, 53, 59, 62, 67, 83, 139, 140, 144, 190, 255, 258, 261, 268, 277, 301, 302, 303
Browne 138, 256, 301
Bruce 173, 301
Bruchium . 73, 111, 116, 117, 118, 119, 182, 263

Brutus 94
Bull Galleries 146
Buono 193, 195
Butler 130, 132, 148, 181, 197, 200, 201, 302
Butte Sainte Catherine 199

C

Caesar 2, 3, 4, 9, 73, 81, 82, 83, 92, 93, 94, 96, 98, 102, 116, 118, 158, 181, 243, 266, 279, 281, 283, 295, 297, 299, 307
Caesareum 96, 127, 148, 159, 170, 199, 200
Caesarion 93
Cailliaud, Frederic 176
Cairo. 62, 129, 130, 131, 134, 154, 155, 169, 173, 194, 195, 196, 197, 206, 224, 269, 294, 300, 303, 304, 305, 306
Caligula 2, 100, 101, 102, 109, 279, 281, 299, 303
Callisthenes 1, 66, 80, 112, 236, 239, 256, 302
Callixinus 77, 297
Campanian 222
Campanile 202
Campus Martius 98
Canale, Martino da 194
Canopic Gate 161
Canopic Way .. 71, 74, 79, 80, 137, 150, 157, 162, 166, 167, 168, 170, 179, 180, 184, 187, 188, 191, 199, 227, 288, 290, 293, 294, 295
Canopus 71, 107
Capella di San Clemente 194
Cappadocia 2, 42, 53, 100
Caracalla 109, 110, 111, 113, 116, 117, 119, 190, 263, 266, 279, 281
Carbon-14 .... 207, 224, 228, 232
Cardia 2, 19, 41, 233, 236, 245

Index

Caria 82
Carmania 8
Carthage 87, 89, 120, 129, 285, 300
Caspian 7
Cassander 21, 26, 53
Cassas.5, 121, 155, 166, 167, 183, 184, 185, 186, 199, 302
Cassius 2, 94, 266
Castaigne 24
Castel Sant'Angelo 107
Catacombs iii
catafalque9, 40, 42, 44, 45, 48, 49, 50, 53, 54, 68, 146, 259, 266, 272, 279
Cavafy 132
CEA 5
Centanni, Monica 217, 218, 225
Cestius 82, 284
Chaeronea 6
Chaldaeans 13
Champollion 141, 256, 268
Chares 209, 236
Charmion 97
Chatby 85, 86, 160, 173, 286
Chiliarch 234
chlamys 58, 102, 105, 188, 191
Christ 70, 92, 113, 128
Christianity ... 5, 10, 148, 192, 200, 306
Christides, Vassilios 133, 151, 302
Chronicon Paschale 193, 297
Church 88, 113, 127, 135, 142, 193, 195, 196, 197, 198, 199, 200, 201, 210, 230, 231, 232, 263, 297, 299
Cicero .. 64, 84, 259, 270, 283, 297
Cilicia 49, 50
Clarke 5, 9, 32, 139, 140, 141, 142, 254, 255, 268, 302, 303
Claudius 1, 2, 42, 299
Cleitarchus 12, 41, 51, 75
Cleitus 34
Clement of Alexandria .. 113, 192, 266, 297, 308
Cleomenes 23, 38
Cleopatra . 2, 9, 10, 11, 51, 87, 92, 93, 94, 95, 96, 97, 98, 102, 116, 121, 122, 123, 128, 144, 173, 199, 200, 260, 279, 293, 304
Cleopatra Selene 95, 102
Cleopatra's Needles 121, 122, 144, 199
Clitophon and Leucippe 1, 73, 79, 180, 288, 297
Cologne 5, 136, 194, 197, 262, 274, 301
coma 24, 28, 32, 33, 40, 68
Comminelli, Ugo 136, 197, 198
Companions 23, 28, 40, 57, 248
Computer Aided Tomography 207
Constantine 115, 120, 148, 201
Constantinople . 3, 6, 80, 107, 113, 114, 128, 129, 130, 140, 237, 255, 266, 293, 298
Constantius 120, 127, 263
Consul 93
Copenhagen ... 6, 58, 71, 150, 158, 261, 289, 295, 305
Coppola, Alessandra 217, 218, 310
Coptic Church of St Mark 173
Coptic Synaxary 148, 197
Copts 129, 197
Cornelius de Bruyn 10, 11, 199, 302, 310
Cossaeans 12, 13, 36
Craterus 7, 25, 42, 50, 56
Cremona 103
Cretaceous 222, 224, 305
Crete 3, 4, 78, 123, 222, 236
crocodiles 51
cuirass 101, 109, 281
Curtius ... 2, 17, 23, 25, 26, 30, 34, 36, 37, 39, 40, 41, 43, 52, 54, 55, 56, 58, 75, 171, 176, 209, 257, 258, 260, 266, 267, 268, 297

314

Cynegius 125
Cyprus 91, 196, 228, 280
Cyrene 85, 86, 286
Cyropaedia 35
Cyrus 130

D

d'Anville................. 155, 186, 199
Daisios........................ 24, 37, 38
Damascus.................. 46, 49, 280
Danube................................ 6, 12
Darius 7, 8, 12, 25, 58, 209
Daru, P...................... 194, 303
Deinocrates............................. 15
Deipnosophistae .. 19, 31, 77, 234, 236, 237, 239, 240, 241, 242, 243, 245, 246, 297
Delphi 26
Demetrius 54, 55, 64, 214, 299
Demophon 23, 38
Denon 5, 139, 141, 254, 255, 306, 309
Derchain, Philippe 257, 260
Description de l'Egypte 6, 131, 138, 141, 156, 166, 182, 183, 184, 199, 254, 262, 267, 292, 293, 306
Diadochi 26, 160, 252
Dialogues of the Dead . 23, 41, 42, 54, 266, 279, 298
dicasterion 74, 227
Didymus 2, 4, 78, 97, 280
Dio Cassius .. 2, 79, 80, 95, 96, 97, 101, 102, 103, 108, 109, 111, 150, 176, 266, 274, 287, 290, 297
Diocletian 87, 116, 117, 118, 120, 129, 190, 263, 285, 309
Diodorus 2, 12, 13, 15, 17, 19, 21, 22, 23, 25, 26, 27, 30, 36, 37, 40, 41, 42, 43, 44, 48, 49, 50, 51, 52, 53, 54, 56, 58, 62, 71, 73, 79, 82, 105, 143, 146, 154, 161, 163, 171, 176, 179, 180, 188, 209, 237, 244, 252, 256, 257, 266, 268, 272, 286, 287, 294, 297, 304, 309
Diodotus........3, 19, 233, 234, 235, 236, 237, 238, 245, 246
Diogenes 3, 15, 64, 235, 259, 266, 270, 297
Diognetus of Erythrae ...3, 19, 236
Dion 17, 214
Dionysius 19
Dionysus 28, 77, 245, 249
divine honours. 17, 23, 38, 41, 148
DNA 207, 208, 231, 308
Dolomieu........................... 139
Domitian 4
Domitianus, Lucius Domitius . 118
Dorotheus........................ 193, 236
drachm........................71, 74, 104
dromos.65, 67, 146, 272, 273, 274
Dryden, John 172
Dulkarnein...... 133, 135, 170, 262, 275
Durrell, Lawrence 70

E

earthquake 1, 10, 83, 123, 124, 128, 190, 264, 275, 281, 284, 295
Ecbatana........................8, 13, 240
Ecole des Arts et Métiers 5, 158
Edessa 213
Egypt 1, 3, 4, 5, 6, 7, 9, 17, 20, 40, 41, 42, 46, 47, 48, 49, 50, 51, 52, 53, 54, 56, 57, 58, 60, 61, 62, 63, 67, 68, 69, 70, 71, 75, 77, 78, 82, 83, 90, 92, 93, 95, 103, 104, 105, 106, 108, 111, 112, 116, 117, 118, 123, 124, 126, 129, 130, 132, 133, 134, 135, 138, 139, 140, 142, 144, 148, 152, 155, 158, 162, 163, 169, 176, 180, 181, 184, 187,

Index

190, 191, 192, 195, 197, 200, 201, 202, 204, 205, 206, 221, 222, 223, 224, 225, 226, 246, 247, 248, 254, 256, 257, 258, 259, 260, 261, 264, 266, 267, 268, 269, 272, 276, 277, 279, 280, 284, 288, 289, 291, 293, 294, 300, 301, 302, 303, 304, 305, 306, 308, 309

Egyptian Antiquities Commission 6
Egyptian foot 220
Egyptian Gazette 173
El Maraqi Bilad El Rum 176
elephant 57, 58, 59, 69, 70, 71, 102, 104, 106, 133, 190, 260
Eliot, T. S. 130
Empereur 5, 104, 118, 133, 136, 144, 151, 153, 155, 158, 163, 169, 174, 182, 228, 303, 304, 308, 310
Emporium 74, 170
Engels 27, 31, 252, 303
Engramma 220, 223, 225, 300, 301, 305
Ephemerides ... 2, 4, 19, 20, 23, 24, 34, 36, 233, 234, 236, 237, 238, 239, 240, 242, 243, 244, 245, 246, 247, 248, 249, 250, 251, 253, 297
Ephippus 2, 20, 27, 31, 58, 102, 105, 236, 239, 240, 241, 242, 243, 244, 245, 246, 247, 248, 249, 250, 253, 297
Ephorus 239, 241
epigoni 35
Epilepsy 30
Epiphanius 119, 196, 297, 298
Epiphanius the Monk 196
Eratosthenes 235, 245
Erythrae 3, 19, 233, 234, 235, 236, 237, 245, 253
Esagila 13, 249
Etesian winds 71, 96

Ethiopia 12, 62, 143, 177, 256
Ethiopic Alexander Romance 113, 302
Euergetes 77, 78, 238
Eumenes 2, 19, 21, 36, 41, 49, 51, 233, 234, 236, 238, 242, 244, 245, 246, 249, 250, 251, 253, 280, 298, 299
Eunostos 71, 73, 159
Euphrates . 12, 15, 16, 22, 29, 116, 235
Euripides 13, 20, 298
Eusebius. 103, 116, 129, 192, 210, 298
Eutychius 148, 193, 298
Exedra 67

F

Fabri, Félix 197
falciparum 28, 31, 32, 33, 34, 190, 251, 252, 253
Falier, Doge Vitale 201
Faustus 227
Fedak, Janos 85, 146, 160, 271, 303
Firmus 117, 118, 190, 263
Flecker, James Elroy 112
Forlati, Ferdinando 201, 210, 211, 212, 213, 303
France 5, 6, 158, 254, 289
Fraser 5, 51, 55, 64, 67, 73, 76, 96, 123, 133, 135, 142, 144, 149, 151, 152, 159, 170, 171, 172, 173, 174, 175, 201, 210, 248, 256, 258, 259, 261, 262, 264, 267, 302, 303, 304

G

Gabbari 225
Galerius 118, 129
Galice Bey 119, 182, 188, 292, 295, 296
Gallienus 116

Ganges 7
Gate of the Moon 71
Gate of the Sun 71
Gaugamela 7
Gaza 7, 209
Gebel Raghawi 224
Gedrosian desert 7, 34
Genealogiae 235
Georgius 120, 122, 125, 263, 264, 275
Gerdek Kaya 146, 271
Germanicus 100, 101, 279, 281
Geta 109
Giza 82, 283
Goddio, Franck 228, 304
Gorgos 240
Goths 128
Graeco-Roman Museum .. 4, 5, 76, 172, 174, 175, 177
Grand Altar of Alexander .. 77, 80, 295
Granicus 7, 34, 209
Great Harbour .. 10, 71, 73, 74, 92, 95, 96, 136, 170, 182, 199, 228, 263, 293
Greece 4, 6, 15, 41, 42, 47, 94, 101, 102, 140, 145, 254, 298, 301, 302, 303
Greeks 8, 17, 20, 27, 29, 35, 36, 42, 57, 70, 94, 99, 103, 113, 128, 212, 249, 266, 297
Gymnasium 74, 97, 227

H

Haas, Christopher .. 123, 130, 143, 154, 163, 169, 170, 193, 264, 304
Hades 101
Hadra 160
Hadrian 2, 4, 58, 70, 71, 74, 78, 103, 104, 105, 106, 107, 114, 123, 264, 279, 281, 302

Hakim.3, 133, 134, 135, 154, 170, 181, 262, 275, 289
Halicarnassus ... 82, 83, 84, 85, 89, 98, 108, 122, 160, 180, 190, 279, 284, 285, 286, 287
Hamadan, Lion of 146, 271
Hamlet 8, 192, 208
Hammond, N. G. L.19, 20, 41, 54, 234, 236, 238, 244, 245, 246, 247, 248, 249, 250, 304
Hanging Gardens 18, 22, 252
Harrell, Professor James 221, 222, 223, 224, 310
Harrison, Rex 94
Heckel 42, 251, 298, 300, 301, 303, 309
Helena 115
Heliopolis 130, 144, 228, 260
hellebore 30
Hellenion 59, 60, 260
Hellenistic Period 210, 212
Hellespont 50
Henry V 39
Hephaistion .. 8, 12, 13, 15, 17, 22, 41, 56, 234, 239, 240, 242, 244, 245, 249
Heptastadion 71, 89, 155, 169, 254, 285, 291
Heracles 21, 32, 37, 53, 56, 57
Heraclius 129, 130
Heraclonas 130
Hermel 286
Hermitage 87
Herodian 3, 79, 109, 110, 111, 113, 176, 263, 266, 281, 287, 298, 309
Hieronymus 41, 42, 49, 51, 233
Hindu Kush 7
Hippodrome 100
Hirtius 2, 297
History Today 203, 230, 302
Hogarth 5, 123, 152, 169, 184, 187, 188, 191, 264, 275, 293, 294, 304

Index

Homer 15, 35, 47, 61, 63, 80, 271, 278, 298
honey 25, 43, 68
hoplite shield 225
Horton Hospital 32
Hospitaller 83
Hurter, Silvia 57, 304
Hutchinson, Lord 5, 152, 172, 255
Hydaspes 7
Hyginus 235
Hypereides 26
Hypomnemata 244

I

Iliad 15, 35, 47, 61, 80, 298
Imensthotieion 59, 60, 177, 260
India ... 3, 7, 12, 27, 30, 35, 54, 68, 102, 136, 162, 207, 246, 249, 262, 275, 308
Indian Ocean 3, 7, 22, 231, 233, 250
Indica 3, 41, 250, 297, 301
Indus 3, 7, 34
Iollas 26
Ionia 58, 286
Ionic 43, 44, 68
Irwin, Eyles 138, 256, 304
Isis 74, 96, 123, 176, 269, 270, 272
Islam 10
Ismaïl 5, 158
Issus 7, 101, 126, 209
Italy 12, 90, 95, 177, 193, 217, 222, 305

J

Jacobites 129, 197, 198
Jacoby, F. 42, 49, 52, 234, 235, 236, 237, 258, 267, 304
Jerash 87, 88
Jerome 53, 192, 298
Jerusalem 115, 286
Jesus 115
Jewish Quarter 160, 170, 291

Jews .. 73, 103, 130, 149, 154, 160
Joannides 173
John Chrysostom . 3, 80, 107, 113, 114, 125, 127, 129, 147, 264, 266, 275, 276, 281, 287, 298
Jordan 223
Josephus... 3, 22, 73, 96, 160, 170, 171, 294, 298
Julia Domna 108, 109
Julian ... 3, 24, 120, 124, 125, 126, 143
Julius Valerius 1, 113
Jurassic 223
Justin 3, 21, 23, 25, 26, 27, 32, 37, 40, 41, 47, 49, 50, 54, 56, 93, 176, 177, 260, 298
Justinian 128

K

Kalat Fakra 85, 86, 286
Kalish 159
Kanzir 194
Khabbash 144, 260
Kipling 149
Knidos 146, 160, 271
Koldewey. 15, 16, 19, 20, 21, 249, 252, 305
Kom el-Demas 151
Kom el-Dikka .. 74, 150, 151, 152, 169, 199, 262, 274, 275, 290, 293
kopis 212, 213, 216
Koran 133, 135, 261, 262, 298
Koumoutsos, Stelios 174, 175, 176
Kroll 80, 233, 299, 305
Ktistes 210

L

L'Élite café-bar 174
La Cause 5, 140
La Prise d'Alexandrie 196
Laboratorio di Analisi dei Materiali Antichi 218

Lane Fox 29, 53, 56, 215, 230, 234, 303
Larissa 20, 236
larnax 214
Last Plans 40, 82, 244, 283
Late Period .. 60, 62, 63, 144, 258, 269
Latin Cemeteries.... 177, 228, 276, 281
Lauer 5, 64, 65, 258, 259, 270, 272, 305
Lausiac History............... 192, 298
Lazzarini, Dr Prof. Lorenzo... 218, 223
Lebanon 85, 86, 112, 224, 286
legionaries 220
Leo Africanus 5, 133, 135, 137, 141, 197, 261, 264, 273, 277, 300, 307
Leo X 5
Libanius 3, 125, 126, 146, 176, 191, 200, 298
Liber de Morte. 23, 25, 26, 38, 41, 55, 176, 251, 298
Library . 35, 73, 96, 181, 238, 250, 283, 288, 297, 299, 301, 304, 307, 309, 310
Libya 25, 128
Lion Tomb 160
Livy 96
Lochias peninsula 71, 73, 125, 159, 160, 161, 168, 170, 173, 179, 180, 182, 191, 193, 197, 291
London. 15, 27, 32, 60, 62, 79, 87, 125, 135, 138, 162, 163, 180, 185, 194, 195, 196, 197, 201, 203, 211, 230, 234, 249, 250, 254, 256, 257, 258, 260, 261, 263, 277, 280, 284, 288, 291, 292, 293, 294, 295, 298, 300, 301, 302, 303, 304, 305, 306, 307, 308, 309
Louvre 5, 194, 272
Lucan 3, 81, 82, 83, 84, 89, 92, 176, 179, 181, 266, 282, 283, 284, 286, 295, 298, 299
Lucian 3, 11, 23, 38, 41, 42, 54, 176, 266, 298
Lucillus of Tarrha 4, 78
Lusignan, Pierre de 228
Lycia 91
Lydia 4
Lysander 17
Lysimachus 39, 58, 133
Lyson & Kallikles, tomb of 213, 217

M

Macedon ... 6, 9, 20, 25, 26, 42, 46, 49, 50, 52, 55, 68, 82, 110, 113, 115, 177, 213, 214, 245, 266, 279, 282, 283, 302, 304, 308
Macedonian shield 211, 219
Macedonians .. 7, 8, 17, 20, 24, 39, 40, 42, 46, 47, 53, 54, 55, 61, 68, 109, 176, 236, 240, 242
Machaut, Guillaume de ... 196, 305
Macrinus 111
Macro 101
Mahmoud 5, 71, 72, 119, 124, 133, 150, 151, 152, 158, 159, 160, 161, 162, 163, 165, 167, 168, 169, 170, 171, 179, 182, 183, 184, 187, 188, 192, 198, 228, 230, 261, 274, 289, 290, 291, 292, 294, 295, 305
malaria .. 28, 31, 32, 33, 34, 40, 68, 190, 251, 252, 253
Mallian 30, 207
Mamelukes 134, 136, 155, 228
Manin, Leonardo Conte . 202, 203, 204, 205, 207, 230, 231, 305
Mankiewicz, Joseph 94
Marcus Aurelius 113
Marduk 12, 13, 16, 20, 23, 249
Mareotis 70, 125

Index

Mariette....6, 63, 65, 66, 145, 146, 147, 259, 269, 270, 271, 272, 273, 274, 305
Mark Antony 9, 78, 94, 95, 96, 97, 98, 99, 100, 279, 280, 299
Marlowe, Christopher 227
Marmol...135, 137, 173, 198, 261, 307
Marr & Calisher 29, 34
Martyrion of St Mark 192, 193
Massaga..............................34, 209
Mauretania 102
Mausoleum. 78, 83, 84, 85, 89, 98, 100, 106, 109, 113, 120, 122, 125, 126, 127, 128, 129, 133, 145, 146, 148, 160, 169, 170, 172, 179, 180, 188, 190, 200, 219, 226, 264, 265, 279, 281, 284, 285, 286, 287, 295
Mausolus 82, 83, 84, 108, 180
Mayer, Luigi 6, 119, 166, 167, 183, 185, 191, 293, 306
McKenzie, Judith ... 125, 162, 306, 310
Medina 129
Mediterranean 7, 35, 41, 70, 71, 75, 85, 87, 92, 93, 98, 123, 124, 134, 140, 157, 195, 219, 221, 222, 226, 262, 286, 301, 307
Medius..20, 22, 26, 29, 32, 36, 37, 236
Meleager 39, 40, 68
Melkites...................................129
Memphis 9, 20, 50, 51, 52, 57, 58, 59, 60, 61, 62, 64, 65, 66, 67, 68, 69, 74, 75, 76, 143, 144, 145, 176, 180, 181, 190, 248, 257, 258, 259, 260, 265, 266, 269, 276, 277, 278, 280, 287, 288, 289, 295, 304, 305, 308, 309, 310
Menelaus 76
Menidas..............................23, 38
Messenia 19

Metz Epitome 25, 43, 58, 105, 209, 251, 298
Michael bar Elias................. 171
Minutoli, Heinrich 176
Mithraeum 127
Mohammed 5, 129, 149, 155, 166, 182, 292, 296
Mohammed Ali.. 5, 149, 155, 158, 166, 182, 292, 296
Mohammed Ibn Kathir el Farghani 148
Monico, Patriarch 206
Moon Gate 79, 288
Moralia 15, 26, 30, 38, 41, 55, 209, 244, 246, 249, 299
Mørkholm 59, 106, 133, 306
Moslems 194
Mosul....................................... 149
Moustafa Pacha 178
Multan 30
Museum . 5, 58, 73, 104, 140, 144, 162, 219, 303, 306, 309
Mycenae 172
Myra 91

N

Nabi Daniel 6, 148, 149, 150, 151, 152, 158, 170, 172, 173, 261, 262, 273, 289, 290, 291
Naples 206, 220
Napoleon 5, 6, 107, 134, 138, 139, 142, 155, 156, 158, 163, 182, 191, 199, 254, 261, 267, 277, 292, 293
Napoleon III................. 5, 158, 289
Narbonensis 103
Narses 117
Nearchus.. 3, 7, 12, 20, 22, 23, 36, 37, 250
Nebuchadnezzar 15, 22, 252
necropolis 5, 44, 60, 62, 69, 71, 76, 85, 86, 160, 173, 216, 257, 258, 268, 269, 277, 286

320

Necropolis 63, 178, 258, 270
Nectanebo .. 62, 63, 65, 66, 67, 69, 127, 133, 141, 143, 144, 145, 146, 147, 190, 191, 229, 248, 256, 257, 258, 259, 260, 262, 263, 264, 265, 267, 268, 269, 270, 271, 272, 273, 274, 278
Nelson 138, 139, 254, 305
Neptune 102
Nero 3, 81, 102, 103, 192, 283, 284
Neuffer, E 240, 243
New Kingdom 60
Newton, Charles 83
Nicaea 2
Nicetas 194
Nike 43
Nikiu, John of ... 79, 194, 288, 298
Nile 7, 9, 25, 29, 34, 35, 51, 52, 56, 57, 58, 59, 60, 69, 70, 71, 79, 93, 100, 106, 107, 130, 138, 139, 159, 175, 224, 254, 258, 270, 280, 304, 305
Norden, F. L. 194, 199, 306
Nysa 249

O

Octavian. 2, 94, 95, 96, 97, 98, 99, 266, 279, 280, 281, 284
Odenath 116
Odyssey 15
Old Kingdom 63, 82, 258, 286
Olympias 6, 26, 47, 53, 55, 62, 257
Olynthus 2, 20, 58, 236, 237, 238, 239, 240, 241, 242, 243, 247, 248, 250, 253
Omar 130
Onesicritus 3, 11, 239
ooliths 222
ORAU 232
Orseolo, Doge 201
Ortelius 5, 136
Osirapis 248

Osiris ... 20, 66, 248, 270, 272, 277
Ostia 87, 285, 300
Ottoman 6, 134, 155, 158, 262
Ottoman Empire 6
Oxydracae 75
Oxyrhynchus 101, 103, 117

P

Padova, Università degli Studi di 217
Pagani, Zaccaria 197
Palazzo del Bo 217, 218
Palestine . 129, 184, 195, 196, 298, 301, 302, 308
palimpsest 48, 49, 50
Palladius 192, 298
Palmyra 116, 117, 177, 263
Paneum 74, 179, 227
papyrus . 1, 59, 60, 73, 76, 78, 101, 103, 108, 117, 150, 238, 244, 274
parabolani 127
Parian Marble ... 4, 49, 52, 75, 176, 258, 267, 280
Paros 4, 49, 52, 75, 257, 267
Passio of St Peter 192
Patrocles 245
Pausanias .. 4, 6, 46, 48, 49, 50, 51, 52, 55, 57, 60, 62, 67, 74, 75, 76, 176, 257, 266, 267, 278, 280, 298
Pearson, Lionel 20, 28, 41, 192, 237, 238, 239, 240, 247, 248, 306
Pella 82, 283
penetrali 81, 83, 97, 287
Pepper Gate 196
Perdiccas 9, 13, 23, 27, 38, 39, 40, 42, 46, 47, 48, 49, 50, 51, 52, 53, 67, 68, 234, 250, 259, 280
Pergamum 77
peribolos 188, 191, 229
Persepolis 7

Index

Persia 7, 12, 35, 95, 117, 136, 262, 275
Persian Empire 7
Persian Girdle 105
Persian Gulf 3, 7
Persians .. 15, 17, 25, 62, 116, 118, 129, 141, 144, 260, 268
Petrie 60, 238
Peucestas 17, 20, 23, 39
phalanx 220
Pharaoh 4, 92, 256
Pharos...35, 71, 74, 77, 87, 88, 89, 90, 123, 132, 136, 155, 228, 254, 257, 262, 285
Pharsalia 3, 81, 82, 84, 92, 181, 266, 281, 282, 284, 295, 298
Pharsalus 92
Philadelphus...4, 9, 53, 56, 64, 67, 69, 74, 75, 76, 77, 144, 179, 238, 246, 257, 259, 260, 267, 270, 278, 280, 281
Philinus 244, 245
Philip II 6, 46, 55, 56, 60, 62, 102, 233, 238, 246
Philip III 39, 46
Philip V 246
Philippi 82, 94, 282
Philo 22, 73, 82, 171, 289, 298, 299, 307
Philopator 2, 78, 97, 179, 190, 279, 280, 282, 284, 286, 295
Philosyrius 87, 88, 120, 285
Phoenician 17, 60
Phrygia 25, 52
Picard ...64, 65, 87, 259, 270, 272, 305, 307
Pisidia 49, 50, 68, 280
Piso 3, 81, 84, 283, 297
Pithon 20, 23, 38, 39, 51
Plato 17, 64, 243
Pleistocene 222, 307
pleurisy 30
Pliny ... 12, 83, 145, 171, 188, 235, 239, 243, 246, 260, 299

Plutarch.... 2, 4, 12, 15, 17, 19, 20, 21, 22, 24, 25, 26, 27, 28, 29, 30, 32, 34, 35, 36, 37, 41, 49, 55, 64, 78, 96, 97, 188, 209, 233, 234, 242, 243, 244, 245, 246, 247, 248, 249, 250, 251, 257, 268, 271, 299
Pococke 6, 137, 138, 161, 162, 163, 183, 184, 199, 256, 292, 294, 307
Poetica Astronomica 235
Poggibonsi, Fra Niccolo of 197
Polemon 46, 48, 49, 68, 280
Polito, Eugenio 219, 220, 221, 222, 223, 225, 226, 307, 310
Pollacopas 16, 29, 36
Pollio, C Asinius 225
Polyhistor 235
Polyperchon 27, 53, 251
Pompeii 58, 101, 214
Pompey 3, 81, 87, 92, 93, 118, 119, 120, 136, 157, 183, 285
Porus 7, 57, 302
Poseidon 74, 87
Praetorian Guard 101, 102
Priapus 77, 127
Procopius 128, 177, 299
Proteas 245
Protectores 117
Proto di San Marco 210, 230
Proverbia 78, 96, 97, 179, 280, 282, 287, 300
Pseudo-Callisthenes... 1, 4, 24, 26, 29, 43, 46, 52, 54, 73, 77, 80, 112, 113, 171, 182, 233, 256, 287, 299, 305, 309
Ptolemaic Empire 4, 84
Ptolemy.... 4, 9, 12, 20, 27, 30, 39, 40, 41, 42, 46, 47, 48, 49, 50, 51, 52, 53, 54, 55, 56, 57, 58, 60, 61, 62, 64, 65, 67, 68, 69, 70, 74, 75, 76, 77, 78, 80, 90, 91, 92, 93, 97, 102, 133, 139, 141, 144, 145, 160, 174, 177,

179, 190, 209, 239, 246, 248, 250, 256, 257, 258, 259, 260, 265, 266, 268, 270, 273, 276, 278, 279, 280, 287, 294, 295, 299, 303, 309
Pyramid 82, 224, 283

Q

Qait Bey 90, 136, 228
quadriga 104

R

Radjedef 224
Razaud 155, 186
Renaissance 157
Rhakotis..... 52, 73, 143, 257, 268, 269, 276
Rhodes 77, 251
Rizan Aneiza 224
Robinson, C. A. 19, 238, 249, 250
Rohlfs, Gerhard 176
Roman Empire. 98, 111, 117, 124, 126, 128, 304
Roman foot 220
Roman Republic 92, 98
Romans 9, 12, 73, 93, 101, 103, 106, 116, 118, 119, 224
Rome 1, 2, 4, 9, 32, 76, 78, 81, 82, 87, 92, 93, 94, 95, 97, 98, 99, 100, 102, 103, 104, 107, 111, 113, 115, 116, 117, 123, 128, 145, 154, 169, 177, 178, 254, 257, 261, 282, 284, 285, 300, 302, 303, 304, 307
Roncalli, Angelo 206
Rosetta 161, 163, 222, 256, 307
Rosetta Gate .. 160, 166, 169, 170, 173, 174, 182, 183, 185, 191, 194, 195, 196, 197, 200, 279, 293, 294, 296
Rosetta Stone. 139, 141, 255, 267, 268
Roxane 27, 39, 42, 50, 53

Royal Quarter. 118, 150, 169, 180, 182, 228, 263
rudist 223, 224
Rufinus 127, 299
Rustico 193, 195

S

Sabina 103
Sacred Band 6
Salt, Henry 162, 164, 166, 171, 188
Samarkand 34, 207, 209
Samuel, A. E. 20, 24, 237, 242, 243, 245, 307
Sandys, George 135, 261, 307
Saqqara ... 5, 6, 60, 62, 63, 69, 145, 190, 229, 258, 269, 270, 276, 277
sarcophagus .. 5, 10, 25, 43, 53, 62, 65, 67, 81, 87, 88, 90, 94, 97, 101, 109, 115, 120, 127, 128, 133, 136, 139, 140, 141, 142, 143, 144, 145, 146, 148, 150, 190, 191, 202, 206, 232, 254, 255, 256, 257, 258, 259, 260, 261, 262, 263, 264, 265, 267, 268, 269, 271, 273, 274, 275, 277, 278, 285, 290, 302
sarissa 219, 220
Satrap Stele 144, 260
Saturn 148, 200
savants 139, 182, 254
Schachermeyr 28, 307
Schilizzi 6, 150, 274, 289
Schliemann, Heinrich 152, 172, 303
Schmidt-Colinet, Andreas. 67, 307
Seleucus .. 23, 38, 39, 51, 133, 245
Sema 78, 80, 81, 172
Senate 98, 107, 108, 109, 113, 148, 266
Seneca 3, 81, 284

Index

Septimius Severus .. 108, 109, 150, 190, 193, 197, 266, 274, 279, 281, 290, 299
Serapeum 6, 63, 64, 65, 66, 67, 69, 74, 103, 104, 118, 119, 127, 143, 145, 146, 147, 157, 159, 168, 181, 183, 190, 229, 269, 270, 273, 274, 276, 278
Serapis .. 20, 23, 38, 57, 65, 66, 97, 110, 123, 244, 248, 249, 250, 277, 278
Seven Wonders 22, 35, 82, 299
Sextus Aurelius Victor 110
Shakespeare 39, 70, 192
Shallalat Gardens ... 160, 182, 183, 191, 228, 279, 294
Shapur 116
Sheikh Mohammed Daniel 149
Sidi Lokman 149
Sidon 44, 45, 58, 105
Sierotka, Michael Radzivill 135, 307
Sinai 130, 224, 308
Sisygambis 25
Siwa 41, 56, 57, 70, 129, 176, 177
Socrates Scholasticus 115, 120, 127, 299
Sogdiana 7
Soma 35, 78, 79, 80, 81, 82, 83, 84, 87, 89, 90, 91, 92, 93, 94, 96, 97, 100, 101, 103, 104, 106, 108, 109, 110, 113, 115, 118, 120, 122, 125, 126, 127, 128, 129, 133, 142, 145, 146, 148, 150, 151, 152, 157, 158, 160, 169, 170, 172, 173, 178, 179, 180, 181, 182, 187, 188, 190, 191, 219, 226, 227, 228, 229, 263, 264, 265, 279, 281, 284, 286, 287, 288, 289, 290, 291, 294, 295, 296
somatophylax 4
Sonnini 138, 142, 256, 308

Soter. 4, 74, 77, 78, 102, 144, 160, 177, 266
Souvaltzis, Liana 129, 176
Sozomenus 123, 124, 264, 275
Sparta 17, 148
Spitamenes 7
St Anthony 204, 205
St Apollonia 211, 215, 219
St Catherine 199
St Claudian 193
St George 197, 199
St Mark 88, 135, 173, 174, 192, 193, 194, 195, 196, 197, 198, 199, 200, 201, 202, 203, 204, 205, 206, 207, 208, 210, 211, 217, 219, 221, 226, 230, 231, 232, 237, 241, 297, 304, 309
St Paul 80, 107, 114, 115, 264, 266, 276, 281
Star of Macedon 214
Stateira 12
Stathmoi 235, 236, 245, 246
Staurcius 195
Stephanus Byzantinus 171, 294, 299
Stoneman ... 26, 29, 43, 46, 52, 53, 56, 73, 77, 112, 143, 182, 257, 266, 268, 276, 308
Strabo. 2, 4, 13, 16, 22, 30, 36, 43, 48, 49, 51, 53, 54, 71, 73, 74, 78, 79, 80, 87, 90, 91, 96, 99, 118, 120, 143, 150, 157, 159, 168, 169, 171, 176, 179, 182, 188, 209, 228, 245, 246, 257, 263, 268, 269, 274, 282, 286, 287, 288, 291, 294, 299
Strattis 20, 236, 237, 238, 239, 240, 241, 242, 243, 244, 246, 247
strychnine 27
Suda . 4, 20, 78, 79, 237, 238, 239, 240, 241, 242, 243, 244, 247, 299

Suetonius ... 4, 81, 83, 84, 97, 100, 101, 102, 103, 150, 176, 235, 266, 274, 284, 286, 299
Sun Gate 79, 288
Suriano, Francesco 197
Susa 7, 8, 12, 13
Syracuse............................ 17, 301
Syria..... 7, 42, 48, 49, 68, 90, 102, 108, 116, 118, 125, 126, 129, 138, 235, 256, 259, 266, 279, 286, 301, 308
Syriac Alexander Romance 55, 66, 80, 112, 113, 287, 302

T

Tacitus 20, 51, 100, 160, 299
Tatianus 125
Taylor, Elizabeth 94
Taylor, Lily Ross 123, 308
Telfer, William 192, 308
temenos 83, 179, 180, 181, 187, 188, 191, 228, 229
Terra Santa 76, 177
Testori, Giulio 220, 225, 300
tetradrachm . 58, 69, 102, 104, 190
The Lost Tomb of Alexander the Great 9, 203, 211, 230, 250, 266, 302
Thebes 6, 28, 34, 57, 64, 177, 245
Thenaud, Jean 197
Theocritus......................... 56, 299
Theodoret............... 115, 147, 299
Theodorus............................. 195
Theodosius. 3, 115, 125, 126, 127, 265, 278, 281, 309
Theodotus 92, 116, 240
Theophilus 126
Thessaloniki........................... 214
Thessaly................................... 92
Thompson, Dorothy..... 60, 64, 65, 145, 230, 259, 269, 271, 308
Thoth 59, 177, 260
Thucher, Hans 197
Tiberius 101
Tiberius Alexander.................. 103
Tibur....................................... 107
Tigris.. 12
Timonium 95, 170, 228
Tintoretto............................... 201
Titus 103, 279, 281
Today Programme................... 230
Toledo 89, 285, 300
Toledo, University of 221, 222
Tower of Babel 12, 15
Tower of the Romans....... 11, 119, 121, 122, 160, 184, 293, 294
Trajan 70, 103
Translazione... 193, 194, 202, 226, 230, 305
Trieste 201, 211, 217, 218, 223, 303
Triptolemus 70
Tritons...................................... 87
Trogus 3, 21, 41, 93, 298
Troy 47, 152, 172
tsunami 10, 142, 168, 190, 231
Tulun ... 3, 119, 133, 170, 291, 296
tumulus ... 44, 60, 76, 98, 178, 179, 276, 282
Turkey 7, 49
Turonian 224
Tutankhamun 207, 231
Tyche............................... 123, 264
typhoid 28, 33
Typhus.................................... 28
Tyre 7, 193

V

Valentine 130
Valentinian 123
Valerian................................. 116
Valloggia, Michel ... 224, 308, 310
Van Egmont 137, 138, 256
van Lyskirchen, Constantin.... 136, 262, 274, 275
Vatican 115, 144

Index

Venetians 173, 174, 193, 194, 196, 197, 199, 201, 221, 226
Venezia, Istituto Universitario di Architettura di 218
Venezia, Università Iuav di 202, 217, 305
Venice 173, 194, 197, 199, 201, 202, 206, 210, 215, 216, 219, 223, 224, 225, 226, 230, 231, 237, 303, 305, 306, 309
Vergina 178, 208, 214, 217, 300
Vespasian 102, 103, 279, 281, 299
Vianello, Gianni 206, 309, 310
Vio, Ettore 201, 230, 309
Vitellius 103

W

Wace .. 6, 143, 256, 257, 268, 299, 309
Welles 76, 267, 297, 309
West Nile Virus 29
Wilcken, Ulrich .. 20, 65, 247, 249, 250, 259, 270, 309
Wilkinson, Gardner 194, 309

X

Xenocles 245
Xenophon 2, 35
Xerxes 13
xyston 220

Y

Yacub Artin Pacha 151

Z

Zarpanitum 248
Zenobia .. 116, 117, 118, 177, 190, 263
Zenobius 4, 78, 80, 96, 97, 120, 176, 179, 182, 282, 286, 287, 288, 300
zeugma 79
Zeus ... 41, 44, 47, 52, 57, 73, 214, 235, 289
Zogheb 6, 150, 151, 152, 261, 274, 309

Printed in Great Britain
by Amazon